Global Problems

The Search for Equity, Peace, and Sustainability

Scott Sernau

Indiana University South Bend

PEARSON

Boston   New York   San Francisco

Mexico City   Montreal   Toronto   London   Madrid   Munich   Paris

Hong Kong   Singapore   Tokyo   Cape Town   Sydney

Senior Editor: Jeff Lasser
Series Editorial Assistant: Heather McNally
Senior Marketing Manager: Kelly May
Senior Production Editor: Beth Houston
Editorial-Production Service: Omegatype Typography, Inc.
Composition Buyer: Linda Cox
Manufacturing Buyer: JoAnne Sweeney
Electronic Composition: Omegatype Typography, Inc.
Photo Researcher: Omegatype Typography, Inc.
Cover Administrator: Joel Gendron

For related titles and support materials, visit our online catalog at www.ablongman.com.

Between the time Website information is gathered and then published, it is not unusual for some sites to have closed. Also, the transcription of URLs can result in typographical errors. The publisher would appreciate notification where these errors occur so that they may be corrected in subsequent editions.

Library of Congress Cataloging-in-Publication Data

Sernau, Scott.
  Global problems : the search for equity, peace, and sustainability / Scott Sernau.
     p.   cm.
  Includes bibliographical references and index.
  ISBN 0-205-34392-9
  1. Social problems. 2. Globalization—Social aspects. I. Title.
  HN18.3.S47 2006
  306.09051—dc22

                                                              2005054602

Printed in the United States of America

10 9 8 7 6 5 4 3   10   09   08   07   06

*To those who wish to understand the problem
so that they can be part of the solution*

Contents

Preface

This is an exciting and ever-changing time to be teaching about global issues and social problems. It can also be a daunting task. There is far more material than can ever be covered in a semester, and the burning issues change with the day's headlines. I hope this book, *Global Problems: The Search for Equity, Peace, and Sustainability,* will make the task of engaging global problems a more manageable one.

The book is divided into three parts, representing what I see as three key dimensions to the current global situation. The first part begins with the challenges of global inequalities: in life chances, wages and work, gender and education. The choice to begin with inequality is not accidental but rather reflects my conviction that inequality lies at the heart of many global problems. The second section focuses on conflict and violence at all levels: from crime to politics, terrorism to war. Violence is closely linked to issues of social justice and human rights, and this connection is made throughout. The final section looks at the issue of sustainability and the problems of urbanization, crowding, and environmental destruction. These problems are immediate but also call on us to look ahead toward the kind of world that we are building.

Each chapter of *Global Problems* begins with a couple of vignettes that typically focus on a distant and less familiar location along with a close-to-home situation that highlights the same issue. I want students to be able to see the interconnectedness of our world and of people leading seemingly very different lives. Each chapter strengthens this local–global connection. The chapters explore social problems by focusing on key theories and enough history to understand the background of contemporary issues. The approach is both multinational and multidisciplinary. Often, I identify both the nationality and the discipline or background of the person cited, so students can get a better sense of the many areas of study that contribute to the whole. I have avoided burdening the text with a bewildering array of citations and have instead focused on the key insights and studies that most clearly inform the topic across disciplines. Both classical and contemporary theorists and writers are noted.

I hope that students will think deeply and care deeply about global problems. At the same time, I do not want to indulge in gloom and doom to the point that the situation seems hopeless, for that can breed apathy and inaction. Each chapter includes and concludes with positive possibilities for global change. The Making Connections section at the end of each chapter offers websites for more information and options for local and hands-on involvement. This section can form the basis for assignments, for further study, or for a class or group project.

This combination of elements allows *Global Problems* to serve social problems courses that seek a truly global perspective and context for analysis as well as courses in global issues, global studies, Third World studies, and international development.

Acknowledgments

Allyn & Bacon has a superb team of professionals who have made my life as an author much easier. Thanks especially go to Jeff Lasser, Senior Editor, for his guidance and gentle encouragement. It helped that he was both enthusiastic about the project and understanding as deadlines sometimes slipped by. It also helped that he was ably assisted by Heather McNally in pulling all the pieces of the manuscript together.

I am also grateful to Theresa Sexton and Audria Mitchell for research assistance in working through, quite literally, a world of data. Finally, special thanks go to the reviewers, who were generous with their praise of the overall project as well as generous with their time in doing a careful reading and suggesting important improvements: A. Ahmad, University of North Carolina; Joan M. Brehm, Illinois State University; Donna Crossman, The Ohio State University; Joanna Grey, Pikes Peak Community College; Curtiss Hoffman, Bridgewater State College; Jonathan London, University of Wisconsin, Madison; James Norwine, Texas A&M, Kingsville; Evan Schofer, University of Minnesota; and Jackie Smith, State University of New York, Stony Brook.

The Global Century

When Bob Dylan sang in the 1960s that the times were "a changing," he was quite right. The times are still changing; only now, they seem to change every year or every few months. The term **globalization** was only popularized in the mid 1990s, but it soon became the favorite label for our age. Our world has been coming together in dramatic new ways.

Globalization is sometimes used to describe just the increasing economic linkages between countries. Yet it is more than that. **Economic globalization** is reshaping our world marketplace. At the same time, **political globalization** is binding the world together in new forms of power and authority relations. **Cultural globalization** means that music, fashion, media, and lifestyles are transported around the world to reshape how people live and even how they think. Economic, political, and cultural globalization are clearly intertwined, but they are also as distinct as their respective U.S. centers: New York (economic); Washington, D.C. (political); and Los Angeles (cultural). They are as distinct yet as interrelated as Tokyo (economic power), Paris (cultural power), and Beijing (emerging political power). By the end of the twentieth century few doubted that globalization, in some form, was here to stay.

Then came September 11, 2001. The world's most devastating terrorist attack, directed against seats of global economic power (the World Trade Center) and political power (the Pentagon), raised new questions. What would the impact of global terrorism be on this shrinking world? Would fear of terrorism restrict the movement of people and products? Even that classic symbol of a shrinking world, the inter- and transcontinental airliner, seemed somehow menacing. The 9/11 terrorist attacks were followed in short order by two wars, toppling the governments of Afghanistan and Iraq, launched by a U.S. government that seemed increasingly eager to use unilateral power and to avoid international agreements and power sharing.

Some have argued that the first great move to globalization that began the twentieth century was stopped, even reversed, by the cataclysm of World War I. The great symbol of globalization of that era, ocean liners such as the *Titanic* and the *Lusitania,* became objects of suspicion, vulnerable to both natural disaster (icebergs) and terror (unannounced torpedo attacks). Is the world of the twenty-first century still coming together, or is it coming apart amidst the flames of nationalism, terrorism, and war?

I firmly believe that globalization will not be reversed in the long term and that new concerns about conflict and terror may even provide a great impetus for global agreements and actions, just as the short-term interruption of World War I soon forced new international agreements, such as the League of Nations and the Geneva Conventions. Economic globalization is not easily reversed. Even as U.S. and British tanks were still rolling across the Iraqi desert, U.S. companies were vying for the rights to secure contracts to rebuild the country and European companies were complaining about being left out. The logic of global capitalism continues to seek new markets and new opportunities.

Similarly, while the Bush administration seemed to prefer a unilateral solution to the Iraq problem, it nonetheless found itself seeking approval of the United Nations (U.N.) Security Council and wooing the support of many small nations. The support of these countries didn't matter much for the military situation, but they greatly added to the sense of legitimacy in the operation. Similarly, some countries that many in the United States would find difficult to locate on the map, such as Djibouti (look north of Ethiopia, next to Somalia), became extremely strategic as staging grounds for special forces and other military action. Cultural globalization is also not easily avoided. Many around the world who opposed U.S. action in Iraq were quick to note that they did not hate Americans or American culture. As one young protestor in Madrid noted in succinct English, "Bush sucks; Santana rocks!" And as this example reminds us, even U.S. cultural influence is increasingly multicultural, a commercial re-exportation of ideas and art forms from around the world.

One reason that globalization will not be reversed is that it is ancient. People have long set out in search of the land beyond the horizon, driven by the desire for commerce (economic globalization), control (political globalization), and sheer curiosity (cultural globalization). Globalization began with the first humans to stride out of Africa. Anthropologists contend that these first human explorers may have reached Australia, across thousands of miles and a strait of open water, in a matter of generations. In time, so-called prehistoric and uncivilized humans—that is, people who lived before the advent of writing and urban life—extended their reach to almost every point on the globe that wasn't buried under a mile of ice.

Early civilizations were far more interconnected than we first supposed. We have learned to think in terms of Western civilization (Europe) and Eastern civilization (China). In fact, the ancient world had at least four interconnected and overlapping centers of civilization.

Mediterranean society included both the northern (European) shore and the southern (African) shore of the Great Sea. The idea that Europe and Africa were different continents would have seemed strange to ancient inhabitants of the Mediterranean region. Rather, they struggled for control, sought commerce, and explored out of curiosity from a circle of competing and cooperating power centers: Athens, Tyre, Alexandria, Cairo, Carthage, Rome, Venice, and many others at various times.

Another cultural center centered on what Europeans later called the Middle East: the Tigris and Euphrates Rivers, the Persian Gulf, and the Iranian plateau. This area included some of the earliest kingdoms on earth (then, the Persian and Parthian Empires), and later became the center of Arab realms, centered on Baghdad, that stretched across North Africa and traded in both the Mediterranean Sea and the Indian Ocean. Parts of this area later became part of several Turkish Empires.

In India, civilization began early along the Indus River. Then power changed hands often, many times due to a series of invaders from the north, mixing Hinduism and Islam and several other faiths but always retaining a particularly Indian flavor.

Finally, for much of the ancient and medieval world, the greatest center of power and culture was China. Originally, this region comprised two centers: one in the north along the Hwang Ho or Yellow River and one in the south along the Yangtze River. In time, these centers merged and drew many of their neighbors into their sphere. Some remained politically and culturally distinct—Japan, Vietnam, Mongolia, Tibet—while exchanging ideas and influence with the Chinese center.

Each of these centers of power and culture, at one time or another, saw itself as the center of the world, an oasis of culture surrounded by barbarians, infidels and heathen, and hostile hordes. Yet while the centers maintained their own cultural distinction, they were always in interaction with one another: trading, fighting, and exchanging ideas and innovations, merchants and spies. The boundaries of cultures, like those of empires were fluid and often overlapping. The Great Silk Road connected the Roman Empire and the Han Chinese Empire, a trade route that, in one form or another, persisted for centuries. Sometimes, they carried on a vigorous traffic in products and ideas with the very nomads beyond their borders that they most despised (Weatherford 1994). Once they became seafaring, traders and merchants from the Phoenicians to the Arabs to the Portuguese carried these products and ideas into exchange with the coast of Sub-Saharan Africa and the islands of what is now Indonesia.

After tenuous connections along icy northern routes, open-water seafaring allowed Europeans to extend their commerce, control, and curiosity to the

Americas. Though they were slow to realize it, what they encountered in the Americas was also a network of empires and cultures with trade routes that spanned North, Central, and South America and the Caribbean. As American gold and silver traveled in European ships to purchase goods in Chinese ports, the great American regional network became fully part of a global world system (Wallerstein 1974).

The continued global extension of commerce, control, and curiosity poses new and changing challenges to students. Economic globalization challenges students to be able to operate both effectively and ethically in the global marketplace. It has been said that one can buy in any language, but if one hopes to sell, he or she better know the language of the customer. This is also true of culture and society. To market global wares, one needs to understand the culture of the customer. To market wares ethically in a world filled with graft and exploitation, one needs to understand a great deal about world politics, society, and economic systems.

Political globalization challenges students to understand the nature of power and the meaning of **global citizenship.** Some have contended that many places have lost their sense of **national citizenship:** the rights and responsibilities that are conferred on those who are part of the nation. Yet we need somehow to claim a new sense of global citizenship: the rights and responsibilities conferred on all who are part of humanity.

Cultural globalization challenges students to understand and appreciate different ways of seeing the world, of expressing themselves, and of building a satisfying life. **Culture shock** is the term applied to those who travel to new locations without adequate preparation and are overwhelmed by the differences. In a globalized world, it is possible to experience culture without ever leaving home. New people, new ideas, new ways of life converge on our communities and challenge our set ideas of how life should be lived. Cultural awareness and appreciation allow us to feel at home in a world of diverse ideas and ways of life.

How do we meet these challenges? First, we must go beyond the "toe in the water" syndrome. This is seen when a student of a foreign language learns just enough to say "No, I don't speak . . ." in the target language, never learning enough to use the language and so forgetting it. A similar process can happen when we learn just enough to feel overwhelmed but never expand our skills and awareness enough to feel conversant in the ways of the world and at home anywhere on the planet.

We must also get beyond the "blue box" syndrome. This is seen in textbooks, where a newly realized issue or group is confined to discussion in boxes (often pale blue, but this depends on the taste of the publisher). For example, the history of the nation is told largely from the perspective of white men (often, politicians and generals), but then there is a box for "Women in History" or "Great

African Americans in History," as though this perspective was an afterthought rather than a central part of the story. Global issues are still often confined to the blue boxes of many texts. The story told is of events and issues within a single country, and an occasional box is included with information on "Marriage in India" or "Education in Japan." One gets the impression that these boxes provide interesting sidelines and tangents but something apart from the real story. Given its size and current world dominance, no place has been a greater offender in this area than the United States. But this denies the reality of our interconnected, interwoven world. A terrorist cell in Frankfurt today is in Boston tomorrow; a virus in Hong Kong yesterday is in Toronto today. There are no sidelines anymore. The entire globe occupies center stage, and the drama is enfolding our lives.

Plan of the Book

Globalization today is fraught with possibilities and dangers, as it has always been. A global reach brings new opportunities for prosperity and progress. It also brings new concentrations of power that monopolize opportunity and deny it to others. Globalization brings the promise of the empowerment of individuals and communities and the integration of these communities into a new world community of exchange and respect. It also brings the harsh possibilities of even greater exploitation of the poor and powerless and exclusion of the mass of humanity from the promised prosperity. Around the world, we see the irony of workers clamoring for jobs in the global economy and leaders begging for global investment while protests grow against international labor exploitation, mounting and unsupportable international debt, and the unchecked power of new and expanding global trade and finance organizations. The world cannot seem to agree whether this powerful genie of globalization is good or evil, but one thing is certain: The genie will not be stuffed back into the bottle. We must make it work for us.

In the chapters that follow, I offer brief overviews of some of the many issues that have emerged in this rapidly changing world. On one level, this book is a story of global problems: poverty, violence, and environmental destruction. On another, it is a story of persistent hope: the continuing search for equity, peace, and sustainability. Part One (Chapters One through Four) focuses on a world in the grip of economic globalization and what it means to build an equitable world amidst vast inequalities. Part Two (Chapters Five through Eight) look at issues of power and conflict: the prospects for a more peaceful world emerging out of the cauldron of war, civil strife, and terrorism. Part Three (Chapters Nine through Twelve) looks at issues of culture and the environment: what it will take to build a sustainable society that can nourish the needs of our grandparents and those of our great-great grandchildren.

Clearly, there are no simple answers. But we must never assume that there *are* no answers. If we must abandon easy answers, we should not abandon hope but go on to tougher questions and seek better, even if they are more complex, answers. Our search for ideas, explanations, and answers will take us across the social sciences: anthropology, human geography and social history, economics, political science, and sociology. We will also need to draw on insight from the natural sciences, especially for understanding the environment within which we must make our decisions. Finally, we will need to reference the humanities and humanistic pursuits: to learn from one another's stories and ideals, as captured in literature, ethics, world views, and the arts.

Again, the goal is not to try to learn everything about everywhere but to weave together the strands we have gathered from many pursuits to speak to the issues raised by a world in search of equity, peace, and sustainability. Certainly, this is a call worthy of our best learning and thinking and our most determined efforts.

CHAPTER 1

Class
A World of Rich and Poor

Cantrall, Illinois

George and Mary Jo Paoni have been looking forward to their retirement. George is leaving his job as a meat cutter, and Mary Jo is retiring from a state government job. They had thought they might leave this farming community outside Chicago and move to Florida. But they may have to adjust their retirement plans to more modest expectations. Their retirement savings aren't looking as healthy as they once did. In particular, they have been hurt by economic downturns in Southeast Asia. How can this be?

The Paonis are conservative Midwesterners who have never traveled outside the United States and have no interest in international finance. George claims that if he wants to gamble, he'll play cards with his friends. What he and Mary Jo hadn't considered is that a large portion of their savings is in a mutual fund managed by A. G. Edwards. This fund specializes in so-called emerging markets. Not that many years ago, they were termed *Third World stocks* and only the most adventurous investors would even consider them. But the term *emerging markets* sounded promising, and indeed, for much of the 1990s, these stocks did very well.

Where are these emerging markets? In this case, they are in Russia, Brazil, and Southeast Asia, especially Indonesia. All of these countries have experienced recession and problems with their emerging markets, problems now reflected in falling stock prices that may affect where the Paonis will retire. George and Mary Jo never realized their future was tied to the future of countries that they were hardly even aware of as they went about their work (Kristof and Wyatt 1999).

Mojokerto, Indonesia

The economic struggles have been even more painful for Salamet, a rickshaw driver in this midsized town east of Jakarta. He has a choice to make that no one would envy.

His mother lies dying on the floor of their home—not just dying but racked by pain from the inoperable cancer that will soon take her life. Salamet can afford the $2-a-month painkiller prescribed by the doctor, but he has chosen not to fill the prescription. It is not that Salamet is calloused toward his mother. Far from it. That is why he broods and struggles with his own pain. His wife, Yuti, points out that if he uses their money to buy this medicine, he will fall behind in payments on the rickshaw. It could then be repossessed, and he would lose the family's only livelihood. An alternative would be not to pay the school fees for their son Dwi, now in second grade. But without the fees, Dwi might be expelled and have no hope for the future.

What should a dutiful son, husband, and father do? Honor his mother and buy the medicine, honor his current commitments and keep up payments on the rickshaw, or look to the future and ensure his son's schooling? Salamet's wife tells him angrily that he must earn more money, but ironically, more investment in this community has meant more rickshaw drivers. That has meant more competition, and now the economic downturn means fewer customers. Salamet has always known poverty, growing up in a family of poor agricultural laborers. (His father fell to his death while pruning palm trees.) He went into the rickshaw business with his stepfather as economic investment poured into this community, creating new businesspeople who wanted to ride rather than walk.

In this midst of all this, Salamet ponders his obligations and his options: Would a reduced dose of painkiller be effective? Would they really expel his son? How close is he to losing his rickshaw and his livelihood? He has not responded to his wife's prodding with angry outbursts and violence, as is common in this town, but he broods over his options (Kristof and Wyatt 1999).

Compared to what Salamet is facing, the options facing the Paolis seem far better: postpone retirement, remain closer to home, scale back their aspirations. Yet they, too, wonder how their future became bound up in the shifting fortunes of a world economy.

Inequalities between and among Nations

The most glaring fact that strikes a world traveler (at least one who ventures beyond airports and look-alike resorts) is that the world is full of inequality. We live on a planet of rich nations and poor nations: glaringly, often grotesquely unequal (see Table 1.1). Upon closer inspection, the inequalities do not fade but rather become more complex.

Even as the aircraft circles over the capital of some poor nation, the tall, gleaming buildings sparkle, the auto traffic forms long lines, and the tiny blue pools of elite hotels and secluded residences shine. Clearly, poor countries have many signs of wealth. The opposite happens in a wealthy country, sometimes even in the trek

| TABLE 1.1 | International Comparisons in Income and Well-Being |

Country	GDP per Capita (Real Purchase Power) 2002	Life Expect. at Birth 2002	School Enrollment Ratio 2002	Human Development Index (HDI) 2002
High Human Development				
Norway	36,600	78.9	98	0.956
Sweden	26,050	80.0	114	0.946
Australia	28,260	79.1	113	0.946
Canada	29,480	79.3	95	0.943
Netherlands	29,100	78.3	99	0.942
Belgium	27,570	78.7	111	0.942
Iceland	29,750	79.7	90	0.941
United States	35,750	77.0	92	0.939
Japan	26,940	81.5	84	0.938
Ireland	36,360	76.9	90	0.936
Switzerland	30,010	79.1	88	0.936
United Kingdom	26,150	78.1	113	0.936
France	26,920	78.9	81	0.932
Germany	27,100	78.2	88	0.925
Mexico	8,970	73.3	74	0.802
Medium				
Bulgaria	7,130	70.9	76	0.796
Russian Federation	8,230	66.7	88	0.795
Brazil	7,700	68.0	92	0.775
Saudi Arabia	12,650	72.1	57	0.768
China	4,580	70.9	68	0.745
India	2,670	63.7	55	0.595
Low				
Pakistan	1,940	60.8	37	0.497
Kenya	1,020	45.2	53	0.488
Haiti	1,610	49.4	52	0.463
Ethiopia	780	45.5	34	0.359
Sierra Leone	520	34.3	45	0.273
Country Averages				
All Developing	4,054	64.6	60	0.663
Least Developed	1,307	50.6	43	0.446
High Income	29,000	78.3	93	0.935
World	7,804	66.9	64	0.729

Source: Adapted from United Nations, *Human Development Report* (2004): Table 1.

between the airport and a downtown hotel. The poor and the homeless shuffle along the streets: sometimes selling, sometimes begging, sometimes waiting. Clearly, rich countries have many signs of poverty.

And while the old adage about the rich getting richer and the poor getting poorer is often repeated, there is always a mix of people and places in between, everywhere. "These poor countries have no middle class, just rich and poor" is something I often hear repeated. Yet travel through the downtown of that capital or major city, anywhere, and you will see people, often in Western-style business clothes, hurrying to work, reading newspapers, riding trains. They buy hot dogs from street vendors in New York, tacos from sidewalk stands in Mexico City, and curried rice from vendors in New Delhi, and then they hurry into one of those look-alike office buildings. These are neither the idle rich nor the idle poor but some version of a global middle class. Better off in some places, more at risk of economic disaster in others, they nonetheless share many of the same worries.

This is the double divide: a big gap between rich and poor nations and a big gap between rich and poor within nations (see Figure 1.1). Working in the gap are many in the middle, wondering if they will ever climb to the top and worrying that they might someday fall to the bottom.

The gap between nations is still greater than the gap within any single country (United Nations 2003). The richest 5 percent of the world's people receive more than 100 times the income of the poorest 5 percent. In fact, the richest 1 percent alone receives more income than the poorest 50 percent of the world's people (see Table 1.2). There is some evidence that income inequality between countries is declining (Firebaugh 2003). This is not true uniformly around the world, however. Incomes in Sub-Saharan Africa have fallen absolutely, leaving much of Africa

The double divide: Great gaps in wealth and income remain between countries, but within almost any country one finds large, and often growing, gaps between rich and poor residents. In New York (left) and in Durban, South Africa (right), the pattern is disturbingly the same.

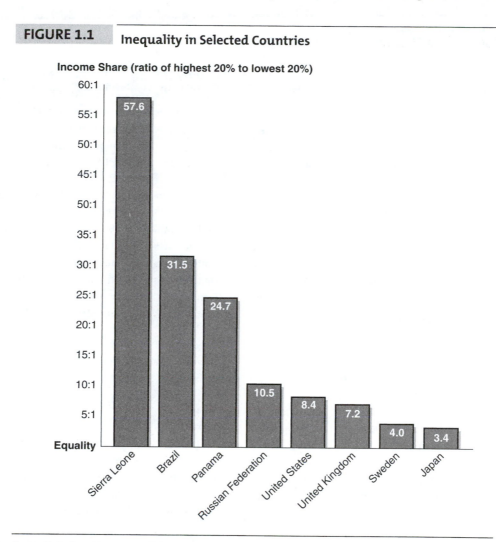

FIGURE 1.1   Inequality in Selected Countries

Income Share (ratio of highest 20% to lowest 20%)

Source: Data from *Human Development Report 2004: Identity, Diversity, and Globalization* by United Nations Development Programme, copyright © by the United Nations Development Programme. Used by permission of Oxford University Press, Inc.

even further behind the rest of the world than in 1990. In 1820, Western Europe's per capita income was only about 3 times that of Africa's; by 1992, it was over 13 times that of Africa, and the gap continues to grow.

The closing of the worldwide gap is due entirely to gains in Asia and in two countries in particular. Both China and India have seen dramatic growth in overall income, with the rate of growth greatest in China. Since these two countries alone account for one-third of the planet's population, this has a big impact on the overall figures. Big gains have also been seen in the city–state of Singapore,

TABLE 1.2	Twenty-Five Richest People: 2004

Rank	Name	Age	Worth ($bil)	Country of Citizenship	Residence
1	William Gates III	48	46.6	United States	United States, WA, Medina
2	Warren Buffett	73	42.9	United States	United States, NE, Omaha
3	Karl Albrecht	84	23.0	Germany	Germany, Donaueschingen
4	Prince Alwaleed Bin Talal Alsaud	47	21.5	Saudi Arabia	Saudi Arabia, Riyadh
5	Paul Allen	51	21.0	United States	United States, WA, Mercer Island
6	Alice Walton	55	20.0	United States	United States, TX, Fort Worth
6	Helen Walton	84	20.0	United States	United States, AR, Bentonville
6	Jim Walton	56	20.0	United States	United States, AR, Bentonville
6	John Walton	58	20.0	United States	United States, AR, Bentonville
6	S Robson Walton	60	20.0	United States	United States, AR, Bentonville
11	Liliane Bettencourt	81	18.8	France	France, Paris
12	Lawrence Ellison	59	18.7	United States	United States, CA, Redwood Shores
13	Ingvar Kamprad	77	18.5	Sweden	Switzerland, Lausanne
14	Theo Albrecht	81	18.1	Germany	Germany, Foehr
15	Kenneth Thomson & family	80	17.2	Canada	Canada, Toronto
16	Mikhail Khodorkovsky	40	15.0	Russia	Russia, Moscow
17	Carlos Slim Helu	64	13.9	Mexico	Mexico, Mexico City
18	Michael Dell	39	13.0	United States	United States, TX, Round Rock
19	Steven Ballmer	47	12.4	United States	United States, WA, Redmond
19	Li Ka-shing	75	12.4	Hong Kong	Hong Kong, Hong Kong
21	Bernard Arnault	55	12.2	France	France, Paris
22	Walter, Thomas, & Raymond Kwok	—	11.4	Hong Kong	Hong Kong, Hong Kong
23	Barbara Cox Anthony	80	11.2	United States	United States, HI, Honolulu
23	Anne Cox Chambers	84	11.2	United States	United States, GA, Atlanta
25	Roman Abramovich	37	10.6	Russia	Russia, Anadyr

Source: Available online at www.forbes.com/maserati/billionaires2004/rank.html.

in Korea and Taiwan, and in urban Thailand. The rural–urban gaps also remains large, however. Most of the gains have been in large commercial cities; rural areas, especially in India, have lagged far behind.

This points to a common problem: Comparisons between countries may mean less than comparisons between groups and regions within countries. Cosmopolitan and high-tech Mumbai (Bombay), India, may flourish along with Seattle, Washington, while the hill country of the northern part of the Indian state of Uttar-Pradesh may languish along with the hill country of eastern Kentucky.

Theories of Class and Economy

The Wealth of Nations: Adam Smith

Why are some nations rich and some poor? This question has puzzled social observers for centuries. One of the earliest attempts to answer this question came from a British analyst, Adam Smith. In 1776, the same year that America declared its independence, he wrote *An Inquiry into the Nature and Causes of the Wealth of Nations* (1937). By this time, a century or more of political philosophers in Europe had debated the nature of the state. Now at the dawn of the Industrial Revolution, Smith pioneered a field that came to be known as **political economy,** which examines the relationship of the political state and the economy, both national and international.

Smith came out of a group of philosophers that became known as the **utilitarians,** very practical-minded people who saw the essence of morality as gaining the greatest good for the greatest number. They believed the way to do this was to allow people to freely pursue their own personal gains, some might even say selfish gains, with as little restraint as possible. Utilitarians believed in individual rights and freedoms: as Thomas Jefferson wrote in the Declaration of Independence that same year, "the right to life, liberty and the pursuit of happiness." (He originally had the word *property* in this sentence.)

Adam Smith believed that these freedoms would also lead to greater wealth. People needed to be free from greedy monarchs who might try to overtax and control commerce (although Smith, unlike Jefferson, remained a loyal subject of the British monarch). He believed in what the French called *laissez-faire,* or that the best government would let capitalists, merchants, and workers pursue their own goals without interference. In a famous phrase, he stated that the "invisible hand" of the market would ultimately turn this selfish ambition into the greatest good for the greatest number. Nations that followed this advice would grow wealthier, such as Britain and the Netherlands perhaps. Those that ignored this advice were doomed to fall into decline, no matter how rich their holdings in land and gold; Spain and Portugal were a case in point. Those who distrusted commerce and believed that society needed the heavy hand of the king and the church to function became known as **conservatives,** and people who followed Smith's ideas about free markets became known as **liberals.** They were indeed the liberal reformers of their day.

This philosophy has seen an enormous revival all around the world, as countries have turned to free trade and free markets in search of wealth. Its proponents are sometimes called **neoliberals** and their views **neoliberalism.** This has caused no end of confusion in the United States, where free trade and laissez-faire capitalism is often the philosophy of political conservatives. (The idea has been around long enough that now it is the **conservative** position.) Unlike Adam Smith, however, U.S. conservatives often want the government to be involved in issues of personal morality, so those who believe in a true hands-off approach to governance are sometimes called **libertarians.**

The Libertarian Party in the United States echoes Adam Smith's belief that giving individuals great liberties to pursue their own ends will ultimately result in greater wealth and greater good. While many are suspicious of the extremes of this position, dissatisfaction with government interference has led many around the world to endorse the free-market, free-trade principles of Smith. This approach is also known as **neoclassical economics,** the economic vision of the early utilitarians.

To be fair, Smith was not as blind to the dangers of laissez-faire capitalism as is sometimes supposed. He recognized that free trade was in danger not just from greedy, manipulative monarchs but sometimes also from greedy, manipulative corporations that might seek great monopolies. Smith, of course, was not thinking of Microsoft but of similar entities of his day, like the Hudson's Bay Company (Korten 2001).

The Misery of Nations: Karl Marx

Three-quarters of a century after Smith, Karl Marx looked at his ideas about the productive power of global capitalism and couldn't have agreed more. Capitalism, Marx agreed, was the most productive engine of economic growth ever conceived. But rather than an "invisible hand" that benefitted all, Marx believed that behind global capitalism loomed deep contradictions that would eventually cause the entire system to unravel:

1. **A growing divide between owners and workers.** Marx contended that every age was divided between those who owned or controlled the productive power of the state and those they depended on for the actual work of production. In the slave societies of the ancient world, such as Greece and Rome, wealthy citizen landowners depended on the work of slaves as well as foreign subjects to produce the wealth that made their cities and rural estates so fabulous. In medieval Europe, the nobility controlled the society through an elaborate hierarchy of power known as **feudalism.** But the wealth of kings and noblemen was dependent on the work of poor peasants. Sometimes, the peasants had a measure of independence,

but many of these were **serfs,** virtual slaves tied to the land and owing everything to the landowner. Marx focused his attention on Europe in particular but much the same arrangements existed in China at the same time as well as in feudal Japan.

Capitalism and the capitalists eventually overturned the feudal nobility, as wealthy merchants and bankers became more rich and powerful than the old nobles. Industrial capitalism, with its demands for large investments in factory production, further gave power to the new capitalist class. They, in turn, depended on industrial workers, the **proletariat,** to do the hard and dirty work of industrial production. But capitalism took an ancient story to new heights: The new capitalists were far richer and commanded more resources than the ancients ever could have dreamed of. At the same, Marx believed that industrial workers were being driven to a uniform level of misery.

2. A continual crisis of profit for owners. The capitalist owners could not sit back and relax in their wealth, however. Capitalism proved intensely competitive. The capitalists always had to worry about being driven out of business by new competition. This competitive struggle forced them to try to increase production by getting more work out of their workers while also cutting costs by cutting wages to a bare subsistence level. The owners would only pay the workers the minimum needed to survive and keep working.

3. Workers driven to the level of subsistence. This is one of the contradictions of capitalism that Marx liked to note. As the system became more productive, the workers did not benefit but became more desperate. Greater productive power stemming from new machinery did not result in rising wages but in more displaced workers. These workers formed a "reserve army" of unemployed who would be eager for any work at any wage. Workers who demanded better conditions were therefore easily threatened with firing and replacement by these desperate displaced workers.

4. Greater solidarity and class consciousness among workers. The capitalists might try to hide the true nature of the system from the larger society by controlling the government and the ruling ideology. The workers could be divided from one another by race/ethnicity and position and told to fear the competition or competition from the unemployed "scoundrels" after their jobs. Nonetheless, the result of working side by side with others in similar situations (unlike peasants, who might be widely separated from one another) would eventually cause workers to see their common condition. They developed a sense of **class consciousness** and ultimately banded together to challenge the system.

Marx believed that ultimately, the only effective challenge would be a revolution that overturned the capitalist system in favor of a system of common ownership for the common good, a system of pure **communism.** In the meantime, however, he encouraged workers and his fellow communists to work with progressive reformers to establish a minimum wage, reduce working hours, ban child labor, and improve the conditions and protections of workers everywhere. These efforts would not solve the problems of a system that is ultimately rotten to the core, but they would raise awareness of the worker's plight and eventually lead to a groundswell of support for a new and better system.

Assessing the Views

So, who is right, or are we all just grasping at theoretical straws in trying to understand a changing world? One view is that Adam Smith was right all along but that his ideas have never been fully applied. Few talk about *modernization* anymore; now the new buzz word is *globalization.* Yet many of the underlying ideas are the same. Perhaps some of the original modernization school was ethnocentric, believing the world should all adopt the ways of the West in general and the United States in particular. Yet, this view contends, modern technology, ideas, and institutions are important because they form the foundation of free and open global trade. Free markets and free trade work, this view contends, at least as long as there are certain modern institutions, such as the World Trade Organization (WTO), to make sure that everyone plays fair.

Adam Smith was basically right about how economies work, it is just that for over two hundred years, governments have been reluctant to step back and allow free markets to do their magic. Global trade will eventually benefit everyone, as it has already benefitted some export-oriented countries in East Asia. Promoting business is good business for all, because wealth will eventually trickle down from rich nations to poor and from rich investors to poor workers. A key step is to limit the power of government and encourage **privatization,** which involves replacing government programs with private enterprise. This view was embraced and exported in the 1980s by Prime Minister Margaret Thatcher in Great Britain and President Ronald Reagan in the United States, where it was dubbed "Reaganomics." It is still seen as an Anglo–American idea in parts of Europe and viewed with some suspicion, but the idea proved popular around the world in the 1990s. All across Latin America, left-wing governments influenced by dependency thinking and right-wing governments bent on modernizing by force have been replaced by governments promoting economic reforms that include privatization, freer markets, and freer trade.

This view has been tempered recently, in accord with Smith himself, who saw dangers in completely unregulated trade. The so-called **third-way economics** of Great Britain's Prime Minister Tony Blair, who first took office in 1997, has been heavily influenced by social theorist Anthony Giddens (1999, 2000).

This approach has called for a smaller but still active government that promotes trade, even as it works to protect the rights of workers and assist those who have not benefitted from globalization. In the United States, President Bill Clinton supported free-trade initiatives—such as the North American Free Trade Agreement (NAFTA), which went into effect in 1994—but sought to include labor and environmental protections. Advised by economist David Ellwood (1988), sociologist Mary Jo Bane, and other social scientists, Clinton proposed reforms to help those for whom globalization was not providing opportunities. Likewise, President George W. Bush champions the benefits of small government and free trade around the country and around the world but has endorsed a "compassionate conservatism" that offers some help to those hurt by global neoliberal economics.

In Brazil, sociologist Fernando Henrique Cardoso studied both Marx and Smith and wrote thoughtful accounts of dependency and development in Latin America as an academic (Cardoso 1977; Cardoso and Falletto 1979). He became a senator, then finance minister, and then president of Brazil. As president from 1995 to 2002, this dependency scholar seemed to embrace the neoliberalism of privatization and free trade. Cardoso contended that his policies were in fact **neosocial,** embracing smaller government and freer markets but, like Clinton and Blair, trying to use the power of government to assist those hurt by these policies while supporting investments in education. Cardoso won great praise for stabilizing Brazil's uncontrolled economy while preserving democracy. But like Bush, he has had to confront how these policies will address the needs of a country in recession.

Another view is that Karl Marx was right all along but that his ideas haven't been fully applied. A popular joke in Russia, as it struggled with the economic transition toward capitalist markets was that "Everything the communists told us about communism was a lie. Unfortunately, everything they told us about capitalism is true." The Soviet government had told the Russian people that communism would bring them prosperity, modernity, and economic equality. It did not. The government had warned that capitalism would only bring poverty, inequality, unemployment, corruption, and crime. It has. What went wrong?

Some argue that communism is inherently flawed—that is it doesn't take into account the realities of economics or human nature (although Marx was an astute observer of both). Others contend that it has yet to be fully tried. First, communism began in the wrong places. Marx looked for revolutions in Germany, Great Britain, and maybe the United States, the advanced industrial nations of his time. Instead, communist systems emerged in Russia, China, Vietnam, and Cuba. Marx did not consider these places ready for true communism. What occurred in these countries was less an uprising of the urban industrial proletariat and more a peasant revolt. Marx himself noted that peasant revolts, though very common throughout history, invariably failed, as the peasantry could not find an effective way to govern themselves without turning to tyrants. (The Greek word originally referred to just this sort of people's leader.) Marx believed that capitalism must emerge first, so that communism could harness its productive might. He also believed that a revolutionary consciousness, one committed to the rights and dignity of all workers, had to be cultivated before a true revolution could occur.

As a result, some are reluctant to call what emerged in Russia and China and several smaller nations *communism*. Marx's communist ideal saw the state, or centralized government, withering away as it was no longer necessary, now freed from its old role of protecting the dominant class. But Russia and China maintained strong centralized and bureaucratic states that only grew. As a result, they are sometimes referred to as **state socialist systems.**

State socialist systems have not fared very well. In 1991, economic and political problems splintered the Soviet system into Russia and many new republics, most of which are gradually moving toward private enterprise systems. The former Soviet bloc of Eastern Europe is also embracing free markets and privatized economies, some with more success than others. China has retained its communist-era bureaucracy but is wide open to foreign capitalist investment and trade. Vietnam and Cuba have retained a few communist slogans but are also courting foreign capitalist investment. To neoliberal economists, this shows the ultimate weakness of communism. To pure Marxists, it only shows that these countries were not ready for true communism and that the capitalist world system wasn't ready to allow them to develop it.

Further, many find that what the communists told them about the evils of capitalism seem to be all too real. Eastern European economies are growing but also growing more unequal with high unemployment. The Russian economy is stagnant with all the supposed evils of capitalism—poverty, unemployment, and corporate crime—but few of the benefits. Capitalist institutions have brought great economic growth to China, but human rights concerns have remained. Moreover, some communist institutions, such as basic health care for all, are now threatened by new divides between rich and poor.

Marxists look at this and say Marx was right all along. Reforms, while important, never fully fix the system. Divisions between countries may be important for a time, but the real, ultimate division is between the rich capitalist owners, who get fewer and richer all the time, and the poor proletarian workers, who become more numerous and more impoverished with each decade. To these Marxists, the world is just not yet ready to embrace a real alternative. World systems Marxists believe that only a worldwide revolution can work; otherwise, communist states in a capitalist world will be pressured to play by capitalist rules. Other Marxists still look ahead to future crises of capitalism that will cause the workers in the advanced industrial states to demand a fundamental change in the system. They are at their strongest in highlighting the glaring problems in our current global economy. The challenge remains to devise and demonstrate a fully workable alternative.

Seeking a Third Way: An Optimal Hybrid?

No economic system is purely capitalist, with no government involvement. Even the earliest classic economists recognized that the government must work to ensure a level playing field by protecting people from crime, coercion, fraud, and the like. Over time, more needs were recognized. In particular, free-market capitalism faces two great contradictions that even its supporters have come to acknowledge.

First, while capitalism is based on the idea of the benefits of vigorous competition, capitalist owners, facing the perils of brutal competition, have always been tempted to use their growing power to limit competition. One powerful corporation will buy out all the others or drive them from the market. This was the charge made against Standard Oil at the beginning of the twentieth century and the charge made against Microsoft at the end of that century. Large corporations also may work together to fix prices or control markets. This was the charge made against the great trusts of the late 1800s, controlled by wealthy bankers, that led to the first antitrust legislation. New concerns have emerged from bank mergers, airline mergers, and colossal media mergers. Competitive capitalism can easily become monopoly capitalism, and the government is called on to maintain competition.

The other great contradiction is that free markets work best under conditions of relative equality yet over time tend to produce great inequality. One could imagine a free-market ideal, proposed by some libertarian, that would have everything provided by the market: health care, education, housing, even parks and recreation. If everyone had equal resources, every parent could shop for the best school, every patient could shop for the best medical care, and so forth. But this would require all to have not only equal incomes but also equal wealth and savings and even equal access to information and transportation. Free markets work on a principle of "One dollar, one vote." What is provided is what people can and will pay for. But if some people have huge resources in wealth, income, education, information, and skills, they can control the markets. Those who do not have these resources have no market power and so, too, as in the case of education, no way to gain resources.

Over time, the governments in capitalist societies have stepped into the breech created by unequal access to resources and resulting unequal opportunities. The first and most enduring of these efforts has been the creation of public education.

Over time, other goods have come to be considered a right of citizenship guaranteed to all, rather than a market commodity, but which goods are included has varied greatly: health care, legal counsel, employment, and so forth. (We will look at each of these in turn in a later chapter.) In the United States, for example, there is a broad consensus that roads should be public (although private toll roads were common in the 1800s) and that farms should be private (although corporate control of agriculture and basic food supply has drawn concern). However, there is little consensus on the right mix of public and private in education or health care.

At the same time, even states espousing communism have often had considerable room for market activity, especially at the small-scale local level. Large-scale agriculture, manufacturing, and retailing may occur on collective farms, state-owned factories, and state-controlled stores, but there is almost always room for small-scale private enterprise in small farms, crafts, and marketing. In general, just as capitalist nations were increasing the role of government in the 1960s and 1970s, many socialist nations were giving expanded freedoms to private enterprise. This raises the question, Is there an optimal hybrid, a system that provides the best of both systems?

The third-way economics of the Democratic Party in the United States and the Labour Party in Great Britain is one example of an attempt to build an essentially free-market system but one in which the government remains active in aiding the disadvantaged (see Figure 1.2). Even the compassionate conservatism of President George W. Bush in the United States proposes something of a hybrid, which strongly stresses private enterprise and free-market approaches but also sees a role for the government, especially in economic development and education. Japan and East Asia have a system with a strong capitalist core but nonetheless have very active governments in promoting national education and economic development.

Many European states, particularly the Nordic counties, see a significantly larger role for government. While their political parties sometimes have the word *socialist* in their names, these are primarily welfare state systems, in which the economy is largely capitalist but the government is actively involved in promoting the welfare of its people, and some measure of equality, through government programs and income transfers.

The most common hybrid around the world looks to markets as economic engines of growth and development (that is, most production is private) but then looks to the government to guarantee certain basic rights and opportunities. Some redistribution is practiced, such as by taxing the wealthy more heavily and offering credits and subsidies to the poor. The scope of this involvement varies greatly: In parts of Europe, these programs are quite extensive; in North America, they are often quite limited.

FIGURE 1.2 **Child Poverty before and after Government Intervention**

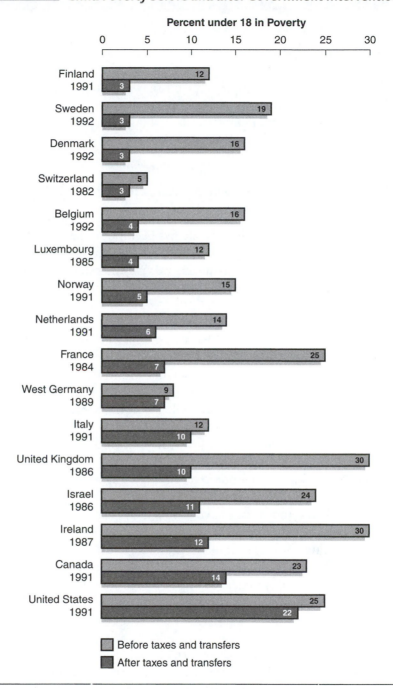

Percent under 18 in Poverty

		Before taxes and transfers	After taxes and transfers
Finland	1991	12	3
Sweden	1992	19	3
Denmark	1992	16	3
Switzerland	1982	5	3
Belgium	1992	16	4
Luxembourg	1985	12	4
Norway	1991	15	5
Netherlands	1991	14	6
France	1984	25	7
West Germany	1989	9	7
Italy	1991	12	10
United Kingdom	1986	30	10
Israel	1986	24	11
Ireland	1987	30	12
Canada	1991	23	14
United States	1991	25	22

■ Before taxes and transfers
■ After taxes and transfers

Source: From L. Rainwater and T. M. Smeeding, "Doing Poorly: The Real Income of American Children in a Comparative Perspective," Luxembourg Income Study Working Paper No. 127, Center for Policy Research, Syracuse University, August 1995; Appendix Table A-2.

An Old Argument: Modernization and Dependency Theories

Why are poor nations poor? Why do they so often stay poor, in spite of what seem to be great efforts to advance? For over half a century, the debate on these points has been dominated by two broad lines of thought: modernization theory and dependency theory.

Time to Clean House: Modernization Theory

The underlying premise of **modernization theory** is that poverty is the basic condition of humanity. People have always been poor. An old adage says that we're born hungry, naked, and crying, and it goes downhill from there. Perhaps the same could be said about humanity in general. We entered the world with great needs, and until we acquired the huge productive capacity of modern society, we lived in poverty.

Modernization thinkers built their ideas on a basic dichotomy between traditional and modern societies that was popular in European social thought in the 1800s, as Europeans and their American counterparts tried to understand the changes brought by urbanization and industrialization. These two forces brought great social dislocations but also incredible productivity; on this point, both Adam Smith and Karl Marx agreed. But what of those societies that did not make the great, often painful leap from traditional society to modern society? With low productivity, they were doomed to stay poor until they changed their ways. To prosper, they needed modernity.

Nations today need modern technology. Peasants working the land—maybe with the help of a draft animal, if they were lucky—would scarcely be able to feed themselves and would have little left over to better their lives; they would remain poor. Artisans and craftspersons using traditional methods might make beautiful things, but they could never make enough of them to raise themselves and their communities out of poverty. They needed industry: tractors, factories, assembly lines, and the energy to drive this production. This was enough for the industrial age of the midtwentieth century, but now with the electronic age, nations also need the computing power and endless electrical grids necessary to organize all this production.

Developing nations need modern ideas. It's not enough just to have the goods without the knowledge and the will to use them. Traditional ideas must go. Traditional values—such as fatalism, patience, humility, communal cooperation, respect for the wisdom of elders and the old order, ties to the land—must be replaced by new modern values—ambition, entrepreneurship, advancement, achievement, and hard-fought competition. The modern ideal (even if rarely achieved) is opportunity for all, regardless of one's inherited status, birthright, ethnicity, or place of origin, but assurances for none. Only hard work and productivity can bring success.

Developing nations need modern institutions. It is no help to believe in education if the schools are all bad. It doesn't help to believe in entrepreneurship if there is no way to begin a business. To prosper, countries need modern governments. Electoral democracy should replace theocracy or monarchy; that is, parliaments or presidents should be put in place of religious leaders and kings. But this is the democracy of Thomas Jefferson and Adam Smith, a limited government that promotes individual freedoms. This government should be free of graft and also of paternalism; it will not promise to repay loyalty with patronage but rather to maintain an open playing field for all. It will be kept in place by a modern electoral process as well as by a free and unbiased press. Business needs to have a secure and stable environment in which to prosper; this requires reliable modern banks and financial institutions, modern insurance companies, and free-market institutions such as stock and commodity markets. Modern schools enroll all children and forego most religious instruction and memorization of ancient texts in favor of learning the skills of the modern technological world.

Together, these views of modernity have provided a powerful vision of progress and prosperity. In the years following World War II, this was the dogma of the United States, Great Britain, Canada, and Australia and, to varying degrees, of Western Europe and Japan. It was encouraged for the newly independent countries of Asia and Africa as well as U.S. allies in Latin America. Mixed with a healthy dose of neoliberal trust in free markets and free trade, this view came to define the **free world.** Modern technology would be brought by multinational corporations building new facilities in the developing world as well as through foreign technical and financial assistance and development loans from new post–World War II institutions, such as the World Bank. Modern ideas would come through Western-model education and Western-dominated global media. Modern institutions would be built with the help of Western managerial assistance as well as through international programs such as the International Monetary Fund (IMF), created at the same time as the World Bank and intended to stabilize national currencies and global economic trade.

Oddly enough, perhaps, modernization thinking also came to define the Soviet model of development, although in this case, it was mixed with the ideas of Karl Marx. Led by the Soviet Union, the communist world was also eager to modernize. Modern technology meant big, state-owned heavy industry. Modern ideas meant the new socialist worker, striving for progress and rejecting traditional religious ideas for a new secular dream of work and opportunity for all, with the rewards of this productivity divided equally. Modern institutions included the complex bureaucratic framework of state socialism, with careful, rational planning ensuring continued gains in efficiency and productivity. These achievements would be exported around the world by Soviet technical advisors and investments and vanguards of enlightened revolutionaries across the globe.

One does not have to spend much time in Latin America, Africa, or South Asia to see that both the capitalist and the socialist visions of modernization have fallen far short of their dreams. To be fair, most in the modernization school of thought always believed that modernization would be slow and painful. But they also believed that progress was inevitable. In much of the world, people are still waiting.

Get Out of My House: Dependency Theory

Since the time of Josef Stalin, national modernization had been a hallmark of the policy of the Soviet Union, but the founder of Soviet communism, Vladimir Lenin, had a slightly different conception of the world. Lenin loved Marxist ideas and preached them with fervor. But influenced by intellectuals among the Russian radicals (Bukharin 1924, 1973), Lenin came to see Marx's picture of capitalist misery not as a state problem, operating within one nation, but as a global problem.

Lenin wrote *Imperialism, the Highest Stage of Capitalism* (1948), arguing that European imperialism—the wild expansion of European empires that was carving up Africa and would eventually help lead to World War I—was driven by the forces of capitalism. Capitalist industry needed new raw materials, more labor, and new markets. Its insatiable thirst for profit drove it on a mad, worldwide chase. But as the industrial empires imported materials, they exported misery. British industry grew while industry in India, a British colony, was crushed. British workers could live better than Marx had predicted only because Indian workers lived so poorly. The squalor, desperation, and misery that Marx had predicted were evident but only in limited fashion in London, because they had been exported to Calcutta. This became the kernel of the idea of **dependency theory.**

Dependency theorists acknowledged that the Western world, or the First World, did bring many things to the poor nations, the Third World, but that most of them were negative and destructive. The destruction came with the European colonial empires but did not leave with them, because new institutions—including multinational corporations, foreign aid, and the World Bank and the IMF—continued to practice neocolonialism. Even after achieving independence, poor countries were hopelessly dependent on the rich. And dependency brought evil in several respects.

Dependency brought exploitation. The poor countries were being ripped off. The terms of trade were rigged against the poor: The rich countries paid them poorly for their raw materials and then sold finished goods to them at high prices. The poor countries were not naturally poor; they had many resources. But the rich countries, not the poor, profited from that natural wealth and left behind little but despoiled, stripped, polluted land when the resources ran out. In the decades following World War II, the rich multinationals came less often in search of raw materials and more often in search of cheap labor, exploiting the people of the land. Once, Europe, Japan, and North America sought out the country that is now Indonesia and once was the Dutch East Indies for its natural rubber. Now, companies such as Nike come to Indonesia to seek reliable, inexpensive labor to stitch athletic shoes made of nylon and synthetic rubber. To dependency thinkers, this shift just perpetuates the gross exploitation.

Dependency has also brought domination. If the terms of trade are so bad and the exploitation so obvious, why don't the poor countries object and throw the multinational companies out? They can't because they are dominated by the vast wealth of these companies and the countries that sponsor them. The newly independent states around the world are not truly independent. They depend on the rich nations for their livelihood (since their independent economies were destroyed long ago by imperial expansion) and so must play by the rules set by the rich. National leaders are bribed or coerced into doing the bidding of rich countries and rich companies, even at the expense of their own people. Those who refuse face sanctions, embargoes, and even outright military intervention.

Dependency has brought distortion. The economies of the poor countries no longer function as an integrated whole; they are entirely structured to serve the needs of wealthy foreigners and maybe a small internal elite. They got help (or borrowed money) to build roads and rails, but the roads and rails mostly lead to port cities to facilitate exports. The goods produced in these countries don't serve local needs, and the local people can't afford them; they are made for foreign markets. The people no longer are self-sufficient but depend on imports from the rich, and so they remain vulnerable to exploitation and domination. And so the cycle continues.

The key to dependency thinking is that the poor were not always poor. They were *made* poor. And this is fundamentally different than the experience of the industrialized wealthy nations. Those countries may also have been undeveloped at one time, with little industry, but they were never underdeveloped. The rich countries developed by stripping wealth from the rest, underdeveloping them in the process (Frank 1967). The poor countries, at least not many of them, cannot do the same, because they are left at the bottom of the heap with no one else to exploit, except maybe their own rural, tribal, or minority populations.

Rooted in Lenin's ideas, dependency thinking gained ground in Latin America, also following World War II. Largely ignored by the industrial West, Latin America had done well in the 1940s, but then new investment and cold war politics seemed to make Latin America more miserable and poor. Dependency theory was clearly the minority viewpoint in industrial North America in the 1950s and 1960s. But as the poor countries remained poor and even got poorer in the 1970s and 1980s, its ideas gained currency. Even the success stories seemed to show failures. Some countries, such as Brazil, saw their economies grow but also the inequalities, and the lives of the poor did not improve. This was the problem of "dependent development" (Evans 1979) or "growth without development."

The most complete extension of dependency thinking came in the 1970s from Immanuel Wallerstein (1974), who in a series of books laid out **world systems theory.** European capitalist expansion began in the 1500s. (You will remember that "Columbus sailed the ocean blue in 1492," and he was soon followed by every European adventurer who could borrow or steal a boat.) Colonial powers created a world economic system that enriched the core nations at the expense of the periphery, their colonies. The world system continues to have a wealthy core supported by a poor periphery. The core of the core has shifted a bit—Amsterdam and the Dutch United Provinces in the 1600s, London and the British United Kingdom in the 1700 and 1800s, New York and the American United States in the 1900s. But the rich have only grown richer while the poor have grown poorer. A small semiperipheral nation, such as Taiwan or Israel, serves a middleman role in advancing the interests of the rich nations.

This was a forceful diagnosis of the world situation, but it proved much harder to find a cure. If modernizationists are still waiting for the promised progress, dependency thinkers are still waiting for the promised alternatives. Socialist China seemed to be charting an independent course but then came to embrace modernization and an export economy after the death of Chairman Mao Zedong. In Cuba in the 1960s, Fidel Castro promised a change but seemed to only move Cuba from dependency on the United States to dependency on the Soviet Union. In the 1980s in Nicaragua, the Sandinista government promised an alternative but became bogged down in corruption and an endless U.S.-sponsored civil war. Nicaragua and Cuba now compete with one another to get more foreign investment. In Africa, the best of theories all seemed to fall under the weight of factional fighting, internal and external corruption, and famine and disease. The search for new ideas continues, and the poor are still waiting.

Looking Back and Looking Ahead

Have people indeed always been poor? The answer to this simple question hinges on what we mean by *poor*. There is an issue of definition and one of judgment. If we mean absolute poverty, or lack of basic needs, then we must note that most of humanity has lived very simply over most history with few material goods. Yet it is not clear that life was always miserable. Many tribal people, that is, living in prestate societies, seemed to have lived quite well. A few still do.

Hunter–gatherers, our earliest ancestors, faced many dangers and challenges. Yet they also seemed to have relished roaming in the openness of the natural world, have had healthy and varied diets of natural plants supplemented with bits of meat, and maybe enjoyed more leisure time to relax, tell stories, and build relationships than most of us will ever know (Sahlins 1972). Simple hunter–farmers and fisher-man in North and South America, in the Caribbean, and in the South Pacific often lived quite well before the Europeans showed up uninvited. Some of those European sailors, in fact, thought they had found paradise. Life for these tribal peoples probably was never pure paradise, but they managed to have a good diet from gardening (horticulture) supplemented by catching fish, seafood, and wild game. They seemed to have had a rich village life, as well, even if almost none were rich by our standards.

The few autonomous tribal peoples that remain in the world may be eager to acquire a shotgun or intrigued by an outboard motor, but they are often also eager to retain their independence and some semblance of their way of life. Certainly, if by *poor* we mean relative poverty, then these people have enjoyed a much smaller gap between the richest and the poorest than in more complex societies.

Did poverty arrive for these societies with European colonization, as the dependency and world systems approaches often contend? For many in the Americas and the Pacific, as well as in Sub-Saharan Africa and parts of Southeast Asia, perhaps it did. They certainly already knew hunger and disease, and all but the simplest and most remote knew warfare. The terrible scourges of famine, plague, and genocidal war were rare, however, and the idea of desperate poverty—going hungry while others ate, going without while others prospered, begging with no accepted social role or vocation—was almost unheard of (McNeill 1963).

But these things did not first appear in 1500. Europe and Asia, and maybe to a lesser extent Mesoamerica from Mexico to Peru, knew these things far earlier. They seem to have come not with the European empires (although the Europeans took them to new extremes) but with the first empires themselves. They came with civilization itself, if by *civilization*, we mean state societies, with cities and rulers supported by large-scale agriculture. They came not with the Industrial Revolution (although it brought a brutal new form of urban poverty) but toward the end of what anthropologists call the **neolithic revolution,** the transition to farming.

Large-scale grain agriculture provided a food surplus that could be stored and shipped and could support mighty empires, from Egypt and Mesopotamia to the great river valleys of India and China. The granaries could support the pharaoh, the king, or the emperor and his armies. The ruler could, in turn, use armed military force to extend territory and bring more people under his (very rarely her) control. Peasants worked the land. They answered to rulers who controlled the land, and their surpluses went to support cities, temples, and armies. Their own diet became dominated by one or two basic foods—often, a grain such as rice, wheat, or maize (American corn). Once drought came, they didn't have a variety of natural foods to which to turn, and they died in mass famines. When war came, large professional armies destroyed the crops. And relative poverty reached extremes. The great rulers lived in fabulous wealth, while the peasants had far less and may have been reduced to bare subsistence or starvation when hard times came.

This was the picture of poverty in the civilized world from about 3000 BCE in the Middle East and China and somewhat later in Mexico and Europe. It is still the picture of rural poverty in much of the developing world. Poor peasants have probably never chosen their fate but had it imposed on them from without. And while few want to remain poor and landless, they may have good reason to fear life in the city. As the cities grew in number and size, rural poverty found a counterpart in urban poverty: begging and work at poorly paid crafts, domestic service, odd jobs, and informal employment. This, too, is as old as the first cities, but it is now the way of life for many of the world's poor. Poor urbanites are almost never content to stay as they are, for they can clearly see what they are missing. They often bear the worst of the modern world's crime and pollution yet see few of its benefits.

Realizing the antiquity of poverty, along with its global spread through colonization, we can see that modernization and dependency have often been processes that occurred side by side. This understanding is important if we are to work for economic development that truly addresses human need.

Modern technology, for better or worse, is essential to our world and people need access to it. A few tribes may want to be left alone (although even the Kayapo of the Brazilian Amazon and the Inupiat of the Arctic have invested in satellite dishes). Poor farmers and poor urbanites need access to technology, only it must be the appropriate technology.

Modern ideas are also growing in importance, even if many of them prove to be more ancient than we originally thought. Once again, these must be appropriate. Much of the world is suspicious of what they are sold as Western popular culture. But they must realize that many in the West, young and old, voice the same suspicions about images of instant gratification without responsibility, about "having it all" at the expense of family, faith, and community. But other presumably modern ideas have roots that go back to our earliest tribal ancestors and strike a chord with people around the world, even if they are often ignored in practice: the dignity and worth of individuals, the rights of women and children, and the importance of opportunities for creative expression for all.

Modern institutions are also needed, even as they often fall short of their ideals. The World Bank, a long-time supporter of free markets, devoted its 2002 World Development Report to "building institutions for markets." Poor farmers and urbanites alike need reliable and accessible financial institutions and affordable credit. Rich and poor alike benefit from a stable currency, a graft-free government, a free and independent press, and a clear and equitable system of laws.

This is the *internal* side of reform and development (Bradshaw and Wallace 1996). Anthropologist Oscar Lewis (1961, 1968) contended that a **culture of poverty** emerged in poor communities in capitalist societies. This culture stressed

fatalism, living for the day rather than planning for the future, and a distrust of outside institutions. Ultimately, Lewis believed, that view was passed on to the children and helped keep them in poverty. Many found Lewis's description compelling, but others saw it as "blaming the victim" (Ryan 1971). They believed that it was not the subculture of poor people that kept them poor but the external structures of a larger society that oppressed and exploited them. Modernization theory is much like the idea of a culture of poverty—in this case, applied to whole societies within a capitalist world. Certainly, we can find many ways in which poor societies need reform, but this can become victim blaming unless we also look at the larger structures, as dependency theory reminds us.

The exploitation of workers around the world can only be changed by new global structures. People and their representatives must also be able to make decisions about their own needs and priorities without facing undue external pressure. Export economies are likely here to stay, but they can be balanced by efforts to meet local needs. A new generation of social scientists have called for development that is both broad based and sustainable (Weaver et al. 1997).

When Markets Fail: Humanizing Development

At the beginning of the twenty-first century, few examples of viable socialism remain. Market economies dominate, even in "communist" China. Yet markets have been slow to deliver the promised benefits to many. As described by former Brazilian president Fernando Henrique Cardoso (1996):

> It's as if the demise of real socialism coincided with some kind of Marx's "revenge." The economy reigns supreme, determining political choices and the limits of social action. And the free market emerges as a leading ideology, fostering competition and an exaggerated, narcissistic individualism that equate the realm of values with the dictates of efficiency. . . . Inherent in the ideal of progress is equity, seen as the convergence of standards of equality of opportunities—or social justice. This idea of equality has nurtured all modern utopias—from the liberal, centered on political equity, to the socialist, concerned with socio-economic equality. Today's demand for equity—denser, more powerful—is searching for new institutional vehicles. It is no longer the monopoly of one group or class. It is now a collective task—to give a human sense to development. (p. 44)

Part of the problem is what's called the **market conundrum.** Markets work best under conditions of relative equality, but over time, they tend to produce conditions of extreme inequality. Pay-as-you-go markets might be acceptable delivery vehicles for food, education, health, and housing if everyone involved had similar market power. Yet in the "one dollar, one vote" logic of the market, some have tremendous power to claim whatever they want while others have no voice at all. The game of Monopoly begins as a free-for-all market and ends with all of the wealth and control concentrated in one player's hands, as the others go bankrupt. Real-world markets, when unregulated, often behave in the same way.

The assumption of market efficiency may also be wrong. Competition can force greater efficiency but can also lead to market inefficiency. Imagine trying to get around town in a city of nothing but competing toll roads: The libertarian's dream would be the motorists nightmare. Competition might be intense, but most of your time would go to paying tolls, and most of what you paid would go to the cost of collecting them. Likewise, four competing toll roads between two cities would likely be disastrous both economically and ecologically. In some cases, people want choice above all, as perhaps in fashion. While we might settle for simple quality clothes, most of us want more choice than the single "Mao suit" of rural China in the 1950s and 60s. But in many other cases, a single quality choice is better than a multitude of poor choices: for instance, one product that lasts in place of ten that don't, one good school in place of six bad ones, or one health insurer that will pay instead of twelve that may not.

Beyond problems of equity and efficiency, there is also the tragedy of the market. Garrett Hardin (1968) wrote about the "tragedy of the commons." He believed that a space that belonged to all would eventually be neglected or abused by all: the collective farm or the world's oceans for that matter. There is also the tragedy of the market, the opposite of Smith's "invisible hand," where individual decisions do not add to the common good but create the worst for all. It may be in my best individual interest to let everyone else use public transit while I drive on open, uncluttered roads. But what happens if everyone decides to do this? Public transit will go bankrupt while traffic jams clog the roads. There is no way out of this by private action, although some have tried helicopters. The only solution is a public commitment.

The ultimate failure of the market can be seen in a basic disjuncture between basic beliefs and everyday life. Despite stereotypes to the contrary, Americans claim overwhelmingly that what matters to them most are family, friends, and faith. Yet most of their time is spent accumulating and caring for material possessions. Somehow, Americans have become captive to the market, and more and more people around the world are experiencing the same fate.

Markets are powerful. But most of what people want, markets cannot provide. Much of what the world is seeking, markets do not provide. Much of the challenge of the twenty-first century will be to tame the markets, promoting equality, opportunity, and second chances while limiting wasteful and destructive choice and agreeing on social solutions. The United Nations has agreed on a series of development goals to focus the world's priorities as it enters the third millennium of the Western calendar (see Table 1.3). With a target date of 2015, time is short, and some locations still have a long way to go before they can rest.

TABLE 1.3 Millenium Development Goals: Status 2004

The chart shows the targets set by the Millennium Development Goals for achievement by 2015.

Goals and Targets	Africa (840 million, Population 2002) Northern	sub-Saharan	Asia (3,738 million) Eastern	Southeastern	Southern	Western	Oceania 8 million	Latin America & Caribbean 536 million	Commonwealth of Independent States (formerly republics of the Soviet Union) 281 million Europe	Asia
POVERTY										
Reduce extreme poverty by half	on track	high, no change	met	on track	on track	increase	…	low, minimal improvement	increase	increase
Reduce extreme hunger by half	low, minimal improvement	very high, no change	on track	on track	progress but lagging	increase	moderate, no change	on track	…	…
PRIMARY EDUCATION										
Universal primary schooling	met	progress but lagging	met	met	progress but lagging	relatively high, no change	progress but lagging	met	decline	met
GENDER EQUALITY										
Equal girls' enrolment in primary schools	met	progress but lagging	met	met	on track	on track	met	met	met	met
Equal girls' enrolment in secondary schools	met	no significant change	…	met	no significant change	decline	on track	met	met	met
Literacy parity between young women and men	lagging	lagging	met	met	low	lagging	lagging	met	met	met
Women's equal representation in national parliaments	progress but lagging	progress but lagging	moderate, no change	progress but lagging	very low, no change	very low, no change	progress but lagging	progress but lagging	decline	decline
CHILD MORTALITY										
Reduce mortality of under-five-year olds by two thirds	on track	very high, no change	progress but lagging	on track	progress but lagging	moderate, no change	progress but lagging	on track	decline	decline
Measles immunization (85% of the population at risk)	met	low, no change	…	on track	progress but lagging	on track	moderate, no change	met	met	met
MATERNAL HEALTH										
Reduce maternal mortality by three quarters	moderate level	very high level	low level	high level	very high level	high level	very high level	high level	…	…
HIV/AIDS, MALARIA, & OTHER DISEASES										
Halt and reverse spread of HIV/AIDS	threatened	some progress	some progress	some progress	significant increase	threatened	threatened	some progress	significant increase	threatened
Halt and reverse spread of malaria	continuing threat	pandemic	met	low level	low level	continuing threat	low level	met	low	low
ENVIRONMENTAL SUSTAINABILITY										
Reverse loss of forests		decline	met	decline	small decline		decline	decline (exc. Caribbean)	met	met
Halve proportion without clean drinking water in urban areas	met	no change	decline	high access but no change	met	met	high access but no change	met	met	met
Halve proportion without clean drinking water in rural areas	high access but little change	progress but lagging	progress but lagging	progress but lagging	on track	progress but lagging	low access, no change	progress but lagging	high access but limited change	high access but limited change
Halve proportion without sanitation in urban areas	on track	low, no change	progress but lagging	on track	progress but lagging	met	high but no significant change	high but no significant change	high but no significant change	high but no significant change
Halve proportion without sanitation in rural areas	progress but lagging	no significant change	progress but lagging	progress but lagging	progress but lagging	no significant change	decline	progress but lagging	decline	decline

= in a particular sub-region, the MDG target has been met, or is on track for achievement or near achievement by 2015.

= progress, but at a rate that is so far insufficient to meet the target.

= areas where there is no change or negative change relative to the target, since 1990, or where current levels are unsatisfactory in comparison with global standards.

A lack of data is shown by a dash.

Sources: United Nations, based on data and estimates provided by: World Bank; Food and Agriculture Organization; UNESCO; Inter-Parliamentary Union; UNICEF; World Health Organization; UNAIDS. milleniumindicators.un.org, Statistics Division of the UN Department of Public Information. Copyrighted by the UN and used by permission.

Fair Trade

- Explore *alternate traders* that may operate in your community or a neighboring city. Alternate traders (sometimes called *fair traders*) attempt to provide an alternative to exploitive international trade relations. They purchase products directly from local producers in low-income countries and communities, often giving special attention to local cooperatives, to women's and poor people's groups, and to products that are produced in socially and environmentally responsible ways. Products include clothing, coffee, and crafts. Often, these are sold with little or no middleman profit, so that a large portion of the retail price returns to the producers.

- Alternate traders with local outlets include Ten Thousand Villages (www.tenthousandvillages.com), SERRV (www.serrv.org), Equal Exchange (www.equalexchange.com), and Marketplace: Handiwork of India (www.marketplaceindia.org). Others can be found at the Fair Trade Resource Network (www.fairtraderesouce.org). Look at these traders' sites for information on fair trade and then check for locations or outlets near you. If possible, visit a store, look at the items (bring your Christmas list if you like!), read the brochures, and talk with store personnel. How do alternate traders attempt to cope with the problems and inequalities of the global economy? Do they provide a viable alternative to the destructive and exploitive aspects of world trade? Why or why not?

The United Nations

- Look at the homepage of the United Nations and the U.N. Development Program (www.un.org). This is "information central" for a host of international issues and statistics. You can focus on a topic of interest such as human rights or gender issues, if you like.

- See also the site for the U.N. Development Program (www.undp.org). This agency of the United Nations collects a wide range of data on global well-being and economic development and publishes the annual *Human Development Report*. What are the key indicators of well-being? Where is progress being made? Where are we losing ground?

CHAPTER 2

Work
The Global Assembly Line

Benin

A slave ship is seized off the West African coast before it can deliver its cargo of human beings. Many are shackled below decks, waiting to be sold. This is not the seventeenth century but the twenty-first century. Slavery has returned.

By some estimates, the illegal trade in humans is exceeded only by the illegal trade in drugs and arms. West Africans, tricked or sold into bondage, are sold to sweatshops, docks, and insurgent armies. In the Brazilian Amazon, debt peons work for huge ranches, bound to the land, without contact with families or homes. Some started so young and so long ago that they have forgotten their names (Le Breton 2003). In Southern Europe, women from Albania and the newly independent Eastern European countries are promised high-wage jobs in Greece and Italy. The women then have their documents seized and are sold as domestics, laborers, and even prostitutes (Karakatsanis and Swarts 2003). Even when authorities deport them, they have often been pulled off trains by traffickers and sent to new locations to be sold again.

Miami

The 2004 meetings of nations from across the Americas to discuss the Free Trade Agreement of the Americas (FTAA) caused quite a stir. The bold idea was to extend the North American Free Trade Agreement (NAFTA), which exists among Canada, the United States, and Mexico, all the way to the tip of South America.

Excitement ran high as proposals were put forward. Could the Americas become a common market as Europe has, moving for several decades toward leading to an expanding European Union (EU)? Miami was pleased to be the host. Maybe this would give it an advantage in the competition with Atlanta and Panama City to become the host city for FTAA institutions, much as Brussels has hosted many EU institutions.

The plan was not without dissent, however. Cuba didn't show up. Costa Rica voiced concerns about market pressures from U.S. media conglomerates. And the streets were filled with protesters. Talks such as these often went unnoticed; the discussions around NAFTA had not raised a stir until much later. But ever since the World Trade Organization (WTO) meetings in Seattle, trade had become a media event. In Seattle, young environmental protestors (a few in whale suits) joined veteran union organizers and self-proclaimed "raging grannies" in chants against free trade and for greater social justice. The protestors also dogged later trade talks in Washington, D.C., and London, spilled out into mass protest in Rome, and then converged on Miami.

A now-familiar pattern repeated itself, as President George W. Bush landed in Chile in November 2004 for the meetings of the Asian–Pacific Economic Cooperation (APEC) conference, a meeting of twenty-one world leaders to promote trade and economic growth. The Chilean government was proud to be the host of the Pacific Rim meeting of countries that control half the world's economy. This event was evidence that it had joined the elite club of wealthy nations. But 30,000 antiwar and anti-globalization protesters were also there. Led by the Chilean Social Forum, one hundred groups opposed to "corporate-led globalization" filled the streets. Why have topics that would have been confined to a macroeconomics classroom suddenly become the rage, quite literally, of the streets?

The Division of Labor

In simpler economies, it is common for many people to be involved in the same tasks. There may be a division between genders and maybe another between nobility and commoners, but economic life is based on just a few divisions. For instance, in hunting-and-gathering societies, all the able-bodied men hunted, all the able-bodied women gathered, and at times, all may have worked together, as in flushing out game or netting fish. In simple horticultural societies, all the men worked in clearing the ground and all the women in planting gardens. In larger-scale agricultural societies, this became more complex. There are noble classes that specialize in warfare (European knights and Japanese samurai) and oversight but never work the land themselves. There are skilled artisans who produce prized products, but their work is usually only for the nobility or elite and so they are few in number. The great majority of people in agrarian, agriculture-based societies work the land. Men and women may work together, as in gathering a harvest or in complementary tasks: plowing, weeding, tending flocks and gardens, and so forth.

Complex societies with more technological economies are based on a complex division of labor. Few of us could maintain anything like our current lifestyle if we personally had to build, maintain, fix, and operate all the material goods that fill our lives. We each specialize in a single pursuit for income, maybe supplemented by hobbies and occasional "moonlighting," and then look largely to markets to provide the diverse goods of our society. This has been true in the industrial world for several centuries, but the degree of specialization and the extent of the markets continues to increase.

Adam Smith: Efficiency

Adam Smith (1937 [1776]) believed that the great efficiency of modern capitalist economies (even as they existed in his day) lay in their complex **division of labor.** Workers could specialize and so be more efficient. In his famous example of a pin factory, Smith noted that even the production of a single industrial pin (what might hold two parts of a machine together) would take one person a very long time, if he or she had to do all the work, from ore to final product. But in fact, each worker only works with a single part of the process. Workers thus become very expert and very efficient in their own parts, and by combining their labor, produce the pins in great numbers at low cost.

The same idea holds for all industrial production. No one at General Motors could produce an entire automobile if he or she had to work alone. Even if the task were given to the most senior engineers, they would take a long time and probably due poor work (as they might not be proficient welders or painters or the like).

Smith saw this ever-increasing division of labor as the key to prosperity. If this efficient production was coupled with efficient markets, so that everyone could have access to the final product, the greatest property would result. But even Smith saw dangers in this. He worried about the collusion of capitalists. Since only the owners would be familiar with the process as a whole, their ability to manipulate production and prices would be increased. Further, since workers would be so specialized that they could not move readily between positions and certainly could not be self-sufficient, he worried that capitalists might also manipulate the **labor market,** the price paid for labor in wages and benefits. It is sometimes forgotten that Smith, the great proponent of free labor and free trade, believed that some government oversight would be necessary to prevent the collusion of powerful interests.

Émile Durkheim: Solidarity

While Smith focused on the economy, a century later, French sociologist Émile Durkheim (1964 [1895]) focused on the effects of a division of labor on overall society. He believed that simpler agricultural societies had strong common bonds, what he called *solidarity,* because so many were engaged in the same tasks. They worked together sometimes, or at least they understood each other and their common concerns. Drought or another affliction for one was common to all.

This solidarity was natural, even mechanical, as people came together without thinking about it. Durkheim referred to it as **mechanical solidarity.** He wondered what would happen to solidarity in modern late–nineteenth century societies. He concluded that they, too, could have solidarity, but it would be of a different type. He called this new bond **organic solidarity** because he believed it was based on a complex division of labor, in which each person contributed his or her specialty to the whole, just as the specialized organs of a body contribute to its overall well-being. People would be bound together because they needed each other.

Max Weber: Work Ethic

Social and political scholar Max Weber also saw a new ethic or sentiment in the new economies; in fact, he believed that a new way of thinking was crucial to building modern capitalist economies. In his classic book *The Protestant Ethic and the Spirit of Capitalism,* Weber (1997 [1905]) argued that in Northern Europe, Protestantism brought a new way of thinking about economic life. Whereas medieval Catholicism was often suspicious of material gain (calling it *avarice* or *greed*) and the desire to advance (calling it *hubris* or *spiritual pride*), Europe's Protestants, beginning in the early 1500s, began to think differently. According to Martin Luther, one's secular vocation was a gift from God and was to be pursued with as much vigor as one's religious duties. According to some Calvinists, wealth was not the root of all evil but could be a sign of God's favor: Had not God blessed Abraham and Solomon with great abundance?

But (and this was crucial) *wealth* did not mean *extravagance.* The Dutch burghers, or rich merchants, and the English Puritans dressed in black wool, not the extravagant colors of silk, satin, and lace that marked the wealthy of the High Middle Ages. To win favor with God and country, they were hard working and shrewd but also diligent and frugal. So what did they do with all that money? If they were true Protestant capitalists, Weber believed, they would reinvest all that money to enlarge the enterprise and make still more money. Weber saw this ethic of frugality and diligence coming to the American colonies, with thinkers like Benjamin Franklin and his famous *Poor Richard's Almanac* (which made Franklin rich, even as he preached frugality).

There are continuing debates about Weber's thesis: Did Protestantism lead directly to capitalism? Or did an emerging middle class, who were not from nobility but certainly didn't want to be part of the peasantry, break with medieval norms to embrace both Protestantism and capitalism? Still, this seemed a powerful combination, and it drove the new American captains of industry during the nineteenth century. John D. Rockefeller, for example, was a staunch and stern Protestant, frugal except in charitable giving, but also a shrewd (some would say ruthless) businessman, who became perhaps the richest man ever. (In real dollars, he was richer than Bill Gates.)

Weber was most concerned about the behavior of the new capitalist *owners,* but his idea, popularized as the **Protestant work ethic,** has often been applied to their *workers.* The maxim for workers is similar, even if the results are often more modest: Work hard, live frugally, invest carefully, and you will advance. In the 1700s, John Wesley, founding thinker of the Methodist and Wesleyan denominations, preached in the slums and flophouses of London a message that seemed to powerfully echo this ethic: Get saved, get sober, and get to work. Some of Wesley's converts indeed learned an organized, methodical (from which we get *Methodism*) way to both worship and work. Some even prospered. Interestingly, Wesley lamented that some lost their religious fervor after they became prosperous.

The ideal of hard work and frugal investment had already been long practiced by Europe's urban Jews, who all through the Middle Ages were a people caught between the medieval estates (or classes of nobility), clergy, and peasantry. In time, the ideal was embraced by Roman Catholics and others, as well. In the United States, it became the ideal for people from all religious backgrounds, preached by populists such as President Theodore Roosevelt, a common man despite his family's great wealth. Some have contended (Bellah 1957) that the Shintoism of Japan and the Confucianism of East Asia espoused a similar ethic that continues to encourage hard work in those regions. Modernization theorists (Wiener 1966) have contended that this ethic of getting ahead through ambition, hard work, and frugality was essential to building a modern capitalist economy.

Karl Marx: Alienation

Karl Marx (see McLellan 1977, 1988) saw many of these same changes in the world of work but mused about the darker side of the changes. He agreed with Smith that the capitalist system of production, coupled with an ever more specialized division of labor, led to greater productive capacity. But he worried that part of this specialization was the deskilling of workers. Instead of a gunsmith knowing how to make an entire firearm, he now punched out a single firing pin to be assembled into a whole that he could not make himself and that he might never even see. Such an individual amplified Smith's concern that deskilled workers were vulnerable workers, who could be replaced just like the cogs in a great impersonal machine.

Marx also believed that the movement from an agrarian to an industrial society could bring greater solidarity among workers. Unlike the peasant farmer, who might work as family units separated, at least some of the time, from their fellow workers, the industrial worker, the proletariat, stood shoulder to shoulder on the assembly line and could forge a common bond of solidarity. But Marx also believed that the work ethic could be manipulated by the capitalist owners to keep workers divided and complacent. Competition between and within plants could keep workers divided, while religious threats and promises could be used to keep them from challenging the system.

Above all, Marx believed that modern industrial workers in capitalist economies experienced profound **alienation.** Work, he believed, was meant to be ennobling and purposeful, a source of pride and accomplishment. But modern industrial workers labored at routine, deskilled, repetitive tasks on minute parts of products that meant nothing to them and that they themselves maybe could never afford. And the truth was, most would never advance, no matter how hard they worked. Work was not just harsh; it was meaningless.

The New International Division of Labor

Around the world, the division of labor continues to become more complex, and new specialists continually emerge. Not just industrial workers but service and professional workers continue to specialize in increasingly more narrow fields. Even highly educated people often know a great deal about a very narrow field of specialty. More and more physicians, for example, specialize in narrow subfields of medicine, and more attorneys practice only one type of law. Every year, the Yellow Pages of the phone book have more categories and subspecialties.

This is one way to cope with an ever more complex world. Having specialists may well be more efficient, at least in some ways, than having many people trying to be generalists. Some also find this degree of specialization quite alienating, however, both as workers and as consumers who are being juggled between specialists.

The division of labor has not only grown within countries, but it has also grown between countries, with different parts of the world specializing in different tasks. The old international division of labor was a divide between producing raw materials and producing finished goods. In European colonial systems, the home country cities produced finished goods—textiles, machinery, and so forth—from the materials produced by the farms, forests, and mines of their colonies. Workers in the colonies were often farmers, miners, and the like, and they provided these raw materials. Finished goods, increasingly industrial products, in the colonies would come from the cities of the home country. In the late 1700s, King George III believed that prosperity for all would come from the great cities of England, such as London, Manchester, and Liverpool, as they produced the finished goods from the cotton, timber, tobacco, sugar, and other products produced by the British colonies.

In 1776, Adam Smith (1937) wrote that this was bad economics: Economies ran best on free and mutual trade, not on royal decrees. The same year, of course, Thomas Jefferson, writing for the American colonies, wrote that this was bad government and should be dissolved. The colonies were declaring independence. It is not a great surprise that the greatest proponents of American independence often came from New England, which was poised to produce its own finished goods.

The new United States opted out of the old international division of labor as a producer of raw materials only to rejoin it as producer of finished goods. Throughout much of the 1900s, raw materials flowed into U.S. cities from Latin America (in particular), as well as Africa, Asia, and the Pacific, while U.S. industry sought to export finished goods around the world. This process continued through World War II, both between Europe and its colonies and between the United States and its less developed trading partners.

This began to change after World War II, however—gradually at first and then rapidly in the 1970s and 1980s. Industry was no longer tied to major industrial centers in advanced industrial countries. Even poor countries could provide electricity for production. New harbors and new container ships could move products easily around the world. New communication systems could keep far-flung factories in touch with distant management centers. Industry could move, and it did. It moved to where manufacturing labor was the cheapest: Latin America, Asia, the Pacific, and in a few cases, Africa. The old industrial centers of North America, Europe, and eventually Japan experienced **deindustrialization,** as their factories moved overseas to **export-processing zones** in developing counties.

The advanced industrial countries became **post-industrial.** As large numbers of workers in poor countries moved from the farm to the factory, many in the richer countries moved from the factory to the office. Professional workers in rich countries today manage, finance, design, plan, advise, regulate, and program production that's carried on elsewhere. Job growth lies in computers, law, banking, accounting, and related fields. Other professional workers serve the financial, health, legal, commercial, and personal needs of postindustrial economies. Job growth also lies in more menial service tasks: cleaning and maintaining those offices, making beds in hospitals and hotels, serving fast food to these new busy workers, and the like.

The new international division of labor is very productive, and so the total productive capacity of the world's economy continues to grow markedly. In many ways, it is very efficient; more is produced at lower costs. It has also produced a new solidarity among groups of workers, including women workers, around the world. And it has produced a new ethic of ambition and achievement.

But many, including many who would never consider themselves Marxists, wonder if Marx may have been right about the alienation inherent in industrial corporate capitalism. Many of these "new economy" workers are profoundly alienated, working ever longer hours at menial and sometimes seemingly meaningless tasks. Old connections of family and village are disrupted in the industrializing world, while old ties between employee and employer are disrupted in the postindustrial world. Ties to the land and to local communities are undermined, as workers find themselves cogs in a huge and often very impersonal machine.

And *efficiency* refers only to means, not ultimate ends. Cigarette factories can turn out cigarettes far more quickly and efficiently than people "rolling their own." Weapons factories can turn out ammunition far more quickly and efficiently than pioneers pouring their own bullets. Yet whether either production enriches or impoverishes the world is not always clear. Nonetheless, the size and power of multinational corporations is staggering. Of the world's hundred largest economic entities, fifty-one are corporations and forty-nine are countries (see Table 2.1).

TABLE 2.1   Top 100 Economies: 1999 (Corporations in bold, italic)

Rank	Country/Corporation	GDP/sales ($mil)	Rank	Country/Corporation	GDP/sales ($mil)
1	United States	8,708,870.00	28	*DaimlerChrysler*	159,985.70
2	Japan	4,395,083.00	29	Poland	154,146.00
3	Germany	2,081,202.00	30	Norway	145,449.00
4	France	1,410,262.00	31	Indonesia	140,964.00
5	United Kingdom	1,373,612.00	32	South Africa	131,127.00
6	Italy	1,149,958.00	33	Saudi Arabia	128,892.00
7	China	1,149,814.00	34	Finland	126,130.00
8	Brazil	760,345.00	35	Greece	123,934.00
9	Canada	612,049.00	36	Thailand	123,887.00
10	Spain	562,245.00	37	*Mitsui*	118,555.20
11	Mexico	474,951.00	38	*Mitsubishi*	117,765.60
12	India	459,765.00	39	*Toyota Motor*	115,670.90
13	Korea, Rep.	406,940.00	40	*General Electric*	111,630.00
14	Australia	389,691.00	41	*Itochu*	109,068.90
15	Netherlands	384,766.00	42	Portugal	107,716.00
16	Russian Federation	375,345.00	43	*Royal Dutch/Shell*	105,366.00
17	Argentina	281,942.00	44	Venezuela	103,918.00
18	Switzerland	260,299.00	45	Iran, Islamic rep.	101,073.00
19	Belgium	245,706.00	46	Israel	99,068.00
20	Sweden	226,388.00	47	*Sumitomo*	95,701.60
21	Austria	208,949.00	48	*Nippon Tel & Tel*	93,591.70
22	Turkey	188,374.00	49	Egypt, Arab Republic	92,413.00
23	*General Motors*	176,558.00	50	*Marubeni*	91,807.40
24	Denmark	174,363.00	51	Colombia	88,596.00
25	*Wal-Mart*	166,809.00	52	*AXA*	87,645.70
26	*Exxon Mobil*	163,881.00	53	*IBM*	87,548.00
27	*Ford Motor*	162,558.00	54	Singapore	84,945.00

The New Frontier: From Hudson's Bay to Land's End

The push for cheaper products and higher profits has long driven industry to try to combine First World technology with Third World labor. The frontiers of industry have been on the move for over 200 years, incorporating slaves, immigrants, migrants, and displaced farmers among others in the search for low-cost labor. When textile mills grew in England in the 1700s, small farmers were driven off their land to make room for more wool-bearing sheep. The farmers, men and

TABLE 2.1   Continued

Rank	Country/Corporation	GDP/sales ($mil)	Rank	Country/Corporation	GDP/sales ($mil)
55	Ireland	84,861.00	78	Honda Motor	54,773.50
56	BP Amoco	83,556.00	79	Assicurazioni Generali	53,723.20
57	Citigroup	82,005.00	80	Nissan Motor	53,679.90
58	Volkswagen	80,072.70	81	New Zealand	53,622.00
59	Nippon Life Insurance	78,515.10	82	E.On	52,227.70
60	Philippines	75,350.00	83	Toshiba	51,634.90
61	Siemens	75,337.00	84	Bank of America	51,392.00
62	Malaysia	74,634.00	85	Fiat	51,331.70
63	Allianz	74,178.20	86	Nestle	49,694.10
64	Hitachi	71,858.50	87	SBC Communications	49,489.00
65	Chile	71,092.00	88	Credit Suisse	49,362.00
66	Matsushita Electric Ind.	65,555.60	89	Hungary	48,355.00
67	Nissho Iwai	65,393.20	90	Hewlett-Packard	48,253.00
68	ING Group	62,492.40	91	Fujitsu	47,195.90
69	AT&T	62,391.00	92	Algeria	47,015.00
70	Philip Morris	61,751.00	93	Metro	46,663.60
71	Sony	60,052.70	94	Sumitomo Life Insur.	46,445.10
72	Pakistan	59,880.00	95	Bangladesh	45,779.00
73	Deutsche Bank	58,585.10	96	Tokyo Electric Power	45,727.70
74	Boeing	57,993.00	97	Kroger	45,351.60
75	Peru	57,318.00	98	Total Fina Elf	44,990.30
76	Czech Republic	56,379.00	99	NEC	44,828.00
77	Dai-Ichi Mutual Life Ins.	55,104.70	100	State Farm Insurance	44,637.20

Sources: "Of the world's 100 largest economic entities, 51 are now corporations and 49 are countries," compiled by Sarah Anderson and John Cavanagh, Institute for Policy Studies, *Report on the Top 200 Corporations*, December 2000. Used by permission.

women, were then unattached labor, who could be employed at low wages in the mill production, either as suppliers of spun wool or as mill workers. The resulting products were then shipped literally around the world, marketed by giant government-sponsored but ultimately private corporations, such as the Hudson's Bay Company and the East India Company.

This pattern continues. Customers who phone in clothing orders to the Land's End corporation are likely to be helped by the wives, daughters, partners, and occasionally sons of farmers, would-be farmers, and once-were farmers in southern Wisconsin. The clothing itself is made in cities and export zones by the wives and daughters of once-rural farming families in Asia and Latin America.

Occasional Help Wanted: From *Bracero* to NAFTA

Industrial demands have kept the United States and Mexico bound in a turbulent marriage of convenience for decades. During World War II, when labor was scarce in the United States, the U.S. government began the *Bracero* **program.** From the Spanish word for *arm*, a *bracero* is a strong manual laborer. The program was so successful that it was extended until 1964. The goal of the program, however, was not to open the United States to Mexican immigration but to maintain a revolving door of labor migrants. Almost a century earlier, the United States had sought a similar arrangement with China to provide temporary Chinese laborers.

When the U.S. economy struck a recession in the mid 1950s and concerns were raised that too many *braceros* were staying on, the government began Operation Wetback. It is not clear if these workers had "wet backs" from swimming across the Rio Grande River, or from hoeing vegetable crops in the hot sun, but this derogatory term for illegal laborers become the title of a massive program that existed between 1954 and 1958. Mexicans working illegally, and many legal workers as well, were rounded up and returned to Mexico. In a few instances, Mexican Americans whose families had been in the U.S. Southwest since the land belonged to Mexico were rounded up and "returned" across the border.

The complexities of recruiting labor migrants in one direction while returning unwelcome workers in the other eventually led to the program's abandonment. In 1964, it was replaced by the Border Industrialization Program (BIP). This program allowed materials to be shipped across the Mexican border to neighboring cities, assembled by low-wage labor there, and then returned to the United States without export duties or tariffs. And so, the *maquiladora* was born, a plant whose only purpose was as an assembly turn-around point for industrial goods, particularly textiles and electronics. Throughout the remainder of the 1960s, *la huelga,* "the strike," raged on in California's farm fields, as Mexican migrant laborers struck for higher wages. The industrial demand, however, was more simply met by keeping the workers in Mexico and moving the products to the United States. Eventually, much fruit and vegetable production also moved south of the border in imitation of the fleeing industries.

In 1993, the North American Free Trade Agreement (NAFTA) was ratified, extending the special trade privileges of the Mexican border cities to all parts of North America. Discussion was renewed in 2001 and again in 2003 over new types of temporary labor arrangements between the United States and Mexico. Most of the laborers in question, however, would be neither industrial nor agricultural but rather low-wage service workers. Cooks, clerks, cleaners, and nannies—these are the jobs that cannot be simply relocated. For production, it is still easier to keep the workers within their own country (though often nowhere near their hometown and family) and to move the products.

Working the Line: Life on *La Frontera*

A thousand-mile chain of twin cities has been created along the U.S.–Mexican border, or *la frontera,* as the Mexicans know it. The cities face each other across this long chain-link line, the "Great Wall of the Americas," in a relationship that is at times symbiotic, at times parasitic: San Diego–Tijuana, Calexico–Mexicali, Nogales–Nogales, Douglas–Aqua Prieta, El Paso–Ciudad Juarez, Del Rio–Ciudad Acuna, Eagle Pass–Piedras Negras, Laredo–Nuevo Laredo, McAllen–Reynosa, Brownsville–Matamoros. As the fastest-growing part of Mexico, this border area is at once the most prosperous and the least appealing.

The twin cities facilitate the movement of products in and out of what in the United States are known as "twin plants" and in Mexico as *maquiladoras.* Juana Ortega works at an RCA plant on the U.S.–Mexican border, one of the first of a series of electronics *maquiladoras* that now dominate the economic life of the city of Juarez. She gets up at 5:00 in the morning to make breakfast for her three children as well as her sister and her uncle. Then she crowds into a van for the ride to work. The plant, like many here, is new and expansive, with an American-style corporate campus. Yet Juana feels her life her is as cramped and stifling as the hot, crowded ride in the van. Says Juana:

> This job is a terror. The noise. The monotony. The constant danger of the machine. . . . In the factory the line is the worst, it crushes your fingers and in the end your mind as well.
>
> They stuff us into vans. They stuff us into factories. They stuff it to you at work. It's stuff! Stuff! Stuff! . . . You work till your bones hurt. You work till your eyes hurt. The engineers make you work till you think you will drop, . . . always watching and hovering, stopwatch and clipboard in hand. (Peña 1997, 6)

Juana goes on to describe acts of collective sabotage against the line, breaking parts and the belts themselves, that workers use to slow its relentless speed-up. Workers play stupid and play sick and sometimes revolt in wildcat strikes against what they see as the inhumanity of their workplace. The plant manager sees the situation differently, however:

> This [repetitive labor] also reinforces discipline and self-worth. We are helping Mexico become more modern. The technology we use here is high-tech. We are upgrading Mexico's technological infrastructure, and this a big part of the progress we are bringing to our good neighbors south of the border. And so this opens up new possibilities for the girls who work for me. I mean, these girls don't have a lot of other options: stay at home, sell trinkets or candies on the street, work at a sewing factory, or, worst of all, prostitution. People accuse us of exploitation, but we are bringing a superior technology good jobs at decent wages, and a better business climate to Mexico. (p. 14)

In contrast, Juana sums up her view of the situation:

> What I regret the most is not the pain of working at something so degrading, so meaningless. It is instead the pain of knowing that we, the laborers, are capable of so much more. (p. 6)

Making It Big: Alcoa and Coca-Cola

Given the sheer size and power of many of the corporate entities that work the border, they quickly give obtain the power to determine the labor market and the futures of entire communities. Alcoa, the aluminum giant whose conglomeration of subsidiaries produce hundreds of products, moved its automotive wiring plant to Ciudad Acuna. In 1996, Alcoa CEO Paul O'Neill, who later became U.S. treasury secretary, boasted at a shareholders meeting of the clean, modern plant and the company's growing profits. He was challenged by a janitor from the plant, who told a different story: wages of six dollars a day, covered-up accidents such as a gas leak that sent one hundred workers to the hospital, and workers so regimented they were each issued an allotment of three pieces of toilet paper. Moved by the charges, O'Neill worked to improve conditions at the eight plants the huge firm (now Alcoa Fujikura Ltd.) owns in the city. Alcoa's wages have risen to the highest in the city but are still too low to bring about change in the ramshackle community:

> In Acuna, as in other border settlements, Mexican workers earn such miserable wages and American companies pay such minimal taxes that its schools are a shambles, its hospital crumbling, its trash collection slapdash, and its sewage lines collapsed. Half of Acuna's 150,000 residents now use backyard latrines.

"Alcuna is a disgrace," notes Mexican historian Javier Villarreal Lozano. "A hundred years ago, U.S. employers would have been ashamed of these conditions. Henry Ford's workers living in cardboard boxes? He'd never have tolerated it. (Dillon 2001, 1–2)

Few of these border plants make anything for the Mexican market. However, a few giants in the interior do, such as Coca-Cola, one of Mexico's largest enterprises. Faced with an epidemic of gastric illness, Mexican governments in the 1950s and 1960s choose to leave the tap water undrinkable and instead encourage bottled water companies and soft drink firms. Mexicans now consume more soft drinks per capita than anywhere in the world, in part because they have few other options. For decades, the great growth industries of Mexico were the water and soft drink companies of Puebla and the beer companies of Monterrey. The breweries, such as Corona, have established an export market around the world, but the soft drink makers have lost ground to the global dominance of Coca-Cola. Coke products are made and bottled within the country but under the close supervision of the multinational giant. Coke is now everywhere in Mexico, sometimes by official mandate. It is a major employer but with extremely low wages and profits that cycle abroad. (Interestingly, Mexican president Vicente Fox was the first in over seventy years not to come through the ranks of the dominant party. Before he was a governor, he was CEO of Coca-Cola Latin America.)

Mall Madness

The Victorians of the late nineteenth century loved fashion and home accessories, and they could find these items in boutique stores in growing urban centers. There, delicate stitching and elaborate feather and floral arrangements were done by very young women: new immigrants in the United States, Welsh and Irish girls in England, and French Canadian girls in Canada.

We still like adornments but now find our boutiques not lining urban streets but side by side in shopping malls. The cultural mix of labor now spans the globe:

Continuing down the mall, the Victoria's Secret store catches everyone's attention with exotic underwear and erotic nightware. Most quickly look away with a bit of self-conscious embarrassment but be bold enough to walk over and turn over the tag under the lace on that exotic underwear: "Made in Israel." Israel? Certainly not in an ultra-orthodox settlement, one would suppose. In fact, they are made by a Jordanian firm who employs veiled Palestinian women to make the delicate stitches, then adds a "Made in Israel" sticker to take advantage of the favorable trade status that Israel has with the United States.

Gawk too long at Victoria's very prominent "secrets" as you walk by and you will fall over the flower stand set up in the midst of the mall. Evoking a bit of the feel of an open-air stall, at least here must be a local product. Don't count on it; turn over the tag on the plastic wrap: "Introducing exclusive bouquets from Colors From the World, specially grown and hand selected in the Andes Mountains of Ecuador." Yes, Ecuador. These bouquets are "specially packed and shipped overnight from Ecuador by Airborne Express" to arrive in this mall only 48 hours after their cutting by Quechua-speaking highland *campesinos*. (Sernau 2000, 54)

Pushed to the Wall: Wal-Mart and the "Big Boxes"

The department store made its appearance in France in the 1800s and soon dominated marketing. By the 1950s, urban department stores were moving to suburban shopping centers, first in California. Soon, marketing planners in cold climates began covering the shopping centers, and the *mall* was born. Around the world, wherever people depend on cars rather than public transit and walking, new U.S.-style malls continue to be built. Yet in some cities, the malls are coming down because they have become obsolete. Some wealthy and trendy shoppers are returning to downtown and uptown department stores, but the biggest push has been to "big box" retail, or massive stores.

The biggest "big box" of them all is Wal-Mart. This chain grew rapidly in rural communities by drawing people from aging town centers. Wal-Mart hires mostly part-timers, sometimes keeping people just below the number of hours needed to qualify for benefits. Many of the store's workers are former homemakers as well as retirees who need added income. Young people and others displaced from the labor force comprise the reminder. Union activity has always been bitterly opposed.

Wal-Mart has moved from small towns to big cities and now around the world. It is the world's single largest marketer of consumer goods. It also employs more people than other company in the world. Its profits have been enormous. If Sam Walton, the founder, were still alive, he would be by far the wealthiest man in the world. As it is, Walton family members, Sam's heirs, comprise five of the ten richest multibillionaires in the world.

The economic power of Wal-Mart is also huge. Building so many stores, it is the world's largest contractor for construction and the building trades. Its market power spans the globe:

Wal-Mart is not just the world's largest retailer. It's the world's largest company— bigger than ExxonMobil, General Motors, and General Electric. The scale can be hard to absorb. Wal-Mart sold $244.5 billion worth of goods last year. It sells in three months what number-two retailer Home Depot sells in a year. And in its own category of general merchandise and groceries, Wal-Mart no longer has any real rivals. It does more business than Target, Sears, Kmart, J. C. Penney, Safeway, and Kroger combined. "Clearly," says Edward Fox, head of Southern Methodist University's J. C. Penney Center for Retailing Excellence, "Wal-Mart is more powerful than any retailer has ever been." It is, in fact, so big and so furtively powerful as to have become an entirely different order of corporate being. (Fishman 2003, 68)

Wal-Mart was not built on fashion or quality. Its foundation is price. Its market position allows it to continue to focus single-mindedly on price. This has benefits for the consumer, but it also comes at a price to the world of work:

> Wal-Mart wields its power for just one purpose: to bring the lowest possible prices to its customers. At Wal-Mart, that goal is never reached. The retailer has a clear policy for suppliers: On basic products that don't change, the price Wal-Mart will pay, and will charge shoppers, must drop year after year. But what almost no one outside the world of Wal-Mart and its 21,000 suppliers knows is the high cost of those low prices. Wal-Mart has the power to squeeze profit-killing concessions from vendors. To survive in the face of its pricing demands, makers of everything from bras to bicycles to blue jeans have had to lay off employees and close U.S. plants in favor of outsourcing products from overseas. (p. 68)

The company that in the late 1980s championed its "Buy American" philosophy now accounts for 10 percent of massive U.S. imports from China. To do business with Wal-Mart, companies must leave home; to ignore Wal-Mart is often to go out of business.

Motorola in Tianjin near Bejing, China, and Wal-Mart in Mexico City. The world of work and trade has been dramatically changed by the globalization of both production and retail. Even though most of the home offices of multinationals are in wealthy countries, the labor sources and the products now circle the globe.

| TABLE 2.2 | Hourly Compensation Costs (in U.S. dollars) for Production Workers in Manufacturing: 30 Countries or Areas and Selected Economic Groups: 1975 and 2002 |

Country or Area	1975	2002	Country or Area	1975	2002
Americas			Europe (continued)		
United States	6.36	21.37	Denmark	6.28	25.16
Brazil	—	2.58	Finland	4.66	21.79
Canada	5.96	16.02	France	4.52	17.27
Mexico	1.47	2.61	Germany, Former West	6.29	25.40
Asia and Oceania			Germany, Unified	—	24.31
Australia	5.62	15.44	Greece	1.69	8.61
Hong Kong SAR (1)	0.76	5.85	Ireland	3.07	15.54
Israel	2.03	10.85	Italy	4.67	15.07
Japan	3.00	19.01	Luxembourg	6.24	18.77
Korea	0.32	9.04	Netherlands	6.58	21.74
New Zealand	3.09	8.65	Norway	6.77	27.11
Singapore	0.84	7.26	Portugal	1.54	5.12
Sri Lanka	0.28	0.49	Spain	2.53	12.02
Taiwan	0.38	5.81	Sweden	7.18	20.27
Europe			Switzerland	6.09	24.11
Austria	4.51	20.83	United Kingdom	3.37	18.03
Belgium	6.41	22.79			

Source: U.S. Department of Labor, Bureau of Labor Statistics, May 2004. Available online at ftp://ftp.bls.gov/pub/special.requests/ForeignLabor/ichccsuppt02.txt.

For years, the progressive corporate leadership of jean maker Levi Strauss in San Francisco resisted taking its production overseas, where wages were (and still are) considerably lower (see Table 2.2). As Gap jeans and others weathered negative publicity about overseas sweatshop suppliers, Levi's held to its all-American image. But Levi's were sold in malls, where sales were declining. Their one hope was to sell their jeans at Wal-Mart. But that would mean cutting costs, and the way to do that would be to move operations overseas. In the early 1980s, Levis had sixty clothing plants in the United States. By 2004, it had none. Like Nike, Levi's no longer makes clothes; it merely imports and labels them.

Made by Small Hands

One of the most remarkable marches in U.S. labor history wound its way from Kensington, near Philadelphia, toward Long Island, just above New York City, at the beginning of the twentieth century. Hundreds of children—many missing fingers, and others hunched over from various disabilities and accidents as a result of their work in the Kensington textile mills—marched under the leadership of Mother Jones, a grandmother and organizer from West Virginia. The children focused on a single demand: They wanted their sixty-hour work week shortened to fifty-five so that they could attend five hours of school a week.

In trying to negotiate this with the mill owners, they had been rebuffed, and so now they marched with banners that read "We Want to Go to School" and "More Schools, Less Hospitals." The children planned to march to Long Island, where President Theodore Roosevelt was vacationing with his own children, who were enjoying pony rides by the beach. Although Roosevelt came from a wealthy family, he was often quite sympathetic to progressive labor causes. But he was also reluctant to see federal government involvement in what he believed were state and local issues. He had signed labor laws as governor of New York, and so he believed the governor of Pennsylvania should champion the children's cause.

The children went back to their sixty-hour week, climbing into and restocking machinery and, like children in Pakistan and India a century later, making carpets. Six years later, the Pennsylvania legislature passed child labor laws, including limits on the work week. And many others who took notice of the children's march—including Theodore Roosevelt's cousin and later First Lady Eleanor Roosevelt—became champions of the child labor reform both in the United States and around the world.

Mills and Mines

Child labor and the struggle to eliminate it has a long history. In many agrarian societies, children are valued farm hands and go to work by middle childhood. In medieval Europe, by age eight to ten, peasant children were typically either working the fields or had been contracted out as apprentices, essentially unpaid labor, to various smiths and craftsmen.

As societies became industrialized, so did child labor become industrialized. Throughout the 1800s, in Great Britain and New England, children were favored to supply looms and machining with thread and materials because they could crawl through cramped spaces, though often at great personal risk. By the late 1800s, immigrant children and young women were the favored workforce for textiles and a host of other factories. A jingle of the time chided the leisure class, "The factory is next to the [golf] links so the children at work can watch the men at play."

In Scotland and Pennsylvania, having children work as coal miners meant that supply shafts could be smaller. At a time when earth removal was difficult and expensive, children could even be lowered into the most difficult pits in buckets

Children have long worked on farms. Industrialization has often been fueled by children working in mines and mills, as seen here in a textile mill in the United States in the early 1900s, and in contemporary Bangladesh making cigarettes (right).

to bring up the ore. When Japan began catch-up industrialization at the end of the nineteenth century, it also found children to be a ready and pliable labor force, and many worked to their deaths in the coal mines of "Battleship Island."

Children were also useful in the service economy. Ironically, the Victorian ideal of hearth and home often meant that less privileged children had to leave both for the workforce:

> For every nineteenth-century middle-class family that protected its wife and child within the family circle, then, there was an Irish or a German girl scrubbing floors in that middle-class home, a Welsh boy mining coal to keep the home-baked goodies warm, a black girl doing the family laundry, a black mother and child picking cotton to be made into clothes for the family, and a Jewish or an Italian daughter in a sweatshop making "ladies" dresses or artificial flowers for the family to purchase. (Coontz 1992, 11)

Hooked by the World Economy

Reformers in advanced industrial societies elsewhere began to denounce the practice of child labor. The ideals of universal education and school as the appropriate place for all children were promoted. Yet the old practices have persisted, and more children are now at work around the world than ever before.

According to the International Labour Organization (ILO), there are 153 million children working in Asia, 80 million in Africa, and 17.5 million in Latin America (2002). A large majority of these children (70 percent) work in agricul-

TABLE 2.3	Children in the Worst Forms of Child Labor

Worst Form of Child Labor	Global Estimates (in millions)
Forced and bonded labour	5.7
Forced recruitment into armed conflict	0.3
Prostitution & pornography	1.8
Illicit activities	0.6
Trafficked children*	[1.2]
Subtotal	8.4
Children in hazardous work	170.5
Total	178.9

Notes: *The number of trafficked children is not included in the total number of children in the worst forms of child labour.

Source: Adapted from ILO, *Every Child Counts: New Global Estimates on Child Labour,* ILO: Geneva (2002), Tables 9 & 10.

ture, fishing, hunting, and forestry (ILO, 2002). Another 9 percent work each in manufacturing and in services such as wholesale and retail trade and restaurants and hotels. An estimated 6 percent of child workers are in community, social, and personal services. Four percent work each in transportation, storage, and communication and in construction, mining, and quarrying. By far the worst forms of child labor range from forced and bonded labor to prostitution and pornography (see Table 2.3).

The demands of changing economies and the perils of family poverty place many children at risk of cruel exploitation. Ten million children are in chronic labor bondage in India alone. More than 1 million children work squatting before dusty looms in Pakistani carpet factories. Pakistani children sew soccer balls for Nike, Adidas, and other foreign contractors for as little as six cents an hour. Working a ten-hour day to stitch one ball, each worker receives sixty cents for an item that wealthier parents will buy for thirty to fifty dollars. The balls enter the United States tariff free and proudly announce "hand made." No mention is made of whose hands. Schanberg (1996) reminds of us to think of those hands:

> Silgli is only three, barely able to hold a needle, but she has started to help her mother and four sisters in India; together they can earn 75 cents a day. Sonu spends his days cutting chicken feathers for shuttlecocks in a worker's slum riddled with tuberculosis. Amir left school after the third grade and now spends his days sitting on a concrete floor using his feet as a vise while sharpening scissors and tools for a Pakistani metal shop for 2 dollars a week. (p. 41)

These situations are not limited to South Asia. Children also work in Honduran factories that make trendy garments, in Brazilian orange groves that supply American breakfast tables, in toy factories in China and Thailand, and on assembly lines in Indonesia. Yet it is in South Asia where the extremes of poverty combine with a history of child labor to produce some of the greatest abuses:

> In India the vista of child labor are much the same: eight-year-olds pushing wheelbarrows of heavy clay across brickyards; four-year-olds stitching soccer balls with

needles longer than their fingers; fragile-looking girls carrying baskets of dung on their heads; little boys hacking up sputum as they squat before their looms, trying to do good enough work to avoid the masters blows. All this takes place against a backdrop of rising affluence enjoyed by the privileged classes—lavish villas with high walls topped by iron spikes and satellite dishes on the roofs, luxury cars driven by liveried chauffeurs. (Schanberg 1996, 45)

In Lahore, Pakistan, child labor is driven by both domestic and external pressures. Brick making is an ancient enterprise that employs hundreds of children. This is not making mud pies. Children mold and form a thousand bricks a day, set out to bake in the hot sun. A family of five working together can earn about one dollar per day. A major export of the region is hand-woven rugs. The carpet makers start as early as age three. The biggest selling point abroad is the number of stitches per centimeter (hundreds), as this denotes a hand-stitched rug. The only hands small enough to work these tiny stitches belong to the very young. A small carpet that takes weeks to make may net a vendor thirty dollars, of which fifteen may go to the workers (Garrels 2002).

Reformers are trying to change these systems, as well. New informal schools allow children to work a few hours less per day so as to attend a few hours of school. Some schools are no more than covered porches, but for many of the young children, this is their first chance to hold a crayon instead of a needle. Unlike the madrassah schools, which only teach memorization of the Koran, these schools teach basic literacy and math, practical skills, and for a few, a chance to go on to regular education.

A Trade Free-for-All

David Ricardo: Comparative Advantage

The much-touted benefits of world trade are based on an idea that goes back to David Ricardo. Ricardo extended the idea of the division of labor to nations and regions (1996 [1817]). Just as Smith believed that national prosperity would come from each person working in his or her area of expertise and then exchanging goods in a free market, so Ricardo believed that national specialization, coupled with vigorous trade, was the recipe for world prosperity. Each area of the world should do what it does best, where it has a **comparative advantage** over others. For example, it makes no sense for Scottish farmers to try to grow bananas and coffee (in a greenhouse perhaps) when they can raise sheep for wool. With the money they get from the worldwide wool market, they can purchase their morning's coffee and bananas from somewhere where their production is cheapest— Central America perhaps.

If each place in the world does this and the wheels of trade keep turning, then the world will have the most efficient, most productive system possible. Free markets will foster this, since the place with the greatest comparative advantage in a product will be able to market the best quality at the lowest price. This seemed highly logical and formed the basis for many national economies. Of course, small countries often became highly dependent on one or two products in which they seemed to have a clear advantage, and this made them vulnerable to sudden shifts in the market (just like overspecialized workers).

This new international division of labor, however—with its emphasis not on finding cheap materials but on finding cheap labor for assembly—puts several new twists in the doctrine. What if the comparative advantage of a nation is in providing a cheap, docile labor force that won't demand higher wages or better conditions? What if the advantage lies in lax environmental laws, insufficient labor protections, and many desperate people looking for work? This is the darker side to comparative advantage.

Chain of Production around the World

TOYS. The search for this elusive comparative advantage keeps many producers traveling the world, always trying to stay ahead of the competition (and often the regulators and union organizers). The manufacturers of toys, which are cheap and easy to ship but labor intensive to make, have often made the global trip:

> Turn into Kaybee toys and examine the array of action figures, stuffed animals, and this year's "must have" items. Note the pre-school aisle (the 3 and 4-year-olds know it by the bright primary colors), edge past the young girls in the hot pink aisle (they know Barbie lives there), don't get run over by exuberant boys in the khaki aisle (it's hard to play quietly with GI Joe, who is stationed here). If you did this fifty years ago you would have found items made in Ohio, Pennsylvania, and the industrial heartland. A decade later, a great deal would have said "Made in Japan." Yet another decade and the stamps would have read "Made in Taiwan, ROC" and "Made in Hong Kong." Now overwhelmingly the labels you find on everything in this store read "Made in China." . . . A full 40% of all toys sold in the U.S. are made in China, and this grows every year. A trans-Pacific entrepreneur described his frustration with rising wages and rising costs in Taiwan, and his eagerness to move operations to the welcoming, dependable production facilities of Guangzhou (colonialists called it Canton) and on to the special economic zones of Fujian. His product? Tiny clothes and plastic guns and boots for GI Joe. The country that only three decades ago trained its children to fight against a feared invasion by real GI Joes (then fighting in Vietnam) now outfits the doll. A country that Westerners associate with the all-purpose all-blue Mao suit now sports row after row of inexpensively but brightly dressed young

women stitching, molding, trimming, not only GI Joe's gear but also Barbie's entourage of sequins, satins, and shiny silver and bright pink accessories. (Sernau 2000, 52–53)

ELECTRONICS. A microchip is a classic example of a high-value item that, by its very nature, is small, light, and easy to transport. In the 1980s, many were assembled by young Asian American women, including immigrants and Southeast Asian refugees, staring into microscopes in the area near San Jose, California, that was dubbed "Silicon Valley." By the 1990s, it was cheaper to have the work done on the other side of the Pacific, in places such as the Philippines and Malaysia. The plant arrangement, even the workforce, looked almost the same. Currently, global microchip maker Intel seems also to favor China as a location, with plants near Beijing, the global industry boom-town of Shenzhen near Hong Kong, and the free trade zone near Shanghai.

Larger electronic consumer items rarely have a single manufacturing location. Whether the brand name is American (RCA) or Japanese (Sony) or European (Thompson), the parts come from all over the world. For television sets, "Made in the USA" became "Made in Mexico" by the 1980s, but this has since become the more mysterious "Assembled in Mexico from parts of various manufacture." The final assembly occurs in plants just over the Rio Grande River from the United States, but parts stream in from all over the world.

TEXTILES. Textile manufacturing has long depended on a steady supply of cheap labor, most often from young women. In the late 1700s, farm girls came to the mills of Massachusetts. In the 1800s, new mills emerged in Tennessee and Alabama and also drew young farm girls. By the 1900s, the growing garment trade required waves of Southern and Eastern European immigrant workers to supply the sweatshops of New York. As the century spun on, new labor came from Asia and Latin America.

Over time, it became easier to move the factories than the workers. Ironically, workers now sometimes lose their jobs to the very lands from which they came:

El Paso, Texas—Ernestina Miranda left Mexico for the United States in 1979 in the trunk of a car. She found a job sewing blue jeans in one of the dozens of clothing factories here. Work was steady, six days a week, 12 hours a day. She married and bought a trailer—without running water or electricity—on a plot of land. She was awarded citizenship in the late 1980's. Now, those blue jeans jobs that brought Mrs. Miranda and thousands of others like her north have gone south, to Mexico.

"My American dream has turned into a nightmare," she said, over a glass of strawberry Kool-Aid in her listing trailer. Until recently, she had made a life on $7.50 an hour. She has become a temporary worker in a plastics plant that used to be based in Michigan, earning minimum wage, no benefits, no security. Her husband, Miguel, is unemployed. The mortgage on the slapdash home is in peril. "I worry about the future," she said, echoing the sentiment of blue-collar and increasingly of white-collar workers from Los Angeles to Detroit, people who find their jobs being shipped to countries where wages are a small fraction of theirs. When VF Jeanswear, the maker of Wrangler and Lee jeans, announced in September that it was moving the last of its jeans production and more than 1,000 jobs to Mexico, it was the death of that industry in a town once known as Blue Jean Capital, U.S.A. Levi Strauss, Sun Apparel, Wrangler, Lee and Farah do not make jeans here anymore. (Le Duff 2004).

Textiles have joined the growing list of products that are assembled around the globe. In *Coat of Many Countries,* Josh Freed (2004) follows the manufacture of a sport coat across the planet. The Canadian manufacturer gets the wool from Merino sheep in Australia and ships it to India to be spun on the great high-speed, high-technology machines that have replaced the simple spinning wheel shown on the Indian flag. Ironically, that wheel was Mahatma Gandhi's famous symbol of self-sufficiency and independence. But now, the coat components keep moving: The shoulder pads arrive from China, the lining from Korea. They meet the cloth in Hamburg, Germany, only to be loaded on trucks and shipped deep into Russia, where border guards are bribed along the way. In central Russia, Soviet-era factories have been retooled to sew and stitch the sport coat by female workers so desperate for employment that they now work for lower wages than those in India. The coat makes another brief appearance in Canada to get the one accessory made there: buttons molded in a factory so automated that labor costs are not an issue. The coat then makes its final trek south of the border to a store in New York.

FOOD. Not only what we wear and what we watch but increasingly what we eat is not so much grown as it is assembled:

The catfish are trucked from the fish farms to the factory where they await the assembly line. The workers—also women, also black, also poor—are ready for them in their waders, looking like a female angler's society. But these women mean business. The fish come down the line, slippery and flopping. The sawyer grabs the fish and lops off their heads with a band saw, tossing the bodies back onto the line while the heads drop into a bucket. Down the line, women with razor-sharp filet knives make several deft cuts to eviscerate the fish and turn them into filets to be frozen. Many of the longer-term workers have lost fingers, especially to the saws. The company says they fail to follow directions and that they get careless. The women say they are overworked. They say they get tired. They say they slip in the fish guts that fill the floor. But through it all, the assembly line, like Paul Robeson's Ol' Man River, "just keeps rolling along." The line that threads between these rows of black women is operated by a tall white man who supervises from a raised control booth, adjusting the speed of the line and noting the workers' efforts. One watches and wonders: is this the face of the new South or the old South? And what of what Marx called the "social relations of production"; is this the assembly line of the future or the plantation of the past under a metal roof? (Sernau 2001, 61)

The scene behind the counter at a fast-food restaurant also bears much more resemblance to an assembly line than to a kitchen. Ground-up beef parts from three continents become hamburgers, and chemically altered oils from North and South America and Africa coat precut potato fragments and are whipped into shakes by workers following exact procedures as they stand in rows of standardized machines. This process was first refined by McDonald's:

"They called us the Green Machine," says Jason Pratt, recently retired McDonald's griddleman, " 'cause the crew had green uniforms then. And that's what it is, a machine. You don't have to know how to cook, you don't have to know how to think. There's a procedure for everything and you just follow the procedures." (Garson 1988, 17)

This process has since been emulated by scores of competitors as fast food, and the procedures now permeate many parts of the service sector (Ritzer 2000; Schlosser 2001).

Ordering the World Market

The International Monetary Fund

At the end of World War II, the leaders of the capitalist world met at Bretton Woods, a resort in New Hampshire, to discuss the shape of the post-war global economy. It was becoming clear that no amount of sputtering determination on the part of Prime Minister Winston Churchill was going to hold together the British Empire in its current form. The Warsaw Pact provided for economic as well as military cooperation among Eastern Europe and the Soviet Union. But the Western allies were fearful of global economic chaos and of the formation of military–economic blocs, such as the just-defeated Nazi Europe and Japan's Asian "co-prosperity" sphere. The alternative was to create international organizations to regulate world trade and the global economy. Several semi-independent organizations were formed, dominated by Great Britain and the United States. The **International Monetary Fund** (IMF) was created to regulate the world's currencies. Its original task was to avoid runaway inflation, collapsing currencies, and to facilitate trade by establishing exchange rates between currencies. One tool the IMF had to achieve this was lending money to prop up struggling economies.

Over time, the lending function become the dominant one. In order to get IMF loans, countries must agree to certain reforms, known as *structural adjustment*. Typically, they are called on to reduce government spending, including on social programs, and to privatize. **Privatization** is the turning over of certain government-controlled functions to private enterprise, including banking, oil refining, and manufacturing. Often, governments are also encouraged to devalue their currencies to make their exports cheaper abroad.

The philosophy of the IMF from the beginning has been deeply rooted in neoclassical economics: Reduce government and encourage free markets and free trade as the route to economic stability and prosperity. The long-range consequences of this policy remain a source of intense controversy, and the short-range consequences are also mixed. Big, wasteful governments with inefficient programs, patronage jobs that build political support by hiring friends of the party in power, and reckless monetary policy such as paying debts by printing worthless currency have benefited from readjustment. At the same time, IMF demands have often included cutting food programs for the urban poor, cutting agricultural subsidies for poor farmers, and even cutting expensive health and education programs. Often, the poorest citizens have borne the brunt of the pain in these policies.

Opponents of free-trade doctrine often call for the abolition of the IMF. Others see the need for such an organization but call into question its absolute devotion to free-market, free-trade policies; to "shock therapy" which eliminates many government programs overnight; and to rapid transitions to market economies (Stiglitz 2002).

The World Bank

The Bretton Woods framers of the new world order believed that newly independent and other developing countries would need outside capital to fund their development. They created the World Bank to provide loans for development projects to speed the growth and modernization of supposedly backward economies.

In its early years, the World Bank seemed to favor large, showy development projects, such as huge dam and highway projects. Newly independent governments also favored these projects as symbols of national strength and pride. Unfortunately, many never delivered all the economic returns that had been envisioned. Governments were saddled with the massive debt incurred without the revenue to pay the debts. Often, the governments needed to turn to the IMF to restructure their debts and their economies.

Over time, the World Bank learned from its early mistakes and sought more local participation, encouraged smaller projects, and insisted on stricter environmental standards and economic accountability. Big dam projects and expensive showpieces were increasingly rejected for funding. Despite these reforms, the World Bank still has many critics, who argue that it lures poor countries into deep debt while ignoring more innovative micro projects that actually employ and empower local people.

From GATT to the WTO

Accompanying the effort to stabilize the world economy has been the effort to encourage and stabilize international trade. For centuries, this had been done through **tariffs.** The very first law the new U.S. Congress passed, signed by newly inaugurated President George Washington, was a tariff law that protected new U.S. industries from cheap European imports.

Tariffs did two things: They allowed local industries to develop by making imported items more expensive, and they raised revenues for the new federal government. Early American manufacturers accused the huge British corporations of dumping products at less than cost in an attempt to put them out of business. It appears this is exactly what they were doing in the early 1800s, and tariffs compensated for it. In a time before the federal income tax, tariffs also provided the national government with much of its operating revenue.

Over the course of the nineteenth century, tariffs remained one of the most controversial aspects of political campaigns and national policy in the United States. Exporters, such as Southern cotton growers, wanted low tariffs in both the United States and Europe, so that they could export their own goods cheaply and in turn cheaply import what they needed to expand. Growing local industries and eventually labor called for higher tariffs to protect manufacturing jobs.

Around the world, tariffs became the way that young countries—such as the many Latin American countries that became independent in the 1820s—could raise revenues and control imports. When rebels or outside powers wanted to seize revenues, they attacked and seized the tariff collections in customs houses. When the British and U.S. governments were concerned about Latin American and Caribbean countries failing to pay their debts, they sent in the marines to seize tariff revenues. But few challenged the right of governments to collect these revenues or to protect fragile, local industries in their early stages.

In the decades following World War II, the controversy over tariffs was settled in favor of what become known as the **Washington consensus:** the neoclassical view that trade was good and tariffs that limited trade were bad. **Free trade**—that is, trade free from regulations and tariffs—became the accepted doctrine. In 1947, this doctrine was institutionalized in the **General Agreement on Trade and Tariffs (GATT)** accords. GATT allowed some limited protections to be gradually phased out, but the overall goal was low or no tariffs and free trade.

In 1994, GATT was replaced by the **World Trade Organization (WTO)**, which monitors trade practices around the world. Countries that place too many or unfair limits on imports can face punitive tariffs on their own exports. If countries can prove dumping in the WTO courts, they can place tariffs on these items or limit their export. Otherwise, the main rule of the game is free trade. Countries are also limited in their ability to keep out imports based on environmental or labor concerns or "unfounded" concerns over products' safety.

The tit-for-tat of world trade can be complex and far reaching. Angered over France's protection of its own farmers and its tendency to favor agricultural imports, such as bananas, from its former African colonies rather than from Latin America, the United States put temporary punitive tariffs on French cheese and champagne. In 2002, President George W. Bush put protective tariffs on imported steel. The U.S. steel industry had been in decline for decades. Critics of the industry said the problem was out-of-date mills and techniques that couldn't compete with newer Japanese and European plants. American steel makers and organized labor claimed the problem was dumping of foreign steel at below cost to drive out U.S. suppliers. The domestic complexity of tariffs was seen in that the steel tariffs were popular with steel makers and their workers, who said they were saving the industry, but unpopular with automakers and their workers, who claimed that higher steel prices raised the prices of their cars, both domestically and for export. The WTO accepted the tariffs as temporary measures but ruled against their extension. In response to these now illegal tariffs, France temporarily put tariffs on U.S. farm products. Clearly, much more is at stake than the price of brie in Los Angeles or the price of Wheaties in Paris. How far can governments go to protect their workers and their industries?

A common complaint is that the WTO still operates by the "golden rule": Those players who hold the most gold make the rules. The United States and European countries have found many arguments for exceptions for their own protected industries. Japan and China have used a long tradition of cooperation (some would say collusion) among government, banking, and industry to hide subsidies and anticompetitive actions. Small countries usually do not have these options and must dance to the tune of the more powerful players.

A Trade Fair-for-All

Everyone loves a fair. Whether a small country affair or a great global exposition, a fair is a place of coming together, showcasing the new, and buying and selling. The entire global economy has become one great world's fair, with technology and new styles on display every month.

Trade is a force for change. Every country that has been drawn, willingly or unwillingly, into the world economy has changed rapidly. Japan was revolutionized from agrarian isolation to industrial might in a matter of decades following the visits of U.S. Commodore Matthew Perry in the 1850s. Perry had come demanding, with great courtesies and great guns, an opening of trade relations. Certainly, China has been undergoing a commercial revolution as sweeping as any Mao-inspired revolution. India is racing to catch up. Latin America, from Mexico to Brazil to Chile, is also being completely rebuilt for participation in global trade. Africa alone has been largely passed over, except for raw materials, but this seems certain to change as the search for cheap labor pushes on.

The great world's fair of the twenty-first century has brought more products to more people than ever before. It has motivated economic, social, and sometimes political reform. The two great Asian powers, India and China, along with a half dozen or so small Asian nations have used the work and income provided by this fair to make significant reductions in poverty. Yet this fair, like the fairs of old, also has its underside. Global profits have created an international elite club of billionaires, while workers around the world continue to struggle under long hours and low pay. The burden of work falls unevenly, leaving some to toil far from their homes and families while others are idled in by-passed places. Can this fair be made more fair?

Trade could be used as a force for positive change. Countries wishing to participate in the WTO could be expected to sign labor and environmental accords. Instead of being required to weaken their protection of both workers and the environment, as the WTO has sometimes insisted in Europe, participants could be required to strengthen these protections. To join the great fair, countries could be required to agree to certain conditions for the global assembly line: no child labor, no banned chemicals, proper waste disposal, minimum wages, inspection and enforcement of local ordinances, national laws, and global accords.

Before this can happen, however, the powerful players and wealthy nations will need to rethink the very foundations of the organizations that govern the world of work and trade. Is the goal to promote trade, at whatever cost? Or is the goal to promote development—economic, social, cultural, and human—and to use work and trade as tools in that process?

Global capitalism hasn't been pretty. But then neither were the attempts to build great spheres of influence that led to World War II or to defend the aging empires that helped spark World War I. Economic globalization is likely, at least in part, to be here to stay. People have come to depend on the global supermarket to supply their needs.

Yet our greatest needs are still often best met locally: quality face-to-face education, quality personal health care, quality housing, livable communities with safe and pleasant spaces and good infrastructure. Most of humanity's history is one of largely self-reliant communities who traded mostly for novelties, adornments, and luxuries. This is a pattern to which we may need to return, at least in part. Of course, this shift in priorities would also mean that the more affluent consumers would need to do with fewer novelties, adornments, and luxuries and invest instead in the lives and development of communities close to home and far away.

MAKING CONNECTIONS

World Mart

■ Walk through your favorite shopping mall or "big box" retailer. Examine the "Made in" tags. What countries are represented? Are certain products centered in certain locations? What might these locations offer manufacturers? You may also be able to do this assignment in your own clothes closet.

Want Ads

■ Look through the "Help Wanted" section of your local newspaper or that of a neighboring city. What types of jobs are common? What types of qualifications are sought? What types of employment are scarce? What can you find on opportunities, qualifications, and wages in manufacturing jobs?

ILO

■ Go to www.ilo.org for information on the U.N.-affiliated International Labour Organization (ILO). This site has information and articles on globalization, child labor, women's work, AIDS and work, global wages, and dozens of other topics. What are some of the new and continuing challenges that workers face across the continents?

Students Against Sweatshops

■ In recent years, students on many campuses have become active in the antisweatshop movement. Go to www.studentsagainstsweatshops.org, the site of United Students Against Sweatshops (USAS). A quick browser search will also take you to the sites of independent Students Against Sweatshops organizations in Canada, California, Iowa, Harvard, and so forth. On the USAS site, note "Get Involved" and "Take Action" sections. Affiliates are also listed. Does your campus or community have a related chapter? If so, talk with the leadership about local issues. What current issues are featured on the national website? How do they propose taking action?

Free the Children

■ Go to www.freethechildren.org, the website of an organization that was founded by a Canadian boy, Craig Kielburger, when he was twelve. He traveled the world for the cause of freeing children from forced and bound labor and won the support of many international human rights leaders. The organization, however, still depends heavily on the involvement of children, as well as their teachers and supportive university programs. Learn more about the group's history and work at its site. Notice information on specific projects and how to get involved, including a university toolkit. What are some ways to start or support a local chapter?

CHAPTER 3

Gender and Family
Overburdened Women and Displaced Men

Benton Harbor, Michigan

When she got pregnant the first time, at age 15, Rashonda Jackson of Benton Harbor never considered marriage. Nor did she give much thought to abortion or adoption. There was never really any doubt about what she would do. With her parents' blessing, and that of her church, Rashonda had a baby boy, Shannon. It was enough to gain her entry into the least exclusive club in Benton Harbor. Single motherhood. This could be the single parent capital of the United States, a struggling rust belt town where an astonishing eight out of every ten families are headed by a single parent. The vast majority are single mothers, often in their teens or early 20s. (Landsberg 1998, B1)

Tokyo, Japan

He averages 12-hour work days, followed by an obligatory round of drinks with co-workers and a long commute home. She dutifully waits up for him to return and prepares breakfast in the mornings. Then retirement rolls around and he discovers he's a stranger to his own family. The result is a phenomenon Japanese are calling "vintage year divorce," the fastest-growing component of a marital break-up rate that has doubled since 1975. And reflecting larger changes in society, the divorces are more likely initiated by women, often after 20 years or more together. "Expectations are definitely changing. Many people are putting their happiness first, and if they think they won't find that in their marriage, they get out," said Atsuko Okano, 49, a divorcee and founder of a divorce counseling service, Caratclub. (Pearson 2004, B6)

Milwaukee, Wisconsin; Flint, Michigan; and Amazonia, Brazil

Dugout canoes ply the waters of the upper reaches of the Amazon River and its tributaries. They carry a myriad of hues for painting faces and potions mixed from exotic herbs. These are neither for some sort of war party nor for a "medicine man" or tribal shaman. This is the Avon lady.

Avon is big business in the Amazon. It's a huge industry all across Brazil, and the Amazonian Avon ladies are coordinated from high rise offices in São Paulo. Brazil has more Avon beauty consultants (over 400,000) than it has soldiers.

What do Amazonian women buy from these Avon armies? Lipstick, of course, and a bit of eye shadow. Even in the rain forest, a Brazilian woman must look her best. They also buy skin creams that lighten the skin, essentially by burning off the outer-most layer. Color is important in Brazil, and lighter skin tones are often the most prized. The Amazonian women might do better, it would seem, with the Skin So Soft creams that are reputed to repel mosquitoes. They pay with what cash they have on hand or perhaps offer a chicken in exchange. The Avon lady then returns to her canoe. She has hired a paddler so that she can hold an umbrella over her head for protection from the sun (one doesn't want to get too dark) and sort her wares for the next stop (Royle 1996).

Selling cosmetics is big business. In 1996, U.S. citizens alone spent eight billion dollars on cosmetics, two billion more than the United Nations–estimated annual amount needed to provide basic education for everyone in the world (United Nations 1996).

In the film *Roger and Me* (1989), Michael Moore noted the many families of laid-off auto workers in Flint, Michigan, who had turned to selling Amway. He featured the former host of a feminist talk radio show, who had turned to Amway color analyzing to determine a woman's color "season." (There's not much opportunity for this in the Amazon, where they are "summers.")

In the TV program *Surviving the Good Times* (2000), Bill Moyers showed the story of struggling laid-off workers from the engine manufacturer Briggs and Stratton in Milwaukee, Wisconsin. Terry Neuman's survival strategy was to borrow money from a relative to buy her initial stock and become an independent salesperson for New Skin cosmetics. Unfortunately, many of her friends and neighbors were also laid off and she lost her investment.

Around the world, massive changes are taking place in the relationship between work and family and in that between men and women. It is not the change envisioned by feminists in the 1960s, nor is it merely a backlash against those changes. Rather, this odd mix of global economy, global culture, and global politics that we have come to call **globalization** is changing men's and women's roles across the continents. Unexpectedly (though it shouldn't be, given trends already afoot in the 1960s), women's roles are becoming ever broader and more encompassing and men's roles are becoming more limited and constricted, at least for certain men. This is not a story of female triumph, however, for only occasionally do women receive the full benefits of their new roles. Often, they end up overburdened, just as men find themselves displaced.

Nietzsche Undone: From Superman to Supermom

The idea of women's liberation is much older than we usually imagine, but the idea of men's liberation may be older still. The ideal man of Athens was free from male drudgery, like plowing the rocky Greek soil, to discuss matters of importance in the city marketplace, to trade and converse, to worship on the hillside, and to vote in the assembly. The ideal man also tended a rural farmstead, so he could stay close to the land and know the joy of picking his own olives and stomping his own grapes. Meanwhile, the ideal Athenian woman, at least in the male mind, was largely cloistered to home, tending a narrow range of domestic duties as befit her temperament. Likewise, the Renaissance man of fifteenth-century Italy knew the pleasures of both the city and the countryside and appreciated the best of each. He also knew the pleasures of both mind and body and indulged both, and he was equally adept in science, art, and politics. Of course, managing the affairs of such a man about town was no small task, and so it took many a domestic woman.

When German philosopher Friedrich Nietzsche envisioned the emboldened *überman,* it was clearly a super-*man* in most respects. All along, women have sought to challenge this, but only the rare woman has succeeded. Elizabeth I of sixteenth century England danced, romanced, conspired, and maneuvered her way through the worlds of politics, art, theatre, and global exploration, but she was always one mishap from losing the throne. She also chose to forgo matrimony as part of her having it all. Sor Juana Ines de la Cruz of seventeenth-century Mexico likewise probed the worlds of art, literature, and science, also by forgoing marriage in what appears to have been, at least initially, a marriage of convenience to the church. By the 1800s, the numbers of women adventurers and explorers, philanthropists and activists had increased, but we still remember them in part because they were so few: Lucy Stone, Susan B. Anthony, Jane Addams, Virginia Wolf, and Amelia Earhart.

The rising influence of well-educated and influential women in the 1800s was matched by the Victorian ideal of womanhood and emphasized that a woman's loftiest aspiration should be motherhood. Queen Victoria of England may have ruled an empire that stretched around the world, but she was often admired for her matronly ways and being the mother of many. The Victorian woman of Great Britain and the United States was expected to follow this queenly example. She should have many children and devote herself to their nurture. Her husband would dutifully devote his time to their economic comfort and sustenance. A man's home was his castle, and his wife's time went into maintaining that castle for her prince and his children, with ample help from servants and day laborers. Of course, only the upper classes and the small, well-off middle classes of the time could attain this cultural ideal. The reality for most women was more like the life of Cinderella before the fairy godmother showed up. Domestic tasks without the help of servants were long and arduous.

It is also misleading to simply note that many women did not work outside the home. In fact, businesses were often family businesses and farms were family farms, with women contributing a great deal of the labor and expertise needed for economic survival, even if they were not listed as landowners or business owners. Typically, women from all classes but the most elite were involved in economically productive activity, even if it was not wage labor. Only the wealthiest families could afford to have women in hoop skirts in grand Victorian homes or plantation houses supervising the work of others while doting on their children, even if this was the cultural ideal.

Women also began the movement into wage labor early in the United States and European industrial periods. Women—especially young, unmarried women from lower-income backgrounds—often went to work in the mills that were becoming common in the United States and Western Europe from about 1840. Textile mills, in particular, were major employers of women, almost as industrial extensions of the textile work that women had often done in their homes. By the turn of the twentieth century, a full one-fifth of U.S. women were in the paid labor force; many of these were immigrant women, trying to help their families survive and become established in growing U.S. cities. Women from middle-class backgrounds were expected to leave the labor force upon marriage. Often this was even required in certain professions, such as teaching. (Male teachers could continue teaching after marriage, as long as they could support their families on the meager wages.) If a middle-class woman lost her husband to death or desertion, she was often placed in a very difficult situation and often turned to so-called quiet employment, such as using her Victorian home as a boarding house, to gain needed income.

In the 1920s, U.S. women worked sometimes as an expression of newfound independence (as they did again in the 1970s) and sometimes as a way of trying to share in the highly touted prosperity of the Roaring Twenties, which was not reaching everyone (as they did again in the 1980s and 1990s). Women in the 1930s often worked out of necessity, as the hard economic times of the Depression forced many to postpone marriage or to replace or supplement the lost income of unemployed and underemployed husbands (a pattern that also returned in the 1970s).

World War II provided the global cataclysm that shattered entrenched powers, including male power, and opened new doors to women. American and European female labor force participation reached its peak in the war years of the early 1940s. Now, it was women's patriotic duty to go to work to keep the industrial "arsenal of democracy" churning while the men were at war. Women worked in heavy industry as Rosie the Riveters. They also worked in meat packing and as bus drivers and "milkmen," fulfilling traditional male-dominated service roles.

When World War II ended, European countries that had lost huge portions of their manpower to war casualties—Germany and the Soviet Union, in particular—continued to need and encourage women in industry. In the United States, however, women workers were told to go home. Millions of servicemen were returning home and looking for college educations and jobs. Women were encouraged to make room for them. Female university enrollments declined, and female labor market participation plummeted.

Correspondingly, women married younger than ever before, and after years of declining fertility rates, they again started to have more children and at a younger age. The Victorian ideal of the domestic woman whose sole devotion was to home and family was revived, but now a growing middle class meant that more families could live this ideal. Women in the paid labor force were accepted, especially in female-dominated occupations, but mostly with the understanding that they were waiting to get married or wanted to buy a few extras. Their employment was acceptable as long as it did not involve taking "men's work."

Suspicion of career women was often fierce, as in Merle Miller's 1954 rebuke in *Esquire* magazine to "that increasing and strident minority of women who are doing their damnedest to wreck marriage and home life in America, those who insist on having both husband and career. They are a menace and they have to be stopped" (quoted in Miller and Nowak 1977, 164). In contrast, *Look* magazine extolled the newly domestic woman in 1956, although in language that acknowledges that she was different from the women of preceding decades:

> The American woman is winning the battle of the sexes. Like a teenager, she is growing up and confounding her critics. . . . No longer a psychological immigrant to man's world, she works, rather casually, as a third of the U.S. labor force, less towards a "big career" than as a way of filling a hope chest or buying a new home freezer. She gracefully concedes the top jobs to men. This wondrous creature also marries younger than ever, bears more babies and looks and acts far more feminine than the "emancipated" girl of the 1920's or even 30's. Steelworker's wife and Junior Leaguer alike do their own housework. . . . Today, if she makes an old fashioned choice and lovingly tends a garden and a bumper crop of children, she rates louder hosannas than ever before. (quoted in Friedan 1963, 52–53)

Much of the social life of the 1950s United States can be seen as a grand attempt to reverse the irreversible. Even in the 1950s, a full one-third of the U.S. labor force was female (and most were not working casually). Growing numbers of other women, many with significant education and work experience, found complete devotion to home less than satisfying (despite the "hosannas"). Yet this cultural vision of the domestic woman was so strong that many people were shocked when young women, as well as less-than-content older women, rejected the old-fashioned choice and followed in the footsteps of the emancipated girl (often their own grandmothers) of the 1920s and 1930s. They returned to higher education in large numbers in the 1960s and to the professional workforce, including the "big career" in the 1970s.

In one sense, the return of large numbers of women to the paid labor force was merely a continuation of earlier trends in the century, trends that had their roots in the expansion of industrialization. Yet there was something new: An increasing portion of these working women were seeking true careers, rather than temporary or low-wage employment. In 1900, wealthy women often received a good education, but it was intended to provide refinement—to make them more elegant, more cultured, and sometimes more pious domestic women. There were exceptions, including the women who left home to become missionaries and the extraordinary group of wealthy, highly educated women that advanced both social work and public health practices and progressive social theory at Jane Addams's Hull House in Chicago. These women were few, however. Poor women, on the other hand, often worked for wages but received little education.

The idea of large numbers of career women pursuing higher education and then using that education in professional employment was new and even shocking. But over time, this new idea transformed many occupations. Law was once a male-only domain, but law schools now enroll about as many women as men, and significant numbers of these women are older, returning students. Law school, with its emphasis on reading, writing, and communication skills, has been more permeable to women than engineering, where entrance often depends on early encouragement to pursue science and higher mathematics. Medical schools, with similar entry requirements, have been slower than law schools to enroll large numbers of women, but in 1996, over 40 percent of medical doctorates went to women (U.S. National Center for Educational Statistics 1999).

Instead of Superman, we found Supermom. But we also realized what classical Athenians, Renaissance Italians, and all the rest of the men's movements overlooked: You cannot fundamentally change the role of one gender without bringing about major changes in the role of the other. Liberation must go both ways. A second lesson is that liberation confined to a privileged class cannot triumph. This was understood by nineteenth-century feminists who worked for civil rights and progressive reforms. It was beautifully exemplified by the mid-twentieth century's greatest feminist, Eleanor Roosevelt (though she may have preferred a different label). Somehow, this idea got lost in the individualism of the 1970s and the corporatism of the 1980s. Then, the liberation of privileged men often came at the expense of poor women, and the liberation of privileged women in the later portion of the twentieth century seemed to come at the same price. Supermom felt guilty because deep down, she knew that she couldn't do it all without basic changes in society—essentially, in men's roles and expectations—and that she could only do what she could because of the added burdens of her poor sisters.

Masculinity as Vulnerability: The Harder They Fall

Around the world, male privilege is persistent but precarious. Respect, prestige, privilege, and power go to *successful* men, not necessarily to all men. In an article called "The Good Provider Role: Its Rise and Fall," Jesse Bernard (1981), one of the first prominent female sociologists in the United States, noted that successful men were told to use their advantages to be good providers to their families. This was not just an ancient idea but actually gained acceptance in the 1800s, as the agrarian partnership of men and women gave way to a market economy dominated by business-*men*.

But not all businessmen proved to be successful. Some never reached their dreams; some fell on economic disasters. Whether for economic or personal reasons, many men found themselves unable to fulfill the good provider role and withdrew from the competition; frequently, in a time when divorce was rare, they simply abandoned their families. The good provider role seems to have had many deserters. Although these deserters were clearly vulnerable to downturns and wounded by social expectations, in one sense, they were still privileged relative to their women. The men could move and start over, but the women they deserted were often left raising families with little means of support. In Latin America and to a certain extent in much of Africa and Central Asia, the idea of the man as provider and protector is culturally well established. But there, too, the number of deserters seems to be increasing.

Some men were always vulnerable because of their race, ethnicity, or class. African American sharecroppers and Irish American stockyard workers could never support their families in the proper style and either had to forgo family life or admit to being less than good providers (Bernard 1981). Currently within the African American community, men are more likely than women not to finish school and not to be employed. Men are far more likely to be incarcerated, as well. As black women struggle to maintain their families and communities without large numbers of contributing men, it is not clear that they are therefore privileged. It is clear, however, that poor black men are particularly vulnerable to loss and humiliation. In societies that accord other men respect, advantage, and power, they find only disrespect, disadvantage, and disempowerment.

This is increasingly true not just of U.S. black men but also poor black men in Brazil, the Caribbean, in Europe, and across Africa. The vulnerability of manhood is realized by Latino men in both North and Latin America, where changing economies limit their ability to be good providers. It is also increasingly realized by working-class white men, both in North America and now across Eastern Europe, who are far more aware of their vulnerability than their privilege.

In an era of heavy industry, men from low-income backgrounds often found their best opportunities in manufacturing. If these were unionized jobs with relatively high wages, they contributed to the male advantage. Men in these jobs earned considerably more than women in routinized clerical, service, and domestic positions. Yet as these unionized heavy industry positions become scarce, the men and their industrial skills are extremely vulnerable to termination, protracted unemployment, and new employment at far lower wages. Women in industry are also vulnerable, but those with skills applicable in the service economy may have more secure employment than the men of their families and communities. The men may still have certain privileges, than the women, such as greater freedom from family responsibilities, but they are most acutely award of their vulnerability. Their severe class disadvantage trumps their gender privileges.

This phenomenon is not purely new. In the 1800s, the paneled offices and the boardrooms—as well as the decrepit boarding houses, flop houses, and rescue missions—were all dominated by men: either men who had reached the top or men who had hit bottom. The place of women is also changing and in similarly complex ways. Women today are more likely to be seen in the boardrooms, but they are also more likely to be found in the rescue missions and the homeless shelters, not always as "sisters of mercy" but sometimes as guests.

Tired, Stressed Women and Angry, Alienated Men

Changing gender roles in the workplace are tied to changing gender roles in the home and family, with a change in one realm often forcing a change in the other. For example, women's growing economic independence has made it easier for them to leave abusive and unsatisfying marital relationships. This, along with other social and legal changes, is one factor in the rising world divorce rate. At the same time, the high divorce rate means that women are often left as sole custodians of children, often with limited child support and sometimes with limited income-earning potential of their own. The result is what has been termed the **feminization of poverty,** with the group most at risk of poverty being single mothers and their dependent children (Sidel 1996).

Women's expanded role in the workforce has often not meant a relaxing of expectations for their family and domestic activities, such that many face a double burden of home and work responsibilities. Women still often have the primary responsibility for the care of children as well as the care of older adults in the family. Women also still often shoulder the largest portion of the upkeep of the home, even when they are working full time (South and Spitze 1994; Stapinski 1998). Arlie Hochschild (1989) has termed this the "second shift" and noted the anger and frustration that women often feel when they find they are still doing the major portion of housework on top of their paid work.

This is a cross-cultural and almost worldwide phenomenon. Around the world, women spend more total hours in work than men, and mothers work the most of all (Scarr, Phillips, and McCartney 1989). In Japan, a majority of women are in the paid workforce, but they face wage discrimination that is the greatest in the industrial world and barriers to upward mobility that are blatant by Western standards. Once married, they are still expected to be devoted wives and mothers who give all their effort to the home, even after a full day of work. Latin American women, now entering the paid labor force in ever-greater numbers, likewise face what they call the *doble jornada,* or "double-day's journey". *Machismo,* that swashbuckling blend of male authority and male privilege in Latin America, appears to be breaking down, as more Latin American men regularly interact with their children and help around the home (Gutmann 1996). Even so, the main domestic responsibilities still fall to the women, even those who are the primary wage earners. In Western Europe, where gender role changes have been most pronounced, the gaps in wages and workload are smaller but still present. Like North American and Latin American men, European men are more likely than ever to play and interact with their children but no more likely to participate fully in their daily care. Likewise, they are more likely than ever to help their wives and female partners at home but no more likely to shoulder all domestic tasks equally.

Sometimes, this is a pretty clear story of continuing male privilege. Other times, it is also a story of male alienation and vulnerability. The changing global economy is displacing many men, especially low-income and working-class men, from their traditional roles, even as it is overburdening women with new and double roles. Around the world, men who depended on strong backs and arms for their livelihood have been displaced by automation in industry and mechanization in agriculture, as well as by the constantly shifting nature of global production. Steel workers in Gary, Indiana; Bethlehem, Pennsylvania; Manchester, England; and the former East Germany have all been idled by new more automated Japanese plants and by products that replace steel with molded plastic parts from Guangzhou, China. Dock workers in Baltimore, Maryland; London, England; and Gdansk, Poland have been idled by container ships that load and unload the world's wares with a single crane. Small farmers in Minnesota, Brazil, the Philippines, and South Africa have been idled as corporate-controlled heavy machines work the land in their place. Cattlemen in Montana watch their ranches turn to condo developments, while cattlemen in Sub-Saharan Africa watch their range land turn to desert.

Sometimes, these men find alternate work. Security guards are in high demand in crime-plagued cities like Gary, Indiana; St. Petersburg, Russia; and Johannesburg, South Africa. Security seems to be manly work, although it is typically low paying in each location. Other men may try criminal activity or a variety of odd jobs—day labor, seasonal or informal construction work, small repairs, and sales. The alternative is often chronic unemployment: sitting around the tavern, the pub, the street corner, the village center, or the diner amidst abandoned buildings, drinking coffee, beer, vodka, or homemade brew and talking about hard times with other men. These men don't feel privileged; they feel humiliated and disgraced or alienated and cheated. As one church conference in Washington, D.C., noted, they're not deadbeats, just dead broke. Given the high rates of suicide, alcoholism, disease, and violent crime among these men, sometimes they are also soon dead. In *Families on the Fault Line*, Lillian Rubin (1994) quotes the unemployed Tony Bardolino:

> I was just so mad about what happened; it was like the world came crashing down on me. I did a little too much drinking, and then I'd just crawl into a hole, wouldn't even know whether Marianne or the kids were there or not. She kept saying it was like I wasn't there. I guess she was right, because I sure didn't want to be there, not if I couldn't support them. (p. 219)

Ironically, if there are women in the lives of these displaced men, they are often overburdened. They may have become the major wage earner for the family. Assembly plants in export-processing zones in Mexico, the Caribbean, and across East Asia are often reluctant to hire unemployed men, who may tolerate

Global economic changes have often displaced men, such as these day workers in Austin, Texas, from many of their traditional roles and jobs. At the same time, they are often overburdening women who often keep traditional roles and add new workplace demands, such as these women at a computer chip facility in China.

too little and demand too much. These plants prefer to hire young women. Strong backs aren't needed to assemble electronic components—just nimble fingers, keen eyesight, and endless patience. Young women bring these skills plus the willingness to work without complaint. Other plants draw on traditionally female skills, such as sewing seams in textile plants. Women in these plants often earn very little by Western standards, but they may become the major wage earners in their families, replacing the income lost by unemployed fathers and husbands. Patricia Fernandez-Kelly (1983) quotes Teresa in Juarez, Mexico:

> There were about seventy women like us sewing in a very tiny space. . . . When I was sixteen I used to cut thread at the shop. Afterwards one of the seamstresses taught me how to operate a small machine and I started doing serious work. Beatriz, my sister, used to sew the pockets on the pants. It's been three months since we left the shop. Right now we are living from the little that my father earns. We are two of nine brothers and sisters (there were twelve of us in total but three died when they were young). My father does what he can but he doesn't have a steady job. Sometimes he does construction work; sometimes he's hired to help paint a house or sells toys at the stadium. You know, odd jobs. He doesn't earn enough to support us. (p. 119)

Regardless, it is not easy for many men to step into what they have always thought of as female roles: taking over domestic tasks and child care. So, these also remain primarily female activities. Left with no roles, the men seek alternate gratification or just leave altogether. Faced with double and triple roles, the women may feel crushed by the added burdens. The men may be as likely to feel resentful of the women as grateful. Somehow, the world has changed, and it is hard to know who to blame. The women may blame the men for not "doing something for themselves." The men may blame other racial/ethnic groups: Displaced white men in both the United States and South Africa frequently blame black workers, and displaced black men in both the United States and East African cities frequently blame Asian entrepreneurs. The men also may turn to ultranationalist politicians and leaders, as they have in the United States, in Russia, and recently even in Austria, Fiji, and France. They may also blame women—the feminists, perhaps—for undermining the status they once knew.

Middle-class and upper-middle-class career men with children face stresses of their own. They often are expected to have the same single-minded devotion to their careers as the 1950s man, who was supported by his "domestic woman." But now, the men are also expected to invest themselves more in the duties and demands of parenting. They face their own set of unrealistic demands and guilt as they confront what Hochschild (1997) calls "the time bind." The very expectation that childrearing is primarily a female endeavor can limit the options of men: Even when paternity leave is offered, the very few men who take it may be subject to suspicion or ridicule (Hochschild 1997). When British Prime Minister Tony Blair and his wife had a baby, the joke was who should take the leave; as a well-paid attorney, she earned far more than he did as prime minister! Sweden is being forced by more conservative members of the European Union to reduce its generous maternity and paternity leave policies, which will bring it in line with new budget-cutting priorities. Finding more equitable, more satisfying ways of combining work and family remains one of the challenges of this century for men and women, for their employers, and for their governments.

Women, especially rural women, are still the poorest of the world's poor, because they often bear heavy family responsibilities with only meager resources. In some urban areas, women are now more employable than men, but they see little of the benefits of this, for their new incomes often go to supporting struggling families. Urban women have made substantial movement into middle-class employment but found it hard to continue to move up to top positions. Men still dominate in positions of power and privilege, although many poor rural and urban–industrial working-class men have lost ground. While they may be inclined to blame this loss on women's gains, most have lost out to global technology and global marketing, both still controlled largely by wealthy and powerful men.

Locked In and Shut Out

In ancient times, raids sometimes killed the men and captured the women. Modern colonial and corporate raids often do the same, albeit figuratively. When local systems collapse under more powerful international forces, it is often the men's roles that are the most completely erased. This is exactly because men tend to hold the positions of power, influence, and independence that are usurped by new forces and new masters. The men's roles of authority and autonomy are replaced by more distant authorities. The women's roles of caretaking and daily providing are still needed, however, and so are harnessed to the new system. Poor women become locked into the global economy, and poor men get shut out. Because the women are closer at hand than distant and abstract forces, they may become the objects of men's anger, frustration, and violence. While this violence is abhorrent and its consequences devastating, it must be recognized as a secondary reaction of the powerless to subtler but more powerful violence.

Examined side by side, common themes emerge from these repeated refrains. Women frequently bear the brunt of poverty. They continue to have the primary responsibility for the care of children, as well as of sick and elderly family members. They continue to face discrimination and handicaps in the labor market, and attempts to gain greater education, independence, and upward mobility are frequently met with suspicion and outright hostility on the part of employers, fathers, husbands, and others. "When people who've had a little bit of education suddenly start acting uppity, they get slapped down," Jesus Sanchez told his daughter in the Mexico of a generation ago (quoted in Lewis 1961). "Take a look in the mirror and tell me what class you belong to, what your place is in society" (p. 482). Versions of these harsh words are still heard in many places and many families, especially in regard to ambitious daughters.

In increasing numbers of homes, the men are just not there at all. Whether divorced, deserted, or just abandoned for long periods, the women carry on without male support. North Americans denounce "deadbeat dads" and "absentee fathers," Latin Americans murmur about the *machos* who prefer the streets to home, and Africans wonder why their traditionally strong families are now so often supported by networks of female kin with few men to be found. These female-headed families are sometimes called **matriarchal,** a term that is misleading because it implies that the women are powerful when in fact they are often overworked, overburdened, and victimized. A more accurate term is **matrifocal,** which means focused or centered around the mother and female kin. These families are increasing in number on every continent.

So, where are these men: the deadbeats, the dead broke, the *machos,* the bums, the deserters? The world has never lacked for individuals who have a difficult time enduring great responsibility, and cultural patterns around the world certainly contribute to this. But again, we would do well to look beyond personal and cultural peculiarities for structural causes. In their defense, many men have been displaced by forces they cannot control and may only partly understand. Traditional male roles—especially those that involved strength, independence, bravery, and self-reliant providing—have been severely undermined. Despite cultural variations, male roles in many societies have emphasized just these traits (Gilmore 1990). The man comes home from the hunt, the battlefield, the voyage, or the marketplace, tired and bruised, but loudly tosses down the goods and enjoys the acclaim of a waiting family and community. No more.

The unemployed steel worker in Gary and the laid-off auto worker in Flint, who once won approval for their ability to withstand the heat and grime and physical demands of their professions, now find themselves competing with teenagers for minimum-wage jobs that the teenagers do better. These men subsist on severance, on savings, and on women's employment. They drink beer, watch sports, and think about how they have become a liability rather than an asset to their families. The same story is repeated in East Africa, where proud herders who once withstood the heat and grime and physical demands of their profession now are idled on government supported settlements, where they drink homemade beer and come to the same conclusion.

Women often find themselves locked in: locked in to a home full of never-ending demands or locked in (sometimes literally) to the demanding drudgery of an electronics or textile plant. Men often find themselves locked out: locked of the labor market and eventually out of their families. Fatherhood around the world is shifting. While some men have the skills and background to become the nurturing, involved "Cosby-style" dad, many others find they are no longer needed or respected, no longer capable, at either the demands of the new marketplace or the new home front (Furstenberg 1988). They become bitter, or despondent, drunk or violent, or they just disappear. While the women may at least have the support of matrifocal families, these men may have very little at all. Some may follow any of a variety of organizations, usually with a clear list of enemies and an angry agenda, but most have only the comraderie of the street corner.

The new global middle classes clearly have access to more opportunities, but these opportunities come with their own anxieties. The new middle classes—whether they are African American, Polish American, Mexican, South Korean, or Indian—are often painfully aware of the precariousness of their position. A sudden economic downturn can result in an equally sudden plummet from privilege (Newman 1988). Raising children, who were ultimately an economic asset in agrarian societies, is an expensive and demanding proposition for the urban middle class. Often, it requires two incomes from two separate professions. This creates demands that are very different from the side-by-side economic efforts of earlier families (Hochschild 1997).

It has been suggested that the very idea of a career was created for a man who was largely exempted from family responsibilities (Slater 1970). This is not likely an option for a career woman. She faces criticism and guilt for neglecting her work if she invests too much at home and for neglecting her family if she invests too much at work. The man feels that security in this precarious situation can only be won by making a heavy investment at work, yet he knows that he is now also expected to be available at home. The challenge lies in how quickly we can open nongendered opportunities and how thoroughly we can make these opportunities family friendly.

The Feminization of Migration

In their book *Global Woman: Nannies, Maids, and Sex Workers in the New Economy,* U.S. social commentator Barbara Ehrenreich and U.S. sociologist Arlie Hochschild (2003) have compiled accounts of how wealthier countries in the last decades have been flooded with immigrant female domestic workers, creating what some are describing as the "feminization of migration." Labor migrants have traditionally been men. For instance, Chinese laborers in the United States in the 1800s were overwhelmingly unmarried men. In Southern Africa, men have long left home to work in mines and industries. Men from South Asia and Northern Africa have traveled to the Persian Gulf to work in the oil industry. Traditionally, women were left at home to care for the children and elders and to wait for the return of their men. Increasingly, it is the women who are leaving.

The first large-scale migration of women on their own was out of Ireland in the 1800s. Young Irish women traveled to England and France and then to the United States in large numbers. Some worked as shopgirls and mill workers, but the largest portion worked as domestics. The Irish maid became a common feature in large, posh Victorian homes. Ironically, it was the movement of women into professional positions in Europe and North America that led to the recent surge in international domestic migrants. The Latina domestic in the United States and the Turkish domestic in Germany have become commonplace. This pattern is now expanding around the globe, as pockets of prosperity become magnets for domestic workers from less-thriving economies. Filipina maids have become common in Hong Kong (Constable 1997). Sometimes, the mix is unusual, as is this Sri Lankan's in Jordan:

> In a sitting room in a wealthy neighborhood of Amman, the Jordanian capital, three Sri Lankan maids—Mala, Manike, and Coomari—sit on plump couches, sipping sweet Arabic tea. Madame Shama is serving, for a change—and translating from the housemaids' acquired Arabic. The women are here to explain why they've traveled thousands of miles to work for a hundred dollars a month. In a word: family.
>
> "I love them so much and I was so desperate to make anything possible for them to live better and eat better and learn better," says Coomari. "And I thought, it's only two years. Maybe it will be worth it." (Tolan 2003)

Increasingly, it is not the male overseas laborer who supports the household back home but the female:

> By almost any measure, the housemaids' salaries are tiny—some as little as 30 cents an hour, plus room and board, for 14-hour days of cooking and cleaning. Yet these women have been able to save for new homes in their villages. Their income now makes up the largest share of Sri Lanka's foreign exchange. And as services that used to be taken for granted now keep their families alive, the women see themselves differently. (Tolan 2003)

Global Family Changes

Marriage and Divorce

Around the world, people are marrying later and divorcing more often. The changes in the last half of the twentieth century were most dramatic in the United States, but mirrored changes took place first in Europe and somewhat later in Latin America and Asia. Modernization theorists tried to divide the world into *traditional* and *modern* patterns of family life, describing a great transformation from traditional family life of large **patriarchal** (male-dominated) extended families to modern arrangements of smaller nuclear families, as described in the work of prominent U.S. social theorist Talcott Parsons (1964) and family sociologist William Goode (1963). This can be misleading, however.

The glimpses we get of family life in simpler societies suggest a more complex pattern. Hunter–gatherers seem to have married for love and lust, raised small nuclear families with the help of close community and perhaps grandparents, and occasionally divorced and remarried, all much the same as today (Fisher 2004). In family life, at least, it seems that prehistory repeats itself. The story of Nisa of the Kalahari Kung people (Shostak 2000) is full of falling in and out love, of happy and unhappy marriages, domestic violence, and interpersonal struggles and intrigue. Her life could serve as the plot for any modern American soap opera, except the actors would need to wear even fewer clothes.

In simple horticultural societies, such as were common in Sub-Saharan Africa and across the Pacific as well as in the Americas before Columbus, people tended to marry early and to have to consider family obligations. But they still exercised some choice, and wives often wielded considerable power and influence. In a significant number of these societies, the couple would live with the wife's family, a system anthropologists call **matrilocal.**

With the expansion of agriculture and its demands, agrarian (agricultural) societies developed, having characteristics that we have come to consider traditional: male-dominated, extended families with arranged marriages. Marriage was a union of families. It was about economic considerations, such as control of the land and inheritance, and as such needed to be strictly controlled. Romantic love was known and even celebrated in song and tale, but it was also dangerous. People who fell in love with the wrong people threatened the stability of the clan or kingdom. From Camelot's Guinevere and Lancelot to Shakespeare's Romeo and Juliet, romantic love brought war and disaster. Tales from Asia, such as the tragedy of the Jade goddess, suggest the same. People knew of love but feared it (Fisher 2004).

Men were traditionally concerned about legitimate heirs and property. Social position and land were matters of inheritance, and marriage was a way, often the only way, to secure one's future. Female virginity before marriage was essential. Women were often closely guarded, cloistered, or veiled, and after marriage, their role was focused around the home and farm. Women were often viewed as property, like land, with few rights of their own, and in some societies, such as in the Islamic world and parts of Africa, wealthy men could own more than one wife. This was forbidden to Christians but often occurred informally in Europe and Latin America, as wealthy and powerful men took mistresses. Children have traditionally been viewed as the most valuable property to come from marriage, and large families with many children to work the land and provide security in old age were prized.

Industrial changes shattered much of this pattern:

Under the impact of industrialization the family in newly developing societies be-comes more egalitarian, emotionally freer, and less sexually stratified. The mys-tique of male dominance that had for generations kept the female in a subordinate position becomes tarnished, and women, supported by an ideology of sexual equality, challenge their husbands' omnipotence, often with success. The sceptre of patriarchal authority does not exactly fall from nerveless male hands; some-times the wife, emboldened by her new freedom of power, snatches it brusquely from her husband's grasp. More often, however, a process of negotiation takes place during which men agree, though not without some reservation, to share power with their wives. (Rosen 1982, 3)

Family patterns do not change overnight, however, and around the world, changes are still taking place. Families are smaller and more flexible. Arranged mar-riage is still practiced in Asia, particularly in India, but instead of children being betrothed at eight and nine, arrangements may be made between the families of two college graduates, each of when can claim veto power over the match. For the 5,000 years that agrarian societies dominated much of the world, marriage was about property, work, and kinship obligations. Romance was a dangerous game for the wealthy. Companionship came from same-sex peers. Increasingly, or maybe once again, marriage is about romance and companionship for young people around the world. This makes marriage more optional. Many are waiting longer to marry and are thus more likely to engage in marriage-like behavior, such as liv-ing together.

Marriages based on romance and companionship may be more appealing, but they are also more fragile. World divorce rates continue to rise. In the United States, the divorce rate has been increasing since the late 1800s. It reached a peak in 1946, only to drop markedly during the 1950s. For a brief time, earlier ideals of motherhood and family again dominated, and divorce carried a great stigma. This changed during the 1960s, and divorce again peaked in the 1970s. Divorce rates in the United States have plateaued since that time. Divorce has likewise in-creased in much of Europe. However, U.S. divorce rates remain the highest in the industrial world (see Figure 3.1), in part because marriage remains very popular in the United States. Northern Europeans are slower to marry in the first place and so less likely to have a formal divorce. The Roman Catholic Church has long held a strong stance against divorce, and rates are lower in staunchly Catholic countries, such as Ireland, Italy, and Poland. Yet numbers can be deceiving: In Italy, cohabitation outside marriage and church-sanctioned annulments of mar-riages mean that coupling and recoupling can occur without formal divorce.

For a long time, the lowest divorce rates in the industrial world were found in Japan. The reason for this, however, was not necessarily happier marriages but a

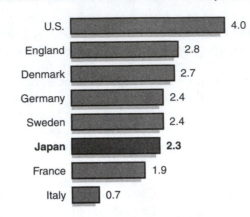

Divorce Rates for Selected Countries (cases per 1,000 people)

U.S. — 4.0
England — 2.8
Denmark — 2.7
Germany — 2.4
Sweden — 2.4
Japan — **2.3**
France — 1.9
Italy — 0.7

Note: France, Germany and Italy data are for 2000, Denmark and Sweden, 2001, all others, 2002.

Source: Data from Japanese Ministry of Health, Labor and Welfare; Council of Europe, Associated Press. Figure from *South Bend Tribune,* January 18, 2004, p. B6.

strong stigma against divorce coupled with lower expectations for marriage. Consider the following:

> Yuri Uemura sat on the straw tatami mat of her living room and chatted cheerfully about her 40-year marriage to a man whom, she mused, she never particularly liked. "There was never any love between me and my husband," she said blithely, recalling how he used to beat her. "But, well, we survived." A 72-year-old midwife, her face as weathered as an old baseball and etched with a thousand seams, Mrs. Uemura said that her husband had never told her that he liked her, never complimented her on a meal, never told her "thank you," never held her hand, never given her a present, never shown her affection in any way. He never calls her by her name, but summons her with the equivalent of a grunt or a "Hey, you." In short, the Uemuras have a marriage that is as durable as it is unhappy, one couple's tribute to the Japanese sanctity of family. (Kristof 1996, 33)

Not all Japanese couples are this distant of course, but it is a common pattern, particularly among an older generation:

> Osamu Torida furrowed his brow and looked perplexed when he was asked if he loved his wife of 33 years. "Yeah, so-so, I guess," said Mr. Torida, a cattle farmer. "She's like air or water. You couldn't live without it, but most of the time, you're not conscious of its existence." The secret to the survival of the marriage, Mr. Torida acknowledged, was not mutual passion. "Sure, we had fights about

our work," he explained as he stood beside his barn. "But we were preoccupied by work and our debts, so we had no time to fool around." (Kristof 1996, p. 34)

The demands of work and obligation are a common theme. But these hard-working marriages have also proven quite durable. Why? we may ask:

It does not seem that Japanese families survive because husbands and wives love each other more than American couples, but rather because they perhaps love each other less. "I think love marriages are more fragile than arranged marriages," said Tomika Kusukawa, 49, who married her high-school sweetheart and now runs a car repair shop with him. "In love marriages, when something happens or if the couple falls out of love, they split up." (Pearson 2004, B6)

This was once also common in the West, and it is now also changing in Japan. Most new divorces are now initiated by women who are tired of being after-thoughts in their husband's busy lives. It's still not simple, however:

Divorce remains a financially precarious road for most Japanese women, who tend to face fewer job opportunities and wage discrimination, particularly when returning to the workforce at a later age. "If women were more financially independent, I think the divorce rate would probably be double what it is," said Okano of the Caratclub service. (Pearson 2004, B6)

Divorce rates are also climbing all across Latin America, in spite of a strong Catholic and agrarian heritage. Only the semiarranged marriages of India seem to be particularly enduring. But the pattern seems inescapable: Only people who marry out of obligation seem to feel compelled to remain together. People who choose to marry and choose whom to marry sometimes choose to break up.

The emotional struggles of divorce may confront men and women equally, but the economic consequences do not. Since men more often command greater economic power and since women often have the primary responsibility for children, divorce places many women and their children at risk for poverty. This feminization of poverty is becoming a global phenomenon.

Parenting

Changes in work and marriage have also complicated the task of parenting. Mothers have long worked with their children close at hand, and many still do: with young children playing in the back of the vendor's booth, in the shade next to the farm field, next to the loom and the cookware at home. At any Latin American, African, or South Asian market, there are a lot of children: the older ones sewing, painting, or stacking fruit and the younger ones watching the crowds slip by. Itinerant vendors have it harder, as they sling their small children on one side and dangle their wares from the other.

This arrangement becomes more complicated as work pulls mothers into less family-friendly environments. In Europe, governments eager to get children on a strong start and to encourage births provide a generous maternity leave followed by heavily subsidized child care. Mothers (and often fathers, if they wish) can spend the first year with their babies on full or near-full pay and then leave their growing infants in the hands of caregivers at a variety of day care settings, such as France's heavily subsidized *ecoles maternelles*. In China and India, the caregiver is more likely a grandmother or other older family member. In the United States, the pattern is mixed. Many also turn to grandmother. Low-income parents may find some help with subsidized day care, while others either use private day care, trade shifts between parents, or seek home-based jobs that can be done with children alongside.

The challenges grow for single parents, who don't have a partner to help. In the United States, single parenting is the single greatest risk factor for poverty. In the chapter-opening Benton Harbor example, a common cycle is seen: Women in communities in which few men have stable employment eventually begin their parenting alone or with an unreliable partner. The single parent, in turn, may find it even harder to escape the poverty of the community. The connection between single parenting and poverty is mediated by the surrounding society. Single fathers in the United States, a small but growing group, are less likely to be poor than single mothers (U.S. Census 2004), since men tend to earn more, and can often only get custody if they can show economic stability.

Public policy also makes a huge difference. Sweden has one of the world's highest rates of single parenthood, yet also one of the lowest rates of child poverty. How can this be? First of all, many single mothers in Sweden do have a partner present but have chosen not to get married. Even when the woman is truly on her own, the choice to have a child is often made later in life, when she is more financially stable. Finally, a strong system of government supports for children—health, education, and child care—make it easier to raise a child without a partner. In Africa, Latin America, and low-income communities in North America, single mothers most often depend on a network of family and neighbors to informally provide support and child care.

The greatest challenges are those that face young single parents, or teen mothers. The patterns here are more complex than they may first appear. Despite the tremendous alarm of concern over teen mothers, as seen in Benton Harbor, the teenage pregnancy rate in the United States is at an all-time low. Why, then, the alarm? It is also true that teen marriage is at an all-time low, so that over 95 percent of births to teenagers occur to single mothers. In earlier times, including the 1950s, it was not uncommon for a woman to be married at eighteen and to be pregnant at nineteen, or perhaps the other way around. So, there were lots of teen mothers, but they were older teens and they were married, even if many of those marriages were unstable. Births to teens are increasingly to unmarried teens and sometimes to younger teens, a pattern first seen in the United States but now becoming common elsewhere. A teen mother at thirteen or fourteen is much less likely to have completed secondary school and be ready to begin parenting than a teen mother at eighteen or nineteen.

The main reason that younger girls are getting pregnant is that they can. In most societies of the past, a girl of thirteen or fourteen would not have yet menstruated. Some experimented sexually and others were sexually abused, but they didn't become pregnant because they weren't biologically able. In a pattern not fully understood, a high-calorie, high-nutrient diet, coupled with a low level of exercise, has resulted not only in a higher proportion of body fat among young women but also younger menstruation and the possibility of pregnancy.

In simple horticultural societies, it was not uncommon for girls to first menstruate at fifteen or sixteen and to be married by sixteen or seventeen. Premarital pregnancy wasn't a problem. Agrarian societies continued to marry off most young women at a young age and strictly chaperoned the rest to avoid pregnancy. In situations where chaperoning failed, marriage quickly followed an unexpected pregnancy. The so-called shotgun marriage was common in colonial America, where it seemed to carry little stigma (Coontz 1992), and again became common in the 1950s in the United States (Rubin 1976). With the average age at menstruation around thirteen and the average age at first marriage creeping up to twenty-six, U.S. women now have a thirteen-year window of possibility for premarital pregnancy.

After a brief rise in teen pregnancy in the early 1980s, the rate is again falling in the United States, due it seems both to greater emphasis on sexual abstinence by some and to greater attention to contraception by others:

> Researchers often sum up the findings in one tidy phrase: "less sex, more contraception." But there is nothing simple about their puzzlement over the reasons.
> "The default position is 'Yahoo, let's have sex,'" said Sarah Brown, director of the private, nonprofit National Campaign to Prevent Teen Pregnancy. "It takes some motivation in a highly sexualized culture for teenagers not to have sex. To use contraception takes a lot of motivation."
> "I think there's something very profound going on. I don't think anybody understands in depth this change in teen culture." (Bernstein 2004)

This pattern has prevailed in much of Europe for some time, where beginning sexual activity is planned and preceded by a contraceptive decision. The United States has one of the highest rates of teenage pregnancy in the industrial world because it neither chaperones as is common in Asia, nor has the broad and open availability of contraception common in Europe. Thus, U.S. teenagers are seemingly getting mixed messages about the onset of sexual activity. Just as this double message seems to be declining in the United States, it is increasing in Latin America. Traditional chaperoning and early marriage of girls is declining, but many families are reluctant to talk about contraception (*South Bend Tribune* 2005). As a result, unmarried teenage pregnancy rates are growing in many Latin American cities and among some U.S. Latinas. As education about AIDS (acquired immune deficiency syndrome) grows in Latin America, there is a gradual movement toward more open discussion of safe sex. AIDS is a huge concern in Africa, but poverty, limited choices, and limited information still lead to high rates of young pregnancy. At the same time, AIDS has brought to modern Africa what was the most common reason for single parenting in the United States and Europe a century ago: the death of a parent.

As rising divorce rates, falling marriage rates, and delayed marriage make single parenting more common around the world, governments and communities are confronted with the task of easing this burden for both single parents and their children. Rising unemployment and underemployment, coupled with disabling diseases, also mean that in many communities (and in poor communities, in particular), even extended and two-parent families may have only one wage earner, and this person is increasingly likely to be female and poorly paid.

The Continued Perils of Being Female

Feminist Theory and World Feminist Movements

The United Nations *Population Fund 2000* report noted that conditions for women around the world have improved since 1994, when 179 countries pledged to do more for their women. Yet the report also noted that throughout the world, women continue to be victims of violence, sexual exploitation, and discrimination—at great cost both to their own well-being and to their countries' economies. The report cites links among abuse, illness, early death, dangerous abortions, and personal degradation:

- One in three women will experience violence during her lifetime, most often at the hands of someone she knows.
- Two million girls under age fifteen are forced into the sex trade each year.
- Complications from pregnancy and childbirth kill 500,000 women each year.
- Lack of obstetric care is the primary cause of 8 million stillbirths and newborn deaths each year.
- One-third of pregnancies each year (80 million) are unintended or unwanted.
- Of the 50 million abortions each year, 20 million are unsafe, leading to 78,000 maternal deaths (United Nations 2000).

Women have been gradually moving into prominent positions in governments around the world (see Figure 3.2). Overwhelmingly, however, most heads of state, judges, and legislators are still men. Asia and Europe have seen a greater rise in female representation in government than have Africa and the Americas.

Women also still earn less than men, on average, around the world (see Table 3.1). This gap has been closing, in part due to the displacement of men from secure employment, as noted earlier in this chapter. In fact, most of the gains of U.S. women relative to men have been the result of men losing high-wage unionized jobs. Europe has a somewhat smaller gender-wage gap than North America. Japan, which has less class inequality than much of the industrialized world, has greater gender inequality. Japanese women report many hurdles to advancing to upper levels in the business world, and Japanese women's earnings are well below those of Japanese men.

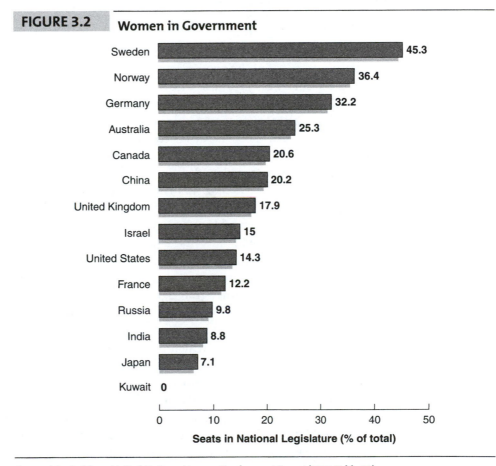

FIGURE 3.2   **Women in Government**

Seats in National Legislature (% of total)

- Sweden — 45.3
- Norway — 36.4
- Germany — 32.2
- Australia — 25.3
- Canada — 20.6
- China — 20.2
- United Kingdom — 17.9
- Israel — 15
- United States — 14.3
- France — 12.2
- Russia — 9.8
- India — 8.8
- Japan — 7.1
- Kuwait — 0

Source: Adapted from United Nations, *Human Development Report* (2004, Table 29).

| TABLE 3.1 | Gender Pay Gap in Selected Countries | | |

Country	Gender Pay Gap (%)	Country	Gender Pay Gap (%)
Japan	34.7	Germany	19.4
Argentina	32.7	Greece	16.2
South Korea	26.0	Italy	14.3
United Kingdom	24.3	Spain	13.2
United States	24.0	France	10.8
Thailand	21.4	Denmark	10.4
Austria	21.1	Belgium	7.3
Netherlands	21.1	Portugal	5.9
Ireland	19.8		

Source: Commission of the European Communities 2002, *Implementation of gender mainstreaming in the Structural Funds programming documents 2000–2006.*

For at least the first 5,000 years of civilization, which were characterized by large-scale agrarian and pastoral societies, men dominated both the economic and political life of most societies. Feminist theorists have referred to this as our "legacy of patriarchy," or male control and dominance. While some feminist writers have ascribed this patriarchy to a particular history of religious and political thought in the West (Gimbutas 2001), it has been the pattern as well across North Africa, the Middle East, and most of Asia (Ruether 2005). Patriarchy, like racism, is about more than individual attitudes. Rather, it refers to the structure of institutions and whole societies in ways that subordinate women, children, and anything considered feminine.

A worldwide feminist movement has grown to challenge these structures. The women's movement in the United States first emerged in the 1840s and was associated with movements for the abolishment of slavery, temperance (the banning of alcohol, consumed mostly by men and which led to abandoned families and domestic violence), and to suffrage (the right to vote). The road was a slow one: Abolition came in 1865, but the right to vote for U.S. women was not national until 1920. Interest in the prohibition of alcohol came and went. Suffrage movements also grew in Great Britain, which did not grant women the right to vote until 1927.

The U.S. feminist movement again gained strength in the 1960s and 1970s, alongside other movements for greater equality and civil rights. Today, women's movements have emerged in Latin America and in Asia. The U.N. Conference on Women stressed the link between women's rights in particular and human rights in general. Hillary Clinton spoke of this connection in her address to the group:

I believe that, on the eve of a new millennium, it is time to break our silence. It is time for us to say here in Beijing, and the world to hear, that it is no longer acceptable to discuss women's rights as separate from human rights. These abuses have continued because, for too long, the history of women has been a history of silence. Even today, there are those who are trying to silence our words. The voices of this conference and of the women at Huairou must be heard loud and clear:

It is a violation of human rights when babies are denied food, or drowned, or suffocated, or their spines broken, simply because they are born girls. It is a violation of human rights when women and girls are sold into the slavery of prostitution. It is a violation of human rights when women are doused with gasoline, set on fire and burned to death because their marriage doweries are deemed too small. It is a violation of human rights when individual women are raped in their own communities and when thousands of women are subjected to rape as a tactic or prize of war. It is a violation of human rights when a leading cause of death worldwide among women ages 14 to 44 is the violence they are subjected to in the own homes. . . . If there is one message that echoes forth from this conference, it is that human rights are women's rights—and women's rights are human rights. (Clinton 1995, 5–6)

Only recently has there been much talk of a men's movement, or a masculinist movement. In his book *Iron John*, U.S. poet Robert Bly (1990) called men to get back in touch with their masculine side, not the "savage man" who is brutal and violent but what he termed the "wild man," who enjoys his masculinity. A Maasai elder, in an ancient East African herding society known for the bravery and fierceness of its *maroni* warriors, makes a similar distinction: A good *maroni* fearlessly takes up his spear and shield to face the enemy or the lion, a good *maroni* readily lays down his spear and shield when nurture rather than valor is called for, and a great *maroni* knows when to do which. The growth of the Promise Keepers organization for evangelical Christian men and the Million Man March for African American men showed renewed interest in male roles and men reclaiming their responsibilities. Both movements, however, seem to have stressed reclaiming earlier roles and responsibilities, which may not be available or even desirable for men in a changing world economy and culture.

Feminist movements continue to work for the rights of women. But feminist theory has also gone on to reconsider how societies construct their ideals of masculinity and femininity and often devalue the latter. In some times, there may have been utility in assigning women as nurturers and tenders of the home and community and having men specialize as warriors, physical laborers, and procreators. But the contemporary world has less need of all three men's roles. Societies, communities, and families are going to be forced to rethink and broaden the roles for both men and women and to welcome and assign equal value to the contributions of each.

Women's Shelters

■ What does your community offer for women's shelters for abused, homeless, or troubled women? Check your local United Way or directory of social services to see what is offered in the area. Also ask about advocacy and information programs offered locally on domestic violence, sexual assault, and gender issues.

Women's Health Services

■ What does your community offer for women's health services? Check for a local chapter of Planned Parenthood (www.plannedparenthood.org) and find out what it is doing to deal with the problem of unplanned pregnancy. Look at the site under "International." What is being done internationally? Are there other organizations active in your community or schools, such as "abstinence-only" groups? How do the philosophies and approaches differ?

NOW

■ Go to the website of the National Organization of Women (NOW) at www.now.org. Find a local chapter and visit it, if possible, to discuss issues. On the website, click on "Global Feminism" for articles and gatherings from around the world.

UNESCO

■ Look at the site for the United Nations Economic and Social Council (UNESCO) at www.unesco.org. Among the many topics addressed is the International Women's Day activities and programs. What aspects of gender are being addressed? What are the major concerns?

CHAPTER **4**

Education
Access and Success

DATELINE

Kisangani, Congo

Mauwa Funidi is a college graduate who works in a college library (Kristof 1997). She has a good education and what looked like a good job that would secure her place in the middle class of her country and provide for her extended family.

But the Congo is a troubled place. After its independence leader, Lumumba, was killed, the Congo was ruled by an absolute dictator, Mobuto Sese Seko (1967–1997). Mobuto ruled for most of the first three decades that the Congo was a nation, following its colonialization as a vast private estate of the king of Belgium. Since Mobuto's death, the resource-rich country has been torn by civil war, refugee crises, and foreign intervention.

Mauwa's library has almost no books; none have been purchased since 1982. Books aren't much in demand, since university classes rarely meet. Even if the library had books, many of the people couldn't read them. Many places in the country are too dangerous for children to attend school, and so literacy rates are falling along with incomes. Mauwa's own salary has plummeted to eleven dollars a month and often goes unpaid. Her extended family, once prominent and not stifled by unemployment, cannot count on her to provide for them. Instead, they must look to her sister, who has a more lucrative job at the Take-a-Peek bar.

Many in the Congo hope that education will be the answer to national development and personal success. But Mauwa already has a good education. There is simply not enough national stability and infrastructure for her to use it.

Islamabad, Pakistan

President Mousharaf called for the opening of new public schools and for a revision in the curriculum of the *madrasah,* the religious schools whose primary focus is the painstaking memorization of verses from the Koran. The memorization of sacred or revered texts has been the focus of many educational systems since ancient times, but there is a new concern with the *madrasah:* The subtext of these schools is Islamic fundamentalism and anti-Westernism (and maybe a negative view of Mousharaf's cooperation with the United States).

Pakistan, a very poor nation of 138 million people, one of the ten most populous nations in the world, will not find it easy to educate all of its children. According to the United Nations, only 40 percent of Pakistan's school-age children attend formal schooling. The *madrasah* have often made up some of the difference and sometimes are the only places that girls learn literacy skills. Pakistan faces a big gender gap in education: Only 45 percent of the population is literate, and female illiteracy is twice that of male.

Pakistan also faces the problem that many poor rural and urban families depend on their children to work and contribute to the family income. Pakistan is often cited as one of the countries with the worst child labor abuses, but having children work is part of their society, as it is in many societies.

These issues highlight the dilemmas of many countries around the world, including advanced industrial countries: How can we educate all children, rich and poor, male and female? And what should they learn? What should the standards be, and who should decide on the curriculum?

The Foundations of Education

The idea that children belong in school is actually quite new. For most of the human experience, formal education was for a select few. Most learning was practical and occurred between parents and children, apprentices and masters. Beyond this, value was given to the ancient stories, verses, and rules that defined a people and their culture. Even the simplest bands often have esteemed storytellers who guard the ancient wisdom. For instance, the oral stories of Dreamtime among Australian aborigines are complex, vivid, and highly valued as a source of understanding. In larger groups, tribal elders, both male and female, have guarded the ancient stories and passed them on through long practice of memorization.

At first, writing didn't help much. A written text could replace a human memory, but writing was a complex and hard-to-learn business. It was limited to a few dedicated scribes who worked their styluses over clay tablets first in Sumer, then wrote on papyrus in Egypt, and later wrote on paper in China and parchment in European monasteries. They kept accounts, they copied laws, and they began to write down the ancient tales of heroes, victories and calamities, the sacred verses, and the honored proverbs. Mastery of this material, *education,* could be a means to advancement.

At several times in the history of China, the imperial bureaucracy was filled by merit; only those who passed the entrance exams were given positions. For centuries, however, the civil service exams consisted mostly of showing that one had memorized the writings of Kung Fu-tse (Confucius) and other important texts.

In ancient Greece, knowledge was highly valued, but schooling was associated with leisure. As such, it was the pursuit of aristocrats and their children and a few esteemed philosophers, some who opened their own schools, many who tutored, and most who were quite poor. In 343 BCE, Philip of Macedonia could afford to hire Aristotle to tutor his son, Alexander, in social and natural philosophy. From Aristotle, Alexander learned political theory, biology, astronomy, and mathematics, but he also needed to study the arts of cavalry and infantry offense to lead the campaigns that would make him Alexander the Great.

One of the great things that Alexander did was to found a city on the Egyptian coast that, like many others, he named after himself. Alexandria became a center of learning. It gathered a great museum, not just a collection but a research laboratory of sorts, where the muses inspired wise minds. It also had a great library, filled with great scrolls in many languages; some had new ideas in science and philosophy, and many had ancient sacred and honored texts. The librarians were no slouches, either. One, a fellow by the name of Eratosthenes, measured with incredible accuracy the circumference of the world based on measurements of the inclination of the sun's rays.

But libraries are expensive and difficult to maintain. The one at Alexandria fell into ruin and burned. The next great centers of learning were Islamic universities—in some ways, the world's first. These great centers of learning gathered what had not been lost from ancient Greece, including the wisdom of Aristotle that Alexander had carried across the Middle East. They had the mathematics of Pythagoras and added the "new math," disciplines like algebra.

European learning was centered in the great monasteries for close to eight hundred years, but gradually, in the newly powerful cities, new universities emerged: Bologna, Oxford, Cambridge, the Sorbonne, and so forth. Still, learning remained largely the domain of priests, monks, sometimes nuns (such as Sor Juana) and other religious specialists, a handful of scribes and philosophers (in Europe now called *Doctors of Philosophy*), and the children of aristocrats. The subjects also changed little. The first universities in the United States all had similar curricula: theology and sacred texts, mathematics, rhetoric, and the ancient languages of Latin and Greek, mostly useful for reading ancient texts and tales. However, most children learned as they had before: from their parents and elders and from master tradespeople.

By the 1700s, the key to education for laborers in Great Britain did not lie in the great universities of Cambridge and Oxford but in **apprenticeships**. In these outgrowths of the medieval guilds, the skills associated with trades were learned from master tradespeople. In the colonial United States, apprenticeships also flourished but with the added expectation that basic literacy and math skills should also be taught to help the apprentice become an effective tradesperson and citizen. In fact, across the southern U.S. colonies, where slavery flourished, slaves and apprentices often worked in similar trades, both bound to their masters. The apprentices were taught the skills, including literacy, that would be expected of a free citizen; the slaves were not.

Not everyone was satisfied with this system. A bright, young printer named Benjamin Franklin had gone as far as the apprenticeship system would allow, but all of his flair for science, math, and language would not be enough to get him into a university. He persuaded the prominent citizens of Philadelphia to sponsor an academy that would be open to all, regardless of family status or religion. (Gender and race remained contentious well into the late 1800s.) Franklin envisioned a more practical education, stressing English skills rather than Latin. The sciences would also be prominent, each with a practical application: biology for agriculture, astronomy for navigation, chemistry for pharmacology, and physics for engineering. Eventually, his academy would provide the foundation for the University of Pennsylvania, although it would be decades before his more practical curriculum would dominate, even in public universities.

In a similar spirit, Thomas Jefferson claimed as his greatest accomplishment not writing the Declaration of Independence or serving as U.S. president but founding the University of Virginia. He built it in the classical style he had found in his own studies at Williamsburg. But he envisioned providing an education for all with the interest and ability, one rooted in the practical needs of a democracy. Education for democracy was also the driving vision of the great progressive reformer John Dewey, who was working at Columbia University in New York around the turn of the twentieth century. He argued for active learning, not rote memorization, as a route to active, informed citizenship.

These changes were slow to reach much of the rest of the world, which by Dewey's time, was dominated by European colonial powers. The epitome of cultured education, limited to a tiny elite, was education at one of the famous universities of Europe (a goal also sought by many in the United States). When schools were founded in Asia and Africa, they were typically based on the model of the colonial power. Thus, British education dominated in India and East Africa, while French education prevailed in French West Africa. The language, the history, even the uniforms were those of the colonial power. Many were mission schools, designed to teach religious values. In Latin America, religious orders also dominated the schooling, and both religious- and government-sponsored education followed European models: first Spanish and later British and French. In Central Africa, the Belgians maintained control of the vast Congo, in part by providing elementary education to all who could reach a school but secondary education only to Europeans.

Everywhere in the colonized world, secondary education was for the few and higher education was only the dream of a small elite. Again, most people continued to learn as they had for centuries from family, elders, and master tradespeople. When Africa and Asia emerged from colonial control in the mid to late twentieth century, one of the most pressing problems for the new governments was how to teach the masses, as well as what to teach them.

And Who Will Care for the Children?

In the poorest and most rural parts of Latin America, South Asia, and Africa, the struggle has always been to get every child to school. Just like on the historic U.S. frontier, the local school in such an area may be small and poorly equipped—a one-room schoolhouse, if that—and larger schools offering higher levels of education may be just too far away. For many rural U.S. children, the problem was also that they were needed on the farm, whether that farm was their family's homestead or whether their families were sharecroppers or migrant laborers on the land of others. Providing consistent schooling for all remains a struggle in many place in the United States.

In poor, rural regions of the world, this struggle is greatly magnified (see Table 4.1). Children's labor is needed, especially as farm laborers. And when the

TABLE 4.1	Gender Inequality in Education: Primary School					
	Primary School Net Enrollment Ratio		Primary School Net Attendence Ratio (%)		Share of Primary School Entrants Reaching Grade 5 (%)	
	(1998–2002)		1996–2003		1997–2003	
Countries and Territories	Male	Female	Male	Female	Admin. data	Survey Data
Sub-Saharan Africa	64	59	60	56	63	83
Middle East and North Africa	82	76	82	76	91	91
South Asia	88	75	78	71	60	91
East Asia and Pacific	92	92	—	—	94	—
Latin America and Caribbean	95	95	92	92	82	—
CEE/CIS	89	86	79	77	—	96
Industrialized countries	95	96	—	—	—	—
Developing countries	86	80	76	72	78	89
Least developed countries	67	61	61	56	64	79
World	87	82	76	72	79	89

Source: UNICEF, January 2005, "Monitoring the Status of Women and Children: Education." Available online at www.childinfo.org/areas/education. Used by permission.

TABLE 4.2	Gender Inequality in Education: Primary and Secondary Enrollment

Rank	Net Primary Enrollment[b,c]		Net Secondary Enrollment[b,c]		Gross Tertiary Enrollment[c,d]	
	Female Ratio (%) 2000/01	Ratio of Female to Male[e] 2000/01	Female Ratio (%) 2000/01	Ratio of Female to Male[e] 2000/01	Female Ratio (%) 2000/01	Ratio of Female to Male[e] 2000/01
High human development						
2 Sweden	102	1.00	99	1.01	93	1.54
8 United States	93	1.01	85	1.00	94	1.35
9 Japan	101	1.00	101[g,h]	1.01[g,h]	45	0.86
22 Israel	101	1.00	89	1.01	67	1.38
53 Mexico	102	1.01	61[g]	1.03[g]	21	0.95
Medium human development						
72 Brazil	97	1.02	74	1.08	21	1.29
77 Saudi Arabia	57	0.92	51[g]	0.93[g]	26[g]	1.49
Low human development						
176 Niger	28	0.68	4	0.66	1[g]	0.34

a. Data refer to estimates produced by UNESCO Institute for Statistics in July 2002, unless otherwise specified. Due to differences in methodology and timeliness of underlying data, comparisons across countries and over time should be made with caution. b. The net enrollment ratio is the ratio of enrolled children of the official age for the education level indicated to the total population at that age. Net enrollment ratios exceeding 100% reflect discrepancies between these two data sets. c. Data refer to the 2001/02 school year. Data for some countries may refer to national or UNESCO Institute for Statistics estimates. For details, see http://www.uis.unesco.org/. Because data are from different sources, comparisons across countries should be made with caution. d. Tertiary enrollment is generally calculated as a gross ratio. e. Calculated as the ratio of the female enrollment ratio to the male enrollment ratio. f. Data refer to the 2000/01 school year. g. Preliminary UNESCO Institute for Statistics estimates, subject to further revision. h. Data refer to the 1999/2000 school year. i. The ratio is an underestimate, as many students pursue their studies in nearby countries. j. Data refer to the 1998/99 school year. k. Census data. l. Data refer to a year between 1995 and 1999. m. Survey data.

Source: Columns 1 and 3: UNESCO Institute for Statistics 2004a; *columns 2 and 4:* calculated in the basis of data on adult and youth literacy rates from UNESCO Institute for Statistics 2004a; *columns 5, 7 and 9:* UNESCO Institute for Statistics 2004c; *columns 6, 8 and 10:* calculated on the basis of data on net enrollment rates from UNESCO Institute for Statistics 2004c. Table adapted from United Nations, *Human Development Report 2004: Identity, Diversity, and Globalization,* Table 26, pp. 225–228, by the United Nations Development Programme, © 2004 by the United Nations Development Programme. Used by permission of Oxford University Press, Inc.

farm economy breaks down, children are often needed as family wage earners. Even if Pakistan can provide schools for all, it will be real struggle to get all the children to those schools. It is not that parents don't care about their children's education but that every family member, including the very young, is needed to help provide income and food as well as to look after siblings while parents are away seeking food and income.

Schools are more available to everyone in urban areas around the world, which is one of the attractions of city life for rural migrants. Yet even in the cities, schools in poor neighborhoods are often poorly maintained and poorly equipped. Absenteeism is high, as children are still needed as laborers, working as street vendors, sewing and helping run family businesses, and tending to younger siblings while parents are at work. This is common in the burgeoning cities of Latin America, as well as in parts of Africa and Asia and even Los Angeles and New York.

Education around the world is also very unequal by gender (see Table 4.2). When resources are scarce, families may have to decide which children will have the privilege of education and which will be needed to work to support that education. Often, it is boys who are given the chance to pursue education. In many cultures, young men are more likely to stay close to home, to bring a wife into the family, and to support their parents in their later years. Girls may marry out to become part of another family, and so educating them is seen as a poor investment. Also, in cultures in which men interact in the marketplace and the community and women remain almost entirely at home, men are seen as needing at least basic math and literacy skills to buy and sell without being cheated, while women are believed to have less use for education. Interestingly, in cultures in which women remain to support their parents and men go live with their in-laws, as well as in places in which women traditionally have had more prominence in the marketplace, the educational gap between boys and girls is also the smallest.

The United Nations Children's Fund (UNICEF 2005) has implemented several programs that share the goal of eliminating gender disparity in education. One program, called the *25 by 2005 Initiative*, focuses on improving educational opportunities for girls in twenty-five of the countries judged to be most at risk of failing to achieve this goal, including eight West African countries (see Figure 4.1).

While providing all children a primary education is difficult, providing them a secondary education has proven even harder (see Table 4.3). Around the world, about two-thirds of all children never receive a high school education or its equivalent. Secondary schools are often far away for rural children. Poor urban children are

FIGURE 4.1   **Countries Selected for Accelerating Progress on Girls' Education**

Afghanistan	India
Bangladesh	Malawi
Benin	Mali
Bhutan	Nepal
Bolivia	Nigeria
Burkina Faso	Pakistan
Central African Republic	Papua New Guinea
Chad	Sudan
Dem. Rep. of the Congo	Turkey
Djibouti	United Rep. of Tanzania
Eritrea	Yemen
Ethiopia	Zambia
Guinea	

Source: UNICEF, January 2005, "Monitoring the Status of Women and Children: Education." Available online at www.childinfo.org/areas/education.

| TABLE 4.3 | **Secondary Enrollment Levels** |

Rank	Net Secondary Enrollment Ratio[b,c] (%)		Children Reaching Grade 5 (% of grade 1 students)	
	1990/91	**2001/02[d]**	**1990/91**	**2000/01[d]**
High human development				
2 Sweden	85	99[g]	100	—
8 United States	85	85[g]	—	—
9 Japan	97	101[g]	100	—
22 Israel	—	89	—	99
53 Mexico	45	60[g]	80	90
Medium human development				
72 Brazil	15	72[g]	—	—
77 Saudi Arabia	31	53	83	94
Low human development				
176 Niger	6	5	62	71

a. Data refer to estimates produced by UNESCO Institute for Statistics in July 2002, unless otherwise specified. Due to differences in methodology nd timeliness of underlying data, comparisons across countries and over time should be made with caution. b. The net enrollment ratio is the ratio of enrolled children of the official age for the education level indicated to the total population of that age. Net enrollment ratios exceeding 100% reflect discrepancies between these two data sets. c. Enrollment ratios are based on the new International Standard Classification of Education, adopted in 1997 (UNESCO 1997), and so may not be strictly comparable with those for earlier years. d. Data on net enrollment ratios refer to the 2001/02 school year, and data on children reaching grade 5 to the 2000/01 school year, unless otherwise specified. Data for some countries may refer to national or UNESCO Institute for Statistics estimates. For details, see http://www.uis.-unesco.org/. Because data are from different sources, comparisons across countries should be made with caution. e. Data refer to the most recent year available during the period specified. f. Data refer to the 2000/01 school year. g. Preliminary UNESCO Institute for Statistics estimate, subject to further revision. h. Data refer to the 1999/2000 school year. i. Data refer to the 1998/99 school year. j. Census data. k. Data refer to a year between 1995 and 1999. l. Survey data.

Sources: Columns 1 and 3: UNESCO Institute for Statistics 2003a; *columns 2 and 4:* UNESCO Institute for Statistics 2004a; *columns 5–10:* UNESCO Institute for Statistics 2004c; *column 11:* calculated on the basis of data on tertiary students from UNESCO 1999. Table adapted from United Nations, *Human Development Report 2004,* Table 11, pp. 176–179.

needed for work and child care by the time they leave the primary grades. And in locations where good jobs are scarce, the practical benefits of a secondary education may not be obvious. Even in the United States, poor communities with few job opportunities and high unemployment among adults often have the greatest difficulty keeping their children in high school through graduation. It is too easy for children, and sometimes parents, to look around at the lack of economic opportunities and ask, What's the use?

What constitutes the best route for completing a secondary education varies greatly around the world. In Europe, vocational programs and apprenticeships, both with traditions going back centuries, often begin in secondary school. Children who do not do well on tests or do not have an early desire for higher education are moved into vocational tracks and apprenticeships that will prepare them for trades. Japan and much of Latin America also use this model. In the United States, tracking is less formal and apprenticeships are often limited to a few trades. Yet some time in high school, children are often still divided into college-bound and vocational tracks, which may be very different.

The United States offers the opportunity to go to college to a larger portion of its students than almost any other country (see Figure 4.2). This opportunity is somewhat less common in Europe and even in Canada. In Japan, the opportunity

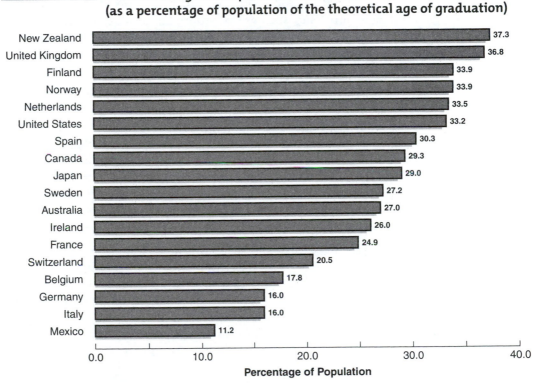

FIGURE 4.2   **Bachelor's Degree Recipients: Selected Countries, 1999 (as a percentage of population of the theoretical age of graduation)**

Country	Percentage
New Zealand	37.3
United Kingdom	36.8
Finland	33.9
Norway	33.9
Netherlands	33.5
United States	33.2
Spain	30.3
Canada	29.3
Japan	29.0
Sweden	27.2
Australia	27.0
Ireland	26.0
France	24.9
Switzerland	20.5
Belgium	17.8
Germany	16.0
Italy	16.0
Mexico	11.2

Percentage of Population

Note: Includes graduates of any age.

Source: Data from Organization for Economic Cooperation and Development. Figure from National Center for Educational Statistics. Available online: http://nces.ed.gov/programs/digest/d02/ch_6f.asp.

to get into a respected college is very limited and intensely competitive. In many poor countries, university education is limited to a very few.

The paths between these programs and between school and work are varied. There is worldwide agreement, at least at the national level, about the importance of education. There is much less agreement, however, about the related questions of How much? For whom? and Of what type?

Education around the World

Great Britain

Well into the 1800s, education was still primarily an avenue for the elite in Great Britain. Most factory workers and farm laborers had little formal education and were likely to be illiterate. Children of the elites went to private boarding schools, called *public schools,* such as Eton and Exeter. These schools prepared them for admission to an elite university, such as Oxford or Cambridge, and for a career. Such an education was especially important for the younger sons of landed gentry, who would not inherit the land and so needed a profession in law, medicine, government, the church, or the military. As fewer of the elites were large landowners, passing on privilege to their children increasingly meant giving them an elite education.

The boarding schools in Great Britain still flourish. Though few are quite as exciting as the fictional Hogwarts known to Harry Potter fans, Britain's new rich see them as a way to give their children elite breeding, profitable acquaintances, and an entry into the upper level of British society. Admission into Oxford and Cambridge is still coveted. Most government officials, as well as business executives, can claim an "Oxbridge" degree from one of these two universities, just as many Americans seek an Ivy League education.

At the same time, there has been an effort in Great Britain to extend the reach of popular education. As early as the 1800s, Robert Raikes began the Sunday School movement. This was not about religious education, although it had a strong moral component. Rather, Sunday was the only day that poor, young laborers were not working in the mills and factories; so it became their one day for school. Across Britain, historic efforts for universal primary education were often coupled with efforts to limit child labor: Children could only be in school if they weren't already in mines, mills, and sweatshops.

State-supported day schools now educate over 90 percent of British children, for whom an invitation to Eton may be as remote as an invitation to Hogwarts. College entrance is competitive, with the government paying most costs for those who do very well on the exams. As occurred in the United States during the Reagan administration, government support for higher education began to decline in Great Britain in the 1980s, with a greater financial burden falling on the students themselves (Gutek 1997).

Japan

Education has long been valued in Japan, but it, too, was originally for only a small elite. In the early 1800s, most Japanese children worked alongside their parents on peasant farms. Industrialization brought even harsher work, as children were used to dig coal in narrow mine shafts and to work in new industries, much as they did at this time and earlier in the United States and Great Britain. Industrialization also brought the need for a more educated population, and in 1872, the first laws were passed for mandatory basic education as part of Japan's governmental reforms.

With roots in earlier Shinto and Confucian models, Japanese education traditionally stressed discipline, order, and harmony (some would say conformity) and a great deal of study and memorization. Beginning in the late 1800s, however, Japan became much more enamored with Western science than Chinese Confucian texts, and the focus of study shifted to math and science, where Japanese students continue to excel. Standardized tests, now becoming popular in the United States, have also played a major role in Japanese education, especially in moving students on to higher levels.

Japanese high school graduation rates are high (over 90 percent, higher than in the United States), but space in major universities is limited. This means that less than half of high school graduates can go on to college (Okano & Tsuchida, 1999). (In the United States, almost two-thirds do.) This makes the university entrance process of supreme importance among the Japanese. It is not based heavily on family wealth or on a well-written essay or portfolio; rather, standardized test scores are the key criteria. Without high test scores, options for college are limited, even for the wealthy.

Japanese high school students not only spend more time in school and study longer than their U.S. counterparts, but they may also attend Saturday "cram schools" to give them an edge on the tests. Japanese schools also tend to have fewer electives and extracurricular activities, as they might distract students from the core subjects. Given the intense competition to get into key universities, U.S. observers are sometimes surprised to find how relaxed the atmosphere in Japanese colleges is, with students often studying less than their U.S. counterparts. Having been admitted, Japanese students seem to often feel that they have arrived. They have honored their family and secured their future and so can now relax a bit after the intense entrance competition. Major Japanese corporations have often recruited directly from the major universities and then offered their new hires essentially lifetime job security. Thus, while Japanese students have felt much more stress than U.S. students as they have tried to enter college, they have felt much less job and career stress as they have left. Students who do not get into a major university are not abandoned, for Japan also has an extensive apprenticeship and worker training program.

One reason for the traditionally high level of Japanese industrial productivity and quality appears to be that their workers are so well educated, especially in math and science, compared to those in many other countries. For a while, many in the United States looked at Japanese successes in international test scores and in industrial productivity and innovation and wondered if Americans should adopt a more Japanese model. At the same time, educators in Japan have often visited the United States in hopes of adopting ideas for Japanese schools, making them more flexible and creative and offering more interaction and less rote memorization. Even though U.S. students lag behind their Japanese counterparts all through school, they seem to do very well in graduate school and in entrepreneurship, which require self-initiative and creative risk taking rather than memorizing answers.

In many ways, while it has been a study in contrasts, the U.S. and Japanese systems are starting to look more alike. Many U.S. proposals for school reforms are for measures already in place in Japan, such as greater use of rigorous standardized tests, longer school days, a "back to basics" curriculum with fewer electives and more emphasis on math and science, school uniforms, an emphasis on order and respect, and a greater emphasis on parent involvement in their children's education. At the same time, while proud Japanese parents still come to hear their uniformed children sing the school song in heartfelt unison, Japanese schools are becoming more flexible and have a new regard for hands-on learning.

Interestingly, after years of recession and efforts to become more efficient, Japanese firms no longer automatically hire all the available top university graduates and are becoming reluctant to assure them lifelong job security. Japanese college graduates may soon feel the same career uncertainties that have been common in the United States.

Russia

Czarist Russia did not experience the profound industrial changes and reforms that altered Great Britain and the United States during the nineteenth century. While Russia had a long tradition of literature and arts (think of the many great Russian authors and composers), the vast peasantry could never read or appreciate these works, and education for the masses was not encouraged.

One of the great changes promised by Vladimir Lenin and the Bolshevik Communists, who took control during the Russian Revolution of 1917, was education for all. Education would not only be the basis for technical advancement, as

Russia was eager to catch up to Western Europe, but it would also be a moral force as it created "the new socialist man" (although the communists also tended to be strong proponents of education for women). Study in the traditional subjects would be wedded to study of Marxist–Leninist doctrine, and instead of educating the elite, the schools would produce a new generation dedicated to the advances of the working class and international communism.

By the time Josef Stalin took control in 1924, the international emphasis had declined and pride in Russia was a core tenet. The horrors of World War II only increased this nationalist emphasis. By the 1950s, Americans saw Soviet education as filled with propaganda. Students not only learned the Marxist–Stalinist ideology in school, but after school, they donned uniforms as Young Pioneers and learned group work, leadership, and the glories of socialism. To be fair, U.S. education in the 1950s was also filled with nationalism and the glories of capitalism. Washington and Lincoln looked down from the walls in place of Marx and Lenin, the textbooks often commented on U.S. successes and Soviet failures, and after-school activities involved flags and uniforms and pledges in the Boy and Girl Scouts in place of the Young Pioneers.

Soviet education was highly centralized and very inflexible, but it had some great technical successes. The launch of *Sputnik* and the Soviet lead in the space race were often seen as evidence of strong Soviet science education; in fact, these events sparked a new interest in science education in the United States, as it sought to catch up. In the 1980s, Mikhail Gorbachev's *glasnost,* or "openness," meant new openness in the school curriculum, as well.

The break-up of the Soviet Union in 1991 meant further changes in education. New textbooks were much more muted about the glories of communism, but Russian achievements—great authors, composers, scientists, World War II heroes, and cosmonauts—were still featured prominently. Today, the Russian government must contend with other problems: how to encourage entrepreneurship in a system that has traditionally held this in suspicion, how to continue to provide virtually free higher education to highly qualified applicants amidst declining government revenues, and how to provide jobs for a highly educated population that is living in a stalled and declining economy.

Mexico

For over the thousand years preceding the arrival of the Spanish in the early 1500s, the Pre-Hispanic Mexicans—the Amerindian peoples of Mesoamerica, such as the Aztecs and Mayans—valued education greatly. It consisted largely of studying astronomy (with related mathematics) and memorizing ancient tales, just as with many other ancient peoples. Yet the accomplishments were substantial. The Mayans used place value and the zero perhaps before the people of India and certainly before

Arabs and later Europeans adapted its use. They precisely calculated the orbit of Venus long before Copernicus ever ventured his theory about planets orbiting the sun.

Mesoamerican education was heavily class based, training warriors, priests, administrators, and merchants for their roles. Yet it could also be a means of advancement for those who were especially promising. Following the Spanish conquest, education become the privilege of the Spanish elite, not for peasants and certainly not for "Indians." The Catholic Church dominated Spanish education for the entire 300-year colonial period, from the 1520s to the 1820s.

Mexican independence fighters in the early 1800s, although they were Catholic and included prominent priests, were influenced by European enlightenment ideas of broad-based secular education for all. In the 1860s, President Benito Juarez, of Zapotec Indian ancestry, sought reforms that would remove the church's influence in education and expand education to all, including the indigenous population. These ideas, among others, sparked a civil war with Mexican conservatives backed by the French Foreign Legion, about the same time as the U.S. Civil War. Juarez won and public education was expanded, but the struggle to provide public education for all continued through the Mexican Revolution, a decade of turmoil between 1910 and 1921.

Providing public education is a goal enshrined in the Mexican constitution, but the struggle to achieve this goal still continues (Gutek 1997). Mexicans are guaranteed six years of public primary education. Yet rural schools, especially those in remote and non–Spanish speaking areas, often only include three grades and sometimes only one. Education therefore means traveling long and difficult distances. Secondary education is competitive, especially the later years leading to college.

Getting into college is not that difficult for urban residents. The Autonomous University of Mexico (UNAM) in Mexico City, is one of the largest universities

The contexts in which children learn vary greatly around the world, as seen in these classrooms in Japan and in Nicaragua.

in the world, with as many as 300,000 full- and part-time students, thanks in part to largely free tuition. But students struggle to pay for living expenses while studying, key classes are often full or not offered, strikes are not uncommon, and many students never graduate. The title of *Licensiado,* essentially one who holds a bachelor's degree, is coveted in Mexico and is used as a personal title, much as *Doctor* is used in the United States. A more secure education is offered, for those who can afford it, at private universities such as the Technologico de Monterrey, from which many of Mexico's business leaders, and increasingly now its political leaders, have come.

Mexico continues to expand higher education and to offer an increasing range of private business and technical schools, often with strong English components. But like many developing nations, it struggles to employ all of its graduates, especially in secure, well-paying professions.

India

India is a huge country of close to 1 billion people, and so everything comes in large numbers. India may have more software engineers than any country in the world, including the United States. But, because of lack of jobs, India "exports" many of its highly trained technical and health professionals. Well-educated Indian physicians, businesspeople, and technical experts are found all across Europe and parts of Asia and Africa, and Indian Americans on the whole are the single most educated U.S. immigrant group. Yet literacy in India is only about 50 percent, which means half a billion illiterate people.

Most Indian children receive some primary education, but classes are often very large, with as many as sixty students, and attendance can be unreliable. Many children, and especially girls, have to work to help support other family members. In some states of India, where male dominance has been the rule for centuries, the female illiteracy rate is very high. In others, such as Kerala in southern India, where women have traditionally held prominent positions, the educational levels of girls and boys are much more equal.

Only half of Indian youths go on to secondary school, and a university education is a coveted opportunity. Yet even for a university graduate, the job market may be tight, and having a career may mean leaving the country for another location, where technical skills and mastery of English are valuable commodities.

Germany and Northern Europe

Compared to the U.S. system of education, the German system can seem extremely regimented. Children do not begin school until about age seven but by age ten are already taking examinations that will help determine their future careers. The main secondary school, *Hauptschule,* prepares them to pursue a technical and vocational education. A smaller, selective track, *Gymnasium,* is rooted in a classical education that will be the basis of a future university career. The decision is not final at this early age, for there are a number of "bridges" from one track to another, but increasingly the paths diverge.

Those who do not get into the university track are hardly abandoned, for Germany has an extensive system of technical training and apprenticeship that goes back to medieval guilds. Likewise, the classical university preparation is rooted in the great German universities of the Middle Ages, with a new emphasis on business and technology. Few students come to the end of their career path without a clear direction of where they are headed in the workforce, and Germany prides itself on one of the world's most productive and capable workforces.

The school-to-work transition is even stronger in Sweden, where the government has tried to guarantee that every young person will be on a track that will lead to a productive working career (Nothdurft 1989). Higher education, though often of a technical nature, is seen as crucial, and few Swedes drop out of the system. For those who struggle in the rather regimented system, there are alternative schools and programs, each also tied to a particular niche in the economy.

Beginning in the Clinton administration, U.S. policy also started looking more closely at the school-to-work transition and the congruence between school training and the needs of the workforce. Most Americans, however, are uncomfortable with the amount of government involvement and the degree of early decision making that are part of the Northern European systems.

China

Chinese education is both ancient and continually changing. Chinese Confucian society long honored the scholar as the most respected citizen below the emperor. At various times in China's long history, both the trusted advisors to the emperor and the administrators of regional provinces were scholars who had come up through the ranks of the civil service by passing examinations. These examinations most often tested knowledge of and ability to memorize ancient texts, including poetry, prose literature, and Confucian dissertations on the meaning and achievement of good government.

Kung Fu-tse, the man to whom Westerners gave the Latin name of *Confucius,* lived from 551 to 478 BCE, a period known as "the time of warring states." He wrote about how to achieve good government and with it, a harmonious society. These ideals were not easy to implement, and the rules of scholars were often interrupted by the rules of both foreign invaders and local warlords. Yet the ideal of dedication to scholarship and advancement through formal education remains rooted in the cultures of China, and of much of East Asia to this day.

Another man had a different view of the making of a just and harmonious society. Mao Zedong, the Chinese Communist revolutionary who came to power in 1949, replaced conservative Confucian ideals with revolutionary communist ideals. But Mao also looked to education to advance the nation, in large measure by raising a new generation in the principles of Marxism, as interpreted by in his once-famous "little red book" of sayings. Westerners have often made fun of "Confucius says" statements and either ridiculed Mao's little red book or seen it as dangerous propaganda. Yet the Chinese have long believed that education should shape the heart as well as the mind, perhaps a philosophical version of the basis of many religious schools around the world.

Contemporary Chinese education continues to emphasize moral education, rote learning, hard work, and mathematics. Now, there is an increasing focus on technical training as well. The Chinese Communists placed great emphasis on expanding basic education to everyone, but like most of the developing world, educational quality and availability are much greater in urban than in rural areas. Many Chinese continue to look to formal education as their best means of advancement, even it increasingly involves understanding the intricacies of an export economy, rather than the doctrines of either Mao or Confucius.

Opening Doors, Opening Minds

Human Capital Theory

Is education the key to national development? A strong affirmation of this is known as **human capital theory.** It has been advanced by economists such as Gary Becker (1964), who held joint positions in economics and sociology at the University of Chicago and won the Nobel Prize in Economics for his application of economic theory to social issues. Becker reasoned that just as investments in physical capital (say, a more technologically advanced factory) would increase productivity and efficiency, so, too, education could be seen as an investment in human capital, increasing the productivity and efficiency of humans. Highly educated people can do more and do it better and so contribute more to national development.

This idea has been very influential in national development policy. The World Bank, driven largely by economic theory, often discourages what it sees as wasteful government spending, but it does encourage governments to spend on education (World Bank 2000). The logic is that this is an investment in the future productivity of the country and just as important as building a better power grid or a better road system. In general, few would argue with this logic, and maybe especially few educators, who see this as a strong rationale for public support of education, including higher education. Students paying hefty tuition bills also want to believe this theory: that education is an investment in a more productive and so more lucrative future. And in most ways, it is.

Some countries have used this approach to considerable success. First Japan, then Singapore, and now places all across Asia, including India, have favored strong investment in education (see Figure 4.3). Education has been key in the rise of the standards of living of countries such as Japan and Singapore. Now, many countries in the world, increasingly in Latin America and the Caribbean, as well, tout their highly educated workforce.

Yet for some, the returns on education have been slower. India, with its vast population, has had a difficult time finding productive employment for all of its

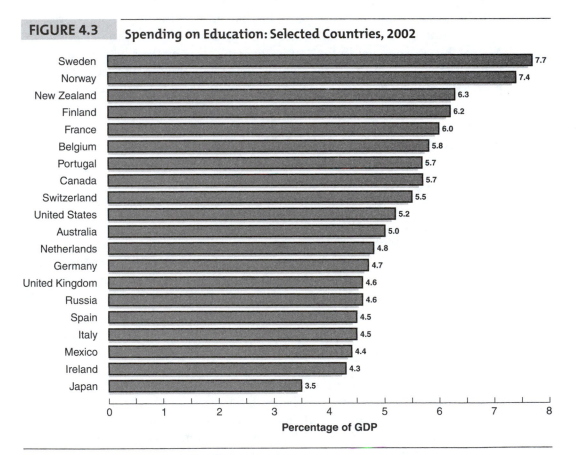

FIGURE 4.3   **Spending on Education: Selected Countries, 2002**

Country	Percentage of GDP
Sweden	7.7
Norway	7.4
New Zealand	6.3
Finland	6.2
France	6.0
Belgium	5.8
Portugal	5.7
Canada	5.7
Switzerland	5.5
United States	5.2
Australia	5.0
Netherlands	4.8
Germany	4.7
United Kingdom	4.6
Russia	4.6
Spain	4.5
Italy	4.5
Mexico	4.4
Ireland	4.3
Japan	3.5

Note: Includes all government expenditures for education institutions.

Source: Data from Organization for Economic Cooperation and Development, *Education at a Glance,* 2002. Figure from National Center for Educational Statistics. Available online: http://nces.ed.gov/programs/digest/d02/ch_6f.asp.

highly educated workers and now "exports" some of its most educated workers and professionals to other places in the world. As noted earlier, Indian Americans are the most educated immigrants in the United States, but many came because they could not use their education to full effect in their home country. The Philippines is another Asian country that tends to "export" educated workers in a "brain drain" to other parts of the world because the economy has not grown fast enough to employ them all.

Even in hard times, education can make people more resourceful and aware, and a good education can be a valued possession in its own right. Retirees traveling to Elderhostels and auditing college classes are not trying to increase their productivity but rather their awareness, intellect, and interest in life. Yet for education to become a true investment in human capital that will offer a return in productivity, it must be connected to a viable means of application. Any college graduate who has graduated into a recession or slow economy will likely agree that education alone is not enough. It must be matched with opportunities for productive application.

The School-to-Work Transition

As mentioned earlier in this chapter the United States started to focus more specifically on the school-to-work transition during the Clinton administration. Does what is learned in school clearly prepare the student for the expectations of the workplace? Are students learning the skills that employers are seeking? Is there a clear path from education to employment?

Recently, many more academic programs in the United States have begun to stress internships and ways to gain practical experience as part of the educational process. At the same time, constant shifts in the state of knowledge in any area and the increasing likelihood that during their careers, workers will go through many positions and maybe even many vocations and professions, each with different skills, mean that learning that is too narrow may not be as useful as a broader education that stresses criticial thinking and communication skills that are useful in many contexts.

In general, European and Japanese educational systems are much more closely tracked than those in the United States and Canada. Students make decisions and take exams at earlier ages that will determine the directions of their future careers. Students in the United States are often allowed to remain undecided longer and to have more second chances in returning to school and in changing programs. At the same time, U.S. students often get less clear career direction and are less likely to be on a path that leads directly to employment; this means they run a greater risk of falling through the cracks in the system. Students in developing countries often face both perils: Programs may be highly selective with few second chances, yet they may also offer few assurances, unless the student is from a wealthy or well-connected family.

Around the world and especially in the United States, there has been intense debate over national standards and international competitiveness. Concern grew in the United States in the 1980s and 1990s that U.S. students knew less, especially in the areas of math and science, than their counterparts elsewhere and that this would hurt U.S. competitiveness. Recently, there has been a strong push to address this with a program of nationally mandated examinations and standards. Most of the world's educational systems are more nationally standardized than in the United States, and many are already much more examination driven.

One reason given for the competitive success of European and Asian advanced industrial economies is the high level of technical and mathematical competence of even assembly line workers. The U.S. system, with its more flexible structure and emphasis on choice and creativity, has proven very successful in promoting a culture of innovation and entrepreneurship, although some have argued it does less well in areas such as quality control.

Elite and Popular Education

Arguments about human capital also hinge on what types of education constitute useful human capital. Human capital theorists are often proponents of **technical education,** the how-to of industrial production and commercial enterprise. Many of the world's educational systems have instead inherited patterns of **classical education,** rooted in the finest ideas and ideals of the past, and **elite education,** intended not to make one rich but to make the children of the rich more refined. From this view, education was not a necessary means to wealth, but wealth was often a necessary means to a quality education. Since the goal of elite education was refinement, rather than productivity, the course of study often focused on rhetoric and refined speaking, the study of ancient texts and languages, and other marks of distinction.

Elite and classical types of education were not limited to Europe but found expression in many of the world's civilizations. Yet once European colonial powers came to dominate the world, the elite education of the dominant powers, such as Great Britain and France, become the model for many educational systems around the world. In Africa, elite students often learned more about the literature and history of the colonial "mother country" than of the cultures and problems of their own communities. In Mexico, in the seventeenth and eighteenth centuries, the elites studied the great writers of Spain and the great Latin classical and ecclesiastical texts; in the nineteenth century, they studied the great thinkers of France and Enlightenment Europe. Rarely did the studies ever turn to the heritage and thought of Mexico itself.

Increasingly, around the world, national texts—many of them approved, produced, and distributed by national governments—seek to produce national patriotism through an emphasis on the story or at least one version of the story of nation building within that country. Schools of technology and industry have also become much more common. The debate remains, however, as to what constitutes a good education. Should it be classical or technical, narrow or broad? Or are these false dichotomies? And of course, whether a student learns to use the proper fork or to use a forklift depends a great deal on his or her social class origins.

Savage Inequalities at Home and Abroad

The type of education a student receives, and the quality of that education, vary greatly depending on that student's position in society. We have already noted the persistent gender gap in education. A persistent gap by region also remains around the world. Namely, children in rural areas are less likely to attend school, less likely to graduate from higher levels, and less likely to have access to buildings and supplies than their urban counterparts. Within urban areas, elite districts and wealthier neighborhoods have the finest facilities, while schools in poor urban areas reflect the distress of the surrounding neighborhood.

This regional difference is somewhat less pronounced in Europe and Japan, where strong national programs and national funding of education have reduced the difference. The regional gap is very marked in Latin America, however, with the exception of a few places with strong national education programs, such as Cuba, or very small size, such as Barbados. In Africa, the regional gap is so great that schools seem to exist in different worlds, with modern schools in the national capital and rural children receiving little or no formal education.

There is also a persistent racial and ethnic gap. Education can reflect a racial hierarchy. Before the dismantling of apartheid in South Africa, the type of school one attended depended on his or her racial classification. Schools for whites were well equipped with books and supplies and had a student–teacher ratio of 18:1. Schools for black South Africans were often in old, dilapidated buildings (or sometimes no buildings at all), lacked basic supplies, and had a student–teacher ratio of 42:1 (World Almanac 1991). A similar situation existed in parts of the United States before U.S. courts demanded desegregation. Schools for African Americans typically had limited facilities, little equipment, and high student–teacher ratios. In rural areas, it was not uncommon for schools for black children to have a shorter calendar, since many children worked in the fields well into the autumn.

Schools in the southern United States began to desegregate in the 1950s following the 1954 *Brown v. Board of Education* decision. By the 1970s, school desegregation orders had reached many northern cities, and angry confrontations shifted from southern states, such as Arkansas and Alabama, to northern cities, such as Boston. South Africa began to dismantle its apartheid laws in the early 1990s and accelerated the process after the 1994 election of African National Congress leader Nelson Mandela to the presidency.

Still, in both the United States and the Union of South Africa, racial and ethnic differences persist. In the United States, test scores and graduation rates for Hispanic and black children continue to lag well behind those for white and Asian American children. A history of social disadvantage is coupled with continued residential segregation and differences in language and culture.

These differences are seen in varying forms around the world. In Latin America, children with strong ties to an indigenous or Amerindian heritage often struggle in schools that were modeled on European forms and European languages, such as Spanish and Portuguese (just as Native Americans in nontribal schools in the United States have often struggled). In Africa and Asia, ethnic minorities often struggle in schools that do not reflect their language, religion, or heritage. These are particularly divisive issues in countries that are trying to forge a common identity out of many diverse groups. Nigeria, the largest country in Africa, has dozens of differing ethnic groups and languages, three major religious traditions (Christianity in the south, Islam in the north, and many traditional African religions in between), and a British colonial past. Indonesia, the fourth-largest country in the world, has literally hundreds of languages and ethnic groups scattered across hundreds of islands, religious diversity (a Muslim majority with Christian, Hindu, and traditional tribal religions all represented), and a Dutch colonial heritage.

In countries such as these, what should be the language of instruction: a national language, such as Basa Indonesian; a colonial language, such as English in Nigeria, or each of the local languages? What religious holidays should be observed, and what ethnic customs and learning styles should be represented? Sometimes, the answers to these questions vary by level. It is not uncommon in parts of the world to find primary instruction in the local language, reflecting renewed local pride and determination; secondary education in the national language, reflecting an attempt at nation building and establishing a common culture; and higher education in a dominant European language, such as English or French, reflecting the realities of international power and resources. From all this diversity, however, a common pattern tends to emerge: Those students who are the most different from the mainstream of the society—in language, religion, race/ethnicity, heritage, and so forth—tend to struggle in the school system and to complete less schooling than their majority-group peers.

All these attributes—race/ethnicity, region, neighborhood, and so forth—are typically intertwined with **social class.** Children of privilege have always received more attention to their education than children of poor and working-class families. For almost four decades now, writer Jonathan Kozol has documented the problems and inequalities in U.S. schools. Kozol graduated summa cum laude from Harvard in the 1960s, was a Rhodes Scholar, and went to work teaching in a low-income public school in Boston's then-primarily African American neighborhood of Roxbury. He was promptly fired for reading his students "unauthorized poetry" and so began a long career in alternative education and critiquing the U.S. educational system. His first scathing critique, *Death at an Early Age: The Destruction of the Hearts and Minds of Negro Children in the Boston Public Schools,* (1967), drew national attention to the problem of central-city schools. Kozol documented not only the poor condition of the schools but also the message conveyed to children in this system that somehow it was they, not society, that was failing and thus to blame.

Kozol's work also drew the attention of international community activist Ivan Illich. Illich, after having worked in many parts of the world, had founded a retreat center near Cuernavaca, Mexico, and was bringing progressive thinkers from around the world to discuss the many vexing social problems of the 1960s. Kozol went to this center, where he met another educator, Brazilian Paulo Freire. Freire's writings had earned him the anger of the generals who ruled his native country, and he was in exile in Mexico. Freire compiled the insights of his experiences in a widely read classic on educational reform, *Pedagogy of the Oppressed* (1968). Freire argued that true education was more than either elite or technical education; it was a liberating experience. He believed that liberation came when oppressed peoples learned the true nature of the system that dehumanized them (and ultimately dehumanized their oppressors, who had to maintain the system). They regained and liberated their humanity through education that included *conscientizacao,* what became known in English as "consciousness raising."

Inspired by Freire's ideas, Kozol proposed to write a second book on education that went beyond calling for greater equality to calling for radical changes in the ideology of U.S. education—from teaching children to accept a fundamentally unjust system to teaching them to analyze and ultimately change that system. Freire warned Kozol that such a book might not be well received, and it wasn't. The book, *The Night Is Dark and I Am Far from Home* (1974), drew angry retorts and far less acclaim. Kozol stopped writing on public education for some time and turned his attention to related concerns, such as adult literacy and homelessness; he also continued to work on alternative education. For a time, Freire joined him in Boston.

Kozol returned to the public schools as a visitor in the late 1980s and was shocked by what he found. As he recorded in his subsequent book, *Savage Inequalities* (1991):

> What startled me most—although it puzzles me that I was not prepared for this— was the remarkable degree of racial segregation that persisted almost everywhere.

> Like most Americans, I knew that segregation was still common in the public
> school, but I did not know how much it had intensified. . . . Moreover, in most
> cities, influential people that I met showed little inclination to address this mat-
> ter and were sometimes even puzzled when I brought it up. (pp. 2–3)

This was segregation not written into law but enforced by divided communities
with little in common. It was inequality that was not based on a national formula
but on the fact that school districts could only spend what local property taxes
generated, and poor neighborhoods had little property of value. Kozol has continued to document how poverty, substandard housing and medical care, and dangerous, segregated, and hopeless neighborhoods deplete the possibilities open to
poor Latino and black children (1995) as well as how children are resistant to
these blights and have an amazing ability to continue to look for hope and new
possibilities (2000).

Pedagogy of the Oppressed

High in the Andes mountains of Bolivia, Quechua-speaking women have long had
little power and little voice. In one program, these women travel long distances
to take part in a brief but intense educational experience based on Paulo Freire's
models. Working in groups, they struggle to write answers on crinkled butcher
paper to questions in Spanish. "Who are the illiterates?" The women think and
write, "Those who cannot read and write." They talk some more and then add,
"Those who do not understand their lives and their situations." The women talk
some more. "The wealthy do not understand our lives and situations; to us, they
are the illiterate ones." The women laugh and then go on with the questions.

In Kenya, a school for girls struggles to keep the girls in and others out, including angry former employers, such as pimps and others in the sex trade. Many
of the girls are homeless, some have children of their own, many have been exploited by various employers in the bustling capital of Nairobi, and few have any
other resources. Rather than trying to keep the girls in school, family members
may try to pull them out, especially if their incomes are needed by the family. Yet
the Mukuru school continues to operate in one of the poorest slums of Nairobi.
Government funding provides about one-quarter of its salary expenses, the U.N.
World Food Program provides hot lunches (which boosts both performance and
enrollment), and private charities such as the Sisters of Mercy provide the remainder. It is a precarious venture, but the staff draw encouragement from seeing
teenage girls who enter looking old and sad and "used up" begin to regain their
youthful enthusiasm and again laugh and sing and learn.

These two schools—one for adults and one for children and young adults—
show some of the struggles of educational systems around the world. The world

is still seeking a pedagogy of the oppressed to reach the poor and the exploited and a pedagogy of the dispossessed to reach those who have lost their homes, cultures, and livelihoods. The elements of that pedagogy are still in process, but the key issues have been well defined.

INCLUSIVE EDUCATION. There must be a place for every child, regardless of gender, region, or race/ethnicity. The world is moving toward an international consensus, affirmed in documents such as the U.N. Rights of the Child, that all children should be in school and in school long enough to keep up with their peers and to progress to higher levels. It is true that for milennia, many children were taught in informal contexts, and there is still a place for family-based learning, for learning from elders, and for learning from practical service in the community. These are all strengths of traditional societies, and rather than be abandoned, they could well be added to the educational systems of modern advanced industrial societies. Japan, perhaps more than any other country, has captured this aspect of both traditional and modern learning.

For almost every child in our interconnected world, however, a meaningful education will involve some formal education. Education must also include adult learners. **Functional illiteracy** in adults is a problem in the United States as well as in the world's poorest countries. Often, the best way to ensure that children will learn to read is to make certain that their parents know how to read, maybe through multigenerational family literacy programs.

EQUAL EDUCATION. Societies have many inequalities in their institutions, but educational inequality perpetuates all the others. It cuts across many of the problems considered in this book. Quality education for girls, who go on to be workers, mothers, and community leaders, is one of the best predictors of population stability, family well-being, and hope for the next generation. Nations with little access to education for women also tend to have exploding populations, high infant and maternal mortality rates, low levels of family well-being, and high rates of worker exploitation. Societies with marked differences in educational access and quality, coupled with intense segregation between racial and ethnic groups, also tend to be marked by turmoil, unrest, ghettoization, and even civil war.

Again, there is broad international consensus on this idea. In the United States, President George W. Bush and then Congress took up the slogan "No child left behind." Yet in countries rich and poor, certain groups and places remain neglected, with crumbling facilities and few resources.

PRACTICAL EDUCATION. If education has no apparent application and hard work in school brings no clear rewards, then it will dismissed by the poor as a worthless investment and will be distrusted by all who don't already have their futures se-cured. Education must include useful skills in communication, analysis and prob-lem solving, and working with complex systems and technology. Some of these skills can be measured by standardized tests, but many can only be assessed by involved instructors working closely with their students, as has typified educa-tion from its beginning.

While the language of national competiveness is often used, in a globalized world of multinational entities, it is misleading to assume that nations compete as single entities. Each student and each community must be able to compete and to cooperate to build a successful future. Learning needs to lead into internships, apprenticeships, entry-level positions, and other opportunities for its useful ap-plication. To be effective, education must open doors.

LIBERAL EDUCATION. This term, as captured in the phrase *liberal arts college,* does not refer to a political ideology but to a broad exposure to the best of human-ity's hopes and ideas. Good education doesn't just train; it liberates, as Freire hoped. Students are learning not just to be workers but also to be citizens.

Too often, this realization has just meant political indoctrination. Students learn a glorified version of their own history—whether in Russia (or the former Soviet Union), China, Great Britain, or the United States—so as to become pa-triotic, nationalistic citizens who will support and advance their country. This as-pect of education has been adopted, as well, by many developing countries seeking to establish and glorify a national heritage. But in a globalized world, students need the broad, inclusive learning that allows them to become global citizens. This means understanding both the rich heritage and the persistent problems of many places and having the critical-thinking skills to address these issues. Effective ed-ucation should also open minds.

MAKING CONNECTIONS

United Nations

- Go to the website of the U.N. Economic and Social Council (www.unesco.org), which has very good information on education, media, and literacy. True literacy is hard to measure and governments often overreport their literacy rates, but this site provides good comparisons. What parts of the world have made the greatest gains in literacy? What parts lag behind? Do you note age or gender differences in literacy?

- Also visit the site of the U.N. Children's Fund or UNICEF (www.unicef.org). It offers good information on the status of children, reports on the Year of the Child, and other material. What are the current key concerns of UNICEF in regard to the well-being of children?

Free the Children

- Go to www.freethechildren.org, the site of Free the Children (which was also noted in Chapter 2). See the section on education, with information on school building projects and school kits. How is this organization seeking to change labor practices end child labor? "Freeing" children may accomplish little unless they can make the work-to-school transition. What are the hurdles that block getting these children into school?

Local Tutoring

- Opportunities abound in many communities for people to tutor both children and adults. This can be a great opportunity to learn firsthand about educational challenges and the possibilities and difficulties of upward mobility. Find out what programs are available in your community from a campus community relations office, local school district, or local public library. Also learn about national programs, such as America Reads and America Counts, that may provide training and stipends to tutors; your campus should have this information.

- Spend time tutoring a child needing extra help, tutoring an adult working toward a GED or improving academic skills, or with a family literacy program that is seeking to improve reading skills for both parents and children. Some programs require an ongoing commitment; others are drop-in or after-school programs that can be visited occasionally. What academic deficiencies is this program trying to address? What did you experience in the diversity of needs, backgrounds, and learning styles? What are the possibilities, as well as the limitations, of this program in promoting academic and career success?

- School districts and community agencies also often have tutoring programs targeted at immigrants, migrant laborers, and refugees. Many of these programs focus on ENL, or English as a new language. Others include a wide array of subjects and academic content support. Some of the English programs, especially those for Spanish speakers, are set up as *intercambios,* where the conversation is half in each language. Each participant in the pair gets the opportunity to teach the other a bit of his or her language while also practicing the other language. What opportunities are available locally? What challenges become apparent in such programs?

CHAPTER 5

Crime
Fear in the Streets

DATELINE

New York and Johannesburg

The world is afraid. It is not clear that life is any more precarious than it has ever been, but stories of new dangers and terrors abound, and safe retreats no longer seem so safe. Sometimes, the responses are innovative.

Some shopkeepers in New York have given up on dogs and are trying tarantulas. They don't eat much and can crawl around jewelry cases and window displays, discouraging breaking and reaching. Tarantulas are actually quite timid, but signs warning about large, hairy, poisonous spiders do get intruders' attention.

In Johannesburg, South Africa, the measures are more extreme. This city, once divided by apartheid, is now deeply divided by extremes of wealth and poverty. Coupled with a high unemployment rates, this is a recipe for a high crime rate. As criminals have become more bold, or maybe more desperate, brazen crimes such as car-jacking have become common. Cars stopped at lights or for any purpose risk being invaded and seized, the owners robbed, kidnaped, or assaulted. Heavy-duty locks don't seem to work well, so drivers now seek the ultimate customization: underbody flame throwers. A tank of flammable material is stored under the car door (one hates to think what happens in an accident), and an igniter and nozzle are pointed out in the direction of the door handle. If anyone unauthorized reaches for the door, the driver hits a button that sends a fireball scorching out toward the attacker. As yet, there is no safety equivalent for those who must ride the bus.

Seeking Security

While some of these attempts at security bring smiles, many are deadly serious. In the United States, the purchase of handguns for home and personal defense is a growing multimillion-dollar business. Long marketed primarily to white men, women and people of color have become the largest target populations. The weapons have also seen a continuing trend to greater lethality: more rounds, more quickly, with more penetrating power.

The results have not been promising: A gun in the home is twenty-two times more likely to be used against a family member by accident (four times) or in a suicide (eleven times) or act of domestic violence (seven times) than it is to be used against an intruder. In 1996, gun-related homicides took the lives of 15 Japanese, 30 British, 213 Germans, and 9,390 Americans (Brady Campaign 2001) (see Figure 5.1).

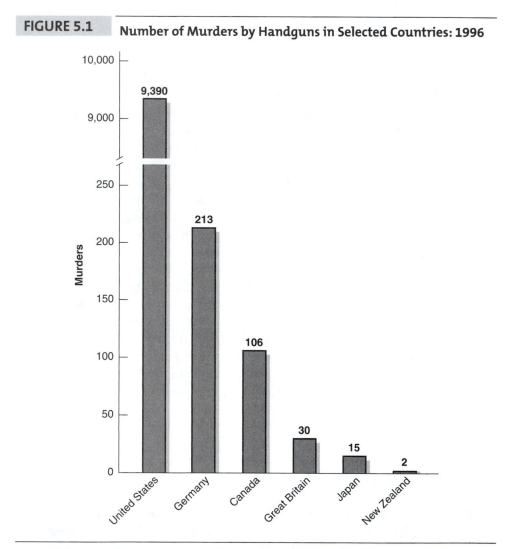

FIGURE 5.1   **Number of Murders by Handguns in Selected Countries: 1996**

Source: Brady Campaign to Prevent Gun Violence (2001).

The problem with using a gun for deterrence is that often only the criminal has a weapon along and is ready to use it at the point of the crime. Some places in the western United States have even tried to reverse a long trend toward controlling the circulation of firearms (the first thing Wyatt Earp and his brothers did when they came to old Tombstone was to ban gun possession in the town), instead encouraging citizens to carry firearms. This has been done in other locations as well. In urban Brazil, women have been known to pull handguns out of their purses in the shopping market to fire on would-be thieves. While this seemed to reduce supermarket theft, the crossfire could be deadly and of limited use against purse snatchers, who ended up not only with the money but also the gun.

Many stores and now many neighborhoods in Brazil have resorted to hiring heavily armed security guards. Likewise, where police protection has failed, neighborhoods in Latin America and Africa often hire private security forces. Traveling in groups in pickup trucks (as do the police in much of Latin America), the forces can quickly turn into vigilante groups that "prevent trouble" by targeting and sometimes killing anyone who is poor and suspicious, including street children.

One of the most extreme examples of this approach is a group called the Sword of the Lord Guards in Lagos, Nigeria, Africa's largest city and one ridden with crime. The Guards ride about parts of the city in the backs of pickup trucks,

As the gap between rich and poor continues to grow, providing security has become a major concern for both businesses and residents in communities around the world as seen here at jewelry store in Mumbai (Bombay), India, and in this vigilante patrol in the "City of God" slum of Port-au-Prince, Haiti.

flashing machetes. At the sight of a local gang, drug dealer, or other potential criminal, the guards leap from their trucks, brandishing a multitude of machetes. They
charge even heavily armed opponents, "counting on the Lord to protect us from
bullets," as one notes, and often hacking the suspects to death. Many believe they
are effective against street crime, although others wonder if they are themselves
just a new form of violent street crime. Regardless, amid rising urban crime rates
and with governments that often cannot afford to staff large and effective law
enforcement agencies, urban dwellers are seeking creative and sometimes violent
alternatives.

Street Crime and Youth Violence

What spurs these waves of urban violence? Poverty is certainly a factor, but places
of great poverty have not always been places of great violence. Inequality appears
to be an added factor—poverty in the midst of wealth, especially sudden wealth.
Equally important are issues of dislocation and unemployment (Wilson 1996).

In places where the rich families have always been rich and the poor families
have always been poor, each may accept their place as inevitable. But when the
rich have suddenly come into their wealth, the question for the others is "And
why not me?" Cities with high unemployment, especially youth unemployment,
leave many seeking alternative ways to use their talents and ambitions. The same
skills that might move someone up the corporate ladder—planning, ambition, net-
working, marketing, and willingness to take risks—might also make one effective in a criminal enterprise. It is all a matter of where the opportunities lie.

In many urban areas, there are decreasing opportunities for newcomers to
use their skills in legitimate ways. Economies based on white-collar services and
management may offer little to those with a less polished demeanor and few formal academic skills. Cities such as New York, which have seen growth primarily
in what has been termed the **FIRE economy** (finance, insurance, and real estate),
leave many "burned" and excluded. According to Phillipe Bourgeois, "Obedience
to the norms of high rise, office-corridor culture is in direct contradiction to street
culture's definitions of personal dignity—especially for males who are socialized
not to accept public subordination" (Bourgois 1995).

For groups such as the young Puerto Rican men that Bourgois studied in New
York, the changing economy has meant huge cultural and social dislocation. The
residential dislocation of movement to and within a large city further interrupts
old networks that might have led to the workaday world of the legitimate economy. Instead, the most immediate opportunities are in the crack cocaine trade.
The work is dangerous and not as lucrative as the young men pretend it is (they're
far from drug lords), but they can get some ready cash and dream of making it

big. The real story is not so much about crack, Bourgois contends, as it is about social marginalization and alienation.

Such dislocation is common around the world. Tijuana is one of Mexico's fastest-growing cities, but many of its new industries prefer to hire young women. For young men, some of the most immediate opportunities are in the illegal trafficking of people, drugs, and other items across the border. Rio de Janeiro and São Paulo, Brazil, are some of the world's fastest-growing cities; São Paulo is now perhaps one of the three largest in the world. New high-rise apartments continue to go up, and new office buildings are being built to serve the computer industry, the growing media, and the agricultural export economy. New cars fill the crowded streets. The middle and upper-middle classes, while always worried about economic crises, continue to grow.

So do the ranks of the poor that fill and surround the cities. Shanty towns fill the lush hills above Rio, looking down on the fabled beaches and bustling streets, but there are few points of access into the legitimate economy. As a result, crime in Rio and São Paulo also continues to soar. Middle-class women wonder whether they should include a handgun in their purse along with the ever-present make-up. And helicopter services for successful businesspeople have become increasingly common in São Paulo as a way to get to work that avoids both the traffic and the crime of the streets.

Brazil's problems are some of the most extreme but also echo the problems of other divided cities, such as Los Angeles, Miami, Detroit, and Washington, D.C., in the United States. These problems are compounded when social and cultural dislocation is joined by political corruption and disruption. The deadliest city in the world is perhaps Bogota, Colombia, with a murder rate more than three times that of New York (and more than thirty times that of Toronto or Tokyo). Bogota is a city divided between rich and poor. It is also a transit point in the drug trade and the capital of a country torn by political violence. Countries torn by war and violent revolt often find this violence taking root in its cities, even after the war has subsided.

Sometimes, the relationships between political and urban violence are transnational. In the 1980s, many young people from Nicaragua, Guatemala, and El Salvador fled the political violence in their home countries. Some went to Los Angeles, where their poverty, dislocation, and familiarity with danger made them prime recruits for urban street gangs. When some of them returned home, they brought with them new skills in urban gang activity, including drugs and violence, that spurred the growth of street gangs in their home countries.

French sociologist Émile Durkheim worried that growing urban areas would be prone to **anomie**, an internal sense of lawlessness and displacement that results as people leave the tight network of their home villages. Durkheim himself focused on suicide, a great concern of his day, rather than drugs or homicide. But his concern that cities would become places of turmoil, both internal and external, is echoed by observers of places like Bogota and São Paulo, New York and Miami.

Yet cities are not always high-crime zones, places such as Tokyo and Toronto are known for their orderliness and relative safety. In fact, some of the most dangerous places in the world, on a per capita basis, are not cities at all but rural areas and villages that have undergone great dislocation and upheaval—political, social, and cultural. Afghanistan remains one of the world's most violent countries, but far more dangerous than the capital of Kabul are the outlying areas, where civil authority is absent or corrupt, the opium drug trade is an enticement, and the line between political violence and criminal violence is often blurred. Rural areas in the United States can also have extremely high rates of violent crime: in the rural Dakotas, in northeast Arizona, in south Texas, and in rural counties all along the southeastern United States (American Demographics, 2000). These all correspond with very low income communities of color and with extremely high rates of unemployment: the Dakota Native Reservations, such as Pine Ridge and the Rosebud; the Navaho–Hopi reservation system in Arizona and New Mexico; the very poor Mexican American communities along the Rio Grande; and what has been termed the "black belt," the very poor African American communities of the southeastern states. Each of these areas has suffered extreme political, social, and cultural dislocation, and each has few opportunities and accompanying high rates of alcoholism, domestic violence, and other turmoil.

International Drug Trade

Opium

Drugs have been bound up in power, violence, and crime for a long time, and these trends often transcend borders. Some of the first international drug lords were none other than the lords of the British East India Company, ultimately making Queen Victoria the top drug kingpin (or queenpin) of her day. In the early 1800s, the British emerged as the top mercantile power in South and East Asia. They were becoming the masters of India (which at the time included what is now Pakistan and Bangladesh) and were eager to build a vigorous trade with the great power on the Asian continent, China. China was rich in porcelain, silk, and many other luxury items that could turn a fine profit for the East India Company.

While the Europeans were fascinated with Chinese luxury goods, the Chinese tended to disdain European imports, and so the British could not find a strong market in which to sell as well as buy. After many tries, they finally found their commodity: **opium.** Opium, and related narcotics such as heroin and morphine, are made from the seeds of a poppy that grows across Southern Asia. In any of its forms, the refined extract of this poppy is powerfully addictive. Opium was being used in medicines in Europe and North America, where it was touted as a cure for many ailments and a good way to soothe the nerves of wealthy ladies (many of whom became addicted).

The addictive power of opium made it a powerful commodity in China. Smoked in special rooms set aside for this purpose, so-called opium dens, it attracted many Chinese customers, especially men, seeking to escape for a moment the turmoil and dislocation of China's crumbling empire. The British traders could bring the opium from poppy fields across South Asia and sell it in China's crowded urban centers. Even as the Chinese government tried to stop the trade, local officials could always be bribed to permit this extremely profitable traffic. They pleaded with the British traders to end this unconscionable trade, but the lords refused.

Finally, the Chinese found an incorruptible official to travel across China and destroy shipments and block further traffic. The lords responded with war. The British justified the Opium War of 1839–1842 on the grounds that China was interfering with British trade, but the trade of note was simply the drug trade. Even though the British did not have vast numbers of troops, it did have a powerful navy, and British steam-powered gunboats could control the coasts and move up and down the great rivers, such as the Yangtze, at will. Chinese resistance collapsed, and the opium trade, along with other trade concessions, continued. China was finally able to ban the opium trade in 1917, only to have it reimposed by the Japanese occupiers in the 1930s. Addictive drugs thus proved not only profitable and a good way to support a war effort but also an effective means of social control.

Profitable drug traffic, once established, is hard to end. In time, opium addiction in many forms found its way around the planet. (The great fictional British detective Sherlock Holmes was portrayed as an addict.) In the twentieth century, heroin, a highly refined extract that can be easily injected, became the narcotic of choice. It was associated with the youth culture in the 1950s and 1960s, claiming high-profile music stars such as John Lennon and Janis Joplin among its addicts. Heroin also become the drug of choice for the dislocated urban poor of Europe and the United States, just as its chemical cousin opium had been for the dislocated urban poor of China.

While opium poppies can be grown in many places, the center of cultivation remains South and Southeast Asia. Poppy cultivation supported the Mujahedeen rebels in Afghanistan, who fought Soviet troops; it briefly supported the Taliban, who for awhile tried to stop the cultivation as un-Islamic); and it now supports regional commanders and warlords in remote parts of the country. Warlords have often found it profitable to be drug lords, as well, and drug trafficking and weapons trafficking often are interrelated. For many years, the center of poppy cultivation was the so-called Golden Triangle, which includes parts of Laos, Thailand, and

| FIGURE 5.2 | Global Opium Production: 2001* |

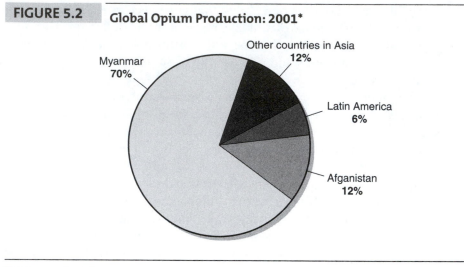

*Total: approximately 1,570 tons.

Source: From U.N. Economic and Social Council (2002). Available online: www.unodc.org.

Burma (Myanmar). The extent of this cultivation has declined, as governments have found that it interferes with other profitable ventures in the area. Yet profits from the poppy trade still find their way to local lords in the region and, by some accounts, into the hands of the military dictatorship of Myanmar (see Figure 5.2).

Cocaine

Perhaps as ancient as the cultivation of poppies in Asia is the cultivation of coca in South America. The leaves of the coca plant can brewed into a tea or chewed to serve as a hunger suppressant and a mild stimulant, roughly equivalent to smoking a cigarette or having a cup of coffee. When the extract of the coca leaf is refined into a powder, it becomes a much more powerful drug: **cocaine.**

Cocaine has a long history and was a common ingredient in many patent medicines. Coca-Cola, first put out as a medicine rather than a beverage, gets its name from two of its original ingredients in 1885; the cola nut and cocaine from the coca leaf. As concern about the dangers of cocaine grew, it was gradually taken out of products. In Coca-Cola, it was replaced with another less potent stimulant: caffeine.

Powdered cocaine became a popular drug of choice in the 1960s, fashionable enough to have songs written about it. About the time that John Lennon discovered heroin, Paul McCartney made the acquaintance of cocaine, perhaps introduced by Bob Dylan. Powdered cocaine was seen as less dangerous than heroin and could be inhaled rather than injected. Always quite expensive, it became the drug of choice for the young and well-off. A modified method of preparing the drug, essentially a cooking process, resulted in cracked cocaine, or "**crack**," which could be smoked. This new form was cheaper and more available and so quickly made in-roads into low-income communities.

The rise of the cocaine trade transformed entire regions in the Andes highlands of South America. Poor farmers in Bolivia found in the coca plant the only crop with a guaranteed world market. Yet farmers rarely saw much of the profit. Rather, they often saw their communities devastated by violence, as drug traffickers fought one another and their governments. Backed by the U.S. military, regional governments made forays into the countryside to destroy crops and refining stations (Weatherford 1986). The center of the cocaine trade fell in Colombia, and entire cities were transformed.

The largest **drug cartel** came to dominate the city of Medellin, Colombia, in the 1980s. Before his death in 1993, Pablo Escobar organized the Medellin traffickers into a cartel that dominated the world market and even Colombian politics through bribery, intimidation, and assassination. No judge, municipal official, or legislator who refused the cartel's money and influence was safe, and many were killed. At the height of its power and wealth, the Medellin cartel became so bold that their schemes were mind boggling. At one point, U.S. and Colombian agents discovered a submarine under construction in the Andes mountains. The traffickers planned somehow to move it down into the ocean and use it to slip under Coast Guard supervision. The Medellin cartel was intensely anticommunist; some dubbed them "cocaine capitalists," for they certainly believed in free trade, and they used their profits to support right-wing paramilitary groups. At the same time, leftist rebels realized the profit potential in the coca plant and also began to use cocaine money to finance their need for weapons and supplies.

Cocaine only turned parts of Colombia into a war zone, and in the form of "crack," it seemed to do the same thing to American central cities. New York, Los Angeles, Detroit, and Washington, D.C., were particularly hard hit. The shock of the crack epidemic filled newspapers with accounts of this powerful new drug, which would drive its addicts to do anything. Also common were stories of "crack babies," born to addicted mothers, who were so physiologically and psychologically scarred that they were presumed to be the next generation of killers.

In truth, crack cocaine, while addictive and dangerous, is probably no worse for the individual than anything smoked in Shanghai, China, in 1850. But it became an epidemic in vulnerable communities, which collapsed under the added weight of addiction. Rival street gangs fought over local control. Money, much of it coming from outside these very poor communities, poured into the illegal economy, just as legitimate sources of income were disappearing. The effects on many low-income, often African American communities were so devastating that some claimed crack was an intentional plan to destroy black America. The desperation and violence of a crack economy had taken hold across many U.S. cities, deepening the already existing problems of deindustrialization and urban dislocation.

The U.S. response to declare a "war on drugs" truly looked like a military operation in parts of Latin America and the Caribbean. Efforts focused on destroying the supply line coming into the United States. Drug interdiction became a primary task of the U.S. Coast Guard. Since drugs were intertwined with politics in Latin America, antidrug activity often involved action against rebels and even governments. The United States accused President Manuel Noriega of Panama of being involved in drug trafficking and used this as part of the rationale for invading the country in 1989 and deposing Noriega.

The United States has also supplied helicopters, night vision goggles, and special forces to Colombia and Bolivia to fight drug suppliers and, by extension, rebel groups who have reputed drug-related ties. These countries, along with Peru, continue to be the center of cocaine manufacturing (see Figure 5.3). Highland peasant farmers are often caught in the crossfire, unfortunately, and complain of the destruction of their farms, whether or not they contain coca plants. Many in Latin America have argued that these dramatic military sweeps distract from the real problem, which is not the growing supply in Latin America but the growing demand in the United States.

FIGURE 5.3   **Cocaine Manufacturing in Bolivia, Colombia, and Peru: 2001***

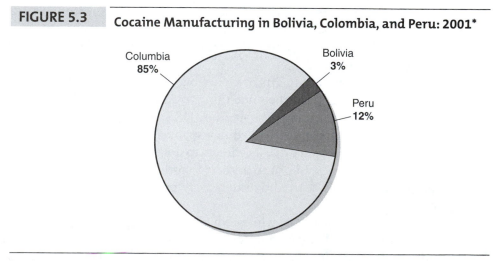

*Total: approximately 1,110 tons.

Source: From U.N. Economic and Social Council (2002). Available online: www.unodc.org.

Cannabis

The **cannabis** plant produces a useful fiber, **hemp;** a quite powerful drug, **hashish;** and a somewhat milder drug, **marijuana.** These drugs also have a long history. They became popular in the United States with the so-called beat generation of the 1950s, and their rates of use soared in the 1960s, as "hash" and "pot" became common terms. Hashish had long been used in South Asia, however, and had a certain appeal for those interested in Indian mysticism, including high-profile international figures. As noted earlier, when the Beatles "turned on" to drugs in the 1960s, the often melancholy John Lennon found heroin and the energetic Paul McCartney found cocaine. But the Eastern-looking George Harrison found hashish.

Much more common was the inexpensive and easily attainable marijuana. Less potent and less addictive (though its dangers and addictive qualities have often been debated), marijuana became a common social drug. Even today in the United States, about one-third of the adult population admits to having tried a form of cannabis, usually smoking marijuana. In fact, politicians who came of age in the 1960s often have to dodge probing questions about their use of this still illegal drug.

Cannabis is grown and trafficked widely around the world. But its ability to grow in any mild climate (or on a window sill, for that matter), has made it less profitable to traffickers. Mexican marijuana coming into the United States must compete with many homegrown varieties.

The legalization of marijuana has long been controversial. Early films such as *Reefer Madness* portrayed it as a powerfully dangerous drug. The most extreme of the purported dangers have not been verified, though medical professionals note that frequently inhaling *any* kind of smoke is not a healthful practice. California and Maine have approved marijuana's use for medical purposes, such as controlling the nausea that comes with chemotherapy, and finding alternate delivery systems to smoking, which is otherwise banned in all forms in hospitals, has been explored.

Various states have explored **decriminalizing** marijuana: that is, it could not be sold commercially and could not be advertised (no "Joe Cannabis" billboards), but mere possession would not be a crime. The most successful experiment in decriminalization has been in the Netherlands, where so-called coffee shops (some of which sell no coffee at all) are allowed to sell small quantities of marijuana and hashish. The product cannot be resold, it must be consumed on the premises, and no disorderly conduct is allowed. Since customers typically walk to these establishments or use public transport, there is also no danger of impaired driving. In the Dutch social context, this has worked very well, and drug use rates for Dutch youths are no higher than those in the United States. The idea that cannabis will be a **"gateway" drug,** leading to other drug use, has probably been diminished, in that the purchase and use of this substance are completely separate from other more potent drugs, which are still illegal. Most significantly, incarceration rates for drug offenses in the Netherlands are a fraction of what they are in the United States.

The most widely trafficked drug in the world is not illegal, except in some Islamic states: **tobacco,** and its addictive stimulant, **nicotine.** Tobacco was first grown by Native Americans in the southeastern area of North America. Like **peyote** in the western part of the continent, tobacco was generally not used as a daily leisure activity but rather for ceremonial use. In the 1600s, the newly formed European colonies needed a cash crop to support themselves, having failed to find gold and other precious items. As tobacco pipe smoking became fashionable in Europe, tobacco became that cash crop for the British American colonies. In the Carribean, it was second only to sugar production.

Tobacco can be grown almost anywhere where the soil will support its nutrient demands, but much of the production remains in the United States, Canada, and Cuba. Cuba's niche is hand-rolled cigars, while the United States has dominated in mass-produced cigarettes. With smoking rates falling in North America, each of these locations is heavily dependent on tobacco exports. Smoking rates are very high in parts of Asia and Eastern Europe: Three-quarters of the men in Vietnam and two-thirds of the men in Russia and China smoke, although the rates are much lower for the women in Asia. In comparison with less than one-quarter of the U.S. population, both men and women smoke.

As a result, large U.S. tobacco companies have aggressively marketed their product overseas, particularly in the growing markets in Asia. The Marlboro man, originally created to get men to smoke what was seen as a women's brand, has been one of the world's most successful advertising images. He still rides the range, but increasingly on billboards across East Asia. Exports have been the key to survival for U.S. and Canadian tobacco-farming communities and have helped the North American balance of trade with Asia. Yet as smoking-related illness continues to climb in Asia, one wonders if this is not continuing a pattern of trade in addictive substances that dates back to the Opium War.

Alcoholism

Despite high-profile challengers, the world's preferred drug of choice for the last 7,000 years has been **alcohol.** The brewing of beer goes back to prehistoric times, probably to the very beginning of the cultivation of grains. Wine production is also ancient. While wine-tippling Romans became part of our lore about wealthy excess, alcohol has also been the drug of choice of the poor.

During the European Middle Ages, grain was hard to store and distribute in a manner that was safe from mold and rats, unless it was brewed into beer. At certain times, European peasants may have gotten large portions of their calories from beer and basically been tipsy for a good share of their working lives (Braudel 1979). Maybe it relieved the drudgery and deprivation that accompanied their lot.

Distilled spirits become common only in the early industrial period, when simple metal machinery became common and inexpensive. Distilled spirits required much less space for the transport of the same amount of alcohol and so lent themselves to wider distribution. Brandy may have begun as a more compact alternative to wine.

The common drink of choice in the seventeenth to nineteenth centuries, however, was rum distilled from sugar cane. Rum figured prominently in a triangular trade that existed among Europe, Africa, and the Americas. Slaves were brought from Africa to work in the sugar plantations of Brazil and Northern South America and the Carribean. Sugar from the plantations was brought into New England by traders and distilled into rum. The rum was consumed locally, exported back to Europe, and used in part to pay off crews on the slave and trade ships and to buy more slaves in West Africa.

Today, any visitor to a duty-free shop in an airport knows there remains a brisk international business in spirits. Wine exports are vital to the economies of France, Italy, Spain, and Portugal and increasingly so to places as diverse as Chile and Australia. Beer exports have long been important to Germany and the Netherlands. Beer was also one of the foundations of economic growth in Monterrey, Mexico, and fueled the development of truck transport and related industries, such as glass making, in the area. Mexican beer exports continue to climb.

The attitude toward alcohol, and thus its impact, varies greatly around the world. Alcoholic beverages are not allowed to be sold in strict Islamic states in the Middle East, except sometimes in stores catering to non-Muslim foreigners. Alcohol is forbidden to Muslims, but adherence to this practice has varied widely around the world. Many Christian-related groups—including Mormons (Latter Day Saints), Seventh-Day Adventists, and some Baptists and Pentecostals forbid or strongly discourage the consumption of alcohol.

The temperance movement against the consumption of alcohol in the United States and Great Britain was strong for nearly a century, from the 1830s to the 1930s, and was closely tied to Christian religious convictions as well as the feminist and abolitionist movements. Revival preachers spoke against the evils of alcohol, but some of the most determined temperance workers were women, who saw doing so as part of overall social reform. Men wasted family resources on alcohol and then became abusive, and alcohol and tobacco had long been intertwined with slavery and other social ills. By 1900, the emphasis had shifted to alcohol and urban poverty and urban decay, as growing immigrant and industrial cities faced mounting problems. Alcohol consumption was banned in the United States in 1920 with the passage of the Eighteenth Amendment, only to be restored thirteen years later with the passage of the Twenty-First Amendment, in part as an effort to revive the Depression-stricken economy.

Alcoholism continues to be associated with a wide array of social problems, from domestic violence to impaired driving. The U.S. Bureau of Justice Statistics (1999) reports that 42 percent of people jailed for violent crimes claimed to have been under the influence of alcohol at the time of the incident. National rates of alcoholism are highest in Russia and parts of Eastern Europe, where a tradition of heavy alcohol consumption, especially for men, has been coupled with political and economic dislocation that has resulted in, among other factors, very high unemployment rates, also especially for men. Extremely high rates of alcoholism have also plagued the native communities in the United States and Canada, similarly coupled with social and cultural dislocation and soaring rates of unemployment. Alcoholism in both Russia and among Native North Americans is also associated with high rates of aggravated assault, domestic violence, divorce, and, striking in both contexts, suicide.

New Recipes: Chemical Agents

Mind-altering substances can also be produced from common substances in the laboratory or someone's modified kitchen. **LSD,** a hallucinogen that can occur in nature due to the action of certain molds and also can be synthesized, was the mind-altering preference of the 1960s. It was often used to attempt to expand consciousness and perception, in ways similar to the use of peyote in the American Southwest and the use of various hallucinogens by shamans and tribal religious specialists in South America and elsewhere (although with far fewer social controls over the use and its results). The use of LSD was popularized and even glamorized by high-profile proponents such as Timothy Leary, and rock songs such as "Lucy in the Sky with Diamonds." But when LSD use became associated with vivid and at times agonizing adverse effects, known as "bad trips," it fell out of favor.

In the 1990s, new **"designer drugs,"** such as MDMA ("ecstasy") and PCP ("angel dust"), gained popularity, sometimes in concert with the rise of a version of international electronic music that became known as *techno.* Powerfully addictive **methamphetamine,** which can be "cooked" in small labs and even home kitchens, has provided a new homemade alternative to the drug trade.

Homemade mind-altering substances are often the preference of the world's urban poor, especially the youth. In an alcove next to a street theater in Guatemala City, a group of ten or twelve boys cluster, many holding plastic bags of a thick, yellow liquid (Konner 1991). The children are homeless except for this alcove, many fleeing families who were abusive or simply too poor to keep them. "The glue makes you loco, crazy," they admit. "It hurts your brain." But it also quells their hunger pangs and boredom, and so its use persists. Glue is cheap and available, sold in plastic bags by adults who clearly know these street kids are not assembling airplane models. Some Latin American street youth have turned from glue to aerosol inhalants, which provide a quicker high and less of a headache. They are, however, equally dangerous, especially in causing long-term brain damage.

Elsewhere in Central America the drug of choice is **bazooka** (a twist on its Spanish name, *pasuco*). Bazooka is generally an ill-defined mix of homegrown marijuana spiked with crack cocaine and sometimes other chemicals, rolled into a fat "joint" to be smoked. Frequent border crossers think it could be the next profitable drug recipe in urban California, Texas, or Florida.

Incarceration around the World

Societies are not only burdened by the effects of crime itself but also by the difficulty and high cost of incarcerating convicts. Nowhere in the world is this a bigger problem than in the United States, where incarceration rates have soared five times as fast as the population to over 2 million people. The United States now holds 25 percent of the world's prison population (BBC 2000), and a greater proportion of its population is behind bars than in any other country (see Figure 5.4).

In the 1980s, the U.S. rate of incarceration was third in the world, behind the Soviet Union and South Africa. Rates in those countries dropped with the break-up of the Soviet Union and the end of apartheid in South Africa; in both cases, there was a release of many political prisoners. Even though crime rates in both Russia and South Africa have grown dramatically since then, the prison populations have not climbed as rapidly. In contrast, in the United States, the prison population grew in the 1980s and 1990s as the crime rate fell.

The single biggest factor behind this increase has been drug sentencing. Tougher drug laws and mandatory sentencing have meant more prison time for more people. In the 1980s, the Reagan administration's "get tough" approach to drugs and crime meant longer sentencing. This trend toward greater punishment for drug offenses slowed down at the beginning of the Clinton administration. But when Clinton was accused of being "soft on drugs" and references to his own college-age marijuana use became common, policy again shifted toward tougher enforcement, including the "three-strikes rule" for those convicted of three felonies. Many drug-related offenses in the United States are felonies. Over 1.3 million of the 2 million Americans behind bars are serving time for nonviolent offenses, usually drug-related crimes. With the second Bush administration, the war on terrorism brought new arrests and detentions, particularly for immigration violations.

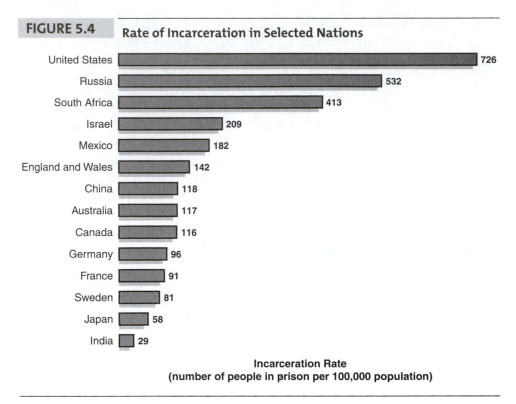

FIGURE 5.4   **Rate of Incarceration in Selected Nations**

United States — 726
Russia — 532
South Africa — 413
Israel — 209
Mexico — 182
England and Wales — 142
China — 118
Australia — 117
Canada — 116
Germany — 96
France — 91
Sweden — 81
Japan — 58
India — 29

Incarceration Rate
(number of people in prison per 100,000 population)

Source: Rate for the United States from *Prison and Jail Inmates at Midyear 2004;* for all other nations, International Centre for Prison Studies available online at www.prisonstudies.org. Incarceration data were collected on varying dates and are the most current data available as of 2005.

A vast racial gap in incarceration exists in the United States, with black men five times more likely to serve jail sentences than white men. Among black men in their twenties, one in three is in jail, on probation, or on parole. In some major cities, such as Washington, D.C., and Baltimore, half of all young black men are in prison or otherwise in the corrections system (BBC 2000). Most of these are due to drug-related offenses. Involvement with crack cocaine, common in black communities, has been a particularly quick route to prison. Drug options more common in wealthier groups, such as the abuse and fraud associated with prescription drugs, are less likely to result in prison time.

The approach to drug use varies greatly around the world. Some countries, particularly in the Middle East and Asia, have very strict drug laws. In many of these societies, drug laws are coupled with strict social controls and expectations that make illegal drug use uncommon. Other countries, such as Thailand and Mexico, which have been transit points for the drug trade, have turned to stricter enforcement, although it has been undermined by corruption (always a problem

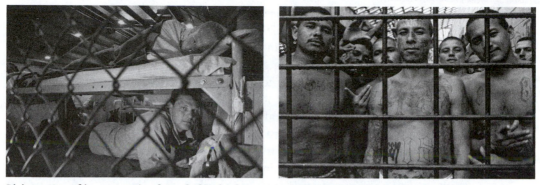

Rising rates of incarceration have led to high costs and crowding in the United States, where these prisoners sleep in 3-tier bunks in California, and in El Salvador, where 540 gang members, many deported from California, are crowded into the Chalatenango penitentiary.

where drugs can generate large amounts of money) and underfunding of law enforcement efforts (Elsner 2005). Many European countries, particularly the Netherlands and the Scandinavian countries, have treated drug use less as a criminal problem and more as a public health problem. As a result, they have invested less in incarceration and more in drug treatment for chronic offenders. The United States, with high rates of urban and rural poverty (like the developing world), extensive personal autonomy and limited social control (as in Europe), but also limited options for drug treatment, has found itself with the worst problem of soaring rates of drug-related imprisonment (Justice Policy Institute 2001).

International Crime Cartels

Crime trends around the world are difficult to gauge. Some locations, such as Southern and Western Africa and parts of Latin America and Eastern Europe, have clearly seen rising crime rates, often as part of political and social disruption and growing inequality. The United States saw a long downward trend in crime throughout the 1990s, but that trend started to reverse for property crime at the beginning of the twenty-first century, accompanying a general economic downturn with rising unemployment (FBI 2004). Fear of crime also seems to have increased in cities around the world, partly as urban dwellers have become less sure they are safe by living in presumably good neighborhoods. The world may not have more criminals than ever before, but it certainly has more weapons as the criminal element is better armed and hence deadlier than ever.

The United States has a long history of urban gangs: Irish, Italian, even Jewish and Polish (Steinberg 1981). What has changed is that urban gangs now often have ready access to high-capacity firearms: automatic pistols, rapid-fire shotguns (such as the infamous "street sweeper"), and automatic and semiautomatic versions of military assault rifles. During the 1980s, the hallmark of gang violence shifted from the switchblade stabbing to the drive-by shooting. Both are dangerous to rival gang members, but the latter also brings far greater dangers to passersby, such as children and neighborhood residents. This pattern has been echoed in Latin America, Africa, and Central Asia, where weapons sometimes originally obtained for civil war and unrest have made their way into the hands of now heavily armed criminal gangs. At times, it is difficult to determine whether a group is a revolutionary army or just a criminal gang, as drug trafficking, weapons, and violence against civilians often characterize both.

One ironic twist to the growth of free markets with less government regulation has been greater opportunities for national and international crime cartels. States emerging from the former Soviet Union—Russia, Ukraine, and Belarus, in particular—saw a surge in organized criminal activity, or "Mafia capitalism." Crimean resorts once favored by communist officials suddenly became the haunts of crime figures in Armani suits, brokering illegal trade and extortion on their ever-present cell phones. China has worried about organized criminal activity in Hong Kong and the former Portuguese-controlled port of Macau. Italy has seen a decline in blatant Mafia activity in the south, but there are new rumors of graft and corruption and possible ties to organized crime at the highest levels of government.

Though the weapons and methods have become more sophisticated and the scope of activity has gone global, the favored criminal activities all have a long history: drug trafficking, prostitution (now often including the global trafficking in women), extortion and kickbacks, and weapons trafficking. New concern has arisen about trafficking in so-called weapons of mass destruction, although most of the trade involves small arms, such as automatic weapons and grenade launchers.

Concern about international crime and international terrorism has also led to a rise in international cooperation among law enforcement agencies. Organizations such as Interpol attempt to coordinate police efforts across international boundaries, although differing procedures and political agendas often complicate international anticrime cooperation.

In Search of Opportunity and Order

What can be done to address the worldwide problem of crime? Political conservatives often emphasize the need to restore order. Police forces must be strict but also efficient and effective, with high professional standards. In much of Latin America, the police now dress in blue combat attire and ride around in the backs of pickup trucks, often carrying automatic weapons. They are an intimating force but also often suspect. They look more like an occupying army than an agent of law enforcement, only a bit more sophisticated than the Nigerian Lord's Army vigilantes.

Mexico has long favored this style of policing, but in major urban areas, at least in the more prosperous areas, the U.S. model of a single or paired police officer with a patrol car (or in some cases, even a bicycle), well dressed and sporting only a small automatic pistol and handcuffs, has replaced this older model. Efforts to eliminate police corruption are difficult, especially where the salaries are very low while the profits in graft, extortion, and bribes are very evident. In Brazil, police in prosperous urban areas have also shifted to a friendlier, more professional look. Those who patrol the poor urban and periphery slums, however, still often look more like a patrol in 1960s Vietnam than a modern police force, as they move through in combat boots and helmets, carrying automatic rifles that are continually pointed into the shifting shadows.

Criminologist James Q. Wilson has written about the need to restore order to urban spaces as part of restoring urban vitality. In an influential essay called "Broken Windows" (1982), Wilson and George L. Kelling note that signs of urban decay and disorder—broken windows, gang graffiti, and the presence of loiterers—give an impression of abandoned spaces, which terrify law-abiding citizens and welcome further crime. Wilson's ideas were influential in the anticrime administration of former New York mayor Rudolph Giuliani. Fixing up abandoned buildings was not controversial, but heavy-handed police action against the indigent and homeless (who may not have been criminal but gave areas a disorderly appearance) clearly was. Still, many credited the ideas with a reduction in New York's crime problem and an improved image for the city.

While political conservatives have stressed order, political progressives have often championed opportunity—legitimate, hopeful opportunity—as the solution to crime. Sociologist William J. Wilson (1996) has argued that the answer to urban crime and disorder is to open the opportunity structure by supporting educational improvement and full employment policies. He contends that many poor urban residents endorse mainstream values but find no way to live out those law-abiding, family-oriented values in neighborhoods that have been abandoned by legitimate businesses and institutions.

Urban and rural residents who are fearful of crime often speak of their desire for both greater order and greater opportunity. Crime prevention seems to hinge on elements of both. Careful, professional policing coupled with neighborhood involvement, not only builds trust but also reduces the local power of criminals and the attractiveness of crime. Policing efforts that focus on building a sense of trust and security have been effective in communities in both the United States and Europe and might offer hope for Latin America and Africa. At the same, their effectiveness seems also to depend on the availability of legitimate alternatives to criminal activity that offer opportunities for advancement and hope for the future.

Amnesty International

■ This international human rights organization collects data on incarceration around the world and champions the rights of detainees to legal counsel and fair trials. Visit the group's website at www.amnesty.org. What are some of the current issues in crime and incarceration?

Gun Controversies

■ The activities of Handgun Control, Inc., to reduce the prevalence of weapons and gun-related violence in the United States are described at www.bradycampaign.org. The site is named for the efforts conducted in the name of James Brady, who was shot in the attempt to assassinate U.S. President Ronald Reagan. The controversial nature of this work in the United States can be seen in the fact that many websites with names similar to Handgun Control actually belong to groups in favor of private gun ownership. The most complete counterpoint can be found at the site of the National Rifle Association, (www.nra.org), a huge site with many articles on crime and violence from a pro-gun position. How do the two sites differ in their assessments of the nature, causes, and solutions to crime and violence?

Bureau of Justice Statistics

■ Current statistics and trends on crime in the United States can be found at www.ojp.usdoj.gov/bjs. What current trends in crime and incarceration do you note? On what types of criminal activity does the U.S. government focus its activities?

Drug Enforcement Administration

■ Go to the site of the DEA, the main U.S. drug enforcement agency (www.usdoj.gov/dea). Click on the section on "Global News." A world map will allow you to focus on drug trafficking and enforcement anywhere in the world, although from a U.S. government perspective. What places in the world raise the most concern for the DEA? How is drug trafficking related to other social and economic turmoil?

Interpol

■ The international network of police organizations, Interpol, has a site at www.interpol.int. It has a huge amount of information on international crime, including drugs and drug trafficking, money laundering, trafficking in children, as well as international crime statistics. Further information on U.S. and international crime can be found at www.fbi.gov, the site of the Federal Bureau of Investigation (FBI).

CHAPTER 6

War
States of Terror

Monrovia, Liberia

A plane lands in war-torn Liberia, its tail sporting the familiar Nike swoosh. But this plane isn't carrying the expensive sneakers favored by teenagers in West Africa. It's carrying something else favored by urban teens in this country: automatic weapons. This is not a new Nike export; the plane originally had been used to transport consumer goods but then was chartered, no questions asked by a Ukranian underworld arms dealer. He may be dealing with the government, he may be dealing with rebels fighting the government, or he may be dealing with both. The profits are high, and if he's lucky, the plane will return filled with both cash and marketable drugs.

Washington, D.C.

The Pentagon announces its choice of a manufacturer for a new fleet of twenty presidential helicopters, each known as Marine One when the president is aboard. These are no ordinary helicopters. They are well equipped: "The US101 will provide the president of the United States with a state-of-the-art-helicopter, . . . an Oval Office in the sky," said Senator Hillary Clinton of New York (Business Week 2005, p. 1). They are also high security: "The president needs a more survivable helicopter while the nation engages in the global war on terrorism," said John Young, Assistant Secretary of the Navy for Research, Development, and Acquisition, in making the announcement (cnn.com 2005). The cost of these twenty helicopters is six billion dollars. (One might guess that for over one-third of a billion dollars, each these might come "loaded" with options.) This figure is small in the world of military spending, but the prestige factor is high. The company with this contract essentially gets free advertising every time the president is aboard. It will also presumably have the inside track as the Pentagon looks for more high-cost search-and-rescue helicopters.

The bidding war came down to Sikorsky, a Connecticut firm that has built "presidential" helicopters for almost fifty years, and Lockheed-Martin, who had proposed a multinational venture that included British and Italian suppliers. Advocates for

Sikorsky included Congressional representatives from Connecticut and places with Sikorsky plants and suppliers, as well as those who argued that U.S. military spending should be spent entirely within the United States on U.S. contractors. Lockheed supporters included representatives from New York and places where it has suppliers and those who argued that Italy and Great Britain should be rewarded for their support of the U.S.-led war effort in Iraq. The Italian prime minister himself made frequent statements advocating for Lockheed.

Lockheed won the prestigious bidding war and the millions of federal research dollars that went with it. The only consolation for Sikorsky was that the U.S. government is likely to continue to buy hundreds of its Black Hawk helicopters in future years.

How States Made War and War Made States

Why something like war—so costly in lives, investment, and destruction—has been so persistent and so prominent a part of the human experience is a perplexing question. Long-time war correspondent Christopher Hedges (2004) offers a psychological answer: that "war is a force that gives us meaning," turning ordinary lives into extraordinary moments in history and heightening our sense of purpose, honor, heroism, and even passion. American sociologist and social historian of conflict Charles Tilly (1975) contends that the modern world is addicted to war, in part because the modern world is the product of a millennium of wars.

Has warfare always been part of human existence? It is hard to know. While there are some human cultures that seem almost exclusively peaceful, they are rare and usually isolated. (There might have been many more that were not so isolated and so were overrun.) Some ancient cultures, such as the Mayan culture of Mexico, once thought to be very peaceful, have turned out to have been highly involved in warfare.

Even the animal kingdom doesn't offer much hope. Chimpanzees, once thought to be peaceful animals, have been observed attacking other bands and ganging up on individuals, engaging in primal (or at least primate) warfare. There may be a gender issue here: Young male chimps like to shake sticks and intimidate rivals, behavior rarely seen among females. But observers have also noted mother–daughter attack teams. Sometimes, the fight is over territory, but most often, it is over dominance.

Human tribal warfare seems to have often been much the same—sporadic skirmishes over territory and dominance, a chance to prove one's courage, and occasionally, a very human addition: revenge for past grievances. Yet with rare exceptions, tribal warfare did not take many lives. Sometimes, the tactics—ritual announcements and expressions of bravado—even seemed designed to offer maximum opportunities for courage and minimal opportunities for carnage. This changed as large agrarian empires became the norm in the Middle East, India, and China around 5,000 years ago and to a lesser extent in Mesoamerica and the Andes somewhat later. Perhaps warfare is not so much built into our genes as it is built into our societies.

Empires are the result of conquest. In short, they are about war. Kings and emperors are primarily war leaders who derive their power and prestige from conquest. In such a situation, war becomes chronic. Logistics and weather often prevented year-round conflict, so there were seasons of war. The Bible speaks of spring as "the time when kings go forth to war" (2 Kings 11:1). The peasants must have often hoped for a long winter. The great problems for the conquerors were often ones of logistics, such as feeding and moving large armies (and later their horses). The maximum size of an empire was determined by how long it took the king's armies to reach the furthest corner. Paying for a large army depended on success. Tribute and loot from conquered states would pay for an army to march on to new conquests.

As a result, empires fed on invasion. The mighty got mightier, and small tribal entities were engulfed. The reverse was also true, however. Any setback in military fortunes would make it hard to reward one's soldiers and would embolden one's enemies. Empires lived by expanding, but larger areas were harder to administer and left ever-growing borders to defend. As such, all the great empires eventually collapsed, often by some combination of turmoil from within and a new invasion by an enemy from without.

During the Low Middle Ages in Europe, about 500 to 1000 CE (sometimes dubbed the Dark Ages for the collapse of central power and the chronic fighting between rival groups), the problem of raising armies was handled through **feudalism.** China and Japan also used a similar system at times when there was not a strong central ruler. Under feudalism, a king depended on his lords, who may in turn have depended on knights or samurai underneath them, to provide his army. The lords and their knights provided protection to peasants under their domain, although that protection may have been little better at times than a violent crime syndicate offering protection to a businessperson. In return, the peasants and artisans provided the lords and knights with the food and supplies needed to live well and to wage war. Sometimes, the peasants also fought, but the key force was comprised of mounted knights with expensive armor and weapons.

Kings relied on staying in the good graces of their lords to stay in power. As a few kings again grew in power, beginning around 1000 CE and continuing for the next four centuries or so, they were again gradually able to field paid armies answerable only to themselves. As weapons and tactics changed, kings came to prefer armies of professional soldiers hired from within their realm or paid foreign mercenaries. Hired Swiss "mountaineers" with some very nasty pikes and hired Turkish "horse archers" proved very effective against feudal knights, while British yeoman archers, essentially small farmers in service to the king, decimated

French knights in famous battles of the thirteenth and fourteenth centuries. Eventually, the rise of guns and artillery permanently wedded a ruler's fortunes to his ability to mass and arm large armies.

Chronic warfare forced the consolidation of diverse regions into national identities that could muster large, unified armed forces. Those who failed to do so were overtaken by those who succeeded. The modern nation–state was formed. Tilly (1975) contends that "the state made war and war made the state" (p. 42) and that this combination of warfare and state formation reshaped, in fact created, the continent. He writes, "A thousand years ago, Europe did not exist" (1990, p. 38).

A Europe of competing nation states was forged in 500 years of war between 1000 and 1500 CE. Then, the idea was then promptly exported. In 1500, Europe was a continent of small nation–states that looked weak and fractious compared to the great empires in what are now China, India, Mexico, and Peru. But their intense competition gave Europeans a great desire to expand abroad, and their frequent fighting pushed them to develop the means to do so. For the first time, European ships were capable of sailing the open ocean. Ships also always had an important drawback: It was difficult to fight from aboard a ship, as various rams, boarding planks, and catapults all had their limitations. Europe also had another innovation, as artillery had become cheap and effective enough to be a major factor in warfare. Cannons had limitations, too, however; they were heavy and hard to haul over distances—except aboard a ship.

The Chinese had invented gunpowder and the navigation compass and had built some of the first great trading ships, but it was Europeans in small, relatively new countries, such as Portugal, Holland, and England, that turned the combination into world empires. The combination of ships with guns gave the Europeans a portable force that soon spanned the globe. Spanish galleons reached and conquered the Americas south of Florida at the turn of the sixteenth century. Portuguese men of war rounded Africa at about the same time (establishing outposts along the way), drove the Arab traders from the Indian Ocean, and forced their way into Asia. By the mid 1600s, bigger and better Dutch ships fought the Portuguese out of South Africa and the West Indies (Indonesia). They also sailed across the Atlantic to seize islands in the Caribbean and neighboring shoreline (Aruba, Surinam, Saint Martaan, and others) and an island and shoreline further north on the Atlantic (Manhattan and New Amsterdam, later recast as New York).

The most powerful navy of all was created by the British, who used it to build the world's largest empire: North America north of Mexico along with points in the Caribbean such as Jamaica, much of Eastern and Southern Africa (the latter seized from the Dutch), parts of West Africa (Nigeria and Ghana), all of India (including what are now Pakistan and Bangladesh), and trading interests in China, Southeast Asia, and across the Pacific. The process was gradual. Britain spent much of the 1700s in constant war with its great rival, France, eventually winning complete control of Canada and India. The British Empire faced only one great setback: the loss of the American colonies to determined irregular armies with the final decisive help of the French fleet. France retained control of much of Western Africa, many points in the Caribbean (losing Haiti in the second great new world revolt in 1811), in Southeast Asia (including Vietnam), and in the Pacific (including Tahiti).

Empires in Collision

The 1800s were dominated by the struggle to maintain and extend these great empires. European nations vied with one another for dominance around the globe. Spain lost much of its great empire early in century to Napoleonic invasions at home and uprisings in Mexico and South America. It managed to retain Cuba and the Philippines until late in the century. Portugal held on to Brazil until 1822 and struggled to keep its hold in Africa. France gave up its last great stake in North America by selling the Louisiana Territory to Thomas Jefferson and the new United States of America, but it turned to creations such as its famous Foreign Legions (essentially a band of mercenaries) to extend its holdings in West Africa and Southeast Asia.

Africa became the center of a great land grab beginning in the 1880s. Until that time, most foreign possessions were small ports and territories on the coast. The interior of Africa remained, to the Europeans at least, unknown: the "dark continent." Increasingly, however, European states wanted the prestige and access to resources that came with owning a piece of the continent. Britain dominated in the east and France in the west. Germany claimed the remaining portions. These three nations vied for control of weak states in the north, such as Morocco. Belgium claimed a piece out of the middle. The Belgian Congo, operated as the private domain of King Leopold, was many times over the size of its home country, with vast mineral and timber resources. By the end of the century, all of Africa was European controlled or dominated.

Meanwhile, the Russian Empire grew, as the great Eurasian land empire of the czars pushed its control south and ever eastward to capture small states and tribally held territory in the Caucasus Mountains and on to the Pacific. The result was a single land empire greater than any since Genghis Khan (much the same territory, in fact). The expense of seizing and controlling this empire was enormous, however, and some portions were too far away to control. Alaska was sold to the United States to help pay the bills.

The United States built a large land empire by extending control ever westward, adding Texas and then seizing the northern half of Mexico in the war of

1846. During the 1880s and 1890s, the United States completed its own push to the Pacific, capturing vast amounts of tribally held territories in the process. The so-called Indian Wars, made famous by dozens of Western movies, were part of a worldwide movement of powerful industrial states against the remaining tribally held territories in North America, Africa, Central Asia, and Australia and New Zealand.

The nineteenth century ended with one final colonial war, in which the United States seized the Philippines, Guam, and Puerto Rico from Spain and created a partially independent Cuba in the Spanish–American War of 1898. After the terrible bloodshed of the Napoleonic wars of the early 1800s, however, the Europeans avoided fighting great colonial wars with each other for much of the rest of the century.

This relative truce among empires was shattered by the cataclysm of the two great world wars of the 1900s. World War I erupted in 1914 amid jealousies, suspicions, and alliances among rival empires. The Russian Empire was huge and menacing but also impoverished and corrupt and showing signs of crumbling. The Turkish Ottoman Empire had ruled the Middle East since the Middle Ages but was also in decay, "the sick man of Europe." The German Empire was strong in Europe but felt surrounded by enemies and the great reach of the French and British Empires. The final spark was the assassination of the ruler of the increasingly insecure Austro–Hungarian Empire by a Serbian seeking national independence.

By the time World War I ended in 1918, the Russian Empire had been destroyed. It was recast as the Union of Soviet Socialist Republics (USSR), or Soviet Union, following the Bolshevik Revolution. The Austro–Hungarian Empire was split into newly independent states. The Ottoman Empire was also broken up and given to the victorious British and French, who began to carve the area into states and emirates: Iraq, Kuwait, Jordan, Lebanon, and the protectorate of British Palestine. The German Empire was greatly reduced, with Germany being forced to give up its African possessions as well land in Europe to France and to the newly recreated country of Poland, which had previously been swallowed by Russian and German expansion.

In many ways, World War II (1939–1945) was round two in this great battle of empires. Adolf Hitler and his Nazi Party dreamed of re-establishing a third great German Empire, or **Third Reich.** They dreamed of dominating Europe and controlling valuable resources in North Africa and the Middle East, especially petroleum. While Hitler is often accused of wanting world dominion, it appears that the Nazis would have been content to allow the British to maintain a remnant empire, the Japanese to control Asia, and the United States to dominate the Americas. The world would be divided into a few great empires, with the German as the most important. In Italy, Benito Mussolini dreamed of the glories of the Roman Empire and sought conquests in North Africa. In Asia, Japan sought an

"Asian co-prosperity sphere," in which the European powers—Britain, France, and the Netherlands—and the United States would be expelled from Asia and replaced by Japanese dominance under the rule of the Japanese Emperor Hirohito, essentially a greater Japanese Empire. In Great Britain, Winston Churchill promised to prevent the "liquidation" of the British empire. In the United States, Franklin D. Roosevelt envisioned a world of free trade without empires or spheres of control, one in which U.S. commercial interests would likely dominate.

Germany moved to seize the territory it had lost in World War I, and World War II began as Germany invaded Poland. Shortly thereafter, it invaded France and demanded return of lost border territory. Josef Stalin's Soviet Union joined in the invasion of Poland, as it tried to reclaim al the territory of the Russian Empire, including Finland. The need for resources, especially grain and petroleum, led the German Nazis to battle Britain for North Africa and to invade the Soviet Union.

To expand its own empire, Japan seized Korea and gradually extended its control over China, replacing the dominance of the European powers. Needing further resources and especially desperate for petroleum, Japan decided to attempt to disable the U.S. Navy, seize the Philippines, and then drive the European powers, all facing defeat at German hands, from Southeast Asia. The resulting war bled and bankrupted Europe and crushed Japan, and imperial ambitions crumbled. The Philippines became independent. The Dutch East Indies became the country of Indonesia. British holdings became Malaysia and Singapore. In India, Mohandas Gandhi, the Mahatma or "great soul," had been leading a nonviolent struggle for independence. After World War II, he achieved his goal of independence but not of unity: British India split along religious lines into Hindu-dominated India and Muslim-dominated Pakistan in 1947, with East Pakistan later becoming independent as Bangladesh. France fought in the early 1950s to retain French Indochina, but after a defeat at the hands of the revolutionary leader Ho Chi Min, withdrew to allow the independent states of Vietnam, Cambodia, and Laos.

Independence came last to Africa. South Africa became independent as white Afrikaaners gained power and sought to maintain white rule. Franz Fanon (1963), from the French Caribbean, closely watched the struggles of Africa. Seeing the poverty and oppression of those he called "he wretched of the earth," he called on Africans to purge the violence of colonialism with the violence of liberation struggle. Algeria, whose struggle inspired Fanon, fought the French army and European settlers throughout the 1950s and gained independence. Starting with the British Gold Coast, which reclaimed the ancient title of Ghana in 1957, Sub-Saharan Africa began to claim independence as a collage of countries whose borders often followed old colonial lines. The Belgian Congo became independent in 1964 and was renamed Zaire, only to have the name return to the Congo decades later. Whites in Rhodesia, named for British colonial administrator Cecil Rhodes, claimed independence to try to maintain white rule. This hope was defeated in a bloody civil war that gave power to the black majority; the country claimed the name of an ancient African civilization, Zimbabwe. Late to gain independence were the Portuguese colonies of Mozambique and Angola. After achieving independence in 1975, they almost immediately fell into civil war. One of the very last colonies, what had been German Southwest Africa and held by South Africa, finally became independent as Namibia in 1990.

The 1989 escape of Eastern Europe from Soviet control and the breakup of the Soviet Union in 1991 could be seen as signaling the end of the Russian Empire, although fighting in the Caucasus Mountains, including Chechnya, and unrest elsewhere still continue. The end of the era of colonial empires in Asia came peacefully, as Britain returned Hong Kong to China in 1997 and Portugal returned its old colonial port of Macau in 2000.

Throughout this time, **nationalism** remained a powerful motivator. For many, independence brought neither peace nor prosperity. The great irony in Africa is that for many, independence came suddenly and relatively peacefully, as Europeans abandoned the old colonial idea. But im many cases, bloodshed followed independence.

From Limited War to Total War to Cold War

The nature of warfare also continued to change. Military historians speak of the shift from **limited war** to **total war.** Until the late 1700s, most armies were quite small. Europeans in the 1200s dreaded the great Mongol hordes, ravaging their eastern lands, but in fact, Ghengis Khan used relatively small groups of highly mobile cavalry. Limited war often had strict rules of conduct and ideals of honor and glory. The Mongol armies struck terror by violating some of the European rules, but they, too, had their ideals of what made a brave and honorable warrior. European ideals of chivalry, or the ideal knight, were promoted by both church and state as a way to limit the plunder and pillage of a violent age. Likewise, in Japan, samurai knights fought with a strict code of honor.

Warfare always ran the risk of degenerating into wholesale slaughter and plunder. The European Thirty Years War (1618–1648) between Catholic and Protestant factions devastated Central Europe, destroyed thousands of towns and villages, created huge refugee crises, plundered fields and led to famine, and resulted in massive civilian deaths far beyond the number of combatants killed. Yet the ideal of the time and the centuries to follow replaced medieval chivalry with the so-called gentleman at arms, popularized in books such as *The Three Musketeers*, who was loyal to king and honor and country.

Whether or not these ideals prevailed, the armies of the day remained fairly small, with engagements typically in the thousands. Medieval armies were limited by the expense of horses and armor, and armies in the early age of firearms likewise were limited by the expense of these weapons. The preferred tactic was a tight formation on an open battlefield attended by much pageantry. At the least, this tended to keep noncombatants out of the fray, much more so than the siege tactics of the Late Middle Ages.

War was still ultimately about brute force, but codes of conduct were often taken very seriously. At the battle of Yorktown, the final engagement of the American Revolution in 1781, one of the final issues of debate among the victorious French and American commanders was whether the British defenders, outnumbered and hopelessly surrounded, had put up a spirited enough defense before surrendering to be accorded the full honors of dignified defeat, with their own bands playing mournful tunes as they laid down their firearms while their gentleman officers kept their own swords.

Total War

Warfare became increasingly less limited in the 1800s. Napoleon violated the rules by attacking without warning. Commanders of the armies he so defeated complained that this was because he was a Corsican peasant, not a true gentleman. Napoleon used the populist ideals of the French Revolution to advance a new idea: mass mobilization, an entire nation at war. All of France's resources were poured into his war efforts. Armies also grew dramatically in size. Napoleon's Grand Army of the Republic numbered over 600,000 as it marched toward Russia in 1812. This grand army moving east onto the Russian steppe was many times larger than any Mongol horde that had ever invaded from the opposite direction.

Rapid industrialization was also changing the face of war. In many respects, the American Civil War (1861–1865) was a turning point from agrarian limited war to modern industrial total war. The weapons were changing: the first battle of iron-clad ships, the first sinking of a ship by a submarine (hand operated), the first use of arial reconnaissance (hot air balloons), the first use of a machine gun (the Gatling gun), the early use of repeating firearms in place of single-shot weapons, and the use of much larger artillery pieces. Europeans watched Americans slaughter one another on the battlefield in unprecedented numbers and claimed Americans just didn't know how to fight a proper war. The truth was that the American commanders on both sides were well trained in the tactics of the Napoleonic era, but the weapons had become far deadlier in the intervening fifty years.

From the day the first war was fought until the Civil War, the primary weapon had been the spear. The hunter's spear was no doubt the first weapon, and in various forms—short javelins, long pikes, and horse-borne lances—it remained the weapon of choice. Archers launching arrows (modified spears) could be deadly, especially in rough terrain, but battles were usually decided by groups of charging spear men, either on foot or on horseback. Even in the era of firearms, the deciding moment of battle was often the bayonet charge, essentially a long gun turned into a spear. But now the commanders learned, from Gettysburg to Fredericksburg, that charging shoulder to shoulder was certain suicide.

As the war dragged on, the tactics shifted. The Southern states of the Confederacy had the most experienced and capable commanders, with a long history of military service, but the Northern states of the Union had greater industrial might and sought to exhaust and strangle the South. Union ships, increasingly steamers, blockaded the South. Rail links and trains became vital nerve systems. The final and ultimately successful Union commander, General Ulysses S. Grant, had no better success with the frontal infantry assault than his predecessors had had. Rather, he won the Civil War with slow, bloody campaigns that attacked shipping and supply centers, and he increasingly levied massive artillery bombardments against urban centers, as his opponents took refuge in trench warfare. He sent his subordinate, General William Sherman, on a march through the South that ripped up railroad tracks, burned down major cities, and sought to terrorize and demoralize the population. The ideal commander at the beginning of the war had perhaps been General Robert E. Lee, the South's gentleman warrior. But the grim face of war that emerged was that of Sherman, who destroyed infrastructure and displaced civilians, contending simply that "War is hell."

The hellishness of modern war fully dawned on Europe and the world with World War I. This conflict began high hopes for a quick victory, and the first battles included drums and bagpipes and bayonet charges. The conflict quickly moved into a long war of attrition, with soldiers digging ever-larger networks of trenches to hide from ever-deadlier artillery. Coils of barbed wire and newer machine guns made infantry charges hopeless. The first large-scale use of poison gas added to the horror and the misery. Population centers could be bombarded with huge guns or bombed from the air, and each side tried to starve the other with blockages: the British using surface ships and the Germans using submarines. Industrial centers worked around the clock to turn out more and deadlier weapons. The bloodiest battles ever fought were the ultimate result. Some 600,000 died in a matter of days at the Somme, the size of Napoleon's entire Grand Army and more than ten times the dead at Gettysburg. By the times the war ended, nearly an entire generation of Europe's young men had been wiped out.

World War II only raised the stakes to new heights. Nazi Germany claimed it could make war more humane by using brief *blitzkriegs* that would "shock and awe" the enemy into quick surrender. At first successful, their destructive might was soon matched by that of the other large industrial powers: Great Britain, Russia, and eventually the world's largest industrial economy, the United States. To finally win the war, U.S. industry was turning out a major ship every day, along with hundreds of aircraft. As each side tried to destroy the industrial capacity of the other, civilian centers became the primary targets. German aircraft flew daily raids in the "blitz" of London and devastated whole cities, such as Canterbury. German ground forces besieged and starved entire Russian cities, such as St. Petersburg. The Allied powers returned the devastation, bombing German industry and ultimately turning to firebombings, which created huge firestorms and consumed entire city centers and their populations in Dresden and throughout the country. The Nazis retaliated with missile attacks on London.

The same pattern was repeated in the Pacific. Japanese troops displaced, enslaved, massacred, and terrorized civilian populations as a weapon of war, seeking to force surrender through terror. Later in the Pacific War, the U.S. Army and Navy tried the same strategy from the air, seeking to bomb Japan into surrendering. Targeted industrial bombings gave way to massive firebombings, which had an even deadlier effect, for Japanese homes were built of wood rather than the brick, stone, and stucco of old Europe. A single firebombing of Tokyo created a vast firestorm that may have killed over 100,000 people. No poison gas was used in this war, but phosphorus and napalm (a jellied petroleum product) were clearly weapons of mass destruction. The annihilation of cities culminated with two atomic bombings that largely destroyed the entire cities of Hiroshima and Nagasaki, killing well over 100,000 in the short term and far more in the long term from the effects of burns and radiation poisoning. Total war had reached its apex.

Cold War

The realization that weapons technology had reached the point where warring nations could entirely consume one another changed the nature of war. People spoke of the next great conflict, World War III, as a cataclysm that might destroy the planet, and indeed, it could have. But facing this prospect, the next great war was not a total war but rather a **cold war,** a new form of limited conflict.

The United States and the Soviet Union were allied in World War II by virtue of having the same enemies. Once those enemies had been defeated, however, relations between the two countries quickly became strained. The first half of the twentieth century had been a struggle among multiple powers, but in the wake of the second world war, two powers emerged as superpowers and vied for vast spheres of influence, offering differing visions of the postwar world. Yet the spectre of that war, which took the lives of 20 million Russians, coupled with the threat of growing nuclear arsenals, kept the two superpowers from direct open warfare. Instead, the cold war was marked by a battle over influence, by an arms race, and by regional conflicts, or "proxy wars," in which what would have been civil wars became part of the struggle for dominance between the two superpowers.

The first and bloodiest of these conflicts was in Korea. Following World War II, the Korean peninsula was divided into a Soviet-occupied north and a U.S.-occupied south, just as Germany was divided into zones of occupation that became East and West. In 1950, as the zones were looking to become permanent, the North launched a massive invasion of the South, quickly capturing Seoul, the southern capital, and almost overrunning the rest of the peninsula and reuniting Korea by force. The United Nations Security Council, with the Soviet Union absent as part of a boycott over contested procedures, voted to condemn the invasion and help the South. United Nations forces, under the command of U.S. General Douglas MacArthur and made up largely of U.S. and South Korean forces, broke out of their small holdout perimeter and drove all the way to the Chinese border.

The situation had just grown more complex, however, as the Chinese Communists under Mao Zedong had just completed their takeover of China. They announced that if the U.N. forces pushed to their border, they would consider this a grave threat and intervene. This they did, and large numbers of Chinese forces drove the U.N. forces back south, retaking Seoul. A U.N. counteroffensive pushed the Chinese and North Koreans back to the original thirty-eighth parallel. MacArthur wanted to push on, bombing and even invading China, if necessary, to win a decisive victory, such as the victory that had ended World War II. The use of nuclear weapons to speed this victory, as had been done at the end of World War II, was also discussed.

But this was a new age. This see-saw conflict was referred to as a United Nations **police action,** not a war. China was huge and could fight on for a very long time, even in a losing conflict. The Soviet Union had not directly intervened but had recently tested its own nuclear weapons. If it responded to a nuclear attack with a similar counterattack, the world could fall into nuclear war. American president Harry Truman fired MacArthur and returned to the bargaining table. The United States' cold war policy became not the destruction of communism but rather its **containment.** A stalemate ensued and an accord, never signed by South Korea, was drafted in 1953 to accept, for the time being, the current stalemate. This civil conflict and police action cost Korea perhaps 3 million dead, many of them civilians, and devasted the country.

In time, South Korea rebuilt with extensive foreign investment. North Korea remained in the hands of its Soviet-installed leader, Kim Il Sung. On his death in 1994, he passed leadership on to his son, Kim Jung Il, more in the manner of an imperial succession than a communist ideal. Kim Jung Il has continued a repressive regime that has become ever more bankrupt, particularly since the Soviet Union disbanded and North Korea lost its main patron. But this poor country maintains a million-man army and the legacy of years of war preparation: a massive artillery pointed at Seoul, missiles that can reach Japan as well as South Korea (and maybe even the United States), and a nuclear program geared to producing nuclear weapons. The spectre of an unpredictable leader in a reclusive state with little to lose, heavily armed with the world's deadliest weapons, is one of the cold war's great legacies.

When Communist forces took control of China in 1949, the Nationalist government fled to the island of Formosa, which had been a Japanese possession for much of the century. The Chinese Communists lacked the naval power to invade, especially with a U.S. fleet blocking the strait. The Formosa-based government became Taiwan, the Republic of China, and long claimed to be the rightful government of the entire country. For two decades, it was treated by the United States as the rightful government of China in exile, and it held China's U.N. seat. Thawing relations with mainland China in the 1970s led to a "two China policy" and then full recognition of the Communist government in Beijing. The Chinese government considers Taiwan to be a renegade province of China and demands its reunion with the mainland. Many Taiwanese would like to see Taiwan formally independent, but it remains as it has for over fifty years as a small, prosperous entity left in political limbo.

The other great Asian cold war battleground was Vietnam and Indochina. France had administered Vietnam as three colonial departments, but the independence plans of the late 1940s looked to forming a unified country. The dilemma for Western Europe and the United States was that the hero of independence and likely winner of any election was Ho Chi Min, who was considered a communist. In fact, while Ho was heavily influenced by Marxist theory, he was also a Vietnamese nationalist, who sought to chart a course that was independent of both China and the Soviet Union. The compromise plan of 1954 was by now a familiar pattern: Vietnam would be temporarily divided into a northern sector under Soviet influence and a southern sector under the influence of the United States and its allies. When the division again appeared to be becoming permanent, however, Ho's followers formed the Vietcong, supported by the north, and Vietnam plunged into civil war.

What would have been an isolated civil conflict in a poor, remote region took on global dimensions as the United States came to view this fight, like the one in Korea, as a struggle to contain communist expansion. This required trying to support a series of increasingly corrupt South Vietnamese governments and the ever-increasing presence of U.S. forces. After over a decade of war and losing over 50,000 soldiers, the United States agreed to a peace treaty in 1973 and withdrew it forces. When the peace collapsed in 1975, so did the South Vietnamese government, but the United States did not reintervene.

All of Vietnam became communist, and spillover wars toppled the governments of Laos and Cambodia, which had also become the site of a proxy war, with Soviet arms supplying forces battling CIA-supported opposition and U.S. bombing. Cambodia fell under the control of a particularly brutal revolutionary group, the Khmer Rouge, which followed a twisted version of Maoist peasant communism. Namely, it depopulated the cities to return the country to its agrarian roots, killing anyone it considered an enemy of the revolution. As many as 2 million people died in the "killing fields" of a Cambodian holocaust. This bloodshed was finally stopped by a Vietnamese invasion. China, which had supported the Khmer Rouge, responded with a brief invasion of Vietnam, which was heavily supported by the Soviets. Meanwhile, border conflicts developed along the Soviet–Chinese border.

While the Western alliance of Europe and the United States still spoke of the communist bloc as a single entity, it was clear by the 1970s that old animosities and new rivalries divided the communist states. Vietnam, like China, has since pursued economic reforms that have moved it closer to the capitalist world economy, while Cambodia has struggled to rid itself of the Khmer Rouge and establish a mixed economy democracy. In the 1990s, U.S. President Bill Clinton visited Vietnam, a sign of warming relations. All of the countries of Indochina remain among the poorest in Asia and the world.

The cold war legacy in the Middle East and South Asia is less obvious but equally enduring. India and Pakistan remained rivals, with border disputes that were never resolved at the time of their partition in 1947. This was a legacy of colonialism but took on a cold war character, as the Soviet Union tended to back India, resulting in U.S. support for Pakistan. India and Pakistan fought four regional wars and now face each other with their respective arsenals of nuclear weapons.

In the Middle East, the Israeli–Palestinian conflict also emerged out of the ashes of colonialism. The land had been part of the Ottoman Empire but then fell under British control. The British essentially promised the same land to both their Arab allies in the world wars and to European Jews escaping the ravages of the holocaust and European anti-Semitism. The United Nations tried to divide the land, not very large, between the two groups but war quickly broke out, given the fervor of Zionist Jews to quickly create a homeland and the anger of the Palestinian Arabs who were displaced. The Soviet Union backed the Arab cause, especially when it was led by Arab socialists such as Prime Minister Nasser of Egypt, and the United States strongly backed and armed the Israeli effort. Again, a regional dispute over the spoils of former empires turned into a cold war battleground.

In Iraq, the United States first supported the anticommunist Baath party. Yet strong U.S. support for the Shah of Iran led the Baath leadership, including Saddam Hussein, to turn to the Soviets. When the Iranian Revolution toppled the Shah and brought the anti-American Ayatollah Khomeini to power, the United States again shifted and began to support and arm Saddam Hussein as a bulwark against radical Muslims. In Afghanistan, the Soviet Union resorted to invasion to try to support an unpopular client government. The United States supported the collection of Islamic resistance groups known as the *mujahadeen*. With U.S. support, they ultimately forced a Soviet withdrawal but then fell into fighting among themselves. Control finally went to Pakistani-borne fundamentalist movement, the **Taliban.** In both Iraq and Afghanistan, the United States ultimately invaded to topple governments that were in many ways relics of cold war politics.

In Latin America, struggles between elite land-owning families and displaced individuals, between military and civilian governments, and between different philosophies of development, some of which were a century and half old, took on new importance as cold war battles. The United States helped topple left-leaning elected governments in Guatemala in 1954 and Chile in 1973, which were replaced by procapitalist military dictatorships as a way to prevent communist (and hence Soviet) influence in the Americas. The Soviets backed successful revolutions in Cuba and Nicaragua and an unsuccessful one in El Salvador. The United States backed opposing forces and counterrevolutions. In Cuba in 1961, the CIA supported a failed invasion of Cuban exiles at the Bay of Pigs, seeking to topple Fidel Castro. In Nicaragua, the United States overtly and covertly aided the Contras, who sought to topple the Sandinistas, a leftist government that had taken its name from an anticolonial nationalist.

While all these global regional struggles made the cold war a true world war, like the first two world wars, this one's primary focus remained Europe. At the end of World War II, U.S. and British troops had moved into Germany from the west while Soviet troops had advanced across Eastern Europe. Both sides were determined to have friendly governments with kindred systems of government in their zones of control. Germany was divided into occupation zones: The Soviet zone became East Germany, and the U.S./European zone became West Germany. Berlin was also divided, and West Berlin became an island of Western and U.S. control in the midst of East Germany. The Soviet Union promoted communist governments in the Eastern European countries under its control, many of which had some socialist sympathies. Together with the Soviet Union, Poland, Hungary, Czechoslovakia, Romania, Bulgaria, and East Germany formed an alliance known as the **Warsaw Pact.** To counter this alliance, the Western European countries allied with the United States to form the **North Atlantic Treaty Alliance (NATO).**

Just as at the beginning of World War I, Europe was divided into hostile alliances, but now with the realization that a full-scale war could destroy the continent. British Prime Minister Winston Churchill warned of an "iron curtain" descending on the continent, and this became the metaphor for the time. The iron curtain became a visible wall down the middle of Berlin in the early 1960s, as the Soviets attempted to prevent East Berliners from fleeing into the more prosperous West. Vast armed forces faced each other on either side of the iron curtain.

NATO, fearing the larger size of the Warsaw Pact forces, refused to rule out nuclear retaliation for a Warsaw Pact invasion.

The 1960s saw tense standoffs, especially over the status of Berlin. NATO airlifted supplies to its isolated half of the city to get around an embargo. Tensions eased a bit during the late 1960s and early 1970s, as U.S. President Richard Nixon, famous as a staunch anticommunist, decided on a policy of **détente,** or limited cooperation, to ease tensions. Tensions again mounted in the late 1970s over Afghanistan.

In the 1980s, President Ronald Reagan dubbed the Soviet Union an "evil empire" and accelerated the arms race. Yet the Soviet Union was changing. After a series of turnovers in leadership, Mikhail Gorbachev come to power and declared new policies of *glasnost* (openness) and *perestroika* (economic reform and restructuring). The Soviet Union started to make moves toward reducing its military arsenal and challenged the United States to follow suit. At the same time, *glasnost* and *perestroika* set in motion a series of events that few could have predicted. Hungary tested the new openness by allowing people to move freely into neighboring Austria, a seemingly small shift. But like a small hole in a dike, this small movement soon became a flood of people from all over Eastern Europe, and the Soviet Union did not move to plug the breach. Soon, it was pointless to try to blockade other borders; the iron curtain was being shredded. The Berlin Wall was deemed to serve no purpose and was no longer defended. Soon, mobs were physically tearing it down. The decade that began with talk of an "evil empire" ended with the Warsaw Pact dissolving, borders opening up across Europe, and Germany ready to forge ahead toward reunification.

Two years later, in 1991 the Soviet Union unraveled after a failed coup attempt against Gorbachev. The republics that made up the Union of Soviet Socialist Republics began to declare independence. The first to go were the small Baltic republics of Latvia, Lithuania, and Estonia, which had been forcibly pressed into the Russian Empire, briefly independent, and then reconquered by Stalin. When the republic of Russia itself, led by Boris Yeltsin, a Communist Party member known for divergent ideas, declared itself independent, the Soviet Union was over.

Some declared that the United States, NATO, and the Western alliance had triumphed. However, upon looking at the tremendous cost of the conflict—the hugely expensive arms race and the cost of proxy wars such as Afghanistan and Vietnam, which had bankrupted the Soviet Union and left the United States with a trillion-dollar deficit—it seemed that perhaps both sides had lost a great deal. As South Asia and the Middle East remain in turmoil, as Africa struggles to get rid of the legacy of cold war–supported dictatorships, and as Latin American commissions find new evidence of proxy "dirty wars" from this period, the shadows of this world war, like the two before, still cast a pall over the planet.

From World War to Regional Conflict

World War I ended with the creation of the League of Nations in 1919 and the hope that this new international alliance would keep the peace. The League was given little authority, the United States refused to join, and peace was short lived. World War II ended with the creation of the United Nations, as well as the International Monetary Fund (IMF) and the World Bank, and the hope that development, trade, and arbitration would replace global conflict. The cold war ended with the hope for a "new world order" and a "peace dividend" and saw the creation of organizations such as the World Trade Organization (WTO) to orchestrate this new world of prosperity and freedom.

In fact, the hope that World War I would be "the war to end all wars" was shattered by the rise of fascism and militaristic states. The hope of stemming global conflict at the end of the World War II was dimmed by the emergence of superpower rivalries. The optimism at the end of the cold war was soon beaten down by a world of regional conflicts and the rise of international terrorism.

Yugoslavia, a post–World War I creation, also came apart in the early 1990s—not peacefully but rather amid a vicious civil war characterized by atrocities such as **ethnic cleansing.** African conflicts were no longer strategic and were largely ignored until the Rwandan holocaust of 1994 claimed the lives of half a million people. New states often fell into the hands of authoritarian leaders who could not hope for world domination but often had old scores to settle with rivals and sought national glory and regional power through war and repression. While peace studies programs continued to emphasize U.S. and Russian relations and cold war ideas such as deference, it was becoming increasingly clear that a new world disorder of regional and civil conflicts was becoming the norm.

Regional conflicts and civil and ethnic strife have a long history, but they were often overshadowed by the rules of empires and superpowers. Rome tried to enforce a rule of order within its sphere of influence, the *Pax Romana*. Likewise, Ghengis Khan and his grandson, Kublai Khan, enforced peace and order within their vast domain even as they pursued conquests beyond it. The British saw their empire as extending order, decorum, and peace to a world of small rivalries. The United States and the Soviet Union both tried to bring a semblance of order and control to their spheres of influence. With these powers removed, old rivalries reemerged and new ones were created and manipulated by the ambitious.

Regional conflicts have always had a way of involving the prevailing power. In the middle of the first century BCE, the Roman General Pompey marched to put down unrest in the East (what we now call the Middle East), and his rival, General Caesar, marched to put down unrest in the West. Both ended up as conquerors who extended the empire to enforce the peace. During the height of their imperial era in the 1800s, the British often moved in to protect their commercial interests, stayed on to arbitrate regional conflicts, and remained as conquerors and administrators. This is essentially the story of the British takeover of India. During the 1900s, the United States often intervened in Latin America to protect its commercial interests and became heavily involved in regional conflicts as a result.

The spectre of **international terrorism** has now added a further dimension to regional conflicts: the threat that they might spawn terrorist actions that will be felt far away, most particularly in the great power centers. The dilemma remains, as the United States has found it very difficult to quickly restore order and then withdraw from places such as Afghanistan and Iraq. One of the great questions for the United States in the twenty-first century is whether it will try to impose order, a *Pax Americana*, as the world's great power (a few have used the now unpopular term of *empire*), or whether it will try again for multinational solutions and organizations.

Small-scale conflicts pose new problems for the global order (see Table 6.1). Most are civil wars, fought by factions within a particular country, but they typically spill over to destabilize entire regions. Fighting in Liberia spilled into Sierra Leone, which in turn led to conflict in the previously stable Ivory Coast. Wars in Central Africa have layered into one another, with factions in one country supporting and occasionally taking refuge with factions in another. Internal and regional conflicts are particularly prone to the use of terrorism as a weapon. Long before Al-Qaeda, Tamils fighting for independence in Sri Lanka "invented" the suicide bomber. In Colombia, long-standing battles among government forces, paramilitary forces supporting wealthy landowners, and two rival guerilla groups have turned the country into a bloodbath of war, terror, assassination, and drug traffic.

Often, it is difficult to tell where war, terrorism, and crime end, as each overlaps the other. One side's martyrs are another's terrorists; one side's freedom fighters are another's criminal gang. Civilians are often caught in both the acts of terror and the antiterror crackdowns in seemingly endless cycles, as has been seen in Northern Ireland and Sri Lanka and most recently in Israel–Palestine and Iraq. British actor and writer Peter Ustinov contended that "terrorism is the war of the poor and war is the terrorism of the rich" (Veterans for Peace 2003).

The preferred weapon for local warlords is often not weapons of mass destruction but children with automatic weapons (see Table 6.2). Watching rival bands of teenagers in West Africa, who wear oversized tee shirts and high-top athletic shoes and fire off irregular but lethal arrays of automatic small arms fire, it can be hard to tell if one is looking at a street gang or an army. In parts of northern Uganda, children spend the night huddled in bus stations and other public places in small cities, not because they are homeless but because their rural families send them into town for the night. In the rural areas, they are vulnerable to

TABLE 6.1	Significant Ongoing Armed Conflicts: 2004

Main Warring Parties	Year Began[1]
Middle East	
U.S. and UK vs. Iraq	2003
Israel vs. Palestinian Authority/Hamas/Hezbollah/Palestinian separatists	1948
Asia	
Afghanistan: U.S., UK, and Coalition Forces vs. al-Qaeda and Taliban	2001
India vs. Kashmiri separatist groups/Pakistan	1948
India vs. Assam insurgents (various)	1979
Indonesia vs. Aceh separatists[2]	1976
Indonesia vs. Christians and Muslims in Molucca Islands	1977
Indonesia vs. Irian Jaya separatists	1969
Nepal vs. Maoist rebels	1995
Philippines vs. Mindanaoan separatists (MILF/ASG)	1971
Africa	
Algeria vs. Armed Islamic Group (GIA)	1991
Burundi: Tutsi vs. Hutu	1988
Democratic Republic of Congo and allies vs. Rwanda, Uganda, and indigenous rebels[3]	1997
Somalia vs. rival clans	1991
Sudan vs. Darfur rebel groups	2003
Uganda vs. Lord's Resistance Army (LRA)	1986
Europe	
Russia vs. Chechen separatists	1994
Latin America	
Colombia vs. National Liberation Army (ELN)	1978
Colombia vs. Revolutionary Armed Forces of Colombia (FARC)	1978
Colombia vs. Autodefensas Unidas de Colombia (AUC)	1990

[1]Where multiple parties and long-standing but sporadic conflict are concerned, date of first combat deaths is given.
[2]2002 ceasefire abandoned; fighting resumed in May 2003.
[3]Ceasefire agreements signed in 2002, but violence continues.
Source: Center for Defense Information, www.cdi.org and Project Ploughshares, www.ploughshares.ca. Available online at http://print.infoplease.com/ipa/A0904550.html?mail-10-14.

the kidnappings of the Lord's Resistance Army. Once taken, the children are often tortured and forced to participate in killings and atrocities until they become calloused killers themselves with nowhere to go but on with the "army." Female soldiers face the added risk of sexual slavery in the armed camps.

TABLE 6.2	List of Countries with Child Soldiers Fighting in Recent and Ongoing Conflicts

Colombia (P,O)

Mexico (P,O)

Peru (O)

Russian Federation (O)

Turkey (O)

Yugoslavia (former Rep. of) (P,O)

Algeria (P,O)

Angola (G,O)

Burundi (G,O)

Chad (G)

Republic of Congo (G,O)

Dem. Rep. of the Congo (G,O)

Eritrea (G)

Ethiopia (G)

Rwanda (G,O)

Sierra Leone (G,P,O)

Somalia (all groups)

Sudan (G,P,O)

Uganda (G,O)

Iran (G,O)

Iraq (G,O)

Israel and Occupied Territories (G,O)

Lebanon (O)

Afghanistan (all groups)

India (P,O)

Indonesia (P,O)

Myanmar (G,O)

Nepal (O)

Pakistan (O)

Philippines (O)

Solomon Islands (O)

Sri Lanka (O)

East Timor (P,O)

Tajikistan (O)

Papua New Guinea (O)

Uzbekistan (O)

Note: G: government armed forces, P: paramilitaries, O: armed opposition groups.

Source: Available online at www.child-soldiers.org/cs/childsoldiers.nsf.

The face of war is ancient, but the faces of warriors are often very young, as seen here in the U.S. army and in boy soldiers in the Congo.

The Global Arms Trade

An added legacy of the cold war is a world awash in weapons. Not only did the United States and the Soviet Union arm themselves to extraordinary heights, but since they found it best not to confront one another directly, their preferred strategy was to arm client states in proxy wars. Soviet arms poured into the hands of leftist governments and rebel movements, while the United States armed right-wing governments as bastions against communism. Many of these weapons remain in circulation.

The deadliest weapon the world has ever known in terms of the sheer numbers of people killed is probably not high tech or a weapon of mass destruction but the lowly AK-47 Kalashnikov automatic rifle. It was designed by Mikhail Kalashnikov in 1947 for the Soviet army, which continued its production until 1960; after that, the other Warsaw Pact countries continued production. Bulgaria still makes and sells the Kalashnikov. There may still be 50 million of these weapons in the world.

Cheap, with an extraordinary rate of fire that makes them deadly at close range, they are the favorite of the world's small arms dealers and their many clients. The Vietcong used the AK-47 against the United States, and the Khmer Rouge used it to slaughter their own population. For a while, every leftist guerilla in Latin America carried an AK-47, and now every well-armed drug trafficker, whether rightist or leftist, carries the same weapon. Afghan warlords and their followers sleep with their Kalashnikovs, and they fill the black markets of Karachi, Pakistan. Somalis fighting for warlord Adid used AK-47s against the U.S. Rangers in Mogadishu, and Baath Party loyalists in Iraq attack with Kalashnikovs. In war-torn regions of West Africa, such as Liberia and Sierra Leone, an AK 47 can be purchased for as little as twenty dollars, less than a bag of rice. Even the poorest warlord can steal enough to arm a cadre of teenagers with enough AK-47s to terrorize a city.

From Baghdad to Bogata to Brazzaville, **small arms** refer to the ever-present combination of automatic assault weapons and rocket-propelled grenade launchers. While they are not much use against a tank, a lucky shot will bring down a helicopter. They are deadly weapons of terror against lightly armed opponents and civilians and bystanders of all types.

Some of the world's hand-held weapons are more sophisticated. Any minor arms dealer in Afghanistan can get you a Kalashnikov or a grenade launcher, but talk longer and bring out more foreign currency and maybe you can get a Stinger: a shoulder-fired, heat-seeking missile designed to bring down high-altitude aircraft. During the Soviet war in Afghanistan, the U.S. Central Intelligence Agency (CIA) found that one of the most effective ways to bleed the Soviet army and to support the *mujadeen* warriors was to supply them with Stingers,

The world weapons trade is big business, as seen here in the huge International Defense Exhibition arms market in Abu Dhabi in the Persian Gulf and in a well-equipped local market vendor in Iraq.

since the Soviets depended on airpower and air supply to fight across the vast, rugged terrain. It proved a remarkably effective tool of guerilla warfare. The only problem is that there is no way to collect up all the Stingers at the conflict's end and bring them home. The high-tech Stinger is not much good in urban combat, unless one's opponent has helicopters, but it would make a lethal weapon for terrorists to use on a civilian aircraft. No one knows how many Stingers are still in circulation.

Small arms are sold by any number of international arms traffickers (see Table 6.3). Larger weapons are sold by governments to allies and increasingly to the highest bidder. Eastern Europe inherited a Soviet arms industry that remains in demand around the world and provides an important source of income. Old-style Soviet and Eastern European automobiles are not exactly popular collectors' items around the world, but many governments are glad to get a good buy on a Russian-style tank. Cheap and durable, old Soviet bloc arms continue to travel the globe.

By far, however, the world's foremost arms supplier is the United States. While many U.S.-manufactured goods have lost ground to foreign competition, U.S.-made arms are still the world standard. Some of these weapons are provided as aid packages

TABLE 6.3	Top Arms-Exporting Countries: 2002

Country	Total Arms Exports (CRS)[1]
USA	$10,241m
UK	$4,700m
Russia	$3,100m
France	$1,800m
China	$800m
Ukraine	$600m
Germany	$500m
Italy	$400m
Israel	$300m

[1]CRS is the Congressional Research Service in the U.S. Figures are taken from a report on arms transfers by Richard F. Grimmett, 22 September 2003, and are in current US dollars.

Source: Available online at www.caat.org.uk/ information/facts-figures/faf-top-arms-exporters.php.

to allied governments. Many, however, are sold to bring earnings as exported goods. The most favored customers are friendly governments that also can pay in cash. Many of the biggest buyers are in the Middle East (see Table 6.4).

The most coveted weapons import, and one with strong U.S. dominance (although there is competition from France, Russia, and even Israel), is the fighter–bomber, a high-speed strike aircraft that can quickly reach targets in a neighboring country or in a remote or rebellious part of a leader's own country. The Gulf, Afghan, and Iraq Wars have all demonstrated the tremendous might of airpower. Before that Israel used U.S.-made strike aircraft to lethal effect against its many Arab enemies.

For many years, the most highly demanded aircraft has been the Lockheed–Martin F-16. There are over 2,000 in the U.S. Air Force and another 2,000 in the air forces of twenty-three other countries (Air Force Technology 2003), but new competitors continue to enter the showroom of this profitable market. Like a classic car, this 1979 fighter keeps buyers coming back with new models that offer a wide-ranging package of options: air-conditioned cockpits, HARM antiradar missiles, stand-off air-to-air missiles, Harpoon antiship missiles, global positioning systems, JDAM satellite-guided bombs, laser-targeting pods, as well as more powerful engines and larger payload capacity. Israel flies more F-16s than any other country besides the United States; in 2003, it put in an order for another 110 planes.

One reason a small country needs so many is that its Arab neighbors continue to order more. A full eighty F-16s, complete with the latest and most powerful General Electric–built engines, went to the tiny United Arab Emirates in

TABLE 6.4	Top Arms Importers and Their Suppliers—Average Annual Figures: 1998–2001

Importer: LATIN AMERICA $0.7 bn		Importer: ASIA $8 bn	
USA	59%	USA	40%
UK	0%	UK	7%
Russia	7%	Russia	24%
France	7%	France	17%
China	0%	China	3%

Importer: AFRICA $0.9 bn		Importer: NORTH AFRICA/MIDDLE EAST $12 bn	
USA	3%	USA	46%
UK	3%	UK	27%
Russia	31%	Russia	4%
France	0%	France	11%
China	14%	China	0.8%

Source: Available online at www.amnestyusa.org/arms_trade/whoisbuying.html. Used by permission.

TABLE 6.5	Top Ten Arms Importers: The Industrializing and Least Industrialized Nations, 1997

Nation	Amount Purchased
1. Saudi Arabia	$22,555,000,000
2. Egypt	$4,495,000,000
3. South Korea	$3,505,000,000
4. Turkey	$3,020,000,000
5. Greece	$2,195,000,000
6. Kuwait	$2,055,000,000
7. Malaysia	$1,920,000,000
8. Iran	$1,780,000,000
9. United Arab Emirates	$1,735,000,000
10. China	$1,610,000,000

Source: Based on *Statistical Abstract of the United States 1998,* Table 576.

2004. Some U.S. allies receive these as part of military aid packages, while others, including petroleum-producing states, can pay as they go (see Table 6.5).

Weapons of Mass Destruction

While conventional arms continue to provide most of the carnage in war zones, new attention has been given to what have become known as **weapons of mass destruction (WMD)**. This term is something of a misnomer. Conventional weapons—such as those dropped from the bombers of World War II, the huge payloads that can be dropped from large bombers such as the B-52 in carpet-bombing campaigns, and the Pentagon's 22,000-pound MOAB (nicknamed "mother of all bombs")—are clearly weapons of mass destruction, but they are not placed in this category. At the same time, chemical and biological weapons are really weapons of mass casuality, but they cause little physical destruction. For a while, these were included as "nonconventional" weapons or ABC (atomic, biological, and chemical) weapons. But the WMD designation has captured the popular imagination, and so the name has remained.

Chemical Weapons

Chemicals have a long history in warfare. The Byzantine Empire defended its shores for close to 1,000 years with a secret substance known as "Greek fire," probably a modified petroleum product a bit like napalm, that burst into flame when it hit water. Regardless of whether it actually sank ships, it certainly terrified enemy sailors.

Incendiaries, chemicals that burst into intense flames that are difficult to extinguish, were used with devasting effect against German and Japanese cities in World War II. Capable of consuming whole cities, they were certainly weapons of mass destruction but were not considered chemical weapons in the same category as poison gas (though huge fires kill many with toxic smoke and fumes). Incendiaries were also used in Vietnam; one of the most famous photos of the time shows a young girl burn victim, fleeing naked from a burning village. Vietnam also saw the use of **defoliants,** chemical agents such as Agent Orange that cause the leaves to fall from the trees and so make hidden troops more visible from the air. Agent Orange has been shown to have many enduring toxic effects, but again, it was not considered poison gas.

The first large-scale use of poison gas was during World War I. The German army began an attack on trenches with the release of green chlorine gas. The lung-searing effects of this strange new weapon sent the defenders fleeing in panic and sent both sides in the war scrambling for more chemicals. One of the favored chemicals was **mustard gas,** a heavier-than-air yellow vapor that sank into enemy trenches. After both sides equipped their forces with gas masks, the gas proved less effective but added one more dimension of horror and misery to trench warfare. Recognition of this led to agreements to ban the use of poison gas after the war, a ban that was observed throughout World War II, perhaps in part because these weapons were not well suited to highly mobile warfare, where attackers find themselves driving right into their poison clouds. Following this war, the United States and the Soviet Union both developed far more deadly chemical weapons, especially new types of nerve agents that killed on contact and could be loaded into bombs, artillery shells, or missiles.

While the world has lived with the threat of incredibly lethal chemicals ever since, their use has been very limited. Communist forces may have used poisons late in the war in Laos. There is good evidence that in Afghanistan, the Soviet Union used **mycotoxins,** mold-based poisons that caused what Afghans called "the bloody diarrhea." When the Iran–Iraq war of the late 1970s and early 1980s fell into trench warfare, Saddam Hussein turned to World War I–vintage mustard gas. When the Kurds in the north of Iraq rebelled following the 1991 Gulf War, he attacked their villages with poison gas from the air in strikes more aimed at spreading terror than defeating armed forces. The United States and Great Britain soon imposed a no-fly zone over the region, enforced by fighter aircraft based in Turkey, and this remained an isolated incident.

While chemical weapons in the form of poison gas have limited use on the battlefield, especially against well-equipped and highly mobile opponents, they do offer great terror value against civilians. The horrors of a chemical release were seen in Bhopal, India, in 1984 where an accidental release from a U.S.-owned chemical plant quickly killed 500. The Soviet Union appears to have suffered several deadly accidents in its chemical weapons programs, which were carefully covered up by the state security apparatus. In 1995, a Japanese religious cult released sarin nerve gas in the Tokyo subway, causing death and confusion.

Many small countries have been interested in chemical weapons, "the poor man's nuclear bomb," since they are cheap to produce yet can inspire fear in potential enemies. One of the greatest fears is that these weapons will be secured by a terrorist group for use in a major urban area.

Biological Weapons

A top-secret aircraft carrier submarine slips close to the California coast. When it surfaces, small bombers with collapsible wings are lifted to its deck. The planes take off and fly over San Diego, where they release their payloads of clay-shelled bombs. The bombs burst open at low altitude, showering the ground with fleas—fleas contaminated with the deadly bubonic plague, "the black death." The fleas bite inhabitants, and soon a terrible scourge of plague is devastating the city.

This is not the plot of the latest James Bond movie or *Matrix* remake. It was an actual attack plan of the Japanese army in 1945, never carried out because the Japanese navy wanted to save its secret submarines for launching *kamikaze* attacks in defense of the home islands. Japan had already secretly used these biological weapons with terrible effect in China, killing unknown thousands. At the time, it was claimed as a naturally occurring disease. At the same time, of course, the United States was working on its own top-secret program of mass destruction, the **Manhattan Project,** and nuclear bombs drove Japan to surrender before the decision to attack with infected fleas and a variety of other deadly biological weapons could be reconsidered.

As biotechnology expands, new concern grows about **biological weapons:** deadly strains of viruses and bacteria that could be spread over a large area or set in motion to spread themselves. Disease has always been a deadly enemy. Attila the Hun had to abandon his invasion of Italy and planned capture of Rome in part because his army was ravaged by the plague in 452. The defenders also believed it to be a divine reprieve.

Disease can also work against defenders. In the Peloponnesian War, Athens's defense against Sparta collapsed in the 420s BCE when a plague (perhaps typhus), arriving on supply ships, ravaged the crowded masses within the walls, killing civilians, soldiers, and even their leader, Pericles. Socrates saw in this horror more of human folly than divine justice. Cortes was able to seize the Aztec capital of Tenochtitlan (now Mexico City) in 1540 in part because the Aztec defenders were ravaged by a smallpox epidemic that killed their emperor and decimated the crowded and besieged city. When the Spanish were largely spared the ravages of this European disease, to which they had partial immunity, it seemed as though their god must be mightier than the patron god of the Aztecs. Likewise, Pizarro and a handful of Spanish adventurers were able to conquer the Incan Empire in part because the Inca were also being decimated by smallpox, which had likewise killed their emperor.

Although in each of these cases, microbes decided the war, none of them were intended actions. Rumors of intended biological warfare have persisted. In 1347, Mongol invaders reportedly shot the corpses of plague victims over the walls of a Crimean fort to spread the disease to the defenders (Weatherford 1994). Whether the plague arrived by catapult or had previously entered through traders, this terrible disease swept into Europe from Central Asia and killed over one-third of the population of the continent before it subsided.

There are multiple accounts of Europeans and Americans attempting to spread smallpox to Native Americans through gifts and trades of infected blankets. Whether such an act of germ warfare ever occurred and whether it was effective (since smallpox travels best person to person) is questionable. What is clear is that smallpox and related infections decimated the native peoples of the Americas and later the Pacific, killing perhaps 90 percent of the original population (Diamond 1997).

The very idea of using biological weapons only made sense in the context of total war and now in the context of terrorism. Pathogens and germs are not easy to control and don't act quickly enough to be useful on the battlefield (even though in both the American Civil War and World War I, the greatest killer was the infection of conventional wounds). These organisms do, however, have tremendous potential for terror and disruption. A minute quantity, easily concealed, could have tremendous impact, especially if it began a chain reaction of contagion.

Key problems have been the issues of storage and dispersal. This is what the Imperial Japanese Army hoped to do with clay bombs and small explosive charges—to spread but not kill the infected fleas. **Anthrax**—a disease caused by a bacterium that can remain dormant for a long period in spore form and then become active once inhaled into warm, wet lungs—has long been favored as a potential weapon and was studied and stockpiled by both the United States and the Soviet Union. Its use in the U.S. mail in 2002 showed both the power and the limits of biological weapons. Anthrax is not highly contagious between people and does respond to certain antibiotics, if treated quickly. Deaths were limited to a handful of early victims who came in contact with contaminated mail. The act completely disrupted the U.S. Postal System, however, and had the attacks continued, they could have disrupted all mail service and the U.S. economy for a very long time. The fact that the agent was a minute powder, easily concealed in envelopes, added to the fear factor and the difficulty of tracing its source.

Other pathogens are harder to control but could be deadlier. By the 1980s, the U.N. World Health Organization had eradicated smallpox, the scourge of the planet for centuries. Since the virus can only live in humans, it became extinct "in the wild" once a worldwide vaccination campaign reached the last villages. It still lived in laboratories in the Soviet Union and the United States, however. Both claimed research purposes but also seemed to worry that the other might try to reintroduce it as a weapon of war. Now, over twenty years later, most of the world is no longer being vaccinated against smallpox and a release of the virus, if it still exists somewhere, could be catastrophic. (Remember the 90 percent fatality estimate among Native Americans). A 1980s triumph, the first complete eradication of a disease by human effort, is now a twenty-first century mystery: Does it remain somewhere, and could someone try to reintroduce it? The prospect is unlikely, but as with the anthrax scare, the power of an unknown, unseen killer has ample chilling effect.

Nuclear Weapons

The weapon that completely changed the face of war—the ultimate weapon of mass destruction, capable of destroying whole cities, whole nations, and maybe life itself—is the power of the atomic nucleus, first harnessed and used during World War II. The United States held a brief nuclear monopoly from 1945 to 1949, and then the Soviet Union surprised the world by testing its first nuclear device. The **nuclear arms race** had begun. The United States then raised the stakes by testing a thermonuclear weapon, a **hydrogen bomb.**

The first weapons worked through **nuclear fission,** in which a heavy, unstable nucleus of uranium or plutonium was split, releasing the energy of thousands of tons of conventional explosives. Thermonuclear weapons began with a fission bomb to generate the huge amount of heat needed to fuse hydrogen into helium. This is the process that drives the sun. Such a weapon could release enormous amounts of destructive energy. Again, the Soviet Union raced to catch up and tested its own hydrogen bomb. Then the bombs became bigger. One Soviet bomb tested was the equivalent of 50 million tons of conventional explosives, or 4,000 times the power of the bomb that destroyed Hiroshima.

The delivery method for these weapons was the intercontinental bomber and carrier-based aircraft, but developing technology in the 1950s produced the **intercontinental ballistic missile (ICBM),** which could be launched from one continent to devastate another. By the early 1960s, the United States had thousands of these weapons, while the Soviet Union only had a handful. There was also a reversal in geographic advantage: The position of the Soviet Union on the edge of Europe meant that most of its armed conventional forces could quickly rush into a European war, which meant the United States had to base forces in Europe or move them across the Atlantic. But it also meant that U.S.-based midrange missiles in Europe could easily strike Soviet territory. The Soviets attempted to gain a similar advantage by placing missiles in Cuba, within close range of the United States.

The resulting crisis produced a classic cold war stalemate. The United States spotted the missile emplacements (it regularly spied on Cuba with U2 aircraft) and demanded their removal. Cuba was blockaded, and U.S. military leaders wanted to bomb the installations before they were operational. Publically, U.S. President John F. Kennedy and Soviet leader Nikita Khrushchev sounded stern and uncompromising. But we now know from their private statements that they secretly wondered if they were blundering into a war that would massacre millions in its first hours. Krushchev pulled the Soviet missiles from Cuba, and Kennedy secretly agreed to remove the U.S. missiles from Turkey, a NATO ally on the Soviet border.

The conflict showed the madness that had entered the world. Both powers had tremendous weapons and were spending huge sums building ever more massive weapons and farther-flung delivery systems. Yet neither side dared to use its weapons. Which side had more and better weapons, a crucial question in all prior conflicts, mattered little when each side had the capability of utterly destroying the other. The policy that resulted was **deterrence,** having the weapons to make sure the other side did not use theirs in a stalemate of mutually assured destruction. This was always an uneasy stalemate, for each side also worried that its massive weapons would be vulnerable to a first strike. Hiding missiles underwater in moving submarines was one answer to this problem, but it only added to the nightmarish quality of the situation: boats like the U.S. Trident submarine, a true doomsday machine, lurking underwater with enough firepower on them to destroy every major city on the planet. Tension mounted in the early 1980s, as the United States accelerated its arms spending, and some members of the Reagan administration spoke of the possibility of a winnable nuclear war. The demise of the Soviet Union brought a moment's respite, as tension eased between the two powers and both relaxed their nuclear readiness.

The problem was that the nuclear "club" was expanding. Both France and Great Britain conducted nuclear tests in the 1950s. China was added in the 1960s. Israel and South Africa secretly developed nuclear weapons in the 1970s and 1980s. The 1990s saw some hopeful signs. One was that Brazil, Argentina, and Algeria all abandoned their nuclear programs. In addition, the new republics that inherited the Soviet nuclear weapons chose to give them up. South Africa dismantled its nuclear arsenal and signed the Nuclear Nonproliferation Treaty.

But new dangers also emerged. India and Pakistan abandoned their pledge not to develop nuclear weapons, and each tested weapons designed to intimate or at least warn the other. Most troubling was that nations with reckless prior records and with possible ties to terrorism became interested in nuclear weapons. Iraq's nuclear program was halted first by an Israeli bombing raid in 1981 and then again by the Gulf War and weapons inspections in 1991. A U.N. program similarly thwarted Libya's interest in nuclear weapons. Iran continues a nuclear weapons program, and North Korea has tested missiles and claims to be very close to nuclear capability. Other countries may decide to follow this path, and the availability of lost or poorly protected nuclear materials worries those who believe they could be acquired by terrorists.

TABLE 6.6	States Possessing, Pursuing, or Capable of Acquiring Weapons of Mass Destruction: 2000			

State	Nuclear	Chemical	Biological	Missile
Algeria	X			
Belarus	X			
Bulgaria			X	
Chile		X		
China	X	X	X	X
Cuba			X	
Ethiopia		X		
Egypt		X	X	X
France	X	X		X
India	X	X	X	X
Indonesia		X		
Iran	X	X	X	X
Iraq	X	X	X	X
Israel	X	X	X	X
Kazakhstan	X			
Laos		X	X	
Libya		X	X	X
Myanmar		X		
North Korea	X	X	X	X
Pakistan	X	X	X	X
Romania			X	
Russia	X	X	X	X
Serbia	X	X		

Table 6.6 provides an overview of which countries possess or seek WMD: nuclear, chemical, and biological weapons as well as missiles to deliver them.

Military Expenditures

"Every gun that is made, every warship launched, every rocket fired signifies, in the final sense, a theft from those who hunger and are not fed, those who are cold and are not clothed."

—President Dwight D. Eisenhower, April 16, 1953

Interestingly, one of the first U.S. leaders to raise concern over the cost of military spending was President Eisenhower, a former World War II general, as he looked at the rising costs of the cold war. In his farewell speech as president on

TABLE 6.6	Continued

State	Nuclear	Chemical	Biological	Missile
South Africa	X	X	X	X
South Korea		X	X	x
Sudan		X		
Syria		X	X	X
Taiwan		X	X	X
Thailand		X		
Ukraine	X			
Vietnam		X	X	
United Kingdom	X	X		X
United States	X	X	X	X

Note: Not every state listed here is actively pursuing or proliferating WMD systems, nor is the list necessarily complete.

Source: Table available online at www.fas.org/irp/threat/wmd_state.htm. Original sources include:
• *A Chemical Weapons Atlas* By E. J. Hogendoorn *Bulletin of the Atomic Scientists* September/October 1997 Vol. 53, No. 5
• *Chemical and Biological Weapons: Possession and Programs Past and Present*
• "The Specter of Biological Weapons" by Leonard A. Cole *Scientific American* December 1996
• Defense Nuclear Agency, *Biological Weapons Proliferation* (Ft. Detrick, Md.: US Army Medical Research Institute of Infectious Diseases, April 1994), page 46.
• *Sources on Tables Listing Countries of Chemical and Biological Weapon Concern Proliferation of Weapons of Mass Destruction: Assessing the Risks* Office of Technology Assessment OTA-ISC-559, 1994 [Angola, Argentina, Brazil, Chad, Cuba, El Salvador, Mozambique, Nicaragua, Peru, and Phillipines are mentioned by a few cited sources as posessing chemical weapons, but most sources do not include them as chemical weapon states, which would bring the total to 29 chemical weapons states].

January 17, 1961, Eisenhower both defended the need to contain the Soviet Union and expressed open worry over the consequences of that effort:

> This conjunction of an immense military establishment and a large arms industry is new in the American experience. The total influence—economic, political, even spiritual—is felt in every city, every State house, every office of the Federal government. We recognize the imperative need for this development. Yet we must not fail to comprehend its grave implications. Our toil, resources and livelihood are all involved; so is the very structure of our society.
>
> In the councils of government, we must guard against the acquisition of unwarranted influence, whether sought or unsought, by the military–industrial complex. The potential for the disastrous rise of misplaced power exists and will persist. (*Public Papers of the Presidents, Dwight D. Eisenhower 1960–61,* pp. 1035–1040).

American sociologist C. Wright Mills (1957) wrote about this **military–industrial complex** that he believed was dominating U.S. society. He saw military leaders, corporate leaders who often depended on military contracts, and political leaders who depended on cold war fears for their positions as forming a power elite that controlled the U.S. economic agenda. Spending by the U.S. military continued to grow and reached a peak during the Vietnam War. It declined, especially in real-dollar amounts, somewhat during the late 1970s. New concerns about the Soviet Union and an attempt to deal with perceived threats through new military superiority during the Reagan administration again lead to a rise in military spending. Military spending in the United States declined following the breakup of the Soviet Union and the end of the cold war. The rise of global terrorism brought a huge increase in U.S. military spending following the attacks of September 11, 2001. The United States was already spending more on arms than all of its adversaries combined. By 2005, the United States was spending as much on its military as the rest of the world combined (see Table 6.7).

TABLE 6.7	Largest Military Expenditures, 2003[1]			
Rank	Country	Level[2] ($ billions)	Per Capita ($)	World Share (%)
1.	United States	$417.4	$1,419	47%
2.	Japan	46.9	367	5
3.	United Kingdom	37.1	627	4
4.	France	35.0	583	4
5.	China	32.8[3]	25	4
6.	Germany	27.2	329	3
7.	Italy	20.8	362	2
8.	Iran[4]	19.2	279	2
9.	Saudi Arabia	19.1	789	2[3]
10.	South Korea	$13.9	$292	2%
11.	Russia	13.0[3]	91	1
12.	India	12.4	12	1
13.	Israel	10.0	1,551	1
14.	Turkey	9.9	139	1
15.	Brazil	9.2	51	1
	Subtotal top 15	723.8		82
	World	879.0		100

1. At market exchange rate.
2. Figures are in U.S. $ billions, at constant (2000) prices and exchange rates.
3. Stockholm International Peace Research Institute (SIPRI) estimates.
4. Data for Iran includes expenditure for public order and safety and is a slight overestimate.

Source: SIPRI Yearbook 2004, Stockholm International Peace Research Institute.

The Last Great War?

German novelist Hermann Hesse, who often wrote of war, speculated that perhaps war, like slavery, would someday be gone from human history. Historian John Mueller (1993) contends that war is a "thoroughly bad and repulsive idea, like dueling or slavery, subrationally unthinkable and therefore obsolescent" (p. 214). Already, formal war, like formal slavery, is disappearing. Yet the end of formal war has not brought world peace, any more than the end of formal slavery brought global economic justice.

Can we build a more peaceful world? The issue is practical as well as philosophical: It is not that violence is nasty and nonviolence is nice. Rather, it is simply that reliance on violence is no longer practical. According to Jonathan Schell (2003):

> If an evil god had turned human society into an infernal laboratory to explore the utmost extremes of violence, short only of human extinction, he could scarcely have improved upon the history of the twentieth century. Totalitarian rule and total war each in its own way carried violence to it limits—reaching what we can call total violence, as distinct from the technically restricted violence of earlier times. Violence was old, but total violence—violence that, as in nuclear conflict, can kill without limit, reaching no decision, no point of return—was new. Rule, when it resorted to total violence, turned out no longer to be rule, for rule is domination over living human beings, and the totalitarian regimes, in their most ferocious epochs, became factories of corpses. (pp. 3–4)

Schell sees hope in the emergence of so-called people-power movements, which are not easily stopped by force. Examples of this are inspiring but uncertain. People power succeeded in toppling the corrupt Marcos regime in the Philippines in the 1980s (where the term was coined) and reversed a corrupt election in the Ukraine in 2004–2005. The crucial moment in both, however, came with the defection to the opposition of key military and security leaders, something that was rumored but never occurred in China's Tiananmen Square uprising.

Others, such as Samuel Huntington (1996), see hope in the triumph of democracy. Allied leaders in both world wars saw themselves as advancing a struggle for democracy that would eventually lead to a more peaceful world, since democracies, where people have some say in their fate, seem less prone to plunging into war than do dictatorships. The Bush administration's doctrine justifying the war in Iraq is based in part on the idea that spreading democracy, even by force, ultimately will bring a more peaceful world. Others worry that part of the Bush doctrine is a new emphasis on **pre-emptive strikes,** attacking a foe in expectation of what might be done in the future, such as the development and use of weapons of mass destruction. The early days of World War I, and in some sense even the

Pearl Harbor attack of World War II, have often been justified by their proponents as pre-emptive strikes to weaken future foes. Neither of these actions, of course, prevented war but led to a chain reaction of expanding warfare.

Others see hope in globalization and the increasing economic interconnection of countries that would make war too risky and too expensive to consider. *New York Times* commentator Thomas Friedman (1999) describes an only partly tongue-in-cheek "golden arches theory of conflict prevention," noting that no two countries with McDonald's restaurants have gone to war against each other. Can it be that simple? Did Baghdad only need a "Happy Meal" to turn things around? Friedman may have a point in the broadest sense that while globalization can stir hatred that breeds instability and civil conflict (Chua 2003), it may make large nations eager to maintain peace and stability, if only to protect world stock markets.

In his book *The Pentagon's New Map*, Thomas Barnett (2004), of the U.S. Naval War College, contends that the world is divided into a **functioning core** linked by globalization and a **nonintegrating gap,** a large swath around the equator that includes most of Africa as well as the Middle East and parts of Southeast Asia, that incubate terrorism and conflict. This is where the world's wars and military interventions continue. The goal of war and interventions, as well as economic policy, he contends, is to shrink this gap. Yet Yale law professor Amy Chua (2003) contends that it is the very attempt to export free-market democracy that is breeding ethnic hatred and global instability. Both may be right, such that the result will not be a great global war but instead a "world on fire" with many smaller conflicts.

In the 1990s, the military task of the United States and its NATO Allies (Canada and much of Western Europe, at the time) shifted from containing the Soviet Union and winning any sort of conventional battle to peacekeeping assignments and interventions in regional conflicts and human rights crises, such as occurred with the breakup of Yugoslavia. Africa continues to provide situations in which Western powers are called on to intervene, sometimes in their own former colonies: Somalia, Rwanda, Liberia, Sierra Leone, Sudan. The tasks associated with peacekeeping can be very different from the challenges of fighting and winning a war, as the United States has found in its occupation of Iraq.

Sometimes, the call for assistance is for natural, rather than humanmade, disasters. Following the terrible destruction in Southeast Asia caused by the tsunami wave of late 2004, many nations not only pledged financial help but used their naval and military air transport capabilities to rush in relief supplies. The U.S. military, with an extensive network of air transport, was particularly needed. Some see this type of effort as a great distraction from the military's main duties. Yet the logistical challenges of natural disasters—rushing in supplies, maintaining communications, moving personnel, keeping the peace, and restoring order—are very similar to the logistical challenges of war. The U.S. National Guard has been used in cases of natural disaster, civil disturbance, and international conflict. Humanitarian relief is still a small task, however, compared to the global investment in military preparedness. The United States pledged $383 million for tsunami relief in 2005, or just over $1 million a day, at a time that it was spending over $1 billion a day—a thousand times the tsunami effort—on general defense spending and close to another $1 billion per day on the Iraq conflict.

Less than one-quarter of the world's military spending would be enough to meet the total U.N. estimate for international development, well-being, and poverty elimination: health, housing, education, and environmental protection. One wonders if such a shift in priorities would not also lead to a much more stable and less conflict-prone planet.

MAKING CONNECTIONS

Peace Groups

- Student interest in war and peace peaked in the 1960s, when many college students faced the possibility of military draft and serving in the Vietnam War. The conflicts in Iraq and the Middle East have renewed interest in peace movements. Are there peace groups on your campus? If so, what forms do they take? Do they have religious or spiritual themes? Are they politically active? Do they include social justice themes or domestic issues in violence?

United for Peace and Justice

- This rapidly growing group serves as a clearinghouse for hundreds of peace groups around the country. See their site at www.unitedforpeace.org. Their issues of concern include Iraq, Israel and Palestine, nuclear disarmament, global justice, and immigrant rights. See if there are activities near you. What groups are involved? What are their current campaigns and activities?

CHAPTER 7

Democracy and Human Rights
Having Our Say

Monrovia, Liberia

Former Liberian President Charles Taylor, indicted on war crimes charges that include the massacre of villagers and the mutilation of children, is condemned almost everywhere in the world. Everywhere except on the *700 Club,* that is. Pat Robertson—U.S. televangelist, entrepreneur, Christian Coalition political activist, and one-time candidate for president—has used the show to praise Taylor and to denounce actions (including U.S. actions) to oust him. "We are trying to oust a fine Christian man, a Baptist, and bring in Muslim rebels. We have no right to do this," contends Robertson. Taylor, who is wanted for atrocities in three countries besides his own (and still wanted for common crimes committed while hiding in the United States) and head of a government that routinely tortures and rapes its own citizens for participating in peaceful protests, "is a fine Christian" and being wrongfully targeted?

Robertson has portrayed the conflict in Liberia as one between Christians and Muslims (in fact, religion has not been a major factor) and calls on his listeners to side with the Christians. Critics note another possible reason for his support: Robertson is the president and major investor in Freedom Gold, a gold mining venture in Liberia made possible by special deals with Taylor, who gets 10 percent of the profits.

What has Taylor done with his take from Freedom Gold? *The Washington Post* (November 2, 2001) and *U.S. News and World Report* (November 12, 2001) reported that he was using the money to invest in diamond production in neighboring Sierra Leone, mined illegally by rebels. The RUF rebels of Sierra Leone recruited young boys, but these were no Boy Scout leaders: Children were kidnaped, sometimes forced to murder their own parents, sent into battle high on "speed" amphetamine drugs that made them feel invincible and kept them addicted, and encouraged to mutilate victims. Ritual cannibalism has been reported, as well. Who would deal with such a group? Reportedly, Al-Qaeda operatives working for Osama bin Laden carried on a lucrative secret trade, selling the diamonds at great profit in the diamond markets in Vienna and (added irony) Tel Aviv. The profits go to support terrorist activity in support of Al-Qaeda's Islamic extremist revolt against what it calls "crusader (European and U.S. activity) and Zionist" (the movement to establish Israel as Jewish homeland) interests everywhere.

Pat Robertson wasn't the only U.S. religious and political leader to have ties to Taylor and the RUF rebels. In the late 1990s, the Reverend Jesse Jackson also paid them friendly visits and encouraged forming closer ties. Only Robertson continued the ties to the very end, however insisting that his business interests were intended only to help the people of West Africa and to spread the gospel. Charles Taylor contends that he is a man of God who has been slandered and misunderstood. Osama bin Laden is hard to reach for comment. Is this a story about religious fervor, commercial greed, political power, historical hatred, ethnic rivalry, international and domestic terrorism, or media manipulation? Quite likely, there are elements of each of these factors, all of which have become entangled in the conflicts of the twenty-first century.

Guantanamo Bay, Cuba

This U.S. naval base on the island of Cuba dates back to days when the United States largely controlled what happened on the island. The United States acquired a long-term lease to the land in 1903 and refuses to give it back to Fidel Castro. The U.S. government pays rent for the space, but Castro angrily refuses to cash the checks.

Following the September 11, 2001, terrorist attacks and the war in Afghanistan, the United States has been keeping prisoners at Guantanamo. Unlike typical prisoners, many of the detained do not know the charges against them, most have no legal council, and the few lawyers involved do not know the charges against the detained. In fact, these people are not considered prisoners of war and thus are not subject to rules regulating such prisoners. The U.S. government claims they are "enemy combatants," a unique status that provides neither the usual protections of civil detainees nor those accorded to prisoners of war.

To try to extract information from the prisoners in their wire "cages" at Guantanamo, they are interrogated. The U.S. government says that it does not allow torture but that prisoners may be placed in "stressful" conditions. This seems to include heat, sleep deprivation, and ridicule—and sex. In some cases, women from private contractors have reserved provocative clothing to use to tease and taunt male detainees during their investigations. In one case, when a detainee refused to open his eyes or to stop praying as a woman touched herself and him, she sought outside advice. Hearing that menstrual blood would make the man ritually unclean under the rules of Islam, she put red ink on him and had his water turned off, telling him that he was marked with blood and would "enjoy the night" with no way to wash it off.

Do such actions constitute torture? They are less severe than the forms of abuse and intimidation that took place at Abu Ghraib Prison in Iraq, yet they are not what one associates with detention and questioning in a democratic society. Does the need of a society to protect itself from terrorism allow for the suspension of the usual rules of arrest and prosecution? Both Canada and Great Britain have used similar patterns of indefinite detention in other locations, and both have been challenged in the courts as violating basic human rights.

Nationalism and the Nation–State

War is only one form of state violence. Often, the worst forms of violence are perpetrated against a nation's own citizens and residents. It may be the bloody violence of a massacre or execution or the more subtle violence of exclusion and repression. The violence within and the search for alternatives is the topic of the next two chapters.

Imperialism drove the nineteenth century; nationalism drove the twentieth. **Nationalism** is the intense belief in the worth, rightness, and glory of one's own nation. **Nation** is itself a slippery term. Used in the context of the *League of Nations* or the *United Nations, nation* simply means an independent entity with full sovereignty; it answers to no higher power, except as it may freely enter into treaties. **Sovereignty,** as we will see, is also a slippery concept. Does it mean a nation can do what it wants, or are we all answerable to a higher moral or social order?

There is an older root of the word *nation* captured in the word *nationality:* people who share customs and culture, maybe language, and certainly identity— an ethnic group. The Latin root of the word refers to *birth,* as one is born into the nation, and implies this older meaning of ethnic identity. Political scientists often prefer to refer to a sovereign government entity as a **state.** For an anthropologist, a *state* is an entity with centralized power and coercive force, something more than a tribe.

I have used the term *state* in these latter two meanings in the last chapter. This can be confusing, though, since people in the United States of America and in Mexico use *state* to refer to a subnational entity, such as a province (and it certainly wouldn't help matters if the *United Nations* starting calling itself the *United States!*). The two terms can be combined as **nation–state,** which is, strictly speaking, a sovereign entity that represents the interests of people who share a common culture, presumably a common language, as well as a common territory.

The trouble for our taxonomy is that this term no longer fits many places, most of which have multiple cultures sharing one land. A single land with a single culture and ethnicity perhaps describes tiny nation–states, such as Slovenia, but not even Belgium and certainly not Switzerland. Japan comes close but certainly not the United States. The nation–state is a fairly recent invention, and it may already be disappearing.

From Bands to States

The simplest way people have organized themselves is what anthropologists call a **band.** It's a small group of people working and traveling together. Hunter–gathers, (what's left of them) often live in seminomadic bands. They don't and can't control all the territory they use. Their decisions are collective, or made by the group. From what we can still see of bands in equatorial Africa and a few remote places, some are obviously more articulate and persuasive than others. These groups are really all adult members—young and old, men and women. This doesn't mean perfect harmony; sometimes it might look more like a contentious family gathering, with sarcasm, insults, and old grievances. All are involved, however. It is participatory democracy.

Once a human group settles down to tend gardens, practice horticulture, or raise animals (which is called **pastoralism**) and the population of the group grows, band leadership becomes more difficult. Not everyone can be heard in one meeting. There are new responsibilities: Horticulturalists have land, often communally owned, to defend, and pastoralists have herds to defend. These groups are often governed as **tribes**. Tribes have recognized leaders who speak for them to other groups and who come together to judge disputes, mark off land, punish offenders, and defend territory. They typically have little permanent power beyond their ability to gather followers and the prestige they have gained over the years.

The tribes most familiar to North Americans are the Native American groups that originally occupied the continent. Some have called these people "the first nations," but they were not nation–states; they were sovereign tribes. Europeans liked to call the native leaders "chiefs," using an old French term (and we're stuck with it), but this can be misleading. To speak of "Indian princesses" is even more misleading, unless one is speaking of South Asia. A better term might be **elders.** Often, there were multiple roles: talking chiefs, the wise ones; war chiefs, the brave ones; and others. Certainly, one person could command great respect. The settlers at Jamestown met the commanding Chief Powhatan, a person of such charisma and political influence that they called the loose alliance of tribes under his control by his name and decided that his daughter, Pocahontas, was a "princess." But even mighty Powhatan did not declare war or make peace; he *advised* war or peace.

When Europeans and North Americans think of tribes, they may also think of Africa, which at the time of the European conquests was, in fact, a huge collage of many forms of government that included bands and tribes. But all our origins are tribal. Europe was also once a land of tribes, and we still call modern nations by their names: the Belgae, the Germani, the Scots, the Britons. Readers of the Jewish Torah and the Christian Bible also know the twelve tribes of Israel, each led by its elders. The "judges" of the book of Judges were elders, or "chiefs," gifted in dispute settlement (wise ones) and in defending territory (brave ones). Occasionally, the related tribes acted in concert under a charismatic leader. Obviously, he was and is more to the faithful, but politically, Moses was much like Powhatan.

A bit more centralized is the **chiefdom,** in which a single leader starts to exercise more central control, commanding armies and perhaps controlling economic life by redistributing goods to those in need. At the time of the Roman Empire, what had been tribes beyond the borders were becoming more organized (perhaps in self-defense) as chiefdoms: The Franks, the Goths, and the various Germanic tribes were, strictly speaking, chiefdoms. This also became true among the Polynesians in the Pacific, again often under the stress of war. Every now and then, a great chief would organize the chiefdoms and looser collections of tribes into a single entity, usually for military purposes. Attila the Hun was a great chief. He brought together a diverse collection of groups and took them on the move, changing the faces of both China and Rome. The man who fought Caesar in Gaul (modern France, named for the Franks), a fellow who would be more famous if he had won (and if modern tongues could pronounce his name), Vercingetorix, was also a great chief. The man who united Hawaii and whom Europeans called "King" Kamehameha, was a great chief. When he first united the nomadic tribes of Mongolia, Ghengis Khan was a chieftan, and he went on to become a great chief.

When the chief became a permanent fixture and passed rule on to his descendants and when he (unlike tribal leaders, these were almost always men) organized a professional fighting force, maybe a standing army, and had other officials under his command so that he could truly *rule* with the power of coercive force, the state was born. A state usually came with agriculture and intense cultivation of the land, as well as a larger population. Typically, it was ruled by a king.

When my children were smaller, they sometimes liked to play King and Queen, with the requisite Princes and Princesses and maybe the dog standing in as a dragon. In the midst of one of these games, there was typically a pause and this question: "OK, I'm the king, but just what does a king do?" This is not easy to answer. Kings rule, clearly. But what constitutes rule? They were the final arbitrators of disputes. King Solomon deciding which woman should get a disputed baby is a famous example, but this would only be likely in a very small realm; otherwise, the king would need to appoint administrators. Kings sometimes embarked on great building projects: the pyramids, the Hanging Gardens of Babylon, the Great Wall of China. But mostly, kings went to war. Kingdoms were built by conquest. To again use a biblical example from the Old Testament, the elder Samuel is recorded as warning the people that if they demand a king, he will seize their finest fields and produce and even daughters for his own use, and he will take their sons for his armies. But he will, they hope, defeat their enemies.

Kings were in an almost common state of war, and so it is not surprising that some were far more successful in this enterprise than others. These kings established empires by conquering other kingdoms. The empires they created, however, were not nation–states but multiethnic, multilingual conglomerations of the tribes and kingdoms that they had overrun. Multiple religions and practices were often allowed, as long the superiority of the ruling city and its ways was acknowledged. The emperor ruled, sometimes with the lesser rulers still in place, as the king of kings or appointed his own staff. Alexander the Great, for example, left local rulers in place throughout the fringes of his empire and appointed his own people to rule Persia in the empire's center. The Romans worked through local kings or their own governors as convenience allowed. From about 2300 BCE—when a tough village kid who took the name of Sargon I conquered a large swath of the Middle East and created the Akkadian, or first Babylonian Empire—until almost 1500 AD, the multicultural empire was the world's usual complex form of social organization. The Mediterranean world saw the Egyptian, Greek, Roman, and Holy Roman Empires. The Iranian plateau and Mesopotamia saw the Babylonian, Assyrian, Persian, Alexandrian, and Parthian Empires. India was consolidated by the Mauryan Empire. Its great emperor, Asoka, converted from Hinduism to Buddhism, renouncing war in the process, but also tolerated as many as 600 different religious practices and languages. The later Mogul Empire included both very tolerant Muslim rulers and at least one "fundamentalist," built incredible structures such as the Taj Mahal, but also allowed the cultural, linguistic, and religious complexity of India to remain. China began to unite under the Shang Empire (about the same time as Sargon in the Middle East), later fell into a series of warring states, and was then reunited by the powerful leader who created the Chin (or Qin) Empire in 230 BCE, about the time that Rome was coming to prominence and from where the name *China* came. His Han successors started to build a more cohesive culture with a greater merging of people and traditions than those in the West, and we still refer to the dominant ethnic group in China as the *Han Chinese*. China remained diverse, however, with multiple religions, languages, and ways of life.

The nation–state, the modern country, emerged from this pattern slowly. Charles Tilly (1990) writes, "A thousand years ago, Europe did not exist" (p. 230). That is, no one had a sense of being part of a common entity, any particular group of countries, nor had any reason to. According to Tilly, "In 990 nothing about the world of manors, local lords, military raiders, fortified villages, trading towns, city-states, and monasteries foretold a consolidation into national states" (p. 230). Rulers dominated but rarely governed. "The emperors, kings, princes, dukes, caliphs, sultans, and other potentates of 990 prevailed as conquerors, tribute-takers, and rentiers, not as heads of state that durably and densely regulated life within their realms" (p. 229). For example, Richard I, the Lion-Hearted, a much admired and famous king of England and leader of the Third Crusade, only spent a few months of his time as king actually in England.

Gradually, over the next 500 years of almost continual war, those rulers who were unable to conquer vast lands found that the best way to consolidate their power was to forge a national identity within their boundaries. This created at least three recognizable nation–states: England, France, and Spain. Each united around a common religion—Catholicism for France and Spain and the Anglican Church for England—and even more slowly around a common language—Parisian French for France, the King's English for England, and Castilian Spanish (the language of Madrid) for Spain. As described by Weatherford (1994):

> Unlike rulers before them, who had been willing to rule over many different nationalities speaking different languages, wearing different clothes, and practicing different cultures, Ferdinand and Isabella installed a new homogeneity that was very much a precursor of the totalitarian movements of the twentieth century. They equated nation, language, race, and religion. To be one of their subjects, one had to speak Spanish and be of European ancestry and Roman Catholic faith. (p. 151)

This, however, was a slow process. Napoleon tried to inspire French national pride and to impose control with a standardized language, laws, and school system. It wasn't easy. He seized Nice from the Italian dukes of Savoy, but to this day, the street names are also given in the local language, Nicoi, something of a French–Italian hybrid. Down the coast, Prince Rainier of Monaco held an independent principality for more than fifty years, and the dialect of the entire region remains distinct. In Spain, as late as the middle of the twentieth century, General Francisco Franco tried strengthen the role of Catholicism as the national church, wipe out regional languages such as the Catalan of Barcelona and the Mediterranean coast, and centralize control in Madrid. To this day, the Basques of northwestern Spain use their own language and agitate for independence. England is still a land of dialects and regional distinctions, and the idea of the United Kingdom of Great Britain and Northern Ireland (the official national title) is even more tenuous as the Scottish seek more legal autonomy, the Welsh work to keep alive their language and culture, and Northern Ireland moves to accords with the Republic of Ireland.

Italy and Germany did not unite into single nations until the 1870s. Both countries retain strong regional identities and north–south distinctions, with differences in dialect and culture. The 1990s saw the dismantling of big multiethnic states into smaller versions of nation–states. The Soviet Union broke up into nationally defined states with nationalist ideologies: Georgia for Georgians, Armenia for Armenians, Estonia for Estonians. The trouble (and it can be real trouble) is that all of these entities still contain ethnic and religious minorities. Yugoslavia, a multiethnic state, broke into small nation–states starting in 1991: Slovenia, Croatia, Serbia, Macedonia. The struggles again mounted over minorities: What about the Serbs in Croatia and the Croatians in Serbia? And Bosnia, with a mix of three nationalities, fell into a terrible civil war. Czechoslovakia managed a rare "velvet divorce" in 1993 when its president Vacslav Havel, refused to try to hold the country together by force. The result was a Czech Republic in the west (which still contains the formerly divided territories of Bohemia and Moravia) and Slovakia for the Slovaks in the east.

While the power of nationalism in Europe has remained strong, it has always had its nobler and baser sides. The twentieth century saw particularly brutal forms of European nationalism. It was a favorite tool of dictators and demagogues, who used national images to win elections, rally masses, and ultimately turn those masses to violence against their neighbors, both internal and external. In the 1930s, Benito Mussolini's Fascists carried ancient Roman symbols and preached the glories of the Italian people and their destiny.

The ugliest yet maybe most masterful use of nationalism was that by Adolf Hitler and the Nazis. They spoke to German anger after the nation's humiliation after World War I and promised a new era of glory for the German people, German culture, and the German nation. All the Germans together, in one greater Germany, provided the excuse for the takeovers of Austria and Czechoslovakia, the invasions of Poland and France (each with German minorities within territory that had been part of Germany), and the expulsion and eventual effort at exterminating of Jews, Gypsies (Roma), and others who did not fit the national ideal.

When Hitler invaded the Soviet Union in 1941, Josef Stalin was not able to rally defenders to the cause of international socialism, especially since much of what the people had seen of Stalinist socialism was brutality and misery. Yet he found he could rally at least the Russian people to a defense of the homeland, Mother Russia. Nazi invaders treated them as inferior people, and the Russians fought back with the same tenacity that had exhausted Napoleon in his Russian invasion. Those who did not rally to the cry of Russian nationalism—conquered Chechnyans, for instance—were deported to the icy east by Stalin.

More recently, in the 1990s Slobodan Milosovich rallied the Serbian people around the idea of a greater Serbia. Serbia was once an important kingdom in the Balkans and had made a heroic defense against Turkish invaders. Now poor and disorganized, Milosovich's idea of a resurgent Serbia struck a chord of national pride. Gradually, it became apparent that Milosovich's nationalism included brutal attacks on Muslims and all non-Serbs in Bosnia and the province of Kosovo. The dark side of nationalism had surfaced once again.

Having faced centuries of bloody conflict fueled by nationalism, many Europeans are turning to a new vision: **Europeanism** and **transnational union.** In one sense, this is not new. For centuries after the fall of the Roman Empire, European states tried to recreate a new Christian empire that would reunite the core of Europe. Despite its power, the attempted Holy Roman Empire never really succeeded, as it was observed by the French writer Voltaire to be "neither holy, nor Roman, nor an empire." Napoleon once envisioned a United States of Europe (of course, with a French core). Hitler envisioned a fascist Europe with a German core.

The new idea of a united Europe is one that intentionally disperses power without a single core. The European Union (EU) has its headquarters in Brussels, Belgium. The European Parliament meets in Strasbourg, France, and its court system is headquartered in Luxembourg. The EU began as a unit of economic cooperation, the Common Market. Economic cooperation has extended now to a common currency, the **Euro.** Political cooperation has included the coordination of common laws and policies, although each member state still retains its own law-making function. There is great ease in traveling across large areas of Europe without customs stops, currency exchanges, and other interruptions. It's similar to moving from state to state in the United States or across the Canadian provinces. (As in Canada, though, the prevailing language may change.)

In some ways, transnational unionism and national splintering complement one another. One reason that tiny European states can thrive is that they are part of a larger economic and political entity. How much this should be a larger cultural entity is more controversial. Usually open Denmark has shown considerable resistance to union, in that the Danes want to retain their Danishness. So, too, for the Finns, who have long been dominated by larger powers and are not eager to lose Finland's hard-fought independence. Even Great Britain has kept a certain distance from the united continent, just as the island does geographically, wanting to maintain strong ties with the United States and other English-speaking countries around the world and not eager to give up time-honored traditions such as the British pound.

How much can one unite economically and politically and still remain unique culturally? Can one be a nation without a state? These are questions that go beyond Europe to a world that is often both coming together and coming apart.

Nationalism and Independence

Twentieth-century nationalism not only fired Europe but increasingly fired the world, often in struggles against Europe. Japanese nationalism glorified the emperor as the embodiment of all that was unique and glorious about the Japanese people. Emboldened by a new sense of national pride, Japanese leaders challenged first Russia in the Russo-Japanese War of 1905 and then the powers of Western Europe and the United States in World War II.

In Vietnam, Ho Chi Min explored socialist ideas but used the power of nationalism to inspire the Vietnamese people throughout the middle of the twentieth century. He called on them to restore their ancient honor and power by evicting the French, the Japanese, the French again, and finally the Americans. One of the great tragic misunderstandings of the Vietnam War was that the United States persisted in seeing it as a struggle of international communism, while for most Vietnamese, it was a struggle for national independence. Commonalities of language, religion, and culture fired broad national aspirations.

One of the most powerful was the idea of Arab nationalism, evicting the Turks, the Germans, Italians, British, and French (at varying times) and creating a common Arab nation under Islam. The most eloquent voice for Arab nationalism was Egypt's President Gamal Abdel Nasser, whose popularity and power in the region was founded on this idea. Egypt even went to far as to merge with Syria to form the United Arab Republic (UAR) in 1958, with the hope that others would join. In fact, the union quickly split apart within three years, although Egypt continued to call itself the UAR until 1970. Instead of a single Arab state that spanned North Africa and the Middle East, what resulted from squabbles among the colonial powers, as well as squabbles among the Arab leaders, was a melange of over a dozen small states, emirates, and sultanates, each with limited power.

Nasser's disappointment was not new. One-hundred fifty years earlier, Simon Bolivar had envisioned Latin American nationalism, a great United States of South America, free from Spain but united with a common language and heritage. What emerged instead in the early 1800s were many small states, often fighting border disputes with one another. Pan-African nationalism faired little better. N'Kruma, a powerful orator and first president of independent Ghana, in 1957 preached a Pan-Africanism that would span all of black Africa, with common goals and cooperation. Africa was instead divided into a myriad of small states, filled with internal conflicts and often at odds with one another. The vision of black nationalism remained and inspired African American leaders in the United States, but its goals remained elusive.

Where a national identity didn't exist, many leaders of newly independent states decided that it had to be created. The country of Indonesia was forged from what had been the Dutch East Indies, a land fought over by colonial powers for centuries. The world's fourth-largest country, it contains hundreds of islands; hundreds of languages and ethnic groups; a Muslim majority with significant Christian, Hindu, and animist minorities; and incredible cultural diversity. In the 1930s, Indonesian nationalist Achmed Sukarno came to the forefront of groups demanding independence, democracy, and national unity. They fashioned a new flag and even a new language. Indonesia needed a language, and it wasn't going to be Dutch. Imposing the main language of Java, which was spoken in the capital and by the largest population, wouldn't work either, as it would likely be just as resented. So a minor language related to Malay was chosen to be Bahasa Indonesian, the language of the country.

When Raden Suharto came to power in 1967 in a bloody coup that took the lives of as many as 700,000 people, he began an enterprise of nation building. Centralization of the economy proceeded, and the schools were mandated to teach a common Indonesian identity. Other entities, such as the former Portuguese colony of East Timor, were added to the nation. Javanese people were transplanted to remote and sparsely populated islands to spread the population as well as to homogenize the culture. Suharto envisioned a united world power. Instead, when he was driven from power in 1998 amid charges of incredible corruption and an economic collapse, the country itself started to fray. Fighting between Christians and Muslims became frequent. Certain ethnic groups, such as Chinese merchants, were targeted for attacks. Catholic, Portuguese-speaking East Timor fought for and finally gained independence in 2001. One reason this was so strongly resisted by the national government was the realization that a chain reaction of independence movements could occur that could unravel the entire country.

The creation of national identity where none has previously existed can be amusing at times, brutal at others. Iraq exists as it does because British colonial administrators drew lines on a map as they divided the former Ottoman Empire. Yet Saddam Hussein sought to create a strong Iraqi nationalism that was distinct from Arab nationalism. In his version, he, as the great father of Iraq, was heir to the mighty Nebucchadezer of Babylon (whose ruins lie within the country) and the great Muslim leader Saladin (who ironically was a Kurd, the group Saddam Hussein attacked with poison gas). The character of the leader aside, it seems quite artificial.

Perhaps nationalism is always based a bit on legend and glorifying a confused past. When U.S. schoolchildren stand and pledge allegiance to the flag under the watchful portraits of President George Washington and Abraham Lincoln, this, too, is nationalism. In most classrooms, the children represent dozens of different nationalities from across the globe, standing on land taken from over 500 different tribal entities. What they have in common are certain symbols and a tradition that is about 225 years old. Many might prefer to term their feelings for the flag *patriotrism*, rather than *nationalism*. The distinction is subtle: Is it that one's own feelings are patriotic and those of his or her enemies are nationalistic? Patriotism, which means devotion to the *patri*, or fatherland, perhaps denotes less of a single ethnic heritage.

Democracy and Its Alternatives

Democracy, or rule by the people, is both an ancient idea and an elusive one. The 1990s saw a great increase in the number of electoral democracies around the world, as authoritarian governments, ruled by unelected powerful leaders, fell in

Eastern Europe and Latin America, while democratic gains were made in parts of East Asia and Africa. Writes political analyst Fareed Zakaria (2003):

> We live in a democratic age. Over the last century the world has been shaped by one trend above all others—the rise of democracy. In 1900 not a single country had what we would today consider a democracy: a government created by elections in which every adult citizen could vote. Today 119 do, comprising 62 percent of all countries in the world. What was once a peculiar practice of a handful of states around the North Atlantic has become the standard form of government for humankind. Monarchies are antique, fascism and communism utterly discredited. Even Islamic theocracy appeals only to a fanatical few. For the vast majority of the world, democracy is the sole surviving source of political legitimacy. (p. 13)

Yet as Zakaria notes, democracy has not always fulfilled its promises. Moreover, many modern democratic systems are plagued by corruption, human rights abuses, misinformation and public manipulation, poor leadership, and suppression of minority rights.

A world of electoral democracies—national governments chosen by popular vote—is new, but the idea of popular participation is not. One could argue that it is not only ancient but even prehistoric. Human bands and tribes often had a process of collective decision making that involved a large portion of the group. This system was often quite informal but not always. The Iroquois of what is now the northeastern United States were led by a variety of male elders, or chiefs, who were ultimately answerable to women *electors* in a system that involved all adult members and included representation at multiple levels: village, clan, tribe, and ultimately the Iroquois confederacy of tribes itself. Some claim that this arrangement (without the female electors) served as a model for the new United States of America; we know at least that Benjamin Franklin admired the Iroquois system.

Tribal democracy gradually gave way in many places to **monarchy,** or rule by a hereditary leader, as kingdoms and empires spread across the planet. The power of these kings nonetheless varied greatly. Kings in the Middle East and the Mediterranean at times ruled as absolute monarchs, having complete authority over the lives of their subjects. The Egyptian pharaohs at the height of their power were considered divine beings who essentially owned all of Egypt, its land and its people, a true and absolute monarch. In other times and places, however, the king was more the great elder above tribal elders, the most revered chief. African kings often held, such a position, and in so far as they hold their offices, they continue to do so. Limited monarchs—ancient kings who were answerable to elders or medieval kings who were answerable to nobles—became the basis of later constitutional monarchies, in which a parliament enacts a code of laws and the king presides over and enforces them, if even in a largely ceremonial function.

In the ancient Middle East, kings often had great authority, but a tradition of laws also emerged. The great Babylonian King Hammurabi set down a code of laws in the 1700s BCE that gave privileges to the wealthy and those of noble birth but recognized certain rights of the poor, as well. Attacks on the person, property, or family of even a poor man would be punished, at least with a fine. Hebrew prophets, who served as royal advisors, reminded kings that even if they ruled by decree, they were still bound to a moral law to protect the poor and powerless and to respect the families and properties of their subjects. This advice was sometimes ignored, but kings who abused their power faced rebellion by religious and military leaders as well as by tribal elders.

About the same time as the Persian kings and the Hebrew prophets, Chinese scholars also pondered the essence of good government. The shadowy figure of Lao Tse—a teacher and maybe a librarian, maybe a retired government official, and certainly a respected elder—is reputed to have fled a China torn by warring states and ruthless kings sometime in the sixth century BCE. Lao Tse believed in limited government, with local autonomy and personal freedom. He denounced the corruption of his day and sought a better way, the *tao*, or way of heaven.

We know more about Lao Tse's somewhat younger contemporary, a scholar and minor government official, Kung Fu Tsu, (551–479 BCE) whom Westerners know under the Latinized name of Confucius. Confucius believed in strong but just government, based on loyalty and responsibility. Children should show respect and loyalty to their parents, women to their husbands, people to their leaders, and all to their king. But in return, each holder of a respected position was bound by obligation to lead firmly but kindly, with moderation and good judgment. Confucius's ideals were not immediately embraced, but his writing was preserved. China's mighty emperor of the Chin Dynasty, hardly a man of moderation and kindness, was not impressed with these ideals and sought to burn everything that Confucius wrote. Later Han rulers saved the remnants of his writing, however, and government officials had to pass tests based on memorizing the words of Confucius, which have influenced centuries of families and governments in East Asia.

The ancient Mediterranean world knew of democracy, though it didn't always approve of it. The most famous ancient democracy was practiced in some Greek city–states, most notably Athens. A **city–state** is a city that functions as an autonomous unit under its own leadership. In the Greek case, the state was small, a city and the land it controlled, and the nation, all Greek-speaking people, was large but mostly defined by a sense of common heritage, rather than a cohesive political entity. The smaller size of the city–state allowed for participatory democracy; everyone could have a say. Well, not really everyone. Women and slaves had limited political rights and no political voice. Free male citizens could serve on juries, vote in assemblies, and help decide the direction of government. By the time of its golden age under Pericles (c. 450 BCE), the Athenian experiment with this limited participatory democracy had reached its peak.

Other systems were also in competition. Sometimes Greek city–states were ruled by kings, and sometimes they were ruled by a group of oligarchs, or wealthy, powerful men. (**Oligarchy** is rule by a powerful elite.) Sometimes the king or the oligarch would oppress the common people so badly they would rise up under the leadership of a **tyrant,** who would lead them in rebellion. The tyrant would then rule as a revolutionary dictator. Some were just, impartial and effective, but many were not (as you can probably guess from the meaning *tyrant* has taken in English). Sparta was largely in the hands of a military dictatorship, ruled by those who had come up through the ranks in Sparta's many wars. The need to hold both conquered slaves and conquered lands under close control meant that the military dominated all aspects of Spartan life.

Greek political philosophers debated which form of rule was best: monarchy, oligarchy, military dictatorship, dictatorship of the masses, or democracy. One of the most famous answers to this question came in Plato's *Republic,* written in 360 BCE. Plato wasn't much of a democrat; he worried that the masses would always fall behind a **demagogue,** someone full of empty but appealing slogans who would appeal to their basest desires—a Milosovich or a Hitler perhaps. Plato believed a ruler should be chosen from among those known for their wisdom and who cared nothing for luxury. Plato's rulers would have great power but no real wealth; they would be too noble to want any. We call Plato's ideal ruler the **philosopher–king,** but this was a not hereditary monarch. The ruler's own children would get no special privileges, nor would any other, for the ruler would preside over a **meritocracy** (rule by the most meritorious) and distribute goods according to need without regard for rank. Plato's ideal rulers were essentially philosopher–communists, an ideal that would have modern appeal but be hard to realize in practice.

Plato had an especially bright "graduate student" by the name of Aristotle. Aristotle believed in more limited government and respect for the rights of free men. His most enduring political idea is that of **natural law:** that ethical principles are apparent in nature to all well-educated, reasonable men and so form the basis of human rights and good government. Aristotle took a job in 343 BCE as tutor for the son of King Philip of Macedonia, a bright lad by the name of Alexander. He went on to conquer most of the Middle East and became known as Alexander the Great. Alexander had great admiration for the culture and learning of Athens; perhaps Aristotle had advised him to be a philosopher–king. But in governance, he seemed to prefer the Persian model of an absolute monarch, who appointed administrators to serve at his whim. His generals continued this pattern after his death. Athenian democracy would later be rediscovered and idealized by Enlightenment Europeans, but as a practical matter of governance, Greek democracy died with Alexander.

Rome began under the rule of kings but for several hundred years was governed as an imperfect republic. Republican Rome was in many ways an oligarchy, with the Roman senate controlled by wealthy men. Yet the Romans loved laws. They wrote a lot of them and created courts to rule on them. Rule by law was important, in that senators were bound by precedent and agreement and could not rule by whim. The laws favored the wealthy but in time gave increasing protection to the poor, or the **plebians,** and even accorded certain rights to slaves and to women.

The Romans never perfected their republic; in particular in times of war and crisis, they often turned to dictators. Their most famous dictator, Julius Caesar, was made ruler for life. His life didn't last when it was rumored that he also wanted to be crowned king; he was stabbed in the senate in 44 BCE. His adopted son, Octavian, won in a rivalry with one of Caesar's favorite generals, Marc Antony, and ruled as Emperor Augustus. Although, the senate continued, with power firmly in the hands of the emperor, Rome went from a republic to a pure empire. The Roman emperors were supposed to hand pick their successors (rather like Mexican presidents for much of the twentieth century). Sometimes this was hereditary, as when a son inherited the throne. Sometimes it went to a great general, and sometimes the army imposed its person in a classic military dictatorship. Some emperors aspired to be philosopher–kings (Marcus Aurelius), some rose through the ranks and were surprisingly adept (Hadrian), and some came to power through intrigue and ruled as madmen (Nero and Caligula). In time, the Roman Empire grew so large that the emperors tried dividing its rule in half, forming one eastern and one western empire. The western empire collapsed around the time of Attila, while the eastern half survived another thousand years as the Byzantine Empire, with eastern-style absolute rulers.

The legacy of Roman law continued to influence Europe, especially through the Roman Catholic Church, and was exported around the world under European colonialism. The key problems of government, however—how to select capable rulers and how to balance power and competing factions—were never fully solved by the Romans. This turmoil accelerated their downfall, and the same unanswered questions continue to beset a world in turmoil.

Medieval European kings were feudal rulers whose rule depended on the loyalty of a hierarchy of nobles underneath them. From dukes to marquises, counts, earls, barons, and on to knights in various times and places, titles still held, though without much authority. This system could lead to ineffective government but provided a check on the power of kings. When English nobles forced King John to sign the **Magna Carta** in 1215, they were protecting their own rights and lands. Yet in time, that document came to stand for the rights of all Englishmen and is now held as one the bases of British democracy. In contrast, in France the king continued to centralize power. Louis XIV was the "sun king" because every matter of state revolved around him personally. Popular discontent meant his successors were deposed in revolutions. In 1776, the American colonies became a republic as did France in 1789, by throwing off the rule of a king. Both countries today have presidential systems, with the executive power held by an elected president. In Great Britain, the king gradually ceded power to a parliament composed of both lords and elected representatives in a pattern of parliamentary democracy.

During this time, political theorists again debated the nature of government and human rights. British philosopher Thomas Hobbes (1588–1679) wrote his classic book *Leviathan* at the time of the English civil war, a struggle between the king and the parliament. Hobbes believed people needed a strong government, and this was best seen in a strong and mighty king, or a *leviathan*. (Since this refers to a sea monster, one wonders about his choice of imagery.) For Hobbes, government was not divinely imposed, neither divine kings nor kings who ruled by divine right, but a social contract entered into by people to protect themselves. In a famous statement, Hobbes contended that the natural state of humans without government was "war of all against all," in which life was "solitary, poor, nasty, brutish and short." Even a strong government that limited individual freedoms was better than this. Although Hobbes argued for a very old form of government, authoritarian monarchy, his language shifted to arguments about social contracts and protecting rights, issues that would be debated for the centuries that followed. Of course, he also wrote at a time when his knowledge of actual human society before the time of European kings was less than the glimpse contained in this chapter.

John Locke (1632–1704), like Hobbes, his predecessor and fellow English political philosopher, saw government as a social contract between individuals. He wrote, however, not to champion a king but to denounce an abusive monarch. As such, his treatises on government were filled with warnings against the excesses of government. According to Locke, the only right to rule came from the consent of the governed. People formed governments to protect their God-given rights: life, liberty, and property. To do this, they sought to create a just system of laws. Kings who did not respect these laws and basic rights had no right to rule.

These arguments will sound familiar to many in the United States because they form the basis of the U.S. Declaration of Independence. In 1776, Thomas Jefferson adopted Locke's ideas to frame his accusations against King George III. Jefferson argued that people formed governments to protect the rights given them by their creator: life, liberty, and the pursuit of happiness (a more lyrical way of denoting property and livelihood). When a government infringed on those, it was the right, even the duty of the people to throw off that government.

Like Locke, French philosopher Jean Jacques Rousseau (1712–1778) wanted to limit government. Unlike Hobbes, Rousseau believed that people in their state of nature were basically noble and good. Society and power corrupted them. If power corrupts, it is best limited, and the greatest possible freedoms should be given to the people. Rousseau also influenced the American revolutionaries, whose success in turn inspired France's own revolution a few years later in 1789.

Debate continued over Rousseau's idea of decentralized power. Jefferson and his "democratic republicans" argued for a decentralized system, with power retained by the states and localities. Federalists, such as Alexander Hamilton and James Madison, argued the need for more centralized control as a way to maintain order. Rousseau's ideas seemed to be more influential in the United States than in France, where even with the king gone, control was still highly centralized in the committees in Paris and soon in the hands of one revolutionary leader, Napoleon Bonaparte.

Authoritarianism versus Democracy

These debates continued into the twentieth century. In Russia, a monarch, Czar (from the Russian form of *Caesar*) Nicholas II, was deposed and executed at the end of World War I. A republican government took power momentarily, only to fall to Vladimir Lenin's Bolsheviks, a group of revolutionary Marxists. Karl Marx had believed that socialist reforms, and even eventually communism, might possibly come through democratic means, especially in places such as Great Britain and the United States, where democratic institutions were well established. Lenin disagreed. As he looked over the ashes of the World War I, he believed that the state of the world had deteriorated so badly that only a revolutionary vanguard, a dedicated few who were truly committed to Marxist ideals, could lead the people to communism through a revolution of the **proletariat** (working class), to be followed by a dictatorship of the proletariat. The government would remain forceful and centralized, but it would use its power to advance, rather than repress, the workers. The Soviet dictatorship was born.

On Lenin's death in 1924, Leon Trotsky discussed a return to earlier Marxist ideals, but Josef Stalin, who ultimately triumphed, sought to strengthen the centralized dictatorship and his own rule, while supporting like-minded governments abroad. On Stalin's death, Nikita Khrushchev returned to the idea that maybe in small countries around the world, electoral processes could bring socialist reforms. Finally, Mikhail Gorbachev argued in the 1980s that Marxist principles and democratic ideals were not incompatible and sought semidemocratic reforms.

Whereas in the United States, socialist or communist economics was typically associated with dictatorship and undemocratic government, in Europe, a variety of democratic socialist parties sought to combine public ownership with democratic government. Some touted the ideals of the young Marx and of Trotsky; others sought to create a new hybrid economy with a democratic base.

In Germany, a monarch, Kaiser (from the German form of *Caesar*) Wilhelm, was toppled at the end of the first world war, and his government was also replaced with a republic. As Germany continued to struggle with the aftermath of the war and a deep depression, however, the party that gradually drew more and more votes was the Nazi Party of Adolf Hitler, which would ultimately dismantle the electoral process for a return to dictatorship under a Führer. The Nazi platform, national socialism, combined state involvement in the economy with a powerful, centralized, and militarized nationalistic dictatorship in a system known as **fascism.**

This system also prevailed in Mussolini's Italy and Franco's Spain. Germany, Italy, and Spain all had ultraconservative right-wing dictatorships, while the Soviet Union had a radical left-wing dictatorship. They were rivals, even before the second world war. The Soviet Union fought a proxy war with Italy and Germany in Spain, with the Soviets supporting leftist republicans and Hitler and Mussolini backing Franco. But they also had similarities; they were essentially **totalitarian,** or extreme authoritarian rule that tries to control all aspects of national life.

Both forms of dictatorship continue to influence the world. Even after the Soviet Union began its reforms, countries such as Albania and North Korea continued Stalinist-style dictatorships. Latin American military governments in the 1950s (Guatemala), the 1960s to the 1970s (Brazil and Argentina), and the 1970s into the 1980s (Chile) often had many of the characteristics of fascist dictatorships. Left-wing dictatorships claimed to rule for the people and often jailed the middle and upper classes; right-wing dictatorships claimed to protect property and champion the needs of business and often jailed labor leaders and labor union members. Both sought to maintain strict control of both the economy and the society, however.

Democracy continues to gain ground, as more governments are based on elections. Zakaria (2003) notes that this is not always "liberal democracy," with a strong respect for human rights and individual liberties. Some of the world's most brutal leaders, such as Hitler and Milosovich, came to power in a democratic process (and some highly respected leaders, such as Pope John Paul II and the Fourteenth Dalai Lama of Tibet did not). Elected leaders in East Asian countries—South Korea, Taiwan, and Singapore, in particular—have ruled with strict laws and limits on freedom of expression, although each country has seen liberal democratic reforms. Sometimes, their leaders have contended that they are not undemocratic, only Confucian: seeking order and demanding loyalty but also feeling the responsibility of a parent to dutifully guide and protect the citizens.

Democratic governments have also been plagued by charges of corruption. Scandals and investigations of government corruption have echoed across Europe, the United States, and Mexico. Charges of corruption have often brought down elected governments. In 1999, one of a series of military coups in Pakistan replaced the elected government, which was charged with corrupt dealings. In Algeria and Turkey, military-backed governments have intervened in the electoral process to prevent the election of people from Islamic militant groups, who are charged with being undemocratic in character, even though they command a large enough following to win an election. What should be done when a group whose ideology indicates it may not retain democratic institutions is poised to win an election? The issue between Hobbes and Rousseau has also returned: In an age of terrorism, how much government control is needed to maintain order?

British Prime Minister Winston Churchill is said to have remarked that democracy is the worst system of government in the world—except for all the others. Democracy is fraught with practical problems, to be sure. How do you create effective government without having autocratic government? Locke was a proponent of checks and balances between powers. This became one of the hallmarks of the U.S. Constitution, a balance among a law-making body (Congress), a law-executing executive body (the president), and a law-interpreting judiciary (headed by the Supreme Court). Ancient Rome had likewise tried to balance different spheres of power, especially the Senate and the consuls and later emperors. Locke favored a strong emphasis on the law-making bodies.

Interestingly, European countries that kept monarchs in power sought a strong balance in their parliaments, and now that monarchs are largely figureheads, actual governing power is largely in the legislative branch, the parliaments. The prime minister is first and foremost a representative of the party that holds a legislative majority. In contrast, countries that abandoned monarchy, such as the United States, created a strong presidency in its place.

Even though the U.S. Constitution devotes most of its space to Congress as the prime organ of government, U.S. presidents have used their position over time to gain greater power. For example, while the U.S. Congress has the power to declare war, the U.S. president is commander in chief of the armed forces. Since no war has been formally declared since World War II, the president now has great discretion in the use of U.S. military force. The War Powers Act of 1973 was an attempt by Congress to reclaim some of this authority.

Parliamentary systems can lead to deadlocks among multiple competing groups or unchecked power when one group holds clear control of the legislature. Power, however, remains in the hands of a group or party. Presidential systems give more direct power to one individual. Most of Asia, including the major powers of Japan and India, use a parliamentary system. Much of Latin America uses a U.S.-style presidential system, and most African countries also use modified presidential systems. The danger in these is that the president personally holds great power, which may be used to create a dictatorship under an electoral guise.

A related problem is the issue of control by political parties. While parties are sometimes not even acknowledged in constitutions, such as the U.S. Constitution, they are major players in most governmental systems. A **one-party system** gives complete control to a single party, even if others are allowed. China continues to be dominated by the Chinese Communist Party, which controls the governing process. For seventy-five years, Mexico was dominated by a single party, which always selected the president. Even Japan's openly contested parliamentary system was dominated for years by a single party.

The United States, Great Britain, and Canada are examples of systems, one presidential and two parliamentary, that have been dominated by **two-party systems,** although the nature and even names of the parties have shifted. An active two-party system can prevent entrenched control by a single faction but may itself become entrenched and eliminate other voices. France and Italy have long had multiple parties competing for control. This can be highly democratic, giving voice to many ideas and groups, but the government can be weak and based on shifting coalitions and complex electoral alliances.

"Dirty Wars": When Democracy Degenerates

With the exception of a handful of Islamic monarchies and emirates, all of the countries in the world have constitutions based on democratic principles. Yet democracy in practice is fragile. Often, democratic documents comprise a thin veneer covering a government run by a "president for life."

Africa, in particular, has been burdened with presidents who never quit. Mobutu Sese Seko ruled the country he called Zaire (Congo) for thirty-five years with complete control of the government and the economy. Daniel Moi ruled Kenya for twenty-five years. Robert Mugabe has ruled Zimbabwe since 1980, and Hosni Mubarak has ruled Egypt since 1981. Typically, these rulers win an election in which the opposition has little opportunity to organize or challenge the system. Saddam Hussein won re-election in Iraq, first winning 97 percent of the vote and then topping that by winning 100 percent in the next "election." While few believe these results, the winner is allowed to claim the title of "president" in international circles.

Often, these rulers claim that only they can keep their countries together. As the ruler consolidates both economic and political power, this becomes a self-fulfilling prophecy. Somalia fell into chaos after the departure of its long-time ruler, Said Barre, while Indonesia struggled through political and economic turmoil to restore democratic institutions after thirty-five years of Suharto.

The other way to power in many countries across South Asia, Africa, and especially Latin America has been through military takeover—what the French have termed the **coup d'etat,** or seizing of the state. During the cold war, seizing power was often done under an ideological guise: either to advance or to prevent communism. In 1954, the U.S. Central Intelligence Agency (CIA) assisted in deposing a leftist-elected government in Guatemala, which led to a series of military rulers that continued into the 1980s. In the 1960s and 1970s, Brazilian generals dominated the political process in that country with brutal suppression of human and political rights.

In 1976, the Argentine military seized power from chaotic political factions. It began what became known as the **"dirty war,"** in which thousands of political opponents, labor leaders, and others considered dangerous were detained and often tortured and killed. To "be disappeared" became a chilling reality for many Argentinians, and bodies are still being found in the ocean and in mass graves. A quiet but persistent protest movement grew with groups such as the Mothers of the Plaza de Mayo, who stood in silent protest with large pictures of the "disapppeared."

In 1970, Chile elected a socialist president, Salvador Allende. After three years of controversial policies, the military, under General Augusto Pinochet, seized power and ruled for the next fifteen years in a regime that likewise targeted labor and opposition leaders. Silent protests took such creative forms as "dancing with the dead," in which wives, perhaps widows, of the "disappeared" danced in the main square with invisible (missing) partners. Pinochet finally agreed to a referendum on his rule in 1988, claiming to be the only one who could retain order in the economy, the military, and the bureaucracy. He lost overwhelmingly, and the democratic process was restored.

Sometimes, dictators are elected in an open process. Hitler and the Nazis won a series of elections in the 1930s, using nationalistic rhetoric to draw support and increasingly blatant acts of terror to disrupt the opposition. Slobodan Milosevic came to power in a similar fashion in Serbia following the breakup of the Yugoslav republics.

One of the most grotesque distortions of the electoral process occurred in the small west African nation of Liberia. The regime of the country's long-time dictator, Samuel Doe, was coming to a close and guerilla forces sprang up to fight over the power vacuum. A tough street kid who had fled to the United States, participated in various petty crimes, and then slipped out of a Massachusetts jail on a rope of sheets returned to Liberia to lead one such group. Charles Taylor, discussed in the opening of this chapter, proved as resourceful and ruthless as any of the local warlords and guerilla leaders. He assembled an irregular force, consisting largely of boys in or near their teens who were recruited or kidnaped into his army. Armed with smuggled AK-47s and RPG launchers, as well as machetes, his "army" moved throughout the country, killing opponents and sometimes whole villages and pursuing a policy of terror that included public executions and tortures, organized rapes, and the mutilation of suspected opponents and their family members. Taylor's army had no uniforms, unless Nike sneakers count, and few supplies, but a mixture of fear, guilt, anger, and drugs drove them on.

As the fighting persisted, international intervention took the form of a West African peacekeeping force in 1995 and a mandate to hold an election in 1997. Charles Taylor ran in the election. His campaign slogan was direct: "I killed your pa, and I killed your ma." The implication was that if he was not elected, he would go on killing. Taylor won. Once in office, he proceeded to organize and support insurrections in neighboring countries: Guinea, Sierra Leone, and the Ivory Coast. The bloody involvement in Sierra Leone, in which cutting off the limbs of children was a favorite terror tactic, finally resulted in Taylor's indictment on war crimes charges. As new rebel groups fought him for the capital of Liberia, West African countries again sent in peacekeepers in 2003.

The Price of Democracy

Is democracy always the best answer to a nation's troubles? In practice, it certainly has been imperfect and even dangerous. Zakaria (2003) claims that if the task of the twentieth century was, in the words of U.S. President Woodrow Wilson, "to make the world safe for democracy," then the task for the twenty-first century is to make democracy safe for the world.

During the turmoil of post–World War II independence, some contended that poor countries needed a strong hand, a development-oriented dictator, and could not yet afford the luxury of democracy. Yet the world's experience has been that dictators often plunder and distort economies and rarely provide a sure route to progress. Argentine political scientist Guillermo O'Donnell (1979) sees democracy as a key element in social development yet also notes that institutions must be built to support the process, and that takes time. A free and independent press that strives for objectivity is one of those institutions that has been fragile everywhere in the world.

What is the price of democracy? In 1959, U.S. social scientist Seymour Martin Lipset noted that as national wealth increased, so did the likelihood of democracy. Political scientists Adam Przeworski and Fenando Limongi (1997, as cited in Zakaria 2003) put an exact figure on it: $9,000. With a per capita income of less than $9,000, a majority of democratic regimes collapse. With an income over this amount, none have.

Yet if democracy is also a major determinate of social progress, as well as its outcome, even poor nations must struggle to gradually build democratic institutions. Countries as diverse as India and Costa Rica have shown that it can be done. With a long history of statehood that included a number of remarkably enlightened leaders, followed by a period of British colonialism that, while very imperfect, included many of the trappings of formal democracy, India has remained democratic since its independence in 1947. This is despite being one of the world's poorest major countries for much of that time and having several major leaders assassinated.

Likewise, Costa Rica, a country of European immigrants who found few native peoples to enslave and imported few slaves, also began early to lay the groundwork for democratic institutions. While other Central American countries were embroiled in revolutions, Costa Rica abolished its army. This was an important signal of its internal as well as its external intentions, for Latin American armies are much more likely to see action against their own people than against foreign armies. While Costa Rica is not much wealthier than its neighbors, it, like India, has maintained very high levels of health care and education and enjoys a life expectancy on par with those of the world's wealthy nations. Democracy does not guarantee economic progress, but it does afford the people a say in how limited resources will be used.

After the Repression

Another precarious question for young democracies is what to do after the repression. Should the emphasis be on bringing the guilty to justice, compensating the victims, or bringing about reconciliation between embittered enemies?

Following World War II, the trials in Nuremberg convicted many Nazi leaders of war crimes. Following this model, after losing power in Yugoslavia, Milosevic was tried for war crimes by the world court in The Hague, Netherlands. In both cases, the accused claimed they were being made scapegoats by the victors. After losing his grip on power in Chile, Pinochet remained a senator, and military leaders were shielded from prosecution as a way of avoiding new trouble. The elderly Pinochet was finally charged with crimes in Spain, since some of his victims had been Spanish nationals.

Following the collapse of apartheid in South Africa, the government created a Truth and Reconciliation Commission. After a period of repression, secrecy, and misinformation, both truth and reconciliation can be elusive. But when they occur, it can be remarkable, as described by Sernau (2001):

> In one case, an old blind, black woman whose son was brutally murdered and who was made to watch the torture and killing of her husband by South African security forces, asked for only three things from the white sergeant who did the killing: that he would help her give her husband a proper burial, that he would come to visit her once a month so she could be "a mother to him," and that someone come and lead her across the courtroom [to give him a hug] so that he would know her forgiveness was real. The courtroom wept, the accused fainted, and someone broke into a chorus of "Amazing Grace." (pp. 272–273)

The Right to Be Fully Human

John Locke and Thomas Jefferson both began their statements on government with a proclamation of human rights. The language of **human rights** has continued to gain currency in the world but is not without controversy.

Nations have long recognized, at least in theory, the idea of **civil rights,** or the rights of citizens. When African Americans sought the right to vote without hindrance and to attend integrated schools and use public facilities, they used the language of civil rights. Their rights of citizenship, guaranteed by the U.S. Constitution and intentionally extended to them by the post–Civil War amendments to that constitution, were being violated. Many around the world still seek full protection of their civil rights, but are there also basic human rights that need to be respected by all governments, regardless of national laws and customs?

Jimmy Carter was the first U.S. president to specifically make protecting international human rights a major foreign policy goal. The Reagan administration retreated from this initially to return to a cold war–based foreign policy, but the demands of addressing humanitarian needs and protecting human rights has continued. During the Clinton administration, NATO, under U.S. leadership, intervened in the fracturing Yugoslavia, claiming to protect the human rights of Bosnians and of Muslims in Kosovo. A remarkable shift occurred in 1994, when U.S. forces were poised to intervene in Haiti to remove a military dictatorship and restore to power to an elected socialist president, Jean-Bertrand Aristide. The United States would intervene again ten years later in 2004—to help remove him from power and the country.

As the political globalization of the world proceeds, more questions about human rights are being decided at the international level. In 1948, the United Nations

Mass public protest has become a popular way to voice opinion ranging from pro-reform "orange revolution" protests in Ukraine (left) to anti-World Trade Organization protests in Seattle (right).

drafted its Universal Declaration of Human Rights, which was followed by statements on the rights of children, women, refugees and other groups (see Figure 7.1).

This trend toward the globalization of human rights has not gone unopposed. One major power that has resisted this movement has been China. While China has opened its economy tremendously in recent years, it has proceeded slowly toward making democratic reforms. Students demanding greater democratic freedoms were brutally repressed in Tiananmen Square in 1989. China has moved toward greater civil rights protections for its citizens but has adamantly contended that pressure based on international human rights is politically motivated, violates its sovereignty, and does not take into account it's unique culture and history. Other countries, most notably Iran, have made similar arguments.

The other major power resisting the move to a more encompassing international law on human rights has been the United States. Only the United States and Iraq refused to sign the U.N. Declaration on the Rights of the Child. The United States has also refused to allow the world court jurisdiction over its citizens. Again, the argument has been national sovereignty and the worry that politically motivated actions would be taken against the United States.

The challenge before the world is that if international institutions and declarations are to be meaningful, there can be no exemptions for powerful nations. Human rights must apply to all of humanity, regardless of national interest and

---

FIGURE 7.1   **U.N. Universal Declaration of Human Rights, First Seven Articles**

Article 1.   All human beings are born free and equal in dignity and rights. They are endowed with reason and conscience and should act towards one another in a spirit of brotherhood.

Article 2.   Everyone is entitled to all the rights and freedoms set forth in this Declaration, without distinction of any kind, such as race, colour, sex, language, religion, political or other opinion, national or social origin, property, birth or other status. Furthermore, no distinction shall be made on the basis of the political, jurisdictional or international status of the country or territory to which a person belongs, whether it be independent, trust, non-self-governing or under any other limitation of sovereignty.

Article 3.   Everyone has the right to life, liberty and security of person.

Article 4.   No one shall be held in slavery or servitude; slavery and the slave trade shall be prohibited in all their forms.

Article 5.   No one shall be subjected to torture or to cruel, inhuman or degrading treatment or punishment.

Article 6.   Everyone has the right to recognition everywhere as a person before the law.

Article 7.   All are equal before the law and are entitled without any discrimination to equal protection of the law. All are entitled to equal protection against any discrimination in violation of this Declaration and against any incitement to such discrimination.

Source: Available online at www.un.org/Overview/rights.html. The United Nations is the author of the original material.

FIGURE 7.2 **The Seven Freedoms**

- Freedom from discrimination—by gender, race, ethnicity, national origin or religion.
- Freedom from want—to enjoy a decent standard of living.
- Freedom to develop and realize one's human potential.
- Freedom from fear—of threats to personal security, from torture, arbitrary arrest and other violent acts.
- Freedom from injustice and violations of the rule of law.
- Freedom of thought and speech and to participate in decision-making and form associations.
- Freedom for decent work—without exploitation.

Source: Available online at www.undp.org/hdr2000/english/slideshow2/slide2.html. From *Human Development Report 2000,* by United Nations Development Programme, copyright © 2000 by the United Nations Development Programme. Used by permission of Oxford University Press, Inc.

perhaps despite the claims of long-defended national sovereignty (see Figure 7.2). German writer Johann Goethe, a contemporary of Jefferson's, put it succinctly: "Above the nations stands humanity."

MAKING CONNECTIONS

Amnesty International

■ This international human rights organization was introduced in Chapter Five. Amnesty campaigns around the world seek to end torture and human rights abuses while championing the causes of political prisoners and other so-called prisoners of conscience. Go to the group's site (www.amnesty.org) to find out the current causes, letter-writing campaigns, and other activities. There may also be a chapter on your campus or in your community. What are their current concerns regarding democracy and human rights?

Human Rights Watch

■ At http://hrw.org, you will find large amounts of information on human rights, including prisons, women's rights, rights and HIV, refugees, children's rights, and so forth, as well as region-by-region coverage of key human rights crises. See the information on "Campaigns" that address the trafficking of women and children, detainees, and other issues. How are they trying to address these problems?

U.N. Office of the High Commissioner on Human Rights

■ Go to www.unhchr.ch for information on many aspects of international human rights, including for women, children and indigenous peoples. This site also offers information on international agreements and human rights training and education. A daily update on human rights issues can be found at www.un.org/rights. On what issues of human rights is the U.N. currently focusing its attention?

CHAPTER 8

Ethnicity and Religion
Deep Roots and Unholy Hate

Sudan and Michigan

The large nation of Sudan is divided into a northern region that is mostly Muslim, dominated by Arabs who control the government in Khartoum, and a southern region that is dominated by black African groups such as the Dinka and Nuer, who are Christian or adhere to tribal religions. Fifty years of civil war that raged with few interruptions from 1955 to 2005 have devastated the south. The Nuer prided themselves on being fierce warriors but had few defenses against a government with modern weapons.

As parents were killed in the fighting, children fled or were sent away by relatives to seek safety. These roving bands of orphans, some no older than six or seven, crossed vast areas of savanna (the Nuer are indeed tough people) and international boundaries, wandering into camps in neighboring countries in the 1980s. These countries, all poor themselves, were reluctant to give the children asylum, as requested by the United Nations. Hearing of their plight, churches in the United States began to sponsor them (Shandy 2004).

Many of these children went to Michigan. They left the hot, dry world of East Africa for the damp chill of the midwestern United States. They came knowing much about survival in the wild but never having been in a school building and never having seen a traffic light, let alone a snowstorm. They became known as the "lost boys of the Sudan." In time, "lost girls" also arrived (Nyabera 2002).

With the fighting in southern Sudan abating, should these children return home? Should they be adopted by families in Michigan or scattered across the United States? Just as a fragile truce was agreed on in southern Sudan, word of horrible atrocities emerged from the western part of the country, a region known as Darfur. Bands of mounted militias, just known by the name of *janjaweed* (literally "bandits" or "wild ones"), rode into villages, massacring, mutilating, and raping and driving the frightened survivors into the desert. Both the militia and victims are Muslim; the janjaweed are drawn from poor Arab communities and linked to the Arab-controlled government, while their victims are black Africans. Racism and the desire to settle old scores may be behind the atrocities as well as government desire to control important regions (Human Rights Watch 2004). Militia attacks were sometimes supported by government planes and used government-supplied arms.

Gradually, countries including the United States began to call these killings **genocide,** or the attempt to wipe out an entire ethnic group or population. The word is an important one, for international accords that emerged after the Nazi holocaust call on countries to intervene to prevent genocide. Large-scale interventions in the Sudan have been few, however.

Minneapolis, Minnesota

George lives in the large community of Liberians that has grown up in Brooklyn Park, a suburb of Minneapolis. Many of these first came as refugees from conflicts and settled in the cold north with help from Lutheran Social Services and Catholic Charities. Others came because family members were already here in a classic pattern of chain immigration. Some are seeking lasting success in this new home; others dream of returning (especially in January) to a peaceful and democratic Liberia.

They have added an interesting and rich texture to this suburb and added to the Africanization of this once largely Northern European city, where the largest minority had previously been Native American. But George is angry with his neighbors. He says they are sending money home that is going to buy weapons for Liberian rebels. He has some sympathy for the rebel cause but also has reason to worry. His family is not safe in Brooklyn Park; they have been kidnaped in rural Liberia, apparently by rebels. He tries to reach them by cell phone but gets no answer. In the city's newspapers, the controversy is whether U.S. Muslims who donate to Islamic charities have been naively funding terrorism. George is worried that his neighbors, with their families safe in the United States, are doing the same.

The tension goes deeper. George and his family are descendants of tribal groups that have lived in rural Liberia for hundreds of years. Many of his neighbors, like the governing elite in Liberia, are Americo-Liberians, descendents of freed American slaves who returned to Africa and founded this country, Liberia, in honor of their new liberty. They did so, however, on land that had been the domain of a variety of related ethnic groups.

Religion and ethnicity can be sources of strength, solidarity, and charity. They are also intertwined in many of the world's trouble spots. Long-time Minnesotans wonder if the Liberians will prove good and permanent neighbors and what this will mean for their community. The Liberians wonder if their country will ever be safe and democratic, a place that lives up to its name and to which they can return. George wonders about his family and keeps calling on the cell phone.

Ethnicity: Ties That Bind and Divide

Theorists such as Karl Marx and Max Weber thought that ethnicity might play a reduced role in the commercial capitalist world of the future, in which trade, not blood, was the primary tie. In some aspects they were right, but the twentieth century also saw a resurgence of ethnic identity and pride.

Ethnicity is based on a sense of common heritage, common culture, what U.S. social theorist Donald Horowitz (2000) calls "the language of a family tie" (p. 3). But ethnicity is also more than this. It not only tells who is "in," or one of *us,* but also who is "out," or one of *them.* Norwegian sociologist Frederick Barth (1969) focused attention on ethnicity as a boundary, a divider between us and them, based on some presumed common ancestry. The common bond may be based in language, cultural practices, and stories or legends of heroic ancestors who did great deeds, were blessed by the gods, sprang from the soil, and so forth. The historical basis of the accounts does not matter as much as the boundary, the sense that others of this group are "our people."

The prehistoric and ancient world was a mosaic of different ethnic groups. We see glimpses of this prehistoric diversity in places such as Irian Jayan and Papua New Guinea, north of Australia, where there are hundreds of different groups, all with their own languages, variations of ritual and religious practices, and tales of their origins. In many places, this persisted well into the ancient world. The complexity of Indian society that often awes visitors is rooted in its history as a subcontinent that has had hundreds of languages, hundreds of variants in religious practice, and both subtle and glaring differences in dress, food, and daily life. As late as the arrival of the Europeans around 1500, the land that would become the United States had at least 500 different ethnic groups, with many more in what would become known as Latin America.

The process of nation building, described in Chapter Seven, has gradually reduced this ethnic diversity. Languages are disappearing at the rate of dozens per year, as elder members die off and younger members of tribal and ethnic groups only know the national language or a regional dialect. Yet there has also been a resurgence of ethnic pride and interest in ethnic identity. In the United States, the Cherokee, Mohawk, Chippewa, and Salish struggle to keep their native languages from dying. In Great Britain, groups likewise struggle to keep the Celtic languages (Welsh, Irish, Scottish) alive amid the universal use of English. Catalans in eastern Spain, Provencal in southern France, and many other languages are being kept alive, not because they are needed for communication but because they carry a group's sense of ethnic identity and heritage, something they are loathe to lose.

About the same time that ethnic diversity was being submerged into the broader ideal of nationhood—essentially, the high tide of European colonialism—another potentially dangerous concept was created: the idea of race. **Race** originally referred to nothing more than a collection of tribes or ethnic groups, as in *the German races.* Gradually, from the 1600s through the 1800s, the term took on a new meaning: a group of people with common physical and maybe psychological characteristics, due to their common origins. Biologists occasionally refer to races of birds or bears, populations of animals that while they are still part of a single species, have come to have easily distinguishable physical characteristics. Most anthropologists now agree that this just can't be done with any sense of precision, given the full range of human diversity. Yet people have tried for centuries, often with strong political and economic motivations.

The Romans would never have thought of themselves as *Europeans* and their southern neighbors as *Africans. African,* in fact, referred only to a single province in about what is now Tunisia. They were all *Mediterranean* peoples. They were very aware of their ethnic differences and held many ethnic stereotypes about Greeks, Jews, Egyptians, Gauls, and so forth. They were often certain that they themselves, as *Romans,* were superior; that is, they were **ethnocentric,** placing their own ethnicity and its ways at the center of the world and judging all others accordingly. Ethnocentrism is not a uniquely European concept; it appears everywhere. The Chinese believed they were the Middle Kingdom, and all around them were inferior habitations of barbarians.

One aspect of ethnic resurgence that we have recently seen is groups claiming for themselves their original names. They want to be known not by the names given them by outsiders (Sioux, Winnebago, Auca) but rather what they called themselves in their own language (Lakota, Ho Chunk, and Haurani, respectively). There's another reason for this shift. The names given to groups by outsiders often translate to something like "savages," "brutes," or "dog-eaters." The names they have for themselves typically translate as "the people," "the real people," or "the first ones." Every group seems to favor itself and be suspicious of others; people are ethnocentric. The ancient Romans were ethnocentric but not racist; they did not have the concept, in fact.

After years of contact and the slave trade, all the many diverse peoples of Africa became "black" and were envisioned as a single race. This was remarkable, given that Africa was a huge continent with the world's tallest (Tutsi) and shortest (the Ete or "pygmy") people and that their skin color ranged from light brown to deep, glossy ebony. At the same time, the tremendous diversity of Europe—from pale blond and red-haired Scandinavians to black-haired and olive-skinned Sicilians—all became "white," another race.

In the United States, this was a convenient shorthand. Most Europeans in the American colonies had come from Northern Europe and were quite light, while most Africans had come from the Bantu peoples of West Africa and were quite dark. Seeing the world in black and white came to make sense. Essentially, however, it was a categorization of privilege, not color. The black race could be enslaved for perpetuity, while the white race could only be held as indentured servants for seven years (Takaki 1993). In time, black and white would divide schools and communities.

New groups were not always welcomed into the white race: Jews and Italians, among others, brought darker complexions and new religious and cultural diversity. In time they "became white"; they didn't grow pale but were gradually accepted into the world of the more privileged (Brodkin 1998). A more elite designation, **White Anglo-Saxon Protestant,** or **WASP,** still kept them out of the most selective groups. Color was a convenient but elusive marker. Some light-complected blacks could "pass" for white, while some Southern European and multiethnic whites were suspected of "being black."

In the apartheid system of South Africa, roughly from 1948 to 1990, racial classifications took on extreme importance as categories of privilege: white, Asian, colored (mix race), and black. Yet even the apartheid-era South African authorities had difficulties, and every year the courts declared some blacks to be colored, some coloreds to be Asian, and so forth. Human ancestry is always complex and often ambiguous. Most of us just take our grandmother's word on who our real ancestors are! Yet around the world, 500 years of European dominance—coupled with earlier events, such as the invasions of Africa by lighter-skinned Arabs and the invasions of India by light-skinned Aryans—means that light is often favored over dark.

Light remains the color of privilege. In India today, seventy years after Gandhi declared all colors and creeds equal "children of God," mothers still purchase creams to lighten their daughters' skin color. Brazil has claimed to be free of the racial segregation and turmoil of the United States. In many ways it has, yet a clear distinction remains. Brazilians don't speak of black and white; they have dozens of color terms, so that a black woman from the United States may find that in Brazil she is no longer black but "coffee without milk." Even the quickest observation, however, shows that the wealthy and privileged of Brazil are overwhelmingly light complected, if not white at least "coffee with lots of milk," while the poorest groups have darker colors and African or Amerindian features.

One's color designation can even change along with social status: Having a college degree can lighten someone a few shades, at least in how he or she is described. As noted in Chapter Three, Brazilians love cosmetics: lipstick, hair color, and especially skin cream. The most favored skin cream doesn't block the sun or repel mosquitoes; rather it burns off the outermost layer of skin to lighten its color. Brazilian skin color comes in many rich hues, but dark-complected women know from the ever-present Brazilian televison and magazines that light is the color of beauty and wealth, and they don't want to be left out.

Faith and Fervor: Religious Diversity

Tribal Religions

The world of prehistoric humanity must have been one of incredible religious diversity. Just as each ethnic group had its own language or dialect—probably related to that of its neighbors but still distinct—so, too, each group would have had its own variant of religious practice, as continues with many tribal groups. This diversity of religious practice, as it survives today, is often just labeled **tribal religions.**

Anthropologists sometimes group many of these as **shamanism** for the informal spiritual specialists, the *shamans,* who exercised spiritual powers. These were often men, sometimes women, and sometimes a "third gender," such as the Native American *berdache,* men who rejected the traditional male roles. These tribal religions are also often labeled **animist,** a belief in spirits and spiritual forces that animate the nature and human world. Among hunter–gatherers whose lives are closely tied to nature, these are typically nature spirits. Among more settled tribal peoples, such as horticulturalists, the important spirits are often spirits of their ancestors, such as the cloud-dwelling *kachinas* of the Hopi.

Often, in both shamanism and animism, there is a strong sense of the natural world. The land is holy, either because it is the place of nature spirits or because it is the dwelling place of the ancestral spirits. This reverence is seen in Native American and African tribal religions, and seems to have been part of European and Asian religions as well. The ancient Shinto religion of Japan retains some of this reverence for nature and the ancestors. Such religious practice often involved an altered state of consciousness, perhaps with the help of mind-altering herbs (mushrooms and so forth) or the mind-altering effects of extreme physical exertion (such as marathon dancing, fasting, body piercing, or enduring the heat of a sweat lodge).

Tribal religions are in slow retreat around the world, as they have been for the last 2,500 years. Nonetheless, tribal practitioners remain in isolated areas. Tribal religion colors the practice of many major religions, such as Latin American Catholicism, and shamanistic practice has again come into vogue. Sometimes, this is part of an ethnic resurgence, as people try to reclaim their dwindling heritage by reclaiming ethnic religious practices as well as language.

Tribal religion is also doing well in some very cosmopolitan places, where it influences New Age religious practice and people seeking new forms of spirituality. The books of Carlos Castaneda reportedly reveal secrets of a South American shaman. There is also the more anthropological work of Bradford Keeney, (1994, 2004) a psychologist who travels the world studying tribal religious rituals and healing. He can also pack a stadium in Miami full of people, swaying and rocking to shamanistic rhythms.

Animistic religions often, though not always, also contain the concept of a supreme spirit or creator. Sometimes, the creator–spirit is remote and can only be accessed through lesser spirits, as was common in West African religion (often known to Westerners only through popularized versions of "voodoo"). Herding peoples in Africa, the Middle East, and Central Asia all seemed to have had a stronger sense of the closeness of one great spirit, who was their own shepherd.

Around 600 to 500 BCE, the world's religious landscape began to change markedly. Scholars and philosophers were asking deep questions about the one behind the many, and about whether religion was about tradition and ritual or about morality and ethics, or both. And they were writing their ideas down. Agrarian empires moved beyond ancestral spirits to worship a pantheon or collection of named gods, often with a ruling god who reigned among the gods, just as the emperor reigned among dignitaries. The lasting effect of this was minimal, however, for when an empire fell, so often did its gods, to be replaced by the apparently more powerful gods of the new conquerors.

During this time period (600–500 BCE and perhaps earlier), Hebrew prophets, seeing portions of the nation fall to Assyria and then to Babylon, wrote about a god who was not defeated even when his people were. This god was also more interested in personal and social conduct, "doing justice and loving mercy" in the words of Micah, than in the specifics of religious ritual. During this time and continuing through the great age of Athens, Greek philosophers distanced themselves from the ancient pantheon of gods. (Socrates was called an atheist for doing this too much.) Greek stoics wrote about "the great spiritual fire" that burned above and beyond the lesser gods and about personal and civic duty as the basis of a religious life. Similarly, Confucius and Lao Tse in China wrote about the "way of heaven" and the duties and ethical living that were to be the hallmark of a religious person. In India, Hindu philosophers organized the diverse collection of practices and beliefs that were coming together into Hinduism. They wrote about Brahman, the eternal one, who was the center and unifier of all things, and how a faithful person should live to attain spiritual advancement. One Hindu prince went further than others in his search for right living and right thinking. Prince Gautama (560–480 BCE) left his throne to fast and meditate on the human suffering he saw. Enlightened as the Buddha, he taught his followers about noble truths and an eight-fold path of right living.

As these ideas spread, they became the basis of the world's first great religions, those that transcended tribal and ethnic boundaries and won converts from many backgrounds. Over the centuries, several more great religions were added. The greatest of all, in terms of eventual numbers of converts, began when a Jewish teacher reclaimed and extended the ideas of the prophets. Jesus of Nazareth (c. 4 BCE–30 CE) claimed that the entire complexity of Hebrew religion was captured in the call to love God with one's entire being and to love one's neighbor as oneself. Jesus' followers—including his most prolific interpreter, Paul of the Roman city of Tarsus—put his life and teachings into the Greek language and in a form that built on Greek philosophy. In three centuries, the way of Jesus the Christ (or deliverer), **Christianity,** had become the religion of the Roman Empire.

Between 570 and 632 CE, another teacher challenged a pantheon of gods to call his followers back to the ancient pastoral or herding idea of one god, the great shepherd. Muhammad put these ideas into his book, the Qur'an (or Koran), which had many similarities to Jewish and Christian thought. He drew a small but fervent following, and the religion of **Islam** was born, soon spreading throughout the Middle East.

Later prophets and teachers extended, reformed, and combined elements of these faiths into Sikhism, Baha'i, and other religions, each with a smaller but dedicated following. The main story since about 600 CE, however, has been the spread of the great religions to all parts of the globe (see Table 8.1).

Christianity

A full one-third of the world claims some type of Christian affiliation. When the Roman Empire split into a western Latin half, centered on Rome, and an eastern Greek half, centered on Constantinople, the Christian church also began to divide into a Latin-based Roman Catholic Church, with the Pope, the Bishop of Rome as its head, and a Greek-based Eastern Orthodox Church, with the Eastern (Byzantine) Emperor in Constantinople and the Patriarch of Constantinople at its head. By 1000 CE, the cultural, political, and linguistic division became an official split, or schism, that still divides Europe into east and west. Just over 500 years later, the Protestant Reformation began in force in Switzerland, Germany, the Netherlands, and eventually England. After a series of struggles, including the bloody Thirty Years' War of the 1600s, Christian Europe was again divided, this time with Western Europe splitting into a Catholic south and a Protestant north.

The original division remains, with Eastern Orthodoxy in its various national forms (Greek Orthodox, Russian Orthodox, Serbian Orthodox and so forth) dominating in Russia and Southeastern Europe. Roman Catholicism remains the dominant religion in Italy, France, Spain, Portugal, Austria, Hungary, and southern Germany (up to a line that roughly marks the greatest extent of the Roman Empire). Among the Protestants, the Lutheran Church dominates in northern Germany and the Scandinavian countries, the Dutch Reformed Church dominates in the Netherlands, the Anglican Church dominates in England, and the Presbyterian Church dominates in Scotland. Two outposts of Roman Catholicism in Northern Europe—Ireland and Poland—remain the most staunchly Catholic countries with the greatest influence of the church in Europe.

TABLE 8.1		**Adherents of All Religions by Six Continental Areas: Mid 2001**						

	Africa	Asia	Europe	Latin America	Northern America	Oceania	World
Baha'is	1,779,000	3,538,000	132,000	893,000	799,000	113,000	7,254,000
Buddhists	139,000	356,533,000	1,570,000	660,000	2,777,000	307,000	361,985,000
Chinese folk religionists	33,100	385,758,000	258,000	197,000	857,000	64,200	387,167,000
Christians	368,244,000	317,759,000	559,359,000	486,591,000	261,752,000	25,343,000	2,019,052,000
Anglicans	43,524,000	735,000	26,628,000	1,098,000	3,231,000	5,428,000	80,644,000
Independents	85,476,000	157,605,000	25,850,000	40,357,000	81,032,000	1,536,000	391,856,000
Orthodox	36,038,000	14,219,000	158,375,000	564,000	6,400,000	718,000	216,314,000
Protestants	90,989,000	50,718,000	77,497,000	49,008,000	70,164,000	7,478,000	345,855,000
Roman Catholics	123,467,000	112,086,000	10,800	466,226,000	71,391,000	8,327,000	1,067,053,000
Confucianists	250	6,277,000	285,554,000	450	0	24,000	6,313,000
Ethnic religionists	97,762,000	129,005,000	1,258,000	1,288,000	446,000	267,000	230,026,000
Hindus	2,384,000	813,396,000	1,425,000	775,000	1,350,000	359,000	819,689,000
Jains	66,900	4,207,000	0	0	7,000	0	4,281,000
Jews	215,000	4,476,000	2,506,000	1,145,000	6,045,000	97,600	14,484,000
Muslims	323,556,000	845,341,000	31,724,000	1,702,000	4,518,000	307,000	1,207,148,000
New-Religionists	28,900	101,065,000	160,000	633,000	847,000	66,900	102,801,000
Shintoists	0	2,669,000	0	6,900	56,700	0	2,732,000
Sikhs	54,400	22,689,000	241,000	0	535,000	18,500	23,538,000
Spiritists	2,600	2,000	134,000	12,169,000	152,000	7,100	12,466,000
Taoists	0	2,658,000	0	0	11,200	0	2,670,000
Zoroastrians	910	2,519,000	670	0	79,100	1,400	2,601,000
Other religionists	67,300	63,100	238,000	99,600	605,000	9,500	1,082,000
Nonreligious	5,170,000	611,876,000	105,742,000	16,214,000	28,994,000	3,349,000	771,345,000
Atheists	432,000	122,408,000	22,555,000	2,787,000	1,700,000	369,000	150,252,000

Adherents. As defined in the 1948 Universal Declaration of Human Rights, a person's religion is what he or she says it is. Totals are enumerated following the methodology of the *World Christian Encyclopedia,* 2nd ed. (2001), using recent censuses, polls, literature, and other data. As a result of the varieties of sources used, totals may differ from standard estimates for total populations.

Source: 2002 Encyclopedia Britannica Book of the Year

In countries other than Ireland and Poland, European Christianity is dominated by state churches that claim huge memberships but have little active involvement. In many countries, affiliation in the dominant or state church is over 90 percent, but weekly church attendance is below 10 percent (Jenkins 2003). A typical Sunday morning may find a Danish Lutheran pastor standing in a huge, ornate church preaching (or more likely lecturing about helping the poor around the world) to fifteen or thirty people. The pastor's salary is paid by the state, so there is no financial worry, and if the pastor is sincere about helping the poor, he or she may garner community respect but little religious fervor. All Danes are enrolled at birth in the Lutheran Church, unless their parents insist otherwise, but few see the need to regularly participate. A similar pattern is seen in much of Catholic Europe, where Catholicism is an important part of national heritage and identity but attendance at mass and adherence to the dictates of the Vatican are very limited.

Some have spoken of a post-Christian Europe, but what has mainly declined is the power of the state church. Many Europeans have spiritual interests and convictions, in spite of mistrust or apathy toward the dominant church hierarchy, and there has been some growth in smaller, more evangelical, gospel-based religious groups. Immigration from North Africa, as well as South and Southeast Asia, has also meant a significant increase in the number of Muslims living in Europe.

In North America, the United States and Canada have historically had Protestant majorities, with strong pockets of Catholicism in French-speaking Canada and in Irish, Polish, Italian, Mexican, Puerto Rican, and Cuban areas in the United States. Latin America has always been overwhelmingly Roman Catholic, given its primarily Spanish and Portuguese heritage. There has been rapid growth of Protestant faiths in many parts of Latin America, however, especially conservative evangelical and Pentecostal groups (emphasizing lively worship and the signs of the Holy Spirit, noted among early Christians at the celebration of the holiday of Pentecost). Places such as Guatemala (where evangelicals include General Mott, noted in Chapter Seven) are now as much as 20 percent Protestant. Because participation in Catholic mass has been declining, on a given Sunday in Mexico, there are more Protestants than Catholics at worship, by some estimates.

Christianity has also seen explosive growth in Sub-Saharan Africa, where many tribal religionists have become Christians, often of the evangelical or Pentecostal forms. The Presbyterian faith and evangelical Christianity have also exploded in South Korea, one of the few Asian nations where this has occurred so massively. Christians are scattered across all of the Asian countries, but South Korea now claims some of the world's largest churches, a few with congregations over 10,000.

Islam

Islam burst out of Arabia shortly after Muhammad's death. Arab conquerors carried it across North Africa to Morocco and across the straits of Gibraltar to all of Spain and even into southern France, where they collided with the knights of the Frankish kingdom. The Moors, a mix of Arabs and North African Berbers, ruled Spain for centuries, until they were gradually driven back and finally expelled by the Catholic monarchs Ferdinand and Isabella in 1491, the year before they sent Christopher Columbus on his famous voyage.

The center of Arab power shifted from Arabia to Baghdad, in what is now Iraq. Persia became Muslim, and Arab traders carried the Islamic faith to their outposts in what is now Indonesia and Malaysia. Many Central Asians converted to Islam. One such group invaded and ruled most of India, where they were called *moguls* (from which we get our name for powerful leaders). One Central Asian group, the Turks, eventually conquered the Arab lands, first as the Seljuk Empire, which battled the European Crusaders, and later as the Ottoman Empire, which ultimately invaded Europe, capturing Constantinople (now modern Istanbul) in 1450 and reaching as far as the outskirts of Vienna in 1688. This was the high tide of the Islamic Empire.

The Ottomans were driven from Vienna by the Catholic Polish cavalry. (It is claimed the bagel owes its origin to pastries shaped like stirrups and baked by grateful Viennese.) A long decline ensued, ending in catastrophe in World War I. Islamic lands fell to European Christians from the time the Portuguese drove the Arabs from the Indian Ocean and the Dutch seized the islands that now comprise Indonesia. The pattern increased when Napoleon seized Egypt from the Turks in 1798, to be followed by the British until Europeans controlled all of North Africa. Following World War I, the entire Middle East was dominated by European powers. They were "infidels" or unbelievers to many of the inhabitants but new "crusaders" in the rhetoric of Osama bin Laden and Islamic nationalists.

Evidence of the high tide of Islamic civilization can be seen in magnificent structures from the Alhambra Palace in Granada, Spain, to the Taj Mahal in India. Having seized the domain of Alexander the Great and the Byzantine Greek Empire and thriving while Europeans were experiencing what would be their Dark Ages, Islamic scientists and philosophers formed an important bridge between the learning of the classical Mediterranean and Middle Eastern world and that of modern Europe (Berkey 2002).

Islamic political power has been in sharp decline for centuries, yet the religion continues to expand. About one-fifth of the world adheres to the Muslim faith. The largest Muslim nation is neither Arab nor Middle Eastern but the country of Indonesia. The second largest Muslim population is in India, where they are a minority in a Hindu country, but such a vast country that even its minorities are huge. Pakistan and Bangladesh, carved as Islamic states from Hindu-majority India, are the next most populous. The Arab nations, with the exception of Egypt, tend to be small in population but are historically important to Islam and now have oil wealth that gives them power beyond their size.

The Islamic belt slices across portions of Southeast, South, and Central Asia; across Iran and the Arabian peninsula; and all the way across North Africa. A rough line across the Sahel, the dry region that separates the Sahara in the north from the wetter country to the south, divides Africa into a Muslim-dominated north and a Christian-dominated south. Sometimes, the line divides countries in two. Nigeria, Africa's most populous country, is roughly divided into a Muslim north, which dominates the national politics, and a Christian south, which dominates the national economy. Rivalries between the two resulted in the Biafran War of the 1970s and continued tension. The line of division also slices into two halves the country of Sudan, a vast country with the largest land area in Africa. The government in Khartoum is in the hands of Islamic nationalists, mostly Arabs, who have been accused of having ties to extremist groups. Southerners include the Dinka, the Nuer, and many ethnic groups, who adhere to tribal and Christian religions. They have fought for independence, or at least autonomy, from Islamic law for years.

Asian Religions

India remains home to most of the world's **Hindus.** Despite being concentrated in a single county, this is still one of the world's largest religions, with 800 million adherents. The large number of Indians living and working overseas has spread the influence of Hinduism well beyond India's borders. Interest has also grown in the ancient practices and ideas of Hinduism. When the Beatles left England to study with the Maharishi Yogi and his adapted form of meditation, transcendental meditation became in vogue, and the Western world reawakened to Hindu ideas. Other Hindu-based disciplines, such as the practice of yoga, also continue to gain in worldwide popularity.

Buddhism began in India but never completely took hold. It quickly spread to other countries, however, and Sri Lanka, Thailand, Burma (Myanmar), and Cambodia are all predominantly Buddhist. Buddhism has had great influence in China, although Buddhism's most prominent spokesperson is in exile from Chinese authorities, the Fourteenth Dalai Lama of Tibet. A contemplative form with fewer rituals, Zen Buddhism, has had great influence on Japan, although given the open-ended nature of Japanese Zen, it is hard to say just how many would consider themselves practicing Buddhists.

The most difficult place to do an accounting of believers of any kind is in China, the world's most populous country. Mao's Communists were officially atheist, and many Chinese claim no religion. There has been a revival of interest in the three "great ways" of China—Taoism, Confucianism, and Buddhism—and there has also been a renewed growth in Christianity. A few Chinese minority groups, primarily along the Mongolian border, are Muslim.

Any accounting of the world's major religions must consider the tremendous intermingling of faiths that has taken place. There are today more Muslims in London, Detroit, and Chicago than in most Arab capitals. There are far more Jews in New York than in Jerusalem, as well as more Hindus than Episcopalians (Eck 2002).

Ethnicity, Religion, and Power

Religious and ethnic diversity have had tremendous power to fuel violence. History is full of accounts of one ethnic group's attempt to subjugate or exterminate another that was seen as threatening or inferior. Ideologies of race and religion have often been used to provide added justification for these acts.

Both Christians and Muslims (and no doubt, many others, such as the Mesoamerican Aztecs) have used religion to justify their conquests. They have also fought among themselves: Protestant versus Catholic Christians, Sunni versus Shiite Muslims and so forth. These conflicts persist in many places in the world: between Catholics and Protestants in Northern Ireland; between Jews and Arabs in Israel and Palestine; among Muslims, Sihks, and Hindus in India and between Muslims and Christians in Indonesia; as well as among Black Muslims and Baptists, Hasidic Jews, and Korean Buddhists, and Presbyterians intermingled in New York.

One way to view these conflicts is to believe they are rooted in human nature and due to the expanse of human history, or ancient hatreds. Harvard historian Samuel Huntington (1996) believes that the post–cold war world will see a "clash of civilizations," in which the great civilizations that have emerged based on religion and ethnicity and that still hold conflicting values will continue to clash in conflict: Western Christian, Islamic, Chinese, Indian Hindu, and so forth.

The history of hate is long, yet so is the history of accommodation. Many religions and ethnicities (more recently, we might add, many races) intermingled in many of the great empires: the Persian, the Alexandrian, even the great Mongol Empire of Genghis Khan and his grandson, Kublai. Even that great modern imperialist, Queen Victoria, spoke of the British Empire as a place of brotherhood between people of many creeds and colors, once petty rivalries were subdued by careful British paternalism (or in her case, maternalism).

Many places known for violence have also had periods of cooperation. When Lebanon burst into violence among Muslims, Christians, and Jews in the 1970s and 1980s, the battles repeated the same bloodshed that had been in this land during the Crusades. Yet for decades, Beirut was known not for hostages and terror but for cooperation and accommodation among all of its religious and ethnic groups, the cosmopolitan "Paris of the Mideast." Yugoslavia fell into war in the 1990s among Orthodox Serbs, Catholic Croats, and Muslim Bosnians. These rivalries went back to the earliest days of the Ottoman and Austro-Hungarian Empires, but Yugoslavia had also known forty-five years of relatively peaceful cooperation before this.

Much hate seems distinctly modern. Donald Horowitz (2000) rooted his theories of ethnic conflict in the idea of competition. Struggles for dominance once a former empire or ruler fell, as well as struggles between people who were fearful that loss in this competition would forever submerge their hopes and their way of life, are what fuel ethnic strife. Economic competition has played a major role in many such struggles. So has political manipulation. Dictators from Hitler to Milosevic to Saddam Hussein have known how to play on ethnic and religious divisions, fears, and rivalries. Promising a better future has long been the rallying cry of politicians, but promising a better future by squashing someone who is profiting at your expense has been a great rallying cry to violence. Merchant minorities, sometimes called *middleman minorities,* who operate businesses amid other groups, have been especially vulnerable. Hitler moved against the Jews in Europe, Idi Amin moved against the Indians in Uganda, and recent violence has targeted overseas Chinese in Southeast Asia. Loss of historical territory, inevitable in a world of shifting boundaries, can also be a powerful rallying cry. In each of these cases, the immediate motivation may have been economic or political, but religion and ethnicity, sometimes combined in a hypernationalism, have proven far more powerful in inciting war—from ancient Sparta, to the Crusades of the 1100s, to modern calls for *jihad* (or holy struggle).

The tragic convergence of these factors was seen in 1994 in Rwanda. Two ethnic groups, the Hutus and the Tutsis, had shared the land for centuries. Under European colonial administration—in this case, Belgian in the early 1900s, which favored one group, the Tutsis at the expense of the Hutus—the divisions and resentments deepened. Upon Rwanda's gaining independence in 1962, the groups had fought, and both sides feared the other. The stage was set. All it took was a group of particularly fiery Hutu leaders, both religious and political, to call their people to arms, to crush their opponents "like insects that infest the land." As the story unfolded, a shocked world saw the scope of the brutality: 1.5 million killed, many hacked to death with machetes as they huddled in churches for protection, while leaders, including a prominent priest, chided the attackers that "the graves are not yet full." The international community was slow to respond and quick to move on to other problems, dismissing this as "ancient hatred" (BBC 2004).

One of the questions raised by this tragedy was how to best respond. The Belgians and French and a handful of United Nations observers were late coming to Rwanda in force, too late to stop the bloodshed. Remembering this, the French were quick to step into Cote D'Ivoire (Ivory Coast), their former colony, when the fighting in Liberia threatened to destabilize that country. Similarly, the British intervened to restore order in their former territory of Sierra Leone. Small African nations have come to look to "big brothers" in times of crisis, but is this a new form of colonialism? The United States, distracted by Iraq and remembering its losses when it got involved in inter-clan fighting in Somalia, resisted sending troops to Liberia, where it had historic ties. Instead, a West African force led by Nigerians intervened. The Nigerians were welcomed but also sometimes mistrusted, as some had ethnic ties to certain factions fighting in Liberia.

Resurgent Fundamentalism

Just as many believed that the power of ethnicity would decline in the modern world, some also believed that the influence of religion would decline. Writing in the 1960s, British sociologist Peter Berger (1967) believed that amid growing modernization and diversity, people would have to hold their beliefs more tentatively and tolerantly; they would become more secular, or at least more liberal, as the "sacred canopy" of religion was pulled back. Similarly, U.S. theologian Harvey Cox (1965) believed that the diverse cities of the world, with their international, cosmopolitan nature, would necessarily become examples of "the secular city."

Berger may have been correct about London, and Cox about Boston in the 1960s, but elsewhere, sentiments were changing. The end of the twentieth century saw a sharp rise in highly conservative, traditional, and literal expressions of religious faith. At times, they have also been militant expressions.

Perhaps it was the pressures of a cosmopolitan, globalizing world that drove the movement. In his book *Jihad vs. McWorld,* Benjamin Barber (1995) sees two opposing forces acting in the world. One, he termed *McWorld:* the capitalist, corporate-controlled, economic uniformity typified by McDonald's and huge corporations. The other, he termed *jihad,* borrowing the Islamic word for "holy struggle," in his usage, referring to all reactionary struggles against modernity and globalization, the fierce call back to tribe and tradition, to religion and noncommercial absolutes.

In the 1980s, the most prominent face of *jihad,* in this sense, was the Ayatollah Khomeini, religious and political revolutionary and leader of Iran, denouncing the United States as the "Great Satan" who dominated and tempted the faithful. In the beginning of the twenty-first century, the most recognizable face of this type of *jihad* is probably that of Osama bin Laden. To him, perhaps, the power of McWorld was best seen in the twin towers of the World Trade Center. Barber fears that both McWorld and jihad may be fundamentally undemocratic—one represents rule by money, the other rule by fear.

The collision between these two forces is not always violent. It may take the form of a cultural clash. Pakistani rock star Joonan fills auditoriums in his home country with people who want to hear his version of international rock and roll, while ultraconservative religious leaders denounce this worldly display, in some cases, calling for a ban not only on rock but all music as "un-Islamic."

What can be misleading in these current examples and in Barber's choice of terms is that this reaction is not unique to Islam. What has been labeled "religious fundamentalism" has taken root around the world.

Fundamentalism originally referred to a type of very conservative, Bible-oriented and largely rural American Christianity. Around the beginning of the twentieth century, U.S. Christians who rejected so-called liberal tendencies in many churches called for a return to the fundamentals of the Bible. These included fundamentals of belief but also often of lifestyle, such as prohibitions against dancing, drinking alcohol, watching movies, and playing cards. These "worldly" pursuits were believed to tempt and distract the true believer. American Christian fundamentalism initially often rejected political involvement as being wordly, although some southern politicians adopted its themes (and fervent style of preaching). Involvement in politics was largely limited to issues such as opposition to the teaching of evolution and to the selling of liquor on Sundays.

This changed in the 1980s with the rise to prominence of Jerry Falwell and the Moral Majority. The early fundamentalists who had found a political platform were likely to be populist Democrats, but in the 1980s, fundamentalist support went to the Reagan administration and conservative Republicans. Falwell's followers still avoided direct political campaigns and instead called Americans back to a more "moral" time, as characterized by traditional gender roles and family structure, traditional (i.e., nineteenth-century) attitudes toward sexuality, and opposition to other trends it considered unbiblical. More direct political involvement came with the creation of the Christian Coalition under Pat Robertson in 1984 and its expansion under Ralph Reed and the presidential campaigns of Pat Robertson, Gary Becker, and others. What became known as the **"religious right"** became a major force in the Republican party and the country as a whole.

Islamic fundamentalism may be an awkward hybrid term, but it captures the notion that many of these same ideas, backed by the Qur'an rather than the Bible, have gained prominence in parts of the Islamic world. This fundamentalism is seen in a form of Islam known as Wahabism, which gained influence in Saudi Arabia and has been exported to other countries through Saudi-supported *maddrassah* schools and religious organizations. This form of fundamentalism also looks to a literal interpretation of the scripture and its direct application to modern life. Like Christian fundamentalism, Islamic fundamentalism is also opposed to alcohol and smoking, to "lewd" publications and movies (and maybe to all movies and theater), to immodest dress, and to many forms of entertainment—in particular, dancing and popular music (in some cases, to all music). It also favors traditional gender roles and provides strict punishment for offenses. In its more extreme forms, this includes cloistering women in their homes, unless they must be out (and then a traditional veiled covering is worn), and forbidding them to drive and in some cases to work. Criminal punishments are based on the Qu'ran and include executions, stonings, and cutting off the hands of thieves and other offenders. Homosexuality and any form of extramarital sex is severely punished.

Many of these fundamentalist practices are seen in Saudi Arabia, although often moderated by local custom. They reached their extreme in Afghanistan under the **Taliban,** which means "student," or one who strictly studies the Qu'ran. Many of these practices are ancient, although over the centuries, a number of Islamic rulers have been extremely tolerant of religious and social diversity. What has gained new attention is that Islamic fundamentalism, like its Christian counterpart in the United States, has grown more political. The Iranian Revolution installed a government based on strict Islamic fundamentalist principles. Many Muslim countries now have Islamic political parties that call for a strict Islamic state, based on fundamentalist interpretations.

Other religions also have their fundamentalist forms. Ultraorthodox Jewish factions also call for a particular type of modesty in dress, traditional gender divisions and family forms, a rejection of certain aspects of the modern world, and a strict and literal reading of the Torah, or Jewish law. In Israel, political parties that wed these beliefs to the conviction that God has promised them all the land of David and Solomon have gained influence in the government.

Hindu fundamentalism would seem to be an oxymoron, given that Hinduism is known as an incredibly diverse and highly tolerant religion. Yet within India, a movement is gaining political and social power that likewise stresses traditional Indian lifestyles, family forms, and gender patterns; rejects certain aspects of the modern, commercial world; and is suspicious of secularists and non-Hindus in positions of power.

It is easy (and maybe it is especially easy in a cosmopolitan university) to condemn fundamentalist movements as shortsighted, anti-intellectual, antimodern, or just out of touch with a changing world. Yet these movements are clearly speaking to the personal and spiritual needs of many people and seem to represent a global hunger for a more stable and more moral social order.

Global fundamentalism also poses some major problems. Barber (1995) suggests they are fundamentally undemocratic. This perhaps remains to be seen. In the United States, Christian fundamentalists certainly endorse the democratic ideals of the U.S. Constitution and often speak of the "Founding Fathers," (even though most historians do not envision George Washington, let alone Thomas Jefferson or Benjamin Franklin, as much of a fundamentalist). Their mix of religion and politics sometimes clashes with the constitutional ideals of the separation of church and state. In addition, they have often objected to the American Civil Liberties Union's idea of free speech and have been vigorous opponents of campaign finance reform.

Islamic parties have been big vote getters in many Muslim nations that hold elections, but the commitment of these parties to continuing a liberal democratic tradition, as opposed to a theocracy of religious leaders and laws, has been questioned. In Iran, a reformist elected government has seen many of its proposals vetoed by religious leaders, who still hold the final authority. African democracies have been more plagued by paternalism and tribalism (i.e., favoring ones own ethnic group), but now, they are seeing new challenges from a fervent and perhaps radical Islamic government in Sudan and a powerful Islamic party in Algeria that the military has kept out of power. Whether the military in Algeria is protecting democracy or subverting it depends on one's view of the intentions of these political entities.

Israel has functioned as a democracy since its founding in 1948, but the so-called religious parties have often sought to conform Israeli law to their form of Jewish religious law and worry about the growing number of Israeli Arabs who can vote. Some wonder if Israel can really be both a Jewish state, defined in religious and ethnic terms, and a modern liberal democracy, with the expectations of pluralism. Likewise, India has been a democracy since its founding in 1947, but the demands of Hindu fundamentalists may run counter to the ideals of a pluralist democracy, which seeks to protect and include people from many cultural and religious backgrounds.

The God of the Poor: Liberation Theology

Not all the mingling of religion and politics has occurred on the religious and political right. There is also a history of blending religious convictions and progressive politics.

Upon his conversion to Buddhism, the Indian leader Asoka (third century BCE) renounced warfare, embraced religious and ethnic tolerance, and sought to alleviate the suffering of the poor. Christian influence in the late Roman Empire restrained the excesses of the emperors and led to the abolition of the gladiatorial games. In the United States during the civil rights movement of the 1960s, many of the challenges to segregation, the demand for voting rights, and the Poor People's Campaign were led by African American religious leaders. Latin American politics have likewise been influenced by liberation theology, a set of ideas coming out of the Catholic Church that, at the core of the gospel, is a message of liberation for the poor and oppressed. Pope John Paul II tried to restrain what he saw as too much political involvement by Catholic clergy, but progressive priests in many countries formed base communities of poor *campesinos* and workers and led campaigns for the poor.

The political landscape of the twenty-first century, however, has been most impacted by religious fundamentalists, especially what some prefer to call **religious extremists,** who hold very strict interpretations of their faith traditions and sometimes appear willing to use force to enforce these ideas. Religion, in this case, is closely allied with nationalism, as in calls for fundamentalists to preserve the United States as a Christian nation, India as a Hindu nation, Israel as an orthodox Jewish state, and Muslim countries as Islamic states under Islamic law. "Hardliners," who combine religion, ethnicity, and nationalism, have been a force in the creation of repressive states, while "extremists" have combined the same elements into national and international terrorism in efforts to topple and remake some of these same states.

Identity and International Terrorism

Revolutionary and State Terror

Terror has a long history. It has been most often used to build states and empires. Cities that resisted Genghis Khan's invading armies in the thirteenth century were often massacred en masse, while those who surrendered were shown leniency, creating a powerful incentive to join rather than oppose the empire. In the twentieth century, state-sponsored terror conducted against enemies of the regime claimed more lives and inflicted more suffering than ever before imagined, even if the exact numbers are hard to tally. An estimated 6 million people were killed in the Nazi holocaust, many millions in the Stalinist purges, several million in China's Cultural Revolution, 2 million in Cambodia's "killing fields," 1.5 million in Rwanda, and these numbers do not include terror in the pursuit of international war. Terror has also been used also to oppose rulers. The *assassins* used carefully planned murders to intimidate and oppose Christian and Ottoman rule. Their leader, an extremist Muslim, used both mind-altering drugs and promises of eternal paradise to motivate the killers.

A Palestinian boy walks along Israel's new security wall that separates his village from East Jerusalem. Fears of terrorism have led to attempts to contain threats, although this can lead to isolation, division, and repression that spur new cycles of terror.

Many troubled locations are trapped in cycles of revolutionary terror, opposing rulers and states, and state repression, including what some would call **state terror.** The classic case has been Israel and Palestine during the *intifada*. Palestinians fighting for groups such as Hamas, Hezbollah, and the Al Axa martyrs brigades all seek an independent Palestinian state, and many also seek the destruction of the state of Israel. They gain support from other Palestinians who may not share their complete political and religious agenda but who have a long history of grievances against Israel and its allies and who respect the utter dedication of these groups, as well as the charitable work they often do in Palestinian communities and refugee camps. Bombings and ambushes have been the favorite tools of their terror.

More recently, the dominant form has become the **suicide bomber**, detonating explosives in crowded places that have been packed into a car or strapped to the bomber's body. Since suicide is forbidden by Islamic law but martyrdom, dying for the faith, is glorified, supporters call these "martyrdom acts," rather than "suicide bombings." To Jewish Israelis, these acts that randomly kill innocent people are the height of reckless, ruthless terror. While their perpetrators agree that terror is the intent, they argue that the victims are not innocent, as they are in collusion with a repressive Israeli state, and that the martyrs are soldiers of faith.

Israel has responded to these attacks with assassinations and targeted killings of suspected leaders and activists in these Palestinian cells, often killing them from the air in attacks that also take the lives of bystanders. Another common retaliation has been the bulldozing of the houses, orchards, and fields of families of suspected terrorists and sometimes whole communities. To the Israelis, these are acts of self-defense; to the Palestinians, they are acts of repression and state terror. In fact, when taken along with the searches, beatings, and humiliation they experience at the hands Israeli troops, these acts justify further acts of martyrdom. Both sides are armed and aided by outside supporters, and the cycle continues, despite attempts to negotiate a settlement.

This same cycle has ripped apart Sri Lanka, the island nation just south of India, for several decades since the 1980s. Once considered a place of peace and tranquility that, while poor, excelled in health and education, Sri Lanka has been shattered by fighting between the revolutionary Tamil Tigers, representing a Hindu Tamil minority with ties to India, and government troops, representing the Buddhist Singhalese majority. The Tamils claimed they were an oppressed minority and sought their own independent state. While some groups worked nonviolently, the Tigers increasingly resorted to horrific bombings that made nowhere on the island safe; they claim to have invented the suicide bomber. Fighting and the state response sent many Tamils into refugee camps, where they were displaced and without work and without much hope. The camps, in turn, became prime recruiting ground for new Tigers, just like the Palestinian refugee camps.

The bloodshed in Sri Lanka never captured the world's press in the same way as the Israeli-Palestinian conflict. A ceasefire was signed in 2001, and the island appears to be returning to an uneasy peace, as Sri Lankans seek to recover from the terror of the tsunami that hit them so hard in December 2004. Still this battle between the Tamils and the Singhalese, between Hindus and Buddhists, provides a powerful reminder that religious and ethnic tensions spilling into terrorism are not limited to conflicts among Muslims, Jews, and Christians.

The Power and Weakness of Terror

The power of terror lies in its ability to grab headlines and command attention. It is not easy to become a famous humanitarian, but it's not all that hard to become a famous (momentarily at least) assassin. There are not many ways that nineteen men from the Middle East could suddenly change the politics and policies of the world's powers and command the attention of the entire world, but the terrorists' hijackings and plane crashes of September 11, 2001, did just that.

The weakness of terror lies in its inability to effect the lasting changes the terrorists and their supporters so desire. The event that has become known just by its date, 9/11, was first and foremost a terrible human tragedy that took the lives of people from around the world—from European financiers to Central American custodians, all working in the World Trade Center. From the perspective of the Al-Qaeda leadership, it seemed to be a great success: the biggest act of revolutionary terrorism ever (it still pales before examples of state terror unleashed during wartime), struck at the heart of the world's superpower and riveting world attention. Yet in terms of achieving the goals of this Islamic extremist collection of terror cells, it was a complete failure.

Intended to divide and undermine the United States, it brought about tremendous national unity and a resurgence of patriotism. Inspired in part by anger over the U.S. military presence in the Middle East, it resulted in the next few years in huge U.S. military deployments in Afghanistan and Iraq. Motivated in part by U.S. support for Israel, it led to greater support for Israel as a fellow country fighting terrorism. Al-Qaeda was angered by U.S. and British embargoes and no-fly zones over Iraq, which they saw as an attack on Arab peoples, but their own attack provided grounds for a new, more aggressive doctrine that resulted in the full-scale invasion of Iraq. Previously, the one truly friendly regime to Al-Qaeda, the Taliban of Afghanistan, was toppled, with many Al-Qaeda loyalists killed and its leadership sent into hiding. In terms of commanding attention, the 9/11 hijackings and attacks were spectacularly successful; in terms of fulfilling long-term goals, they were a complete failure.

The Tamil Tigers had to face the reality that their spectacular "successes" in bombings and killings brought only misery to their people, not liberation, and so they were eventually rejected by most Tamils. Ever more Palestinian leaders have come to realize that their attacks on Israel bolster the position of Israeli hard-liners, who favor repression and expulsion of Palestinians, at the expense of the position of more moderate Israelis. Terrorism has been called "the weapon of the weak," for it has typically been favored by those who cannot field large, victorious armies. As the weapons available to terrorists increase, the world can only hope that both the proponents of revolutionary terror and those of state terror will realize that terrorism is also a weak weapon, one that almost never produces the desired outcome.

Alternatives to Terror

Religion as Resilience

Religious conviction and cultural heritage have also been used to effect nonviolent change and reconciliation. The towering figure of nonviolence in the twentieth century was a small, personally unimposing man, Mohandas Gandhi, whom Indians called the *Mahatma,* or "great soul." Gandhi believed that social change began with an inner spiritual change. "You must be the change you seek" was his famous motto. He also believed that as vital as deep spiritual conviction was, if it was not tied to tolerance and nonviolence, it would become a weapon of destruction.

Gandhi was deeply inspired by his own Hindu roots, especially the ideals of the Bhagavad Ghita, and also by insights from other faiths, notably Christian pacifist and Russian writer Leo Tolstoy and the ethic of Jesus in the Sermon on the Mount. Gandhi called his program *satyagraha,* meaning the energy and power of the soul, driven by truth and love. His campaign of nonviolent resistance to injustice, tolerance for all faiths, respect for all castes and ethnicities, and respect for the cultural heritage of India won worldwide recognition in the early twentieth century and paved the way for India's post–World War II independence.

Gandhi's ideals were not accepted by all, however. Even though he favored a tolerant, multireligious India, he could not prevent the 1947 partition into a Hindu-dominated India and an Islamic state in East and West Pakistan. He was murdered by a Hindu hard-liner who resented his accommodation of Muslims. Yet his ideas lived on to inspire the Reverend Dr. Martin Luther King, Jr. in his commitment to nonviolence as well as that of many lesser known leaders in the American civil rights movement, such as Ella Baker, and many other leaders across Asia and Africa.

In the antiapartheid struggle in South Africa, where Gandhi first started to form his ideas, a nonviolent campaign of resistance was led by Bishop Desmond Tutu of the Anglican Church and Allan Bosak of the Dutch Reformed Church. Throughout the 1970s and 1980s, they held rallies, staged boycotts, lobbied for international sanctions and pressure, and pleaded to the moral conscience of their church members. The apartheid system eventually collapsed in the early 1990s without a violent revolution.

In the late 1960s, the Fourteenth Dalai Lama of Tibet fled the country, as China pressed harder to incorporate the once-independent country culturally and politically into China. Some of his followers proposed a guerilla war in the rugged

Tibetan plateau to try to keep the Chinese out. The Dalai Lama instead chose a pattern of nonviolent resistence and continued dialogue with Chinese leaders. In over thirty years, he has not won independence for Tibet and now often speaks only of earning autonomy. He has, however, become a widely recognized spokesperson for Tibetan Buddhism and its ethic of compassion and a symbol of enduring Tibetan culture. The respect he has garnered in the international community, as well as among his own people, has kept Tibet, once remote and largely unknown, in the forefront of the media throughout the world, forcing Chinese authorities to carefully consider their policies and image in Tibet.

Another leader who has drawn strength from Buddhist conviction (and like the Dalai Lama, has won the Nobel Peace Prize) is Aung San Suu Kyi of Burma. Elected prime minister in 1990 but never allowed to take office by the ruling military junta, who has often kept her under house arrest, she has nevertheless remained a symbol and leader of the struggle for democracy in this Buddhist country that the military now calls Myanmar. Again, she has not won quick results. Yet the charges most often levied by military dictators against the civilian leaders they depose—that they are corrupt—do not work against this highly respected woman. She remains a powerful moral and political force in the country.

Ethnicity as Resilience

Some movements draw strength from ethnic heritage, often with strong ethical, social, and spiritual values but not always rooted in the language of a major religion. The **Zapatista** movement in Chiapas, Mexico, has drawn heavily on Mayan

The desire to have cultural and political autonomy as well as a say in the control of the local economy continues to spur many revolts around the world. The Zapatistas in Chiapas, Mexico, and Karen rebels in the highlands of Myanmar (Burma) depend more on publicity and outside support than they do on their antiquated weapons. Here Subcomandante Marcos leads a Zapatista march and rally in Mexico City, and the young Htoo brothers lead "God's Army" in the Burmese highlands.

traditions and culture in its campaign against what it sees as Mexican government repression and economic exploitation in the very poor state of Chiapas. The movement's charismatic spokesperson has been "*subcomandante*" Marcos, but it insists that the real *comandantes* are the indigenous village elders.

The group looks like a typical armed Latin American rebel group, wearing ski masks and carrying rifles. Yet the rifles are not AK-47s but antiquated hunting guns and sometimes no more than wooden cutouts. Members claim that the masks are to protect them from reprisals and that the guns mere symbols of their determination to fight for their rights in the spirit of other indigenous and populist revolutionaries, such as Emiliano Zapata of the Mexican Revolution. Interestingly, their main weapon seems to be the Internet. Their international friends maintain their website (www.ezln.org) and publish resolutions from the elders and scathing critiques of Mexican society and international capitalism from Marcos. The group has created a new model of resistance: rooted in indigenous culture and beliefs yet very savvy in the use of modern international media and recalling revolutionary heroes while pursuing a largely nonviolent agenda.

Moral Leadership as Resilience

Nonviolent groups are often not as good as grabbing the headlines as their violent counterparts, who get immediate attention with spectacular terrorist attacks and other acts of violence. Even in this, however, some nonviolent leaders, Dr. King and the Dalai Lama among them, have been very effective in getting media attention.

Nonviolent groups are also not as easy for governing authorities to disparage and dismiss. State and federal governments, as well as popular opinion, often dismissed groups such as the Black Panthers as dangerous criminals. Yet this was hard to do with other groups, such as King's Southern Christian Leadership Conference and the hundreds of college students who formed the Student Nonviolent Coordinating Committee. These young people endured attacks and insults to nonviolently insist on desegregation, and their moral power was hard to dismiss.

Gandhi believed that once he had wrested the moral high ground from the British Empire, his struggle would be ultimately won. In South Africa, the apartheid government portrayed Nelson Mandela as a dangerous communist and terrorist, but this was not an easy charge to make against a dignified bishop who spoke eloquently about brotherhood and reconciliation. Similarly, long after many revolutionaries have been forgotten, El Salvador's Catholic archbishop Oscar Romero, killed for his nonviolent defense of the rights of poor *compesinos* (peasant farmers and country people), is still remembered and his ideals pursued.

There is always the danger that nonviolent actions will be overtaken by more spectacular violence. In Kosovo, a nonviolent Muslim movement in the 1980s and early 1990s was founding Albanian language schools and community services in opposition to the government of Milosevic. It was the armed resistance, however, that got the attention and support of Western Europe and the United States and then drew horrible reprisals and repression from the Milosevic government in 1998. In the occupied territories of Gaza and Palestine, Palestinian groups, many with strong Muslim convictions, have organized schools and relief programs, have used boycotts and strikes as major means of protest, and have generally drawn on the arsenal of nonviolence. Some of their fellow Palestinians see these methods as too slow and ineffective, yet had this approach dominated throughout the *intifada,* or uprising, one wonders if the Palestinians would not have been more effective in winning sympathies from moderate Israelis and from world opinion and thus strengthened their claims for independence.

In his book *The Unconquerable World: Power, Nonviolence, and the Will of the People,* Jonathan Schell (2003), Peace Fellow at the National Institute in New York, describes what he sees as a progression from (1) traditional war, now obsolete in a nuclear age; to (2) "people's war," guerilla fights that depend on popular support but often lead to growing cycles of violence, with many civilian casualties; to (3) nonviolent revolution and nonviolent rule. While Schell respects the power of Gandhi's spiritual calling, his call for nonviolent revolution and rule is more practical than theological. Both types of war only lead to mounds of corpses. Only patient, persistent, nonviolent action can preserve both freedoms and traditions and provide what uprisings—popular, religious, and ethnic—hope to attain.

As people look for alternatives to terror in struggles around the world, several repeated lessons emerge:

1. Religious fervor and ethnic identity can both be dangerous when manipulated by demagogues and used to justify attacks on "the enemies of God" or "those who would destroy our people." But these same traditions and convictions can motivate people to make tremendous personal sacrifices, to stand in solidarity with one another, and to seek creative cultural, social, and political alternatives to violence.

2. While nonviolent change may be slow, it is often more enduring than the change brought about by force. Often, it is the only way out of a cycle of terror and repression.

3. The ethic that is rooted in many spiritual traditions and that may be most needed is that of compassion and forgiveness. History can be a great source of wisdom and understanding, but places can also be "sick with history," as the story of myriad grievances. Letting go of these grievances is very hard for the aggrieved and resisted by leaders who know that playing on grievances will build a quick following. Yet as Gandhi learned, tremendous power results when truth is coupled with compassion and forgiveness. The South African truth and reconciliation commission hearings were imperfect, but at times, they produced remarkable results.

MAKING CONNECTIONS

Overcoming Violence

■ The World Council of Churches, an international affiliation of Christian groups, is sponsoring a decade to overcome violence (2001–2010). Themes include the logic of violence, justice, power, identity, and pluralism. Go to www.overcomingviolence.org for current activities and ideas on how churches and individuals can become involved. This multilingual site also includes stories of nonviolent action from the around the world.

■ The site of the World Council, www.wcc-coe.org, also contains links to information about churches around the world. How do various traditions approach the theme of nonviolence? Are there ways that local groups and places of worship are becoming involved?

Plum Village

■ Vietnamese Zen Buddhist monk Thich Nhat Hahn has worked for peace and reconciliation based on the principles of Buddhism for almost half a century. He first worked for peace during the Vietnam War and has continued his efforts in exile in France at a site called Plum Village since that time. Dr. Martin Luther King, Jr., nominated him for the Nobel Peace Prize. Information about his work, about the Unified Buddhist Church, and ongoing efforts for interpersonal and global peace can be found at www.plumvillage.org. What are some of the current emphases at his center? How does it draw on both Bhuddist and Christian traditions?

Tibet

■ The world's most prominent Buddhist leader is the Fourteenth Dalai Lama of Tibet, who received the Nobel Peace Prize for his work for nonviolent solutions in Chinese-occupied Tibet. His ideas and work are featured at www.dalailama.com.

■ More information on peaceful attempts to preserve the cultural and religious heritage of Tibet can be found at www.tibet.com, the official site of the Tibetan government in exile. What solutions are proposed for the situation in Tibet? How do these reflect a commitment to justice and nonviolence?

Chiapas

■ Although the Zapatista Army of National Liberation often looks and sounds like a guerilla army, most of its efforts have been nonviolent and stressed indigenous leadership and principles. These "fighters" have mostly fought for public opinion, with the help of a site at www.ezln.org. The site includes information in English and French as well as Spanish. What are their goals for Chiapas? How are these related to indigenous Mayan communities and their heritage?

CHAPTER 9

Urbanization
Cities without Limits

Mesa, Arizona

This place is big. Just how big, I can't say, since given the rate of growth, my estimate would be obsolete by the time this book reached print, but Mesa is heading toward half a million people. Mesa is also one of the fastest-growing places in the United States. It is already bigger than Minneapolis, and it is bigger than St. Louis. But Mesa is not a *city*, at least not in the way we have thought of cities. It is a suburb of Phoenix. It may be the biggest suburb in the world.

Phoenix sits at the center of one of the fastest-growing metropolitan regions in the United States. Like most Western U.S. cities that boomed after the dominance of the automobile, it is built around great highways and expansive spaces. People moving here don't want to be confined to high-rise apartments in the manner of Manhattan or Hong Kong; they came for sun and for space. As a result, as the Phoenix metro continues to sprawl, much of the growth is in neighboring communities, such as Tempe and Mesa. Mesa is no place to walk, even in the pleasant winter temperatures. Rather, it is a place to drive: past sprawling malls and huge, one-story, "big box" megastores, past ever-new subdivisions, out to your place in the sun.

Is this the good life or the end of community? Will it thrive and bloom in the desert, or will it bake to death in its own greenhouse gases? This remains to be seen. In the meantime, residents can pick up a chilled latte, turn on the air conditioning in the car, and drive out to see the sunset.

Addis Ababa, Ethiopia

There are many things you can't get in this ancient capital, high in the mountains of Ethiopia. But you can have great shoes. Shoeshine boys are everywhere, hauling their equipment and hawking their services. All across Africa, prosperous young people seek American-style sneakers, such as Nike hightops. But older prosperous Africans like nice shoes, and here in this place of dust and rock, where everyone walks everywhere, shoes need frequent shining—hence, the ever-present, hard-working shoeshine boys.

If you have your shoes done, please tip well. This is not because the shoeshine boys are homeless and starving, although many of them live in tight communal quarters and eat very simple local dishes. It is because they have a family to support, often a big family. Most of the shoeshine boys have come from the Ethiopian countryside, where food is scarce and jobs are often nonexistent. They save as much of their earnings as they can and send the money back to their villages. In some cases, they are the major supporters of their families. How poor does one have to be to depend on a shoeshine boy as your family's major wage earner? Ethiopian annual incomes hover at about $350 a year.

Around the world, people are flocking to the cities to seek opportunities. The opportunities they find are modest, however. Some find work with large multinational corporations. More often, they find work in the so-called informal economy, working semi-independently at menial and occasional service jobs, such as shining shoes. For these refugees from rural poverty, the city rarely fulfills its promise of the good life, but they will remain so long as it offers a chance at survival.

Once a month, the shoeshine boys get to go home. They see their families and turn over their savings. Maybe they will play a bit. They might even walk to the top of one of the ridges in this rugged land to see the sunset. They won't need to wear shoes.

The Urban Millennium: Worldwide Urbanization

Somewhere around the beginning of this, the third millennium (for those who follow the Western calendar), something momentous happened that will continue to reshape our times, regardless of the calendar we use. Unlike the new millennium itself, the event wasn't celebrated with fireworks. It was noted mostly by demographers, who are not known to be an overly boisterous bunch.

What happened? We became an urban world. Just over half of the world's population now live in cities and urban areas.

Dawn of the City

In one sense, this was a long time coming. The first cities emerged around the dawn of agriculture, somewhere well before the dawn of the third millennium BCE. We have many accounts of the founding of the early cities, but they are all shrouded in legend: Romulus and Remus being raised by wolves before founding Rome, Gilgamesh descending from the gods to rule Uruk, and so forth.

Probably the first cities were at key points on trade routes, maybe walled and fortified to protect the traders and their goods. The walls of Jericho, one of the world's first cities between 8000 and 5000 BCE, are most famous for falling down, but they must have been an imposing feature on the desert crossroads. Villages had already been around for several thousand years and were growing larger, but the first cities offered a social complexity that was new to the world. Cities were not only centers of trade. Some also became centers of religious observance, and some served as the homes of rulers who could commandeer the surpluses of surrounding fields of grain to support themselves and ruling elites along with religious leaders, craftspersons, and eventually soldiers to secure it all.

The early cities emerged by 3500 BCE throughout the Middle East: in Asia Minor (modern Turkey), all throughout Mesopotamia, and at several points along the Nile River. Somewhat later, great cities emerged along the Indus River, and along the great rivers of China by 2500 BCE. In time, well-watered valleys and lush lowlands in what are now Mexico and Peru would also see the building of great, complex, fortified cities between 500 BCE and 1500 AD.

With cities came civilization. The earliest cities of the Sumerians in southern Mesopotamia, with strange names such as Ur and Uruk, are still being excavated from the sands and the swamps to reveal complex urban networks. It is always dangerous to accord "firsts" to anyone, for history has had many cradles of civilization in many places, but between 4000 and 2000 BCE this was the land of firsts. The Sumerians were some of the first people to use the wheel, to bake bread, and to keep track of it all in writing. The oldest writing samples we have are not great religious texts but something like accounting ledgers stamped on clay. Cities collect an abundance of goods, and someone has to keep track of it all.

Cities have also always provoked considerable ambivalence in people. The book of Genesis in the Bible gives credit for the first city to the murderous Cain and notes how Abraham, the father of Western religion, left the city of Ur and lived in the desert, where he could see the stars and be close to God. His nephew made the bad choice of going to the city, none other than Sodom, whose name has become synonymous with depravity and evil.

Even older than the account of Abraham is the ancient Sumerian (and later Babylonian) story of King Gilgamesh, who ruled Uruk. He was mighty, descended from the gods, but he also grew to be a tyrant and a slave driver. The people were crushed under his demands for higher walls and bigger monuments. Finally, the gods sent someone to be his friend, one equally strong but a wild man who talked to the animals and understood the forest and the desert. To his shame, Enkidu was won over to the attractions of the city (in most accounts, women and baking have something to do with it), but he remained in touch with the wild. Only when Gilgamesh had his friend Enkidu, the wild man, was he whole and humane. It seems that the inhabitants of the earliest cities, telling and later writing one of the world's first epic stories, already sensed that life in a mighty city came at a great price.

Triumph of the City

Ambivalent or not, great civilizations were dominated by great cities. In the Indus Valley of India, by 2500 BCE cities were laid out on careful grid patterns, much like midwestern U.S. cities today. And they included an important innovation that would not appear in many European cities until industrial times: indoor toilets that fed into covered sewage systems. In China, for thousands of years following about 2000 BCE, powerful emperors built ever-grander cities around the area of the current city of Beijing, protected by ever-longer networks of walls and dominated by ever-grander imperial palaces. In Mesoamerica, near present-day Mexico City, the great city of Teotihuacán grew up around the obsidian trade and dominated a vast region about the same time as the rise of Rome before likewise collapsing and falling to northern "barbarian invaders" around 750 AD, several centuries after the fall of Rome.

Rome stands as the ultimate city of the ancient world, with between 1 and 1.5 million people at the height of its population. It was the city of great public works, a huge aqueduct bringing fresh water, "circuses" ranging from gladiatorial games to chariot races to great mock sea battles fought in the flooded Colosseum, a center of a trade network that stretched all the way to China along the Silk Road, and the power center of a mighty empire. Rome was the queen city of the Mediterranean world. It was also a city of beggars and thieves, a city dependent on slaves and on regular shipments of grain from abroad to feed its masses, a city prone to unrest and civil strife, and a place where "all the filth of the empire eventually comes to collect."

These themes continue to be present in ambivalent and contrasting views of cities: as the "pearl" of the region or the exploiter of the region, as the place of noble pursuits or the place of depraved pursuits. Cities have been the centers of great flourishes of thought and culture.

The Golden Age of Athens lasted less than fifty years in the middle of the fifth century BCE between two devastating wars, but for several centuries, the city was the home of great art, science, and philosophy. Aristotle, one of the most famous of the hometown philosophers and scholars, claimed in the *Politics* that one comes to the city to live, and stays to live well. Living well may have been more difficult for the Athenian women cloistered to their homes, for the slaves laboring long hours to support a leisure class, and for lesser cities forced to pay tribute to Athens at the height of its power. Regardless, this one city produced incredible insights into everything from democracy to astronomy to natural history to health care.

In terms of learning, the only rival to Athens was Alexandria, founded by Alexander the Great, on the Egyptian coast. A vast library held books (in scroll form) in many languages from around the world. Moreover, scholars from many places and ethnicities who worked in the library and museum measured the circumference of the earth (Eratosthenes, 276–194 BCE), conducted advanced mathematics (Hypatia c. 370–415), and collected and advanced learning from around the Mediterranean and across the Middle East.

While the European cities fell into decline, cities such as Baghdad flourished with the wealth of empire and carried on the studies of astronomy, mathematics, and philosophy that had begun in the Greek-speaking cities. The European Renaissance was also centered in great (though by our standards, small) cities. Renaissance Florence may have had no more than 70,000 people, but among them were Michelangelo, Da Vinci, Giberti, and scores of artists, writers, and scholars.

One of the most striking features of medieval cities was their compact size. Houses were crowded along tangled, narrow streets. If an original wall still stands, it often encloses a city not much larger than a modest modern neighborhood. For centuries, the only city of any significant size in Europe was Constantinople, the capital of the Eastern Roman and Byzantine Empires, on Europe's eastern edge. Gradually, beginning in the 1500s, growing empires brought growing cities: Seville in Spain, Lisbon in Portugal, Amsterdam in the Netherlands, and eventually London in England. As the British Empire grew, so did the importance and size of London. The matriarch of a global empire, London stood as perhaps the first truly global world city.

Industrialization changed the face of the cities. The first factories were clustered along scattered sites of waterpower, but eventually, cities built on coal power clustered around rail and shipyards. In the eighteenth century, London, as well as Liverpool and Manchester, became cities of industrial might and also of soot and ever-present smoke billowing from "dark Satanic mills." In the United States, cities of mills such as Brooklyn, Yonkers, Hoboken, and Newark grew up around the port of Manhattan. Other major cities also took root around industrial might: Baltimore, Pittsburgh, and Chicago. It was the incredible influx of people from Europe in the late nineteenth and early twentieth centuries, however—many of them displaced farmers, whose own cities could not supply enough jobs—that eventually made New York the world's largest city.

In the late years of the twentieth century, New York was overtaken by another great industrial empire, Tokyo, Japan, and soon by many others. The rush to the cities had begun. Great world cities of over 5 million people now dot every continent, some having doubled in the course of a decade.

World Cities

The pace of global urbanization is staggering. In 1950, the world had one city with over 10 million people: New York. In 1995, it had fourteen. By 2015, at current rates, there will be over twenty-one cities with over 10 million people (see Figure 9.1). Almost all of this boom will take place in the developing world.

In 1950, New York's competition was largely limited to the great capitals of Europe: London, Paris, Moscow, and the industrial heartland of Germany. By the

FIGURE 9.1   Largest Urban Agglomerations: 1950, 2000, and 2015

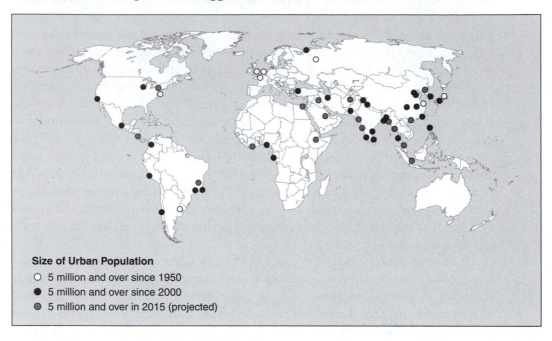

Source: United Nations, *World Urbanization Prospects* (1999 Revision).

turn of the twenty-first century, none of the five largest cities in the world were European: Tokyo, Mexico City, São Paulo, New York, and Mumbai (Bombay). The projected list of the "big five" **world cities** for 2015 would challenge the geography skills of many North Americans and Europeans: Tokyo (Japan), Dhaka (Bangladesh), Mumbai (India), São Paulo (Brazil), and Delhi (India). How many people do you know who could even identify these growing giants, let alone point to each one on a map?

The cities in Europe and North America continue to grow by international **immigration.** A few U.S. cities now grow explosively due to **internal migration,** such as the Phoenix area (noted at the beginning of this chapter) and Las Vegas, Nevada, which grew 83 percent in the 1990s, springing from the desert thanks to the "circuses" of the gaming and entertainment industry and air conditioning. The real growth, however, will be in the "sun belt" of the developing world—the global South (see Table 9.1). Europe, North America, and Latin America are all already at least two-thirds urban, with many countries, including places such as Chile and Argentina, having urbanization levels above 75 percent. Africa and Asia are still two-thirds rural but will be half urban within a decade or so.

| TABLE 9.1 | Top 10 Largest Urban Agglomerations: 1950, 2000, 2015 |

1950		2000		2015	
1. New York, USA	12.3	1. Tokyo, Japan	26.4	1. Tokyo, Japan	26.4
2. London, England	8.7	2. Mexico City, Mexico	18.4	2. Bombay, India	26.1
3. Tokyo, Japan	6.9	3. Bombay, India	18.0	3. Lagos, Nigeria	23.2
4. Paris, France	5.4	4. São Paulo, Brazil	17.8	4. Dhaka, Bangladesh	21.1
5. Moscow, Russia	5.4	5. New York, USA	16.6	5. São Paulo, Brazil	20.4
6. Shanghai, China	5.3	6. Lagos, Nigeria	13.4	6. Karachi, Pakistan	19.2
7. Essen, Germany	5.3	7. Los Angeles, USA	13.1	7. Mexico City, Mexico	19.2
8. Buenos Aires, Argentina	5.0	8. Calcutta, India	12.9	8. New York, USA	17.4
9. Chicago, USA	4.9	9. Shanghai, China	12.9	9. Jakarta, Indonesia	17.3
10. Calcutta, India	4.4	10. Buenos Aires, Argentina	12.6	10. Calcutta, India	17.3

Source: United Nations Population Division, *World Urbanization Prospects* (1999 Revision). Used by permission.

Who is urban and who is rural hinges on debatable criteria, such as the number of communities over 20,000. Many rural people are already dependent on neighboring cities, and in India and China, villages can run together in great agglomerations of population. But a city is distinct from a mere agglomeration of people. It has a complexity and interconnectedness of its own. The exact size of a city depends on who gets counted and who does not (such as people who are displaced or homeless or illegal "squatters"). It also depends on how one figures the extent of a metropolitan region. For example, based on the incorporated city itself, Houston is by far the largest city in Texas, but Dallas–Fort Worth is the largest combined metropolitan area.

The next generation of world cities will be a dizzying array of newborn giants. What do you know about Chongqing and Wuhan? Unless you are from China or you study or do business in East Asia, these could be kinds of soup, for all you know. They are, in fact, Chinese cities of growing industrial might, each with over 7 million people. They are each the size of greater London or Chicago.

Megacities

Who are the actors in this global drama of urban life? Read on for a brief tour of a few of the world's current **megacities.**

TOKYO. Following World War II, Tokyo, the ancient Japanese City of Edo, was a charred husk. It did, however, command a magnificent natural bay on a crowded, mountainous island. As Japan rapidly urbanized, Tokyo grew to become the world's largest city and is likely to remain so well into this century. It is also one of the most crowded and one of the most expensive cities. The land value around the imperial palace in Tokyo is worth more than all of the real estate of some entire countries. Rents are exorbitant, and buying a house is often unattainable.

Yet for decades jobs were plentiful, wages grew to some of the highest in the world, and Tokyo grew to be one of the world's premier commercial and financial centers. Only New York has more major banks and corporate headquarters. The price of this success has been intense air and water pollution and constant crowds. Tokyo's clean, efficient, and profitable subway train system is so popular that the operators have had to hire "pushers" to pack everyone (politely of course) into the train before it continues on a rush-hour commute that seems to have no end. Almost anything from anywhere can be purchased in Tokyo, even air to breathe. Commuters who are feeling faint amid the fumes and crowds of the city can stop and buy a few breaths of pure oxygen to revive their energies and carry them home.

Tokyo can intimidate someone who is unprepared, yet it is also a vibrant, bustling, and hugely productive city. Whether it can maintain its premiere role, as Japan suffers a recession and confronts new competitors, remains to be seen. In the meantime, people cram onto the trains to work twelve-hour days and dream about visiting a Zen garden in Kyoto to meditate and restore their calm.

NEW YORK. For several decades the world's largest city, New York is the only U.S. city likely to remain among the world's "big ten." It is really a vast urban agglomeration that spans several states. Where the New York metropolitan area ends is hard to say, but the core has always been the island of Manhattan. The city grew as a port, with rail lines from Hoboken, New Jersey, and before that the Erie Canal upstate, carrying people and goods inland. The city awed the world from the 1880s on with ever-taller buildings, new and amazing bridges, and growing financial might.

Between 1880 and 1920, 20 million people came through New York's gate of entry at Ellis Island, past the Statue of Liberty (a gift from France in 1884) with its promises to the poor of the world, and into a city of incredible diversity, boasting hundreds of languages. Some went on, but many stayed. Two-fifths of the U.S. population has ancestry that came through this one portal.

Industry spilled over to the manufacturing and shipbuilding of Brooklyn, one of several cities later incorporated into New York, while chemicals and railways went to neighboring New Jersey. Manhattan itself flourished in finance, commerce, and culture, from the theater dominance of Broadway to the Harlem Renaissance of African Americans in the 1920s. Manhattan's financial power became concentrated on Wall Street and began at the same time as did urban decay in Harlem. The skyscrapers still soar on Manhattan's south end and in Midtown, where high property values and solid bedrock allow them. The spaces in between still fill with newcomers in Chinatown and in Harlem, which is again experiencing something of a Renaissance. New vitality has returned to Times Square, shoppers still crowd Fifth Avenue, and art and culture still flourish on Broadway and throughout Greenwich Village and Soho.

Many newcomers, however, now prefer to bypass this crowded core and find their dreams somewhere further out in the metropolitan sprawl. The Flushing area of Queens, home to the 1965 World's Fair, is still a world's fair of newcomers and people from dozens of nationalities and ethnicities. Indian temples crowd near Ethiopian cafes and Chinese markets. New York remains a slice of the world.

It is also a city that intimidates and frightens. The city of dreams is also known as a city of crime and despair, of endless hurry, and of a certain harsh, even ruthless character. As far back as 1916, an anonymous poem, "While the City Sleeps," captured these images:

> Stand in your window and scan the sights,
> On Broadway with its bright white lights.
> Its dashing cabs and cabarets,
> Its painted women and fast cafes.
> That's when you really see New York.
> Vulgar of manner, overfed,
> Overdressed and underbred.
> Heartless and Godless, Hell's delight,
> Rude by day and lewd by night.

Of course, this image may have attracted the curious even as it repelled the cautious. Yet even today, Pico Iyer (1997), the British Indian globe-trotting writer who lives in Tokyo, wonders about New York:

> The lighting is harsh, the contrasts are stark, and the effects are as loud as the tabloid headline in your face. When I think of New York, I think of people with an unearthly pallor, dressed all in black; of black jackets and white ties; black limos and white lies. (p. 80)

In spite of this, New York remains a magnet for capital and for people from around the world, who are sure, to paraphrase the words of the song "New York, New York," that success in New York can translate into success anywhere.

MEXICO CITY.   The middle of Mexico is no place to put a city. The Aztecs were said to have been led here by an ancient prophecy, but they may have been driven here by hostile neighbors. They ended up on a snake-infested island in a large, shallow lake. The lake has all but dried up, leaving Mexico City as one of the few great cities that is nowhere near a major body of water, unless one counts the water below the surface. It is essentially a city on a high-altitude swamp. Yet here, the Aztecs expanded the work of their predecessors to create a city that awed the Spanish conquistadors in 1519, who followed Cortez over the pass between the two volcanoes that pierce the skyline. As reported by Bernal Díaz del Castillo (1963 [1568]):

> And when we saw all those cities and villages built in the water, and other great towns on dry land, and that straight and level causeway leading to Mexico, we were astounded. . . . It was all so wonderful that I do not know how to describe this first glimpse of things never heard of, seen or dreamed of before.

Over time, the lake was filled in, paved over, and pumped dry. But the city continued to flourish. In the early 1800s, Robert Southey could still write, "Queen of the Valley! Thou art beautiful! Thy walls, like silver, sparkle in the sun" (2004 [1805]). For generations, canals sliced through this city (a few remain in the heavily touristed gardens of Xochimilco), giving Mexico City the name of Venice of the New World. The title is as appropriate as ever but not in the original intent. Venice, that medieval city of great canals, is sinking into the ocean. Mexico City is also sinking—a full two stories in the last century—because water is pumped out of the underground aquifer upon which the city was built in an attempt to satiate the thirst of a city of 20 million people.

Mexico City is not a city of skyscrapers. They would sink into the ancient lake and crumble under earthquakes. Mexico City has reason to fear earthquakes, as an unstable lake bed is about the worst place to be in a quake. The 1985 tremor brought terrible devastation. The couple of tall buildings in the city have been built on giant rollers that will rock and roll through an earthquake, a technique now being tried in Japan. With so many people and so much danger in building up, the city sprawls in a great concrete sea that seems to go on for as far as the eye can see. The city now fills the ancient valley and spills over into neighboring plateaus; it climbs up steep mountainsides in communities that cannot be reached by urban services. One of its neighboring cities (one cannot really call this a suburb as it would dwarf Mesa, Arizona) is one of the largest cities in Mexico. Built on the flats of the dry lake bed, Netzahaucoyotl (named for an Amerindian poet, diplomat, and king) claims 3 million people in a vast holding tank of the working poor.

This huge expanse of city has one of the most extensive and least expensive subway systems in the world. But even this system cannot effectively span the sprawl, so urban fringe dwellers ride minibuses that connect to bigger buses or eventually to the subway in multihour commutes over huge distances. The more prosperous people drive along avenues packed in day-long gridlock and contribute to the area's terrible smog. This high-altitude, mountain-ringed environment has some of the worst air in the world. A brown haze with the taste of old tobacco hangs over the city much of the winter, obscuring the view of the great volcanoes. One of those volcanoes continues to smoke itself, maybe in solidarity with the city, and adds to the natural threat.

Market reforms and globalization have brought new industry and commercial activity to the corridors that spill out of this city into the neighboring states. These forces have also widened the gap between rich and poor urban dwellers, and the crime rate continues to rise. The city's streets are threaded by old Volkswagen taxis with the front seats removed to allow passengers to squeeze into the back. Although this seems ingenious, visitors are warned against entering unknown taxis, some of which trap them for a robbery, rather than whisking them to their destination.

A city of poverty, crime, smog, natural hazards, and unsightly sprawl would seem to be a place to flee from, rather than a magnet for much of the country. It is true that Mexico City is also a fabulous collage of varied neighborhoods, great restaurants, and world-class museums and cultural events. But what draws residents is the promise of work. Increasingly, that promise is going unfulfilled, which is why Mexico City will probably never be the world's largest city, as once predicted. The displaced continue further on, to the exploding cities on Mexico's northern border and to bigger promises in the country that lies just beyond.

SÃO PAULO. The quintessential Brazilian city may be Rio de Janeiro, where the mountains meet the beach and the rich and the poor live crammed between them. The capital of Brazil now lies in the interior in the planned city of Brazilia, neatly carved from the forest. But the economic dynamo of Brazil, well on its way to being one of the world's largest cities, is São Paulo. The industry and business in this hardworking city, from computers to automobiles to entertainment, generate much of Brazil's wealth and employ its most prosperous citizens. But the seemingly endless forest of highrises gives way to equally endless slums. The city that is the biggest producer and consumer in all of Latin America is also a city in which two-thirds of the residents are poor.

The poor and the middle class have one thing in common, however: Neither can get anywhere fast in this traffic-choked city. Only the rich, who can afford one of the many helicopter shuttle services, can whisk over the gridlock and the carjackers to get to their board meetings. São Paulo is New York with the heat turned up—a city whose power is obvious but whose charm takes some searching, residing in patient, determined, hopeful, and creative residents.

SHANGHAI. Long China's most outward-looking city, Shanghai is now also China's largest, a vast commercial center whose ties often seem closer to Taipei, Hamburg, and New York than Beijing. The Northern Chinese may look on Shanghai with suspicion: too greedy, too capitalist, too foreign. Yet the residents of Shanghai are proud of their city's place as a center of Asian commerce, a hip yet hard-working cosmopolitan dynamo. Every day, the cities pulses with the pedals of millions of bicycles as its residents commute to work. On weekends, the parks are filled with one-child families, enjoying a brief time off.

The future of Shanghai remains uncertain, however. How large can it grow? What will happen to this city of bicycles as ever more of its citizens can now own automobiles? Will they speed its growth or choke it?

MUMBAI (BOMBAY). When Westerners picture a large Indian city, they often imagine the nuns of Mother Theresa's order, pulling the diseased and the derelict from the gutters to die in peace. That is one face of India, but Indian cities are not dying in peace. India is huge, more populous than all of Africa combined. It has been a largely rural, village-based society, but the rush to the city is on. Calcutta, also largely a British colonial creation, continues to grow. Delhi—the old Delhi that long ruled India and the New Delhi that is now its capital—dominates the north and will soon be one of the biggest metropoles in the world.

But India's most dynamic city may be Mumbai, on the coast that faces the Arabian Sea. It is an economic giant with a global reach. Call a "help" line for your computer, and you may get a young man in Mumbai who speaks crisp English and has a complete command of Microsoft Windows and the problems of gigabyte hard drives. Everything in India comes in numbers that boggle the mind. There are more poor people in this one city than in most countries. There are also more software engineers in this city than in any city in the United States.

LAGOS. This is another site that wasn't meant to be a city. The name Lagos means "lagoon," and the city is built on three low-lying islands, coupled with a sprawl to the interior, with only a handful of bridges to connect the tangled masses of millions of people. This congested bit of coast, chosen by the British navy, is at least as unpromising a place for a great city as, well, the island of Manhattan.

Lagos is now the biggest city in Africa. It is the commercial core of Africa's largest country and will soon be one of the largest cities in the world. It's a city of maddening snarls and tangles and crammed neighborhoods that look and sound like the transported ethnic villages that they are. Even the Nigerian government gave up and moved the capital out of this city. Yet the city adds a million residents each year, all seeking opportunity.

Nigeria has oil, but that provides few jobs. Most of the work in Lagos is what residents create for themselves, as they have for over thirty years. Baker (1974) described the early stages of this population surge in 1970s:

> Lagos was unlike anything I had seen before in Africa; it was more like an overcrowded city in India. . . . People are jammed into this area, almost all of them selling something to someone. . . . Whole sections of the town are devoted to headscarves, and women walk nonchalantly down the street with two- or even three-

foot piles of these scarves on their heads. . . . All night the city is alluring: candle flames flickering in the small shops or on stalls by the roadside, green or pink electric light bulbs casting eerie shadows in beerparlors. (p. 16)

Sprawling and Brawling Contenders

INDUSTRIAL GIANTS. Carl Sandberg (1916), a Chicago-based reporter and writer, wrote about his hometown in these classic lines that celebrate the industrial city:

> Hog Butcher for the World,
> Tool Maker, Stacker of Wheat,
> Player with Railroads and the Nation's Freight Handler;
> Stormy, husky, brawling,
> City of the Big Shoulders.

There is no longer much bellowing and commotion in the stockyards, as occurred in Sandburg's day. Instead, the bellowing and commotion continues on the Chicago Board of Trade, as traders wrestle over the prices and delivery of products. Likewise in Cleveland and Pittsburgh, where smokestacks on the horizon are often dormant but tall office buildings now punctuate the skyline, managing the products that are manufactured elsewhere.

This is no longer just a North American and European phenomenon. Taipei, Taiwan, the city–state of Singapore, and the special port of Hong Kong all grew as industrial giants but have now become largely trade giants, filled with managers debating deals on products made elsewhere. The new industrial giants are often near the old centers: Juarez, Mexico, on the U.S. border, and Guangzhou, China, a short drive from Hong Kong.

CULTURE CAPITALS. Other cities, while active in global trade, draw their prominence from cultural enterprises. Paris, France, and Milan, Italy, are filled with savvy businesspeople, but their draw is as leaders of fashion and style. A new sport coat may be spun in Delhi, India, lined in Seoul, Korea, padded in one of the megacities of China, and then stitched in Novgorord, Russia. But the corporate owners—Canadians, Americans, and Germans—still come to Paris to study next year's styles.

Of course, styles and centers of style may change quickly. Several top corporations are interested in what their French fashion spy can find—in Tokyo:

> Loic Bizel leads visitors through alleys packed with wild-haired youngsters, makes his way into tiny boutiques tucked beneath stairwells and points out fatigue-inspired jackets, handpainted sneakers and plaid miniskirts. . . . "Japan is advanced. What will happen 10 years form now is already in Japan," Bizel said. Fake fur trims, oversized sunglasses, dogs dressed to the T, chains and gemstones embedded in shirts and hats of all shapes are "in." ("Japan the Trendsetter," 2004, p. B-1)

If they can't afford a French spy in Tokyo, trend-conscious businesspeople can at least log on to www.japanesestreets.com. Trend watchers contend that Japan is shifting from being a manufacturing powerhouse to an exporter of culture, tapping into the creativity of the streets in the world's largest city.

Through its power in film and international media, however (and though the French may cringe to hear), the world's cultural capital may be Los Angeles. California styles are sent around the world on film and video. Of course, the styles are not always created in the studios; often, they emerge on the streets of a city where hundreds of cultures and styles mingle.

CITIES OF DESPERATION. No tour of the world's important cities would be complete without visiting those that are truly places of desperation and destruction. Mogadishu, Somalia, remains torn apart by the chaotic violence and unending poverty of that struggling almost-nation. Kinshasha, Congo, has millions of people and almost no jobs, except what can be invented informally. The hospitals there have no doctors, no medicines, and often no lights. Civil war, government corruption, and economic collapse have all but destroyed the urban infrastructure and social structure. In the past, people abandoned collapsing cities to return to the countryside, leaving only the ruins of Teotihuacan or Babylon. Yet in Somalia and Congo, the countryside may be even more dangerous. There is simply no place to run.

Other cities are not collapsing but struggling desperately. Karachi, Pakistan, is on its way to being one of the world's largest cities. It hasn't yet staked a major claim on Asian trade, however, and the national capital is far to the north. The streets of Karachi are filled with millions who face poverty and very uncertain futures. These streets have also become one of the great recruiting grounds for extremist and terrorist organizations.

There may be hope, however, in the incredible resilience of both the cities and their people. Beruit, Lebanon, once the "poster child" for the desolation brought by civil war, is slowing healing and regaining its international prominence. Calcutta, India, still has millions of poor but also millions of middle- and working-class Indians, who are cautiously optimistic about the future.

Cities as Dynamos: Central Places and Hyperurbanization

Whether global urbanization is a cause for hope or alarm or both remains controversial. Can the planet support all these megacities? Can these cities support all their people? "Cities are the fundamental building blocks of prosperity," claims Marc Weiss of the Prague Institute for Global Urban Development, who also notes that the industrial and commercial activities of cities account for between 50 and

80 percent of the gross domestic product (GDP) of most countries (quoted in Zwingle 2002). Canadian urbanist Jane Jacobs (1970, 1984) sees cities as the necessary engines of productivity, creativity, and prosperity for their countries. She contends that places with great cities, such as her home of Toronto, flourish, while those without great, complex cities fall into decline.

Jacobs's ideas represent a line of thinking in geography known as **central place theory.** It suggests that regions need central places where key functions converge, and these central places, in turn, tend to prosper and grow. It is true that for all the squalor and misery in the cities in poor countries (and in parts of many of the cities in rich countries), urban dwellers are better off on many measures than their rural counterparts. They earn more money, they are closer to schools and health clinics and other social services, and they tend to have a better education and longer life expectancy. Even though cities grow little food, the people who live there tend to gather it from many places, and urban dwellers are sometimes less prone to hunger and famine than rural dwellers. For all these reasons, people continue to come to the cities, even when jobs are scarce and life is hard.

Whether the cities will fulfill their promises is less clear. The migrant who leaves southern or north-central Mexico to come to a border town like Tijuana or Juarez will likely earn more money and have more possessions and opportunities than someone who stays behind. At the same time, the migrant will face industrial pollution and urban filth, high crime rates, ugly transient housing conditions, and social dislocation due to living far from his or her family, traditions, and roots. Are the economic gains worth the price? For many, they must be, for people continue to come. And while many return home for visits and pilgrimages and many hope to retire to their home region or village, most continue to work in the growing cities.

A related question is whether the advantages of life in the big cities is due to advantages inherent in city life or the fact that governments tend to neglect rural areas in favor of urban showplaces, especially when those places are also national capitals. From Mexico City to Nairobi, Kenya, urban capitals often gleam with new high rise offices and hotels and impressive government buildings, while rural areas are left to deteriorate. British social scientist Michael Lipton (1977) called this **urban bias.** City life, especially in a state or national capital, is better because governments drain resources from rural areas to invest in cities, where their prestige and power are more likely to lie.

One place where both Lipton and Jacobs agree is that many developing countries are dominated by a single, over-large metropolis. They have experienced **hyperurbanization** (Timberlake 1998), in which the city size is far out of proportion to the level of industrial and commercial development of the country. Further, this growth is often concentrated in a single **primate city** that dominates the economic, political, and social life of the country and often holds a large share of the country's total population. Buenos Aires, Argentina; Quito, Ecuador; Nairobi, Kenya; Abidjan, Ivory Coast; and Bangkok, Thailand all are primate cities in that they are the primary centers of national life. But they are also the "800-pound gorillas" of the developing world. Their demands determine national policy. Also, when they decline, the country declines, and when they are in crisis, the whole nation is in crisis.

Cities in the United States have always had a dispersed urban pattern: commerce in New York; government in Washington, D.C.; rail and foodstuffs in Chicago (as well as Omaha and Minneapolis); film and television in Los Angeles; industry in shifting corridors from Buffalo to Pittsburgh to Birmingham. This is partly a function of size. New York's shipping industry had to compete with other contenders on a long coastline, from Charleston to New Orleans and later San Francisco and Seattle–Tacoma. The cities tended to grow up around resource bases and commercial nodes, with jobs coming first and people following the labor demand.

Many European countries have had much more single-city dominance: Paris, Copenhagen, Brussels. These cities were at least supported by extensive empires or trade networks. In many poorer countries, there is little to support the dominant city but uncertain government investment. Likewise, there is little to support the residents other than what they can create for themselves in the informal economy.

The Shape of Urban Life

Theories of Urban Culture

People have been pondering the advantages and perils of urban life since the time of Gilgamesh. The urban explosion that came to Europe and North America with the beginnings of nineteenth century industrialization (and is now rippling around the rest of the world) brought a new analysis of urban life.

German social analyst Ferdinand Toennies (1988 [1887]) wrote about the shift in social relations from *Gemeinschaft,* the face-to-face world of community, to *Gesellschaft,* the more impersonal and institution-mediated world of society. French sociologist Émile Durkheim (1951 [1897]) wrote about the *anomie,* or internal sense of displacement and rootlessness, that urban dwellers, cut off from village community and tradition, would experience. He believed in changing urban worlds. German social theorist Georg Simmel (1964 [1905]) believed that urban dwellers cope with the onslaught of too many people, sounds, sensations, and demands by becoming more withdrawn and indifferent to external stimuli, including people.

These images of the harried and withdrawn urban dweller still capture many of our negative views of the city. This is how rural Midwesterners may think of New Yorkers, how rural Mexicans often think of *Chilangos* (Mexico City dwellers), how exuberant Brazilians think of *Paulistanos* (of São Paulo), and how rural villagers in Kenya think of the residents of Nairobi. In fact, these stereotypes may have some truth to them. Greeting a New Yorker with a smiling "Howdy, y'all" may not get the desired warm response. Yet we must be careful about too quickly dismissing the vitality and creativity and the distinct variations of urban life.

Upon studying Italian Americans in Boston's West End, U.S. sociologist Herbert Gans (1962) contended that urbanites don't really leave the social life of the village at all; they recreate it, becoming "urban villagers." In big cities around the world, one can enter an "urban enclave" (Abrahamson 1996) and immediately be struck by the sights, sounds, and smells of an ethnic community. The urban villagers may gather on the corners, in the pubs or coffee shops, in the bakeries or delicatessens, or on the steps of places of worship, to chat and gossip, maybe in their home language, just as they or their parents or their grandparents once did in a rural village.

Theories of Urban Structure

This alternative perspective points to the importance of the structure of the city and of people's participation in shaping that structure. Simmel and Durkheim may have been right in suggesting that the city bombards people with strange stimuli and ideas, but Gans and Abrahamson may also be correct in noting that people contend with this bombardment by creating safe and comfortable enclaves, where the traditions and connectedness of community persist.

One of the first systematic studies of urban life and the structure of the city came out of the new department of sociology at the University of Chicago in the beginning of the twentieth century. Robert Park (1967 [1916]) had his students not just sit back behind the gothic walls of this great university but plunge into the heart of the city to drink in the pubs, hang with the gangs, investigate the institutions and explore the ethnic neighborhoods to understand the life and structure of the city. He drew his ideas from **human ecology,** the study of people and their environment, and often borrowed concepts from the new field of **environmental biology.** Park (1914) believed that urban neighborhoods go through patterns of succession similar to the stages of a forest:

- **Invasion:** a distinct new group begins to move in.
- **Resistance:** the established group attempts to defend its territory and institutions.
- **Competition:** the two groups compete for space and control of social institutions such as churches and schools.
- **Accommodation and cooperation:** eventually the two groups settle into a stable pattern of interaction.
- **Assimilation:** as cooperation increases, the two groups begin to merge, eventually intermarrying.

Park believed that while conflict was inevitable, it would lead to eventual accommodation and assimilation. Not everyone examining modern cities is so sure, however. Some groups seem to have been excluded and segregated for a very long time, such as the Jews of pre–World War II Europe and the African Americans of the post–World War II United States. Yet assimilationists who follow Park believe that a new blending of traditions will indeed come in time. In particular, the demands of an interconnected marketplace and the expanse of urban opportunities may overcome people's initial desires to remain in more isolated enclaves (Sanders, et al. 2002).

Park's University of Chicago colleague, Ernest Burgess (1967 [1916]), attempted to describe the sectors of the city, which he believed fall into recognizable zones that form concentric circles: the commercial core, the industrial belt, the zone of working-class housing, the zone of middle-class and upper-middle-class residences, and so forth. This pattern fits older cities built on open terrain (like Chicago) fairly well. Newer urban agglomerations, built around highways and forced into canyons and irregularities (like Los Angeles), fit the pattern less well. One might also need to update Burgess's zones and add a few more: the zone of look-alike condominiums, the zone of endless strip malls, and so forth.

Beginning in the 1960s and 1970s, as cities around the world, and particularly in North America and Europe, went through increasing turmoil, new ideas of the forces that shape cities came to the forefront. These views were shaped more by the political–economy and looked at how power and wealth determine urban structure and life. Neighborhoods are shaped not just by natural selection but by policies of segregation and integration, by which groups hold political clout, by the willingness or unwillingness of banks to offer mortgages, by absentee landlords and by real estate speculators. This line of inquiry continues to be examined by U.S. urban sociologists, British urban geographers, and others with new concerns about how global power and wealth continue to reshape world cities (Sassen 2000). In the twenty-first century, the banks and absentee landlords and real estate speculators may be halfway around the world, yet their impact is felt in the local neighborhood.

Fantasy City: Postmodern Theory

New urban thinking has been influenced by **postmodernism,** that eclectic set of views that challenge modernist assumptions and seek to give voice to other marginalized perspectives. *Postmodernism* has come to mean many things, but it was first used as a description of architectural styles. In the 1950s and 1960s, modern architecture was dominated by what was known as the **international style,** largely because it looked the same everywhere in the world. Buildings were big rectangles, set on their sides in suburban areas and on their ends in the urban core, with rows of look-alike windows and little adornment. The idea was that buildings were great machines and should be built for efficiency with clean lines. The trouble was that many people did not want to work in a machine or live in a city dominated by sameness and uniformity.

Beginning in force in the 1980s and continuing through the 1990s, new buildings again borrowed themes from the past. Skyscrapers were topped with gothic arches and spires, which had not been seen since the Chrysler Building went up in New York in 1931. Courtyards with fountains and pools made a comeback, and echoes of Tudor England, Provincial France, and the Alhambra in Spain graced both commercial and residential buildings. Some believe that this trend has accelerated to the point where we now live in "fantasy cities" (Hannigan 1998), where reality and imagination are blurred.

One of the fastest-growing and most-visited U.S. cities is Las Vegas, a hugely popular and populated collage of Egyptian pyramids, Roman palaces, fake volcanoes, leaping fountains, and suburban green lawns that sprout from the desert like some drug-induced mirage. In Orlando, Florida, the theme parks seem to blend with the city, so that it is hard to tell which is which. The most popular destination in the United States is now the Mall of America in Bloomington, Minnesota near Minneapolis. It's become more popular than the Grand Canyon and Elvis Presley's Graceland combined.

In one sense, the mall is the recreational center of the great marketplaces of the world's great cities, complete with diverse wares and massive entertainment. Yet most malls are also entirely climate controlled and corporate controlled, managed by strict regulations set not by a government but by mall management. This is becoming an international phenomenon. Families play under the Eiffel Tower and the onion domes of St. Basil's (in miniature) in Guangzhou, China, while Tokyo is so full of ornate wedding palaces, fantasy hotels, themed bars, and other buildings evoking every culture that ever was (and a few that never were) that it is often hard to know where the real ends and the facade begins.

Some have suggested that these places are popular because they allow people to escape their fears of crime and disorder in real cities to mingle in spaces that pretend to be cities. Few people walk in the heart of downtown Los Angeles, but "Downtown Disney" in suburban Anaheim is crowded every day of the week. Shut out, as well, are people from the poor and working classes, who cannot afford to access these spaces. It may also prove harder to shut out urban problems than we may think. Prostitutes, many of them from middle-class backgrounds, now work the "avenues" of the Mall of America, just as they do the streets of Amsterdam and Bangkok. Drugs, homelessness, and crime are invading these safe spaces, as well.

The Shape of the City

Autosprawl

Another aspect of urban structure that first struck in U.S. cities and is now appearing in various forms around the world is **urban sprawl.** Sprawl is not just urban growth; it is the spreading of the urban population over an ever-greater expanse. Some U.S. cities, such as Detroit, reached their maximum population in the 1950s and have been losing population ever since. The greater metropolitan area, however, continues to grow in number and certainly in extent. The growth takes place in suburban locations, as well, as more distant ex-urban locations gradually become suburban. As the city itself becomes an ever-smaller and sometimes ever-poorer part of the metropolitan region, it loses power and influence. Meanwhile, farmland and open spaces are lost to suburban housing and shopping.

Early cities had to be compact, since the residents needed to reach all points by walking. The development of the streetcar in the late nineteenth century allowed the expansion of cities, as residents could live further out and commute to work and shopping by rail. Still, the most coveted point was the city center, where the rails converged; it held the most important buildings and the most extensive shopping. This was changed by the dominance of the automobile, however. Gradually, the streetcar rails disappeared between the 1920s and the 1950s, perhaps with the prodding of automobile manufacturers, who were eager to make their product indispensable.

Cars change the basic urban equation. Central city areas quickly become congested with traffic and can rarely provide enough parking for all the cars. Gradually, many stores begin to abandon these areas, and the central cities of big urban

Las Vegas, Nevada (left), one of the fastest growing cities in the United States, and smog-laden sprawl in ever-growing Mexico City (right): Urban sprawl continues to consume land and resources and make life difficult for urban commuters.

areas begin to cater mostly to outsiders who arrive by air; witness the growth of convention centers in many central cities. The centers of smaller cities often just fall into decline. At the same time, cars allow people to move their homes (and their garages), ever further out into new "green fields" and then to travel to suburban shopping surrounded by "miles of free parking." The movement is complete as businesses move out to suburban commercial parks and light industry finds new suburban industrial parks. For many suburban dwellers, there is no need to enter the heart of the city.

This pattern was completed as the U.S. federal government built beltways around large cities in the 1960s and 1970s. These were intended to move cross-country traffic around urban centers on the national interstate, but they quickly became attractions themselves. New **edge cities** (Garreau 1991) sprang up along these beltways, often at the junction of two or more large freeways. These are not suburbs but sprawling, car-dependent conglomerations of office space, shopping, and truck shipping that together often generate far more income than the urban center.

For a century, cities were defined by their tall buildings. Louis Sullivan built the first skyscraper in Chicago in the 1880s. New York dominated in this area for decades, with each new building taller than the last: the Chrysler Building, the Empire State Building, the World Trade Towers. Chicago reclaimed the title of having the world's tallest building with the great black spire of the Sears Tower. In the late 1990s, it lost this title by a few meters to the twin Petronas Towers of Kuala Lampur, Malaysia. But oil money built the Petronas Towers, and cheap oil was already making towers obsolete, even before the Al-Qaeda attacks on the World Trade Center.

The Sears Tower remains as a huge vertical city, a complete entity where thousands can work and live without stepping outside, where one can find anything— anything, that is, except Sears. To find a Sears store, one must go out to the many suburban shopping malls. To find the Sears corporate headquarters, one must head out to Chicago's beltway to a vast corporate office park of postmodern, low buildings, ponds, and open space.

As automobiles dominate more places around the world and as urban dwellers continue to fear crime and congestion, more and more of the world's great cities are continuing to sprawl. Some, like Singapore and Hong Kong, don't have much room to grow and so continue to push upward. In many others, rich and poor alike play a game of leap-frog, each trying to claim its space on the city's edge to find affordable housing or to have "the best of both worlds."

The trouble with life on the edge is that the edge keeps moving. Cities, unlike some physicists' models of the universe, cannot expand indefinitely, and some are showing signs of collapse. In some cases, the privileged are returning to selected urban neighborhoods in a process of **gentrification.** This can bring new resources to old communities; it can also displace the poor who are already there.

How much cities will expand is a matter of political economy as well as human ecology. The future of sprawl will depend in part on the willingness of governments to invest in public transportation, to protect green space, and to limit ex-urban development. It will also depend greatly on the price and availability of oil to fuel long commutes in air-conditioned automobiles.

Global Ghettos: The Spread of Shantytowns

Towers in the sky and periurban sprawl have been competing abodes of not only the captains of commerce and industry but also the world's urban poor. In most cities in poor countries, the poor have crowded into shantytowns on the cities' edge.

As New York grew in the 1890s, poor Irish immigrants, "the shanty Irish," crowded into shantytown shacks of broken boards and castoffs along such outlying derelict areas as New York's Fifth Avenue (near 101st Street). The Irish slums were ruled by "plug ugly" gangsters in hobnail boots with pulled-down caps and a black-jack clubs or pistols in their pockets. Respectable New Yorkers avoided the place. Modern New Yorkers know this same area as a fashionable part of Manhattan, giving a glimpse of how far and how fast this city has grown.

This pattern was repeated across the United States and then across Latin America as American cities boomed. In the rugged, often mountain-ringed cities of Latin America, the shantytowns climb the surrounding mountains. Settlers (**squatters** is a more common term) invade the land, desperate for a toehold on urban opportunity. The shantytowns ring the city and climb higher and higher into the hills, carving out steep dirt roads that often erode. Water and electricity rarely reach these places, and residents must climb down the steep ruts to get to work, to collect water from delivery trucks, and to dispose of any trash they don't want next to or can't use in their "hand-crafted" homes of cardboard, scavenged tires and tin, and occasional bits of wood and concrete.

This is the life above Mexico City, Lima, Quito, LaPaz, and many Latin American capitals. The names given them by their residents are evocative: *Lucha de los Pobres* (struggle of the poor) and *Cuidad de Esperanza* (city of hope). The Brazilian lofty slums, known as *favelas,* are infamous for their size, poverty, and crime. Latin American governments have debated how to deal with this influx: expel the invaders and bulldoze their homes, give them title to the land and try to incorporate them into the urban political process, or just ignore them and let them try their own resources. Often, promises are made and not kept.

One of the few creative and successful efforts has been made by Jaime Lerner, an architect who became mayor of Curitiba, Brazil. Like many Brazilian cities, Curitiba has seen explosive growth—an elevenfold increase in fifty years to over

2 million—and grinding poverty, with the average family income below $100 per week. As described by Palen (2005):

> Nonetheless, Curitiba is a green, clean, and very livable city. It began twenty-five years ago when the mayor, rather than building highway overpasses and shopping centers as was occurring elsewhere in Brazil, instead advocated pedestrian malls and recycled buildings . . . Crime is minimal. People come into the center on a system of express buses running in separate high-speed bus lanes. (p. 330)

In the lowlands of Southeast Asia, the poor cannot gather on the mountainsides; instead, they live on stilts over wetlands and waterways in urban fringe *kampongs*, an Indonesian word. The Latin American poor get slums with a view, and the Southeast Asian poor get waterfront property. The trouble is that the water is often filthy and disease ridden, with floating garbage and dead animals amid the warm currents, perfect for cultivating cholera. Here, the poor do laundry, bathe, and travel in search of urban opportunity. *Kampong*-like slums also crowd the Amazonian and coastal cities of the Brazilian northeast and the low-lying ports of West Africa.

Perhaps the closest the United States gets to a *kampong* is in parts of East St. Louis that lie low along the Mississippi River. Writer Jonathan Kozol (1991) describes neighborhoods where the urban poor swelter in a chemical stew dumped on them from above by industries that probably will not hire them and face authorities that are more likely to close bridges to contain them than to build bridges to integrate them. Children try to play, caught between the asthmatic haze that hangs in the air and the sewage-filled chemical soup that leeches up from the

Poor urban dwellers are often pushed to the periphery as in this favela or highland slum above Rio de Janeiro, Brazil (left), or in this low-lying slum near Lagos, Nigeria (right).

ground. Other low-lying and low-income communities are slung along to the south through the region known as the Mississippi Delta.

Ghettos in the Sky

The Spanish, the Portuguese, and the people in their Latin American colonies believed in the city as the center of power and influence. The central square was the gathering point, and the twin symbols of power—the cathedral and the government palace—often faced one another across this square. The wealthy and powerful lived nearby. Wealthy Latin Americans have therefore been slow to abandon the central city to the poor.

The British and the citizens of their American colonies, however, have always idealized the green countryside and been somewhat ambivalent about the city. So while great mansions were built near the city center, where some still stand as museums, restaurants, and bed and breakfasts, there was an earlier movement outward. Many of the greatest mansions of New York were built far north (at the time) along the Hudson River in the late nineteenth century.

In the United States, where the flight from the central city began early, central cities began to become synonymous with poverty, or the inner city. Urban tenement houses filled with poor immigrants from the 1880s to the 1920s. In the decades that followed, as African American rural farm workers, sharecroppers, and others moved north, they often found places to stay on the edges of the downtowns of major cities: New York's Harlem, Chicago's Bronzeville, Detroit's Near Eastside, South Central Los Angeles, and the heart of Baltimore and Washington, D.C. In the eastern United States, they filled old neighborhoods that had been vacated by earlier immigrants, cramming into the tenements and kitchenette apartments divided out of larger houses.

As the number of low-income newcomers grew, the question of where to house them also grew. In the late 1950s, Chicago's Mayor Richard Daley proposed scattering them in public housing throughout the city. Opposition to this was so intense that he chose instead to build upward, creating the Robert Taylor Homes and Cabrini Green between 1958 and 1962. Highrise poverty was born. Initially, the buildings provided an attractive alternative to tenements and kitchenettes. Yet having so many poor people in one place also proved attractive to the criminal element, rather than to legitimate employers, and the buildings often fell into decay. With the end of the 1990s, the Robert Taylor Homes started to come down, to be replaced by a planned community of multifamily, multi-income housing. Whether this becomes gentrification (the site commands a valuable view of the lake) or recaptures the original vision of mixing low-income families with diverse institutions and opportunities remains to be seen.

Other towers have changed residents as the cycle has continued. The great multicolored towers of Cedar–Riverside in Minneapolis was once filled with low-income residents, many of them African Americans. The towers are again filling, this time with Somali refugees who have come from the East African deserts to the northern U.S. plains, often with help from Catholic Charities and Lutheran Social Services, both active in this traditionally Northern European community. Saturday night finds the towers full of strange new sounds and aromas. Sunday morning finds Somali Christians wrapped in white, lightly woven blankets, which they wear over their Western attire, riding the buses to local churches. Many still hope to return to their troubled country. If earlier patterns hold, many will stay. The question remains, though, what they can make of this "ghetto in the sky" and whether they can find success in this distant city.

For decades, the fortunes of African Americans in U.S. cities have been constrained by intense **segregation.** Cities in the Northeast and Midwest of the United States are often two to three times more racially segregated along black–white lines than their Canadian counterparts; some are as segregated as South African cities at the height of apartheid (Massey and Denton 1993). This intense segregation is lessening, not so much due to policies of integration as to new immigrant influxes that continue to restir the U.S. urban "mixing bowl." Cities from New York to Los Angeles and now even Minneapolis are immigrant metropolises (Nee et al. 1994), with an ever-changing mix of nationalities and ethnicities. Some immigrants find their foothold in enclave economies among their co-ethnics, but the continued changing patterns of international migration continue to stir the pot. Korean, Chinese, and Lebanese Americans often find their niche as middleman minorities, serving a largely black or Latino clientele. Others move quickly from enclaves into new and diverse neighborhoods.

Just west of Cedar–Riverside in Minneapolis, the Phillips neighborhood and Lake Street business district bustle with scores of differing ethnic groups from Asia, Latin America, and Africa in a city that was once more known for blonds and Swedish meatballs. In Chicago, the Near West Side was the traditional home to immigrants. There, pioneering sociologist and social worker Jane Addams operated Hull House from the 1890s into the 1930s, celebrating the many cultures while providing basic health, education, and social services to help newcomers cope with daily life and advance their version of the American dream. Today, this area still bustles with Chicago's Chinatown, Little Italy, Little Mexico, and more. Meanwhile, Chicago's northeast draws new immigrants from India, Armenia, Georgia (in the Caucasus), and elsewhere. Manhattan's Harlem and Chinatown still receive newcomers, but many now find their first homes in the Flushing section of Queens, where dozens of groups intermingle. Each of these has brought new vitality as well as new challenges to their cities.

The difference between a ghetto and an enclave is that the first is forced and often long term, and the second is chosen and typically short term. The difference between a slum and a first start is hope. Assuring that hope is well founded makes all the difference.

Seeking Livable Cities

Cities That Work

Where are the cities that are thriving, livable, and working? Many examples could be touted. One commonly cited is Copenhagen, Denmark:

> Copenhagen is wonderful—a bustling, cosmopolitan city of 1.5 million full of scenic canals, tidy parks, lively squares, relaxed taverns and coffeehouses, well-preserved old buildings, safe streets, cheerful people, and the enchanting 150-year old Tivoli Gardens amusement park.
>
> Yet it is no fairy-tale land: Copenhagen faces many of the same problems that bedevil North American cities. Its richness and vitality stem not from any happily-ever-after magic but from creative responses to difficult urban situations. (Walljasper 1994, p. 158).

Solutions to the problems in Copenhagen have included tax sharing between the city and suburban and rural areas, a view of low-income areas of the city as incubators for people on their way up rather than dead ends, a ban on cars in a network of downtown streets that goes back to 1962, and a view of urban renewal that relies on refurbishing older neighborhoods to maintain their community fabric and architectural integrity, rather than relying on bulldozing the old.

While Europe has had a head start in reclaiming cities as livable, exciting, yet pleasant spaces, the ideas are taking hold around the world. This focus has been dubbed the **new urbanism,** and it has several basic features. Somehow, traffic must be tamed to allow pleasant walking spaces. As much as people love their cars, few want to live in a drive-by city. Rather, pedestrians can meet and mingle, and they can stop and shop.

New Urbanism

New urbanists welcome urban diversity; the eclectic mix of people is one of the attractions of urban life (Duany et al. 2001). Enough order must be maintained so that all people, including young families and the elderly, feel safe. Once basic order and safety have been assured, the more variety the better. (Everyone likes to people watch.) Urban spaces must allow places to pause and rest and enjoy the scene, whether a park or a sidewalk cafe. This can be achieved in the narrowest spaces, a single table on a medieval street, as long as lingering is welcomed. The urban space may shimmer in tinted glass, polished metal, and glistening lights, or it may brood in stone and stucco and half-timbered lodges. Either way, it must be attractive. People do not want to linger and mingle in a sterile, machine-like setting.

New urbanist ideas have taken hold in many cities that are eager to reclaim old industrial districts, renew neglected waterfronts, and bring back a mix of people (and their money) to urban districts. Some of the most dramatic renovations have been in old industrial and shipping sectors: London's dockyards, San Francisco's embarcadero, Baltimore's inner harbor, Montreal's Old Quarter, Cleveland's lakefront, and so forth. In many places, these developments represent a long-awaited rebirth of the city.

Critics contend that the new urbanists are too concerned with appearances and have not dealt with the deeper political economy of the city (Marshall 2001). For instance, the poor and working-class neighborhoods may be displaced to create new playgrounds for the middle classes. Jobs in heavy industry may be lost and, if replaced at all, only by low-wage service jobs that maintain, clean, and service the new urban spaces.

The challenge remains to create cities that work and that work for all sectors. New urbanist designs have restored vitality to old and decayed urban cores. They now need to reclaim vital neighborhoods throughout the city, not posh but pleasant places for people of all ages, incomes, and backgrounds. As we look to the developing world, can we even begin to talk about bringing the finer aspects of culture, social events, higher education, and cross-cultural experiences to the poor, transient, and displaced? Jane Addams's century-old experience at Hull House suggests that this is exactly where to begin—with people who appreciate the finer parts of urban life but have not yet been fully included in the life of the city.

MAKING CONNECTIONS

New Urbanism

■ See the site of the Congress for New Urbanism at www.cnu.org. Here, you will find the principles of this influential school of thought and its current activities. Take the online tour, illustrated with scenes from across the United States and Europe, which places this movement in its historical context and argues that cities can be reclaimed from decline and autosprawl. The site also lists resources, upcoming conferences, local chapters, and ways to get involved. What aspects of urban redesign do they advocate? Do you find their ideas and models appealing?

Sprawl

■ You can learn more about sprawl, transportation, and sustainability at www.newurbanism.org. Note the designs for alternative systems, including urban and inter-city train systems. How do they propose to halt and reverse trends toward ever greater urban sprawl?

Neighborhood Organizations

■ Check with your municipality or campus–community office to find out what neighborhood groups and associations are active in your area. Try to attend one of their meetings or visit their offices. Are they city sponsored or independent? What are their key issues: crime, planning, property values, traffic, or others? Are there ways for citizens and student groups to become involved? Note in particular groups in troubled or transitional neighborhoods and those in neighborhoods bordering the college campus.

Community Revitalization

■ Many low-income individuals and families live in areas of concentrated poverty and limited opportunity. Where are these locations in your community, and what efforts are being made toward bringing positive change? Visit a community center, neighborhood association, nonprofit community development corporation (CDC), or other community-based organization working in a low-income community. Learn about the community demographics: Who lives here (income, race and ethnicity, family composition, many youth or many elderly, and so forth)? Has this changed over time? Is the area undergoing a transition? What is the housing situation? Are there many absentee landlords, subdivided large homes, apartments, public housing, and so on? What, if any, are the areas employers and retailers? What are the most pressing problems, and what is being done to address them? Are local residents actively involved in these efforts? You may find activities in which you can assist, whether on your own or with a group.

CHAPTER 10

Population and Health
Only the Poor Die Young

Houston and Hyderabad

A group of students coming home late from a party are sideswiped by a drunk driver. They are rushed to a nearby Houston hospital for tests. In the emergency room, they are met by a Filipina nurse, who soon brings in a Ukrainian-born doctor. The doctor looks at the injuries and sends two of the students down to radiology for X-rays. The African American X-ray technician is already busy with a chest X-ray, checking another patient for possible pneumonia. The technician works the entire night, but the radiologists, already overworked from growing numbers of complex diagnostic procedures, have long gone to bed. They can rest easy.

The results of X-ray procedures are increasingly digitalized, rather than put on film, and digits can circle the globe at the speed of light. The results are sent halfway around the world to Hyderabad, India, where it is the middle of the day. An Indian physician reads the results and e-mails back a diagnosis. Not until much later the next day are the results confirmed by one of the Houston hospital's own radiologists, who is an Indian immigrant himself.

This type of global exchange is becoming increasingly common. It meets real needs, such as a shortage of specialists, and takes good advantage of time differences. Would U.S. radiologists, who are among the highest-paid specialists, ever find their incomes challenged by less expensive foreign competition? Would Indian radiologists ever find their incomes growing, moving them closer to what their U.S. counterparts earn but further from what most of their fellow Indians earn?

The possibilities are complex and intriguing. They offer new opportunities for India but also real dangers. So many Indian physicians are leaving India, especially rural India, for more lucrative jobs elsewhere that poor Indians who once had access to an extensive national system of clinics are increasingly turning to unqualified "quacks" (Dugger 2004). The situation is even worse in the Philippines and parts of the former Soviet Union, where doctors sometimes find they can earn more money working abroad as nurses than they can working at home as physicians. With new technologies, will they now be able to stay at home and practice international telemedicine? Will U.S. providers seek to lower costs by importing drugs and exporting procedures? Will telemedicine make expertise more available or just make medicine yet more impersonal?

Shanghai

China's fast-growing commercial hub has many things to offer. For instance, it now offers cable access television. Tune in to hear the singing bachelors. This is not some new bizarre blending of U.S. reality television shows, such as *American Idol* and *The Bachelor*. This is the new reality of modern China.

The Chinese bachelors are indeed singing for both notoriety and love. The problem is that there are too many of them. For years, China's birth rate has been skewed toward boys. In some rural areas, there are as many as 134 boys born for every 100 girls. Chinese parents want boys, who will marry and bring wives home to them, not daughters, who will eventually leave them to join their husbands' families. In the distant past, all they could do to achieve this goal was to beseech their ancestors to give them a boy. Rumors of female infanticide abounded. Now, they can turn to ultrasound and other medical procedures to determine the sex of the fetus and then decide whether or not to abort it.

The result is that more boys are born than girls. But these boys are supposed to honor their parents by gaining success in the workplace, getting married, and having children. These singing bachelors have found economic success in Shanghai. But they haven't found wives. After two decades of skewed birth rates, there are not enough women to go around. So the bachelors do what everyone does in Shanghai: They advertise. On cable access, they talk about their successes, their promotions, their wealth, maybe even their new car. And they sing. Interested women can call in. The competition is fierce.

If a singing bachelor is successful and does get a wife and have a child (China still has a one child per couple policy for people in the cities), one wonders, will he wish for a boy or a girl? And what will the parents tell the next generation about the worth and value of each?

World Population Estimates: Counting Heads

How many people are there in the world? The last time I checked, there were 6,419,801,044. Obviously, I didn't count them. You can get the current figure from the U.S. Census Bureau and its world population counter at www.census.gov. The Census Bureau doesn't count either but instead prints United Nations estimates based on census figures, reporting, and estimates from the world's countries, which they update continually based on projections of birth rates.

Attempting precision at keeping this head count is silly in one sense, as we can only estimate and the figure is obsolete as soon as it is posted. Yet it is a reminder

TABLE 10.1	World's Largest Countries: 2004 and 2050

2004		
Rank	**Country**	**Population**
1	China	1,300,000,000
2	India	1,087,000,000
3	United States	294,000,000
4	Indonesia	219,000,000
5	Brazil	179,000,000
6	Pakistan	159,000,000
7	Russia	144,000,000
8	Bangladesh	141,000,000
9	Nigeria	137,000,000
10	Japan	128,000,000

2050		
Rank	**Country**	**Population**
1	India	1,628,000,000
2	China	1,437,000,000
3	United States	420,000,000
4	Indonesia	308,000,000
5	Nigeria	307,000,000
6	Pakistan	295,000,000
7	Bangladesh	280,000,000
8	Brazil	221,000,000
9	Congo, D.R.	181,000,000
10	Ethiopia	173,000,000

Source: Population Reference Bureau, *2004 World Population Data Sheet*, available at prb.org. Reprinted by permission.

of how carefully we have tried to chart and tabulate the world's growing population. What is harder to estimate are the effects that this growth and change will have on our planet.

The world's population, like the world's wealth, is very unevenly distributed. Of the roughly 6.3 billion people on the planet, 1.3 billion are in China. Another 1 billion live in India. Overall, about three-fifths of the world's population is in Asia. The remainder are roughly evenly divided among Europe, Africa, North America, and South America.

The same ratio happens to hold when comparing the largest countries: Of the ten currently most populous countries, one is European, one North American, one South American, one African, and the other six Asian (see Table 10.1). Of these ten countries, two are high income (United States and Japan), two are middle income (Brazil and Russia), and the remainder are low income. One is losing population (Russia), two have stable but aging populations (United States and Japan), and the rest are growing. Nigeria has one of the highest population growth rates in the world. A shown in Table 10.1, its population is expected to more than double by the year 2050.

How many people can this planet hold? No one knows for sure, and that has caused concern for some time.

Marx and Malthus: The Population Bomb Debate

For centuries, leaders saw a growing population as key to their power. The Spartan Greek leaders bribed their handful of citizen–warriors to spend enough time with their wives to procreate a steady supply of new boys to grow into citizen–warriors. They were needed to defend the city and to keep the large population of slaves in line. Too many of the wrong sort could be a problem. The biblical book of Exodus has the Egyptian pharaoh worrying about the rapid growth of the enslaved Hebrew population. Sufficient slaves were needed to do the work, but too many could be dangerous.

For millennia, the world's population grew slowly. Disease and disaster, often humanmade, keep the death rate high. And while the beginning of agriculture meant a larger food supply, it also meant a more concentrated population, sharing their grain supplies with rats and insects and so more disease. The world had about 300 million people by 1000 CE and maybe 500 million by 1500 CE. The planet was well into the 1800s before it passed the 1 billion mark.

At least one person was worried about this growth. British economist Thomas Malthus (1766–1834) noted a trend in human population growth: It was not linear but rather exponential, an upward rising curve that seemed to grow ever steeper. Malthus's mathematical reasoning went this way: The food supply was also growing, but it tended to grow in linear fashion, a straight upward line. Population had the power to grow exponentially: it doubled every so many decades (1926 [1798]).

The power of this doubling is dramatic. The Indians tell a tale of the man who invented chess. For compensation from a grateful king, he asked only for one grain of wheat on the first chess square, two grains on the second, and so forth. This didn't seem like much to ask, except that the amount of grain needed for the sixty-fourth square would be more than all the grain the world has ever produced. The food supply will never be able to keep pace with this exponential growth.

In the 1800s, crowded London and Paris were already showing the strains of a large population. Malthus (1926 [1798]) warned that this was only the beginning. The French have a simple riddle: Suppose you have a pond with a growing water lily patch that doubles in size every day. It will cover the pond in thirty days. On what day will it cover only half the pond? The answer, of course, is the twenty-ninth day. Again, dramatic changes come with exponential doubling.

Malthus believed that since "passion between the sexes" was inevitable—and he wrote before contraception was common—this growth was also inevitable. It would continue until it outstripped the food supply. Then population would collapse through catastrophe: wars over food along with outbreaks of disease and famine. In time, even if things stabilized, the cycle would only begin again. Some say it was Malthus who gave economics its nickname as "the dismal science."

Yet most nineteenth-century leaders were not worried. Napoleon encouraged all French women to do their patriotic duty and bear more French citizens. Only in this way could France match the size of Russia and the German states and send out vast armies. Those vast armies would conquer enough land and seize enough food to feed this growth, and so Napoleon marched disastrously into the vastness of Russia. The British also looked to their empire to help with growth: excess population could be transferred overseas. Britain was small and getting crowded, but who could imagine an end to the vast open spaces of Canada, the U.S. colonies, Australia, and southern Africa? These lands seemed empty by comparison to Europe, and where they were not, they could be emptied through war, removal, and disease.

Another European economic thinker, Karl Marx (1818–1883), also disputed Malthus. People were a land's greatest strength, Marx contended. If they were miserable, it was because they were not able to enjoy the fruits of their labor. Once land and wealth were redistributed to the poor workers, there would be enough for all. Many leaders of poor countries in the twentieth century (and especially those influenced by Marx) continued this line of thought. In China, Mao Zedong claimed that the people, in all their many millions, were the country's glory and power and that the Westerners who sought to limit China's growth were only fearful of this growing power. A similar line came from the other end of the political spectrum. Fascist leaders, such as Fransisco Franco in Spain, banned contraception, claiming it was anti-Catholic but also seeing power in numbers. In Italy, Benito Mussolini, like the ancient Spartans, told Italians it was their patriotic duty to increase their numbers.

By the 1970s, the population growth curve had reached its steepest incline. Doubling was taking place within a single decade. Observers wondered how long it would be before "the pond" was full and choked with growth and at what point no increase in the food supply would be enough to feed the world. The Club of Rome, a group of concerned observers, issued a report on "the limits to growth." The most famous statement on the problem came from Paul Ehrlich in his 1968 book *The Population Bomb*. Ehrlich used the logic of exponential numbers to show the ultimate absurdity of unchecked growth. He pointed out that eventually, each person would have about two square meters in which to stand and nowhere to move, grow food, or otherwise provide for his or her survival. Ehrlich looked at a world of 3 billion and said it simply could not grow to 6. He was, at least in the absolute sense, quite wrong.

The world has passed the 6 billion mark and not yet collapsed. There is enough food for all—at least, if we could get it to them. Yet growth always comes at a price. This planet of 6 billion has overcrowded megacities, eroded farmland and diminishing water supplies, disappearing forests, and many species on the verge of extinction, driven off by the pressure from a single species. What will the price of growth be in the future?

The simple answer is a world of more poverty. By various projections, the world's population will grow to somewhere between 8 and 12 million by the middle of this century (United Nations 2000; see Figure 10.1). A lot depends on the policies of the next few years. But there is agreement on one factor: Almost all of

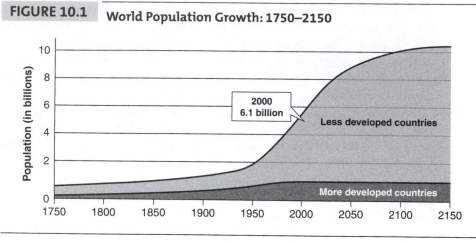

FIGURE 10.1 World Population Growth: 1750–2150

Source: United Nations, *World Population Prospects* (1998 Revision), and Population Reference Bureau, *2004 World Population Data Sheet*, available at prb.org. Reprinted by permission.

that growth will take place in poor countries. The rich have growing economies, while the poor have growing populations. The rich get richer, it seems, while the poor get pregnant. A simple theory proposes to explain this pattern.

Demographic Transition Theory

Demography is the study of human populations: their numbers, movements and migrations, and characteristics, such as age and race/ethnicity. Demographers are particularly interested in the **vital statistics** of human life: births, deaths, and migrations. A **demographic transition** is a change in the pattern of population growth and distribution. **Demographic transition theory** proposes that there is a predictable pattern to population growth as a country develops.

Death Rate and Birth Rate

In many preindustrial agrarian societies, the **death rate,** or the proportion of the population that died in a given year, and the **birth rate,** the proportion of the population that were born in a given year, were both quite high. As long as they were in balance, with similar numbers of birth and deaths, the population remained stable. At some point—perhaps due to better nutrition and sanitation for a larger number of people and the control of certain highly infectious diseases—the death rate began to fall. But people in these changing agrarian societies continued to have large families due to cultural expectations, the hope that children would provide economic security in old age, the need for farm labor, and the uncertainty that their children would survive to adulthood.

During times of demographic transition, with a falling death rate but a very high birth rate, the population soars. This occurred in Europe and the United States in the 1800s and into the early 1900s. European and North American cities grew rapidly, and much of the explosive population growth was channeled into growing industries. The excess population of Europe, those who could find neither land to farm nor industrial work, were "exported" in great outmigrations. They moved to the great open spaces of Canada, the United States, Argentina, South Africa, and Australia, where frontier land—opened in part by the decimation of native populations through European-introduced disease, war, and removal—beckoned to newcomers.

The United States, in particular, took in huge numbers of immigrants for the time: 30 million between 1880 and 1920. These immigrants filled the coastal cities and pushed relentlessly into the interior. The tide of immigrants slowed as the birth rate began to fall in Europe and European-heritage communities in the United States.

For farmers, children have traditionally been a source of pride as well as labor and security. For urban industrial workers in crowded housing, raising children could be more difficult. They could still be a source of labor, however, if they were put to work in the factories. Yet all across Western Europe and North America in the late 1800s and especially by the early 1900s, the idea was taking hold that children should be in school, not in the factory. Putting children through school was expensive. As women's workplace moved from the home farm or family business out into the city, caring for children also became more difficult. Cultural expectations about large families began to shift, interest in contraception (often illegal at the beginning of the twentieth century) grew, and family size began to fall.

As the birth rate fell to the level of the death rate, population growth slowed and the U.S. population level again became stable. This same pattern is being repeated in various forms around the world today (see Figure 10.2 on page 260).

Life Expectancy

Despite ongoing disease and war, death rates have fallen everywhere in the world over the last fifty years. There have been temporary reversals in this pattern in certain locations, including intense civil war and the height of the AIDS crisis in some African nations. Yet even these occurrences haven't changed the overall trend.

An easier figure to imagine and consider than the death rate of so many per 100,000 is **life expectancy,** and this is often used in international comparisons. Life expectancy is an estimate based on projections of death rates, and so it is less

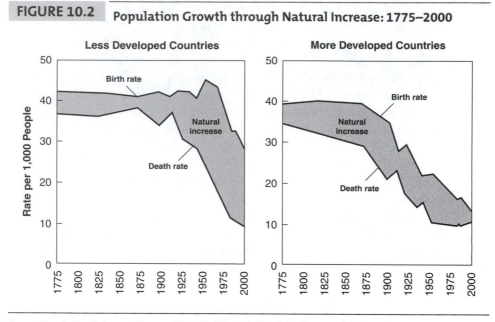

FIGURE 10.2 Population Growth through Natural Increase: 1775–2000

Source: Population Reference Bureau, *2004 World Population Data Sheet,* available at prb.org. Reprinted by permission.

precise than counting the actual numbers of deaths. Even so, it allows us to compare numbers that make sense at the individual level: how long one can expect to live.

Remember that life expectancy is an average. A country in which the life expectancy is 45 probably does not have large numbers of 45-year-olds passing on. More likely, it has a very high rate of **infant mortality,** or the proportion of children who die before reaching their first birthday. Since life expectancy is an average, having a large number of deaths among people of very young ages will bring down the average dramatically, even if the country has some people who reach very old ages.

Japan leads the world in life expectancy, followed closely by the Northern European countries (see Figure 10.3). The United States has a high life expectancy but lags behind. Again, the difference is not so much lifestyle, although it can have some effect. The United States has a higher rate of obesity than most of Europe and certainly Japan, and has had a high-fat diet for a longer time (although others are catching up on this). But Americans are also now less likely to smoke cigarettes than Europeans or Japanese, and smoking is one of the greatest health risks of all. Both Americans and Japanese suffer from work-related stress. The biggest difference is that many more in the United States, especially in poor and nonwhite

FIGURE 10.3   Life Expectancy at Birth across the Globe: 2002

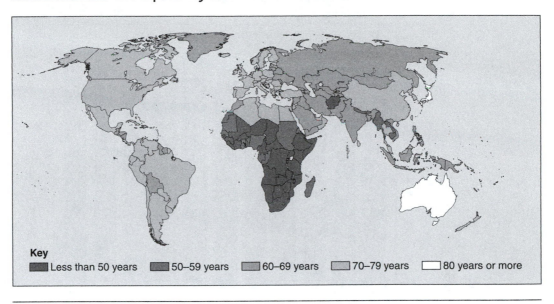

Key

■ Less than 50 years   ■ 50–59 years   ■ 60–69 years   ■ 70–79 years   □ 80 years or more

Source: U.S. Census Bureau, International Programs Center, International Data Base and unpublished tables.

communities, lack good access to quality health care, especially prenatal and early childhood care. This raises the U.S. infant mortality rate and lowers the life expectancy. Worldwide, however, life expectancy is projected to increase in the coming years, from about 64 years in 2005 to over 76 in 2050 (see Figure 10.4 on page 262).

Infant mortality rates have declined dramatically since 1950, particularly in areas of the world such as Africa, in which improved health care has been provided to mothers and children. Regardless, there is a huge gap in infant mortality around the world, ranging from 150 infant deaths per 1,000 births in Liberia to just 3 deaths per 1,000 births in Finland. Africa still has by far the highest infant mortality rate (see Figure 10.5 on page 262).

Fertility Rate

Life expectancy provides a more intuitive way to think about the death rate, and so the **fertility rate** provides a more intuitive way to think about the birth rate. Like life expectancy, the fertility rate is an average projection based on current rates—in this case, the birth rate. The fertility rate is the number of children the average woman will have in a particular country.

FIGURE 10.4   **World Life Expectancy at Birth: 2002–2050**

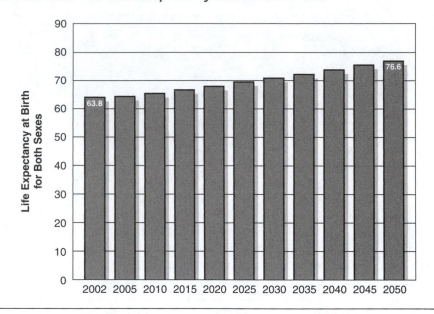

Source: U.S. Census Bureau, International Programs Center, International Data Base.

FIGURE 10.5   **Infant Mortality around the World**

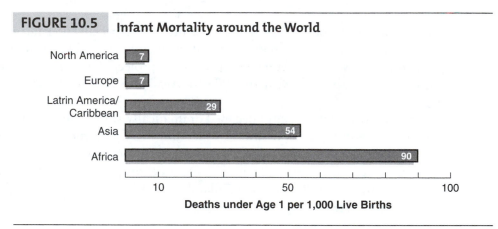

Source: Population Refrence Bureau, *2004 World Population Data Sheet,* available at prb.org. Reprinted by permission.

The fertility rate in the United States around the turn of the twentieth century was close to 6; that is, the average woman bore six children in her lifetime. This would also have been a measure of family size, except that not all of the children survived. Moreover, some may have been "apprenticed out" as young as ten, and the older children may have already been married and having children of their own when their youngest siblings were born to the family (Hareven 1982).

In recent decades, the fertility rate has dropped markedly around the world, from also around 6 to now closer to 3. And as demographic transition theory would predict, this rate is not evenly distributed (see Figure 10.6). Fertility rates in parts of Africa, parts of the Islamic world, and a few locations in South Asia still range between 4 and 6. Meanwhile, fertility rates in parts of Europe and Japan have fallen below 2. The fertility rate makes an enormous difference in a country's future. A fertility rate of 4, with most of the children surviving, will double a country's population every generation; if the mothers begin young, this could be every fifteen to twenty years. If the fertility rate falls below 2 and the country does not experience net inmigration (people coming into the country from elsewhere), then the population will begin to age and decline in number.

Fertility rates are highest in rural areas, in the least industrialized regions, in places with traditional gender roles, and in locations with a strong religious and cultural ethic of the value of large families. The very highest fertility rates are in Islamic regions of Africa, such as northern Nigeria. In the United States, the fertility rate is substantially higher in Utah, with its strong Mormon heritage, than in other portions of the country.

Yet fertility rates have fallen markedly even in parts of the world that have, until recently, stressed the value of large families. The fertility rate for Mexico

FIGURE 10.6   Fertility Rates around the World

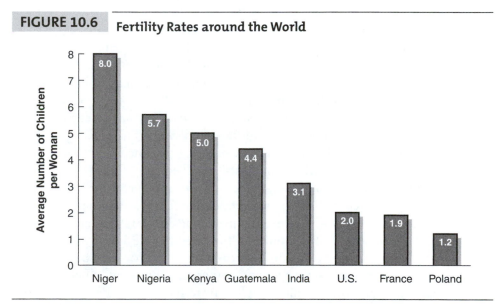

Source: Population Reference Bureau, *2004 World Population Data Sheet,* available at prb.org. Reprinted by permission.

has fallen below that of Utah; for Mexico City, it is approaching the replacement level of 2. The United States hovers right at replacement level with a fertility rate around 2. It grows only due to immigration, and the composition of its population changes accordingly. Groups with higher immigration rates—Hispanics as well as some Asians—grow rapidly due mostly to immigration.

Changing Demographics

In Western Europe, fertility rates are consistently below replacement level. These countries will therefore see aging populations and shrinking populations unless immigration from elsewhere in the world fills this void, a process that would change the religious and cultural complexion of Europe as well as its physical complexion.

Japan has been particularly struck by the "birth dearth." While the Japanese value children, theirs is a very urbanized country, with crowded living conditions and many women in the paid labor force. Japanese parents invest heavily in their children, seeking to get them the best education and preparation, and this makes children expensive. Most Japanese couples only have one or two children, and some forgo having children all together, devoting themselves to professional pursuits. With a fertility rate around 1.7, the Japanese population is aging quickly, and the government has tried incentives to encourage more births. Japan is an ethnically homogenous society that has not attracted or sought large numbers of immigrants.

Heading the list of shrinking countries is the one with the world's largest land area: Russia. The nation, as a single entity, lost just over half its population when the Soviet Union broke up into small republics in 1991. Russia now combines a very low birth rate with net outmigration, as many seek to leave but few seek to come to Russia, with its troubled economy.

The most dire predictions about global overpopulation came in the 1970s, as the planet added people at a faster rate than ever before. That growth rate, about 1.7 percent a year, has since fallen to about 1 percent a year. To understand what these rates mean, try the economists' so-called law of 72. (This works for compounding interest as well compounding population growth.) Divide 72 by the rate of growth to get the time to the next doubling. A population growing at 1 percent will double in about 72 years, at 2 percent in 36 years, and at 4 percent 18 years.

Growth is based not only on the fertility rate but also on the age of the population—a kind of shadow effect of previous growth. Countries with rapidly growing populations have very young populations—lots of children and young people. Even if these young people start to have only a few children themselves, the population will continue to grow for some time, just because there are so many people in their prime childbearing years.

This effect keeps Mexico's population growing. It has also kept China's population growing in spite of attempts (more effective in urban than in rural areas) to enforce a "one-child" per family policy. Even with a declining overall fertility rate, the world population will continue to grow until a larger portion of the population ages past their prime child-bearing years. The most significant effect, however, will be not just in the rate of growth but where it will occur.

By the middle of this century, the world's population will grow from 6 billion to somewhere between 7.5 and 11 billion, depending on how one does the predictions of how fast fertility rates will fall. But virtually all of this growth will be in poor countries. As noted earlier, in today's world, the rich grow their economies and the poor grow their populations. A similar pattern occurs within countries, where urban, two-income, upper-middle-class families tend to have fewer children than rural, low-income and working-class families.

This demographic pattern has important implications for individual countries. Western Europe, Japan, Canada, and the United States all have aging populations and wonder how they will provide for them as retirees, as they continue to comprise an ever-larger portion of the population. These countries also often debate how much they should open their borders to immigration to bring in younger workers and how doing so would affect their societies and economies. Russia, Ukraine, and other parts of the European portion of the former Soviet Union face the prospect of outright population decline—as much as 28 percent for Russia and a huge 40 percent for the Ukraine by midcentury, according to U.N. population estimates. Poor countries, in contrast, worry about how to cope with the demands of a young and growing population. A population with many children needs a large number of schools. Children, like older adults, also require more health care. And as they graduate from school, they need jobs, requiring an ever-expanding economy and labor market.

Changing demographics are also changing the world as a whole. An increasingly larger portion of the world's population will be in Latin America, Africa, and Asia, giving greater numerical clout to these regions. All the world's explosively growing megacities will be in these places. If a large number of people try to move from fast-growing poor areas into slow-growing richer areas, the movement of peoples and cultures will be enormous—a countertide to the large number of Europeans that moved out into the world in the 400 years between 1520 and 1920. Should this occur, it would also mean that despite economic gains in some regions, most of the world's children would be born into poverty. Tremendous economic growth and expansion of social services would be needed just to keep pace.

"Around here," the queen in *Alice in Wonderland* explains, "one must run as fast as one can just to stay in one place." This seems to be the situation for the world and especially for the world's poorest regions. Humanity has experienced 10,000 years of economic growth and incredible invention since the first humans began tending crops. After all that, is the average peasant or slum dweller in the world's poor regions any better off—in terms of nutrition, health, livelihood, and well-being—than the hunter–gatherer who watched the glaciers melt? It is hard to say.

What happened to all that growth and inventiveness? Inequality took some of it. The wealthy of the world are certainly better off in material terms, even if other measures of well-being are less clear. But population growth also used up the benefits of these efforts. We grow more food but have more mouths to feed. We build bigger dwellings but have more people to house. We have faster-paced economies but more people to support. This sense of running just to keep up is most evident in the world's poorest places. Jobs are created but not enough for many new job-seekers. Schools are built but not enough for ever more children. New food and water supplies are tapped but not enough for exploding urban populations.

Prospering places on the planet face their own version of this treadmill, as population and prosperity combine to increase the demands on their environment and infrastructure. New highways are built but can't keep pace with the numbers of new cars and added miles driven. Efforts are made to improve efficiency and lower emissions from those cars, but a 30 percent gain in efficiency is lost to 60 percent more vehicles being driven (Duany et al. 2001). And so it goes, running hard to stay in one place.

It is not clear that crowding is always bad. Some of the most crowded places on the earth—Hong Kong, Singapore, Manhattan—are also some of the most prosperous and economically productive. Congested regions, such as the Ruhr Valley of Germany and Tokyo Bay, have pollution problems but also may offer good health care and nutrition and have healthy populations with long lives. On the other hand, some of the world's most sparsely populated countries—Niger, Burkina Faso, Mongolia—are also some of its poorest. Yet we know that a dense population places great demands on resources and infrastructure. Tokyo and New York thrive by trading their commercial wealth for resources from all over the world, something that is not an option for very poor communities. Rapid population growth, even in a sparsely populated region, can undermine even the most careful of economic plans.

No one knows for sure how many people this planet can support. Previous estimates have tended to greatly underestimate levels of natural resources and human resourcefulness. In the 1800s, some thought the United States could never reach 100 million, since there would not be enough pasture land for all those people's horses. Recall that Ehrlich (1968) did not believe the earth could support its present 6 billion. It is, in fact, supporting that population, though not always very well, and it can no doubt accommodate more. This growth has come, however, at a great price to the natural world—to species that have been driven to extinction, to fossil fuels that cannot be renewed, and so forth.

A crucial corollary to the question of How many? is the question of How much? Americans consume energy and resources at a rate between 10 and 20 times that of Mexicans and 30 to 50 times that of South Asians. If everyone wants to live at the level of consumption enjoyed in the United States, then the planet may not be able to support the current 6 billion, let alone more.

Population Control

Controversy continues to rage over how to best limit the world's population growth and whether this is even desirable or necessary. One view, common in many parts of the developing world, contends that the problem is poverty and economic injustice, rather than population. People are miserable, the argument goes, not because they are too many of them but because they are getting too little of the earth's abundant resources. This idea echoes Marx's contention but is also popular with those who oppose **contraception,** or birth control, for religious and cultural reasons. At the World Population Conference in ever-crowded Cairo, Egypt, the Vatican, drawing on Roman Catholic tradition, found itself in agreement with representatives from many Islamic states (United Nations 1995). People are not the problem; the inequitable distribution of wealth and resources is.

The counterargument has been around since Malthus: No matter how much we increase production or better distribute resources, our efforts will always be outstripped by the exponential curve of population growth. Population is the primary problem.

These two arguments need not be mutually exclusive. If it is indeed true that humanity's inventiveness over the past millennium has been used up by both inequality and population growth so that many people are no better off, then both a more equitable distribution of resources and a slower rate of population growth will be needed to provide a better life for those many people.

Debate also rages on how to best achieve population control. For a time, China used strict sanctions, primarily economic, coupled with a strong push for contraception, including sterilization, to enforce its one-child policy. While this policy has never emphasized abortion, it has tended to be very tolerant of the use of abortion to achieve its target. In contrast, the United States, first under the Reagan administration and then again under the George W. Bush administration, moved to withhold funding for population programs that included access to abortion.

Contraception has been controversial for a very long time. Tribal peoples have used contraceptive herbs, and Greek and Roman women knew of the practice (though the great physician Hippocrates did not want his doctors performing abortions). Contraception was controversial for over one hundred years in the

Population growth by itself does not always create poverty, but large and growing populations can severely strain community infrastructure, as seen here in Dhaka, Bangladesh.

United States. Feminist leaders in the late 1800s and early 1900s went to jail for promoting and distributing contraceptives. If motherhood was a woman's highest calling and civic duty, then contraception was a crime against both nature and the state. Yet even pioneer families in the American West circulated information on how to make homemade condoms.

Contraception became far more accessible with the approval of oral contraceptive pills in Europe in the 1950s and the United States in the 1960s. The media touted this as a "sexual revolution" but what really happened was a "fertility revolution." Fertility rates for U.S. and European women plummeted from the 1950s to the 1970s. Access to readily available and inexpensive contraception, along with the education and social acceptability to use them effectively, has been the key to declining fertility rates.

Attitudes change more slowly than technology, and often men seem more reluctant to accept contraception than women. But even in traditionally "pronatal" countries, where a strong value is placed on large families, attitudes are beginning to change. Phillip, a Pentecostal pastor in Nigeria, comes from a very pronatal heritage, yet his ideas have changed:

My father had just eight acres. It was an average-size farm but not enough for 13 children. In the morning there was just a cup of tea. No lunch. Poverty eats you every day. What made me decide to have a vasectomy was that I wanted to have a family I could raise. My wife was taking pills, and she had high blood pressure. Who am I to my wife? I'm her partner. I'm there to help her. That's what the Bible says. So I read about vasectomy. The only side effect is that you can't have children anymore, and that's the side effect I wanted. (Zwingle 1998, p. 47)

Fertility rates in the United States and Europe did not decline simply because new drugs became available. There were also new attitudes about the role of women and about their place in higher education and careers. This was crucial to the change: *careers*. Around the world, women work in fields and markets with small children tagging along or slung over their backs. Women pursuing higher education and professional employment, however, often choose a smaller family size. The state of women's education in a country is often a very good predictor of its fertility rate. More educated women are more likely to wish to space out their children, to invest heavily in only a few children, to use contraception effectively, and to have the social power to convince others—both the men in their lives and an earlier generation of women—that this is a good approach for them and their families.

Population conferences, such as the one in Cairo, have also often featured controversies over the best route to lowered fertility: improved contraception, improved education, or an improved standard of living. Interestingly, these tend to be inseparable. The most successful approaches have often included all of them.

Women with broader life options chose to limit and space childbearing. They also tend to be healthier and to have healthier children. With more children surviving and more options for the future, the pressure to have many children as a form of "social security" also declines. Even when abortion is legal, in such situations, its rate may actually decline, as women make choices about family size in advance of pregnancy, rather than being pressured to seek abortion after conceiving. Worldwide, the fertility rate is expected to drop below the replacement level by midcentury (see Figure 10.7 on page 270).

Migration

Demographers are interested not only in how many people there are but where are they going. People have been on the move since the first ancestral human strode out of Africa to explore points unknown. Within remarkably few generations, humans were in South Asia and then Southeast Asia. By 40,000 years ago, they seem to have been lashing together rafts and crossing to Australia, with their newly domesticated dogs. By 12,000 to 20,000 years ago, they were crossing the Bering Strait, either on foot or by boat, making their way between the ice and then turning south to seek the bounty of warmer climates.

In the middle of all this movement, two great waves of **migration** stand out. The first came with European colonization of Africa, the Americas, and parts of

---

FIGURE 10.7 Global Fertility Levels Relative to Replacement Level: 2002–2050

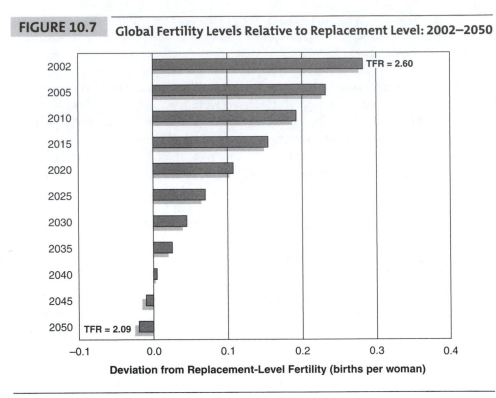

Deviation from Replacement-Level Fertility (births per woman)

Note: Global total fertility rates were derived by calculating weighted age-specific fertility rates from country- and age-specific births and numbers of women.

Source: U.S. Census Bureau, International Programs Center, International Data Base, and unpublished tables.

Asia. Millions of Europeans eventually relocated to these "new worlds." This movement also accompanied the greatest population collapse in history: the decimation of the original peoples of the Americas, particularly through the introduction of Eurasian infectious diseases. The labor shortage that came with this population collapse was filled by exporting poor Europeans and then by moving millions of Africans as slaves across the Atlantic.

The second great wave of movement, larger in sheer number than the first, is occurring right now, as people from Africa, Latin America, and parts of Asia are leaving the troubled economies and dangerous political turmoil of the postcolonial world for safer and more prosperous regions. **Immigrants** leave their home countries to permanently settle elsewhere. **Labor migrants** travel abroad to seek work with the hope of someday returning home. **Refugees** are defined by the United Nations as those who have "a well-founded fear of being persecuted for reasons of race, religion, nationality, membership of a particular social group or political opinion" (UNHCR 2005). If immigrants and labor migrants seek opportunity, then refugees above all seek safety. Those who flee their homes but remain within their countries of origin are labeled as **internally displaced.**

These labels and definitions are sometimes ambiguous: Is someone who is fleeing utter economic collapse and turmoil an immigrant or a refugee? Whether or not he or she will be granted entry and asylum, or the right to remain in a new country, may depend on how this question is answered by the authorities and the courts. The United Nations estimates there are at least 6 million immigrants, 15 million refugees, 42 million labor migrants, and millions (just how many, no one knows) of internally displaced people in the world (UNHCR 2005).

Each of these groups changes their host country or region in profound ways. Having a large number of internally displaced people can destabilize both a government and an environment, as can having a large number of refugees in a poor neighboring country. In Lebanon, Palestine, and Sri Lanka, refugee settlement areas have been places of great poverty and great unrest, serving as recruiting grounds for militants. Refugee camps in Africa have devastated fragile environments and placed huge strains on fragile governments.

When jobs and resources are available, however, immigrants and refugees can also be sources of innovation and prosperity. Immigrants often have a very high rate of entrepreneurship, starting new businesses in new locations, and many working very long hours. The immigrant boom fueled U.S. economic growth and industrial might at the beginning of the twentieth century, and immigrants have also brought growth and prosperity to places such as Canada, Australia, and Israel. But immigrants can also place a great strain on schools and social services, especially if they are concentrated in few locations. Immigration has remade the faces of cities such as Los Angeles and Miami, as well as Sydney, Australia, and Toronto and Vancouver, Canada.

So, from what countries are migrants leaving and to what countries are they going? There are both "sending" and "receiving" countries in all parts of the world. With the exception of Mexico, which is the number-one "sender," the countries with the highest levels of outmigration are all in Asia and Africa. The number-one destination for these countries' migrants is most definitely the United States, which took in over 1 million migrants in 2002 (see Table 10.2 on page 272).

Disease

Infectious Disease: The Kiss of Death

When people travel the world, they take many things with them. The most dangerous things are their breath and their blood. When humans travel and mingle, they often inadvertently transport dangerous microbes: viruses, bacteria, and parasites. Most are annoying, but some are deadly.

TABLE 10.2	Top Net "Senders" and "Receivers" of Migration: 2002

Top Ten Net "Senders"

Rank	Country	Net Migration
1	Mexico	−280,000
2	China	−230,000
3	Tanzania	−180,000
4	Congo (Kinshasa)	−150,000
5	Philippines	−130,000
6	Pakistan	−120,000
7	Kazakhstan	−100,000
8	Bangladesh	−100,000
9	India	−80,000
10	Burma	−80,000

Top Ten Net "Receivers"

Rank	Country	Net Migration
1	United States	1,040,000
2	Afghanistan	300,000
3	Canada	190,000
4	Germany	180,000
5	Russia	140,000
6	United Kingdom	130,000
7	Italy	120,000
8	Singapore	120,000
9	Australia	80,000
10	East Timor	50,000

Source: U.S. Census Bureau, International Programs Center, International Data Base.

Through their activities, humans have often made their communities wonderful breeding grounds for microbes. Hunter–gatherers, however, seem to have been healthier than we first supposed. They ate a diverse, all-organic diet, exercised a great deal, and lived in small, isolated bands that were not the best breeding ground for dangerous microbes. Their greatest danger probably lay in parasitic worms and microscopic organisms that lay in wait in the natural world. Any backpacker who has stopped for a cool drink from what appeared to be a clean stream or lake, only to contract a persistent stomach ailment related to the parasite *giardia*, can understand the danger.

Healthy individuals probably developed some resistance to these dangers, but things got worse when people started rearranging their environments. Domesticated animals became a valuable food source, but living in close proximity to these animals posed a real danger (Diamond 1997). Many of the "poxes" that have plagued herding societies and then traveled to their farming neighbors probably moved to humans from their livestock. Their names still reflect some idea of their origins: *chicken pox* or *cow pox*, which is closely related to one of history's greatest killers, *smallpox*.

Agricultural people, or grain farmers, didn't fare much better. Storing grain was a great way to provide for winter or drought, but it was also a bonanza for rodents. Mice and rat populations soared as these opportunists moved in to gobble stored grain, a year-round food supply. They brought with them a whole new array of microbes, as well as fleas to help transport the infection. People—who were now living in close quarters in villages and, worst of all, in cities—helped by transporting diseases through breath, water droplets in coughs and sneezes, dirty hands, and just plain puss. People were most at risk in poor and crowded urban spaces, where they were literally breathing down one another's necks.

Crowded cities also faced a perennial problem that persists to this day: sewage. Human waste often ran in the streets and seeped into the waterways that provided water for cooking and drinking. The combination was deadly.

Great plagues devastated all of the ancient cities with regularity. Famous plagues killed major portions of the urban populations of Athens, Alexandria, Carthage, Rome, and London. The most intense killer in Europe and Asia was **bubonic plague,** the so-called Black Death. Probably originally a disease of rodents, fleas carried the infection from rats to humans, who then shared it with each other. Whole cities were decimated with regularity in the fourteenth century. Refugees fleeing the cities would carry the infection into the countryside. Then the disease would subside, seemingly in a great divine reprieve. But it would live on somewhere, probably in wild rodents, waiting for the right time to return.

In 1333, the plague took hold of famine-stricken China, whose already weakened population was highly susceptible to infection. The plague moved westward with the caravans of traders and raiders. In what may be the first act of biological warfare, Tartar raiders are reported to have catapulted their plague-ridden corpses over the walls of the trading city of Calla in the Russian Crimean. Traders became infected and brought the plague to Constantinople and Venice. By 1347, the plague had found a home in famine-stricken northern Italy. Its source was still mysterious, and the Jews were blamed for poisoning the wells. In England, one-third to half of the population died, forcing a truce in the Hundred Years' War with plague-stricken France. Malnourished peasants in Russia and Poland succumbed quickly, and the Black Death began an eastward return march.

Before it left Europe, the Black Death had killed perhaps one-third of the entire population in a great demographic reversal. Rising populations suddenly fell. The survivors moved through a world in which labor was scarce, and so wages rose. Whole areas of the countryside were so depopulated that feudal agriculture collapsed. Some think the Black Death may have permanently changed European society. The last major outbreak of plague killed 50,000 in Marseilles, France, in 1720. Bubonic plague is not gone, however. Carefully monitored cases show up every year; today, it is kept in check by human immunities, vigilance, and drugs.

Smallpox is a virus that travels from person to person. Closely related to animal diseases, it came to specialize in human hosts. Waves of smallpox swept over Europe, Asia, and parts of Africa until many people developed a partial immunity to the disease. No such disease and no such immunity ever took hold in the Americas until Christopher Columbus showed up with a few sick sailors. The disease swept the Americas with an intensity only possible for a new invader. When the first lost Spaniards traveled across what is now the U.S. South in the last years of the fifteenth century they found a powerful civilization. Within a couple decades, later explorers found nothing but empty ruins and abandoned pyramids. Groups such as the Natchez had disappeared without a trace.

When Hernando Cortez attacked the great Aztec capital in Mexico in 1521 he had a secret weapon: The city was being devastated by smallpox. The disease killed an Aztec emperor and demoralized the defenders. The Spanish seemed largely immune, as if the gods had abandoned the continent's first inhabitants to favor the invaders. A few years later, in 1533, Francisco Pizarro attacked the vast Incan Empire with a handful of soldiers. He triumphed through treachery and disease. Smallpox killed many of the Inca, including their emperor, and left the empire in confusion and civil war.

A century later, English colonists aboard the *Mayflower* had drifted hundreds of miles off course and were facing starvation in the chill of Cape Cod, Massachusetts. They were saved by finding the food stock of an entire native village that had abandoned the site in the wake of disease, probably smallpox. The colonists took the food, gave thanks for God's provision, and went on to explore a continent that seemed to have been emptied to make room for them.

The emptiness of the Americas was partly due to the fact that its inhabitants had less dense settlement patterns than the Europeans, who cleared large areas for plow agriculture that supported growing cities. But this condition was most likely due to the fact that the region had been emptied by disease. European colonists didn't find an untamed wilderness, they found a continent devastated and depopulated by disease, microbes released when the first sick sailor breathed a sigh of relief at reaching landfall.

Smallpox continued to attack Europe, especially whenever populations were weakened. It became the first disease to be inoculated against, as it was noted that milkmaids who contracted a mild form of cow pox seemed immune to smallpox. When London was hit by smallpox in 1720, the same year of the last outbreak of bubonic plague, inoculations began and eventually reached even the Royal Family. The same year, smallpox struck in Boston, and a Boston clergyman and scientist began giving inoculations, despite intense suspicion. Gradually, the idea gained acceptance. George Washington may have saved the Continental Army from destruction by inoculating his weakened, malnourished troops at Valley Forge.

Smallpox continued to take lives around the world well into the twentieth century. The U.N. World Health Organization eventually launched a massive global campaign to eradicate the killer. Aided by better vaccines and by a virus that only infected humans and so could not hide in animals, the campaign succeeded in 1977, when the last smallpox case was reported in Africa. This was one of the world's greatest successes in fighting global disease.

Ironically, however, the fear of smallpox has returned. After the last naturally occurring case had ended, both the United States and the Soviet Union continued to keep vials of smallpox virus, each fearful that the other might try to use this killer as a weapon. Some of these vials are today unaccounted for, especially those that were part of the Soviet bioweapons programs. The fear that terrorists might get a hold of the smallpox virus and use it with terrible effect against populations that are no longer vaccinated and do not have a natural immunity to the disease has led some to call for renewed vaccination programs.

Cholera is a bacterial killer. It infects the digestive tract and kills through the dehydration that results from uncontrolled diarrhea. Not only is this an undignified way to go, but it is especially dangerous for young children. Cholera epidemics strike with ferocity and then disappear for a while. It appears the bacteria can live in warm water, waiting to be transported and to contaminate a drinking water supply. Once the disease has hit, poor sewage facilities move the bacteria quickly from a diarrhea-stricken victim to the next new host.

A cholera epidemic killed thousands in China in 1830 and then began a spread around the world that would claim the lives of millions over the next twenty years. By 1849, London was finally working on an improved sewage system. The London epidemic was halted by one insightful physician, who removed the handle from a water pump in the center of the most infected neighborhood. Immediately, the new cases subsided and the connection between contaminated water and disease was established, along with the usefulness of careful demographic research!

Yet cholera epidemics continue to kill millions around the world, recurring every decade or so. The bacterium that causes cholera was identified in the late 1800s, and it was discovered that this disease responds to antibiotics. Death can often be averted with simple rehydration therapies. Cholera continues to kill, however, now mostly as a disease of the poor.

The fight against cholera also demonstrates the importance of improved sanitation. Death rates in European and North American cities began to fall long before the advent of antibiotics in the 1940s and later medical advances. The key disease fighter in the early 1900s was the sewer. But around the world, dysentery, cholera, and other diarrhea-causing intestinal diseases remain major killers, particularly of children. Providing a clean, covered water supply is the essential element in preventing these killers.

The other great weapon against disease has been improved nutrition. The great epidemics and plagues often followed famines and wars, times when populations were greatly weakened.

New Threats: HIV/AIDS and Other Diseases

In recent years, the world's attention has been riveted on a new killer, **AIDS**, or **acquired immune deficiency syndrome.** The disease is caused by **HIV**, the **human**

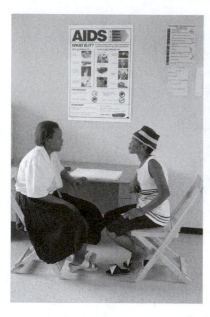

A counselor discusses treatment at Médecins sans Frontières (Doctors without Borders) AIDS clinic in Cape Town, South Africa. Mixe families wait for vaccines at a clinic in rural Oaxaca, Mexico. Providing health care to a shifting population is a difficult challenge in many countries, compounded by growing challenges such as HIV/AIDS and the limited access of rural dwellers to facilities.

immunodeficiency virus, which can remain dormant in the host for a period of months or years before attacking the body's immune system with enough force to cause AIDS. People with AIDS typically die of pneumonia or another infectious disease that takes over once their immune system has been disabled. HIV is spread by exposure to contaminated body fluids, particularly blood. It has most often been spread by sexual contact, sharing of needles by intravenous drug users, and exposure to unsafe blood supplies.

AIDS appears to be another animal to human crossover virus. It is related to diseases that infect felines and primates. Sometime in the 1960s or 1970s, the virus apparently made the leap from animal hosts to humans. The ability of this virus to mutate, or change its form, quickly has been one of the difficulties in creating a vaccine. By the early 1980s, the virus had left Africa and traveled with its human hosts around the world. Over 20 million people have died of AIDS (UNAIDS 2004), and over 40 million are carrying HIV. No place on the planet has been spared this pandemic, but over three-quarters of the cases have occurred in Africa, where the disease began (see Figure 10.8)

The Southern African countries—South Africa, Botswana, Zimbabwe, Zambia—all have HIV infection rates of 20 percent to 40 percent. Thus, an entire generation and much hope for the future is being lost. Government agencies and medical services lack a sufficient number of healthy people to staff them.

| FIGURE 10.8 | HIV/AIDS around the World |

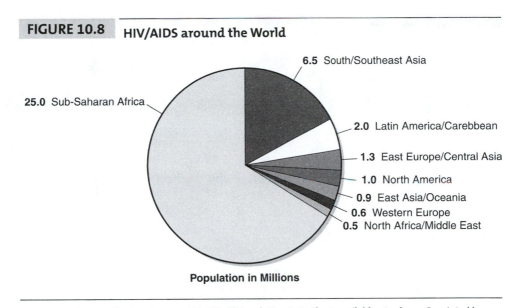

Population in Millions

Source: Population Reference Bureau, *2004 World Population Data Sheet,* available at prb.org. Reprinted by permission.

With over 40 million orphans in Sub-Saharan Africa alone, the social services are overwhelmed to the point of collapse. Since the virus can pass from an infected mother to her child, some of these children were born infected, compounding their needs.

In the tiny country of Swaziland, the HIV infection rate is approaching 50 percent of the population, although many still deny being infected, as it carries a strong negative social stigma (see Table 10.3). Life expectancy in Swaziland has fallen from 60 years to 37 years and could fall below 30. Although growth estimates for all of Southern Africa have been adjusted downward due to the high mortality from AIDS, the population continues to grow due to high fertility rates. Yet unless the spread of HIV can be contained and the survival rate of people with AIDS improved, these countries will become nations of orphans: the eerie specter of a country of children, many of them sick, growing up in a country in which the adult population, and with it much of the national infrastructure, has been decimated.

Many factors contribute to the concentration of HIV/AIDS infections. In the United States, there is such a concentration in the South Bronx of New York. It also contains neighborhoods of orphans and poor children, overwhelmingly Latino and African American, who are raised by grandparents and others. The primary culprit in infecting and killing the adults here, along with persistent poverty, is drug use that includes the sharing of needles, which spreads infected

TABLE 10.3	Top Fifteen HIV/AIDS Prevalence Countries: End 2003

Africa			Outside Africa		
Rank	Country	Percent of Population	Rank	Country	Percent of Population
1	Swaziland	38.8	1	Haiti	5.6
2	Botswana	37.3	2	Trinidad and Tobago	3.2
3	Lesotho	28.9	3	Bahamas	3.0
4	Zimbabwe	24.6	4	Cambodia	2.6
5	South Africa	21.5	5	Guyana	2.5
6	Namibia	21.3	6	Belize	2.4
7	Zambia	16.5	7	Honduras	1.8
8	Malawi	14.2	8	Dominican Republic	1.7
9	Central African Rep.	13.5		Suriname	1.7
10	Mozambique	12.2	10	Thailand	1.5
11	Tanzania	8.8		Barbados	1.5
12	Gabon	8.1	12	Ukraine	1.4
13	Côte d'Ivoire	7.0	13	Myanmar	1.2
14	Cameroon	6.9	14	Jamaica	1.2
15	Kenya	6.7	15	Estonia	1.1

Source: Population Reference Bureau, *2004 World Population Data Sheet,* available at prb.org. Reprinted by permission.

blood. That drug use is sometimes supported by prostitution, which spreads the disease through multiple partner sexual contact (Kozol 1995).

In Africa, HIV/AIDS has spread by various means. Prostitution is common in areas where work keeps men away from their families for months or years at a time. When the men do return home, they may return infected and spread the virus to their wives. The medical system has at times been as much a problem as a help. African hospitals depend more on blood transfusions than their European and North American counterparts, which have access to other treatments and drugs, and African hospitals have found it harder to secure and monitor their blood supply. Risky behaviors—some ancient, such as polygamous marriage, and some more recent, such as roadside and township prostitution—will need to change to control the spread of the disease in Africa. Sometimes, the choices are difficult:

Lillian is a 16 year old orphan in Uganda. Uganda has been cited as a success story in the fight against AIDS, with lower rates of infection than its East and Southern African neighbors, due in part to a government-coordinated campaign.

The campaign for young people is explicit about condom use but stresses sexual abstinence as the best protection. Lillian is a leader in one such program called Straight Talk. The club is a model of its type, yet some members have had to drop out due to pregnancy. The biggest threat is shear poverty coupled with persistent gender inequality. Girls who cannot afford to stay in school are tempted to drop out to become an older man's second or third wife, and to face the risk of HIV infection. Girls determined to stay in school have little means to raise the tuition, unless they take a "sugar daddy" who will pay their fees in return for sex, again placing them at risk of both pregnancy and HIV infection. Lillian's tuition is $30 a month, and her cousins have ideas on how she could raise the money.

"They say 'Why don't you find a sponsor?' I know what they mean. They want me to what so many girls do and get a sugar daddy. You give him what he want, and he gives you what you want." (Lacey 2003, p. 1)

Africa is not alone in terms of the complicated set of risk factors that people face. AIDS came to much of Asia with a vengeance. Thailand, home to an international drug trade and sex trade, was particularly hard hit and has launched a major campaign against HIV risk factors. Other countries, such as China, have been much slower to address the problems. In still others, such as India, the government has made major efforts but the message has been slow to reach the countryside. In some of India's poorest roadside villages, prostitution is almost the only source of income, and girls as young as twelve are quickly maneuvered into becoming prostitutes for those traveling the roads. Similarly, young Thai girls are often sold or tricked into the service of pimps, who confine them in the Bangkok sex trade. In both cases, these girls become new links in the chain of HIV transmission. The highest rates of new infection are now in Central Asia, where new countries spun off from the Soviet bloc face disrupted economies and societies.

The fight against HIV/AIDS must be based on preventing infection, but new drugs also give hope to those already infected. When first released, these drug combinations were so expensive that they were beyond the means of poor people in poor countries. Now, treatment can cost as little as one dollar a day, although this still constitutes the total daily income of the world's poorest billion people.

New dangers for other infectious diseases also continue to surface. A world of people in motion is also a great worldwide web of infection transmission. A "mad cow" in England can spark a global panic in the world livestock industry the next day, and a sick chicken in China can be the start of an epidemic in Toronto within a month.

The world's deadliest year of disease was not during the height of the Black Death but the influenza epidemic of 1918. Spread around the world by soldiers returning from World War I, it killed more people around the world than the war had. The United States lost 115,000 people to combat in World War I and 500,000 to the flu epidemic that followed. No one knows what made this particular flu so deadly. It killed over 21 million people, or 1 percent of the world's population (WHO 2005).

Every year, new influenza strains emerge, many of them in China and East Asia, where close proximity between farmers and livestock, especially chickens and pigs, seems to allow enterprising viruses to adapt to a change of host. Soon, they go on a global tour. The SARS virus shut down global trade in major cities from Guangzhou, China, to Toronto, Canada, in 2003 before being contained by especially vigilant international action. Although no flu-like virus has ever struck again with the virulence of the 1918 strain, world health officials continue to wonder and watch for mad cows and suspicious chickens.

Chronic Disease: Dying by Degrees

Some infectious diseases are not acute killers, like smallpox and the Black Death, but slowly incapacitate their victims over time. With new drugs that contain but do not cure the disease, HIV/AIDS may be shifting from an acute to a chronic infection. TB, or tuberculosis, can be deadly but often has a slow disabling progress. Many of the parasitic infections that have long plagued humans follow this pattern.

The U.N. World Health Organization has targeted a number of these diseases for eradication (WHO 2005). Long underfunded, the efforts have gained a major benefactor from the multibillion-dollar Gates foundation. Other groups have targeted specific diseases. The Carter Center has focused on Guinea worm, which has disabled millions in West Africa. River blindness, transmitted by a biting fly, gradually takes the sight of thousands in West Africa. Young children, some as small as three or four, become "seeing-eye children," whose full-time occupation is to lead blind elders around. The disease thus not only disables its victim but takes the childhoods of these children, who have no time for play or study.

In warm, wet locations, schistosomiasis, borne by snails that thrive in perpetually wet irrigated fields, slowly saps the energy of its victims and is particularly devastating to children. Haitian villages have long known the horror of "monster men," afflicted with a mosquito-borne worm that cause elephantiasis. The lymph nodes in the limbs and groin swell, giving the disease its name. The swelling and secondary infection can be so severe as to cause second-degree burns. The victims not only suffer intense pain but also the social isolation that comes with the disfigurement and horrible odor caused by the disease. Medical workers, backed by foundation money, are trying to get everyone in infected areas to take a harsh pill that kills the young worms and prevents the disease and to eliminate the sewage collection ponds that breed it. Like smallpox, these diseases have no nonhuman hosts to complete their life cycle and can be completely eradicated.

One disease not responding well to global efforts is **malaria,** which is caused by a parasite that is transmitted by mosquitoes. It can be deadly, and even the less-acute forms are often thoroughly disabling. Although it is now concentrated in certain regions (see Figure 10.9), malaria once circled the warm areas of the globe. It was the "fever and ague" that afflicted U.S. pioneers and settlers along river bottoms and wetlands in the southern part of the United States. Even before the doctors of the day understood the disease (they believed a lethal "miasma" arose from stagnant waters and poisoned the air), they had a powerful weapon to combat it. The Amerindians of South America had discovered that a bitter tree bark could cure the disease, and this became the basis of the one of the world's first truly effective medicines: quinine. The well-off took quinine pills, while the poor brewed the coarse bark into a bitter tea. But in any form, quinine was effective—for a while.

Over time, the malaria parasite has grown resistant to quinine, which is no longer recommended for many cases. Malaria was in retreat for a long time, given the spread of effective medicines coupled with the persistent draining of wetlands in many locations. It persisted in the tropics, and a new weapon was deployed in

FIGURE 10.9 Worldwide Distribution of Malaria: 2003

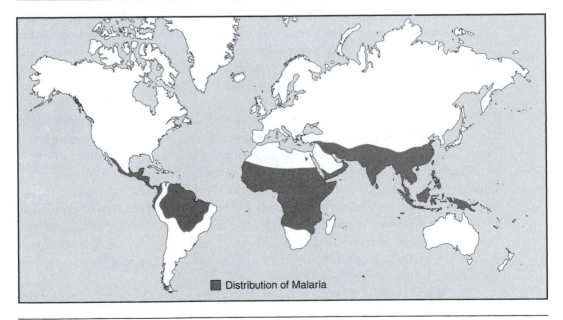

Distribution of Malaria

Source: www.cdc.gov/malaria/distribution_epi/distribution.htm.

the 1950s: DDT. This pesticide was used widely around the world. In prosperous temperate cities, it was a way to control the annoyance of mosquitoes; in poor tropical areas, it became the first line of defense against mosquito-borne malaria. DDT was found to have disastrous environmental and public health side effects, however, and its use has been discontinued in wealthier countries; it was banned in the United States in 1972. It has sometimes been replaced by newer and more expensive alternatives.

A new line of defense against malaria was found in newer drugs such as chloroquine, which treated quinine-resistant malaria successfully. Now these newer drugs are becoming less effective, and a third generation of more expensive drugs is being tested. Poor countries can afford neither the more expensive mosquito control programs nor the more expensive drugs, and so malaria is making a comeback in these regions. Some want to expand the spraying of DDT, even though it has many known dangers to both wildlife and humans.

Many of the world's chronic diseases are not infectious (caused by microbes or germs) but are the result of work and community and lifestyle. These diseases are often very modern. During the height of deep shaft coal mining in the United States, coal miners often were disabled and sometimes dead by their forties, what we would now consider midcareer, due to chronic diseases such as "black lung," caused by breathing coal dust. Careers and lifetimes were even shorter in the coal mines of Japan's Battleship Island at the beginning of the twentieth century. Miners in the great, deep mines of South Africa have long suffered both accidents and chronic infirmities. While conditions have improved in some mines, the occupation remains one of the most dangerous in the world. Occupational hazards are the source of many chronic diseases: Textile workers inhale lint dust, and industrial workers inhale fumes from toxic metals. Some workers are permanently bent, stooped, or partially blinded by working under intense and uncomfortable conditions for long hours.

Communities filled with pollutants are also disabling. In the inner cities of the United States, poor children have extremely high and rising rates of asthma and lung disease. Toxic waste sites are often located near low-income communities.

Much chronic illness is also related to lifestyle. The worldwide spread of tobacco use—particularly in the form of packaged cigarettes that encourage "chain smoking"—is one of the leading disablers and killers. A high-fat diet, often a Western "export," kills and disables through heart disease and stroke. High-sugar and high-calorie diets also contribute to diabetes, a major disabler of African American, Native American, and Native Hawaiian and Polynesian peoples and a growing threat to children and young people.

The World Health Organization (2005) has begun including obesity as a growing threat to people in the more prosperous nations of the world. The United States is a leader in this problem, and many European countries are not far behind. Obesity is also increasing in Latin America and Asia. The spread of "fast food"—high-fat products that are consumed quickly—coupled with the sedentary lifestyle of a video age is exporting this chronic ailment around the world.

Health Care Reform

Every society in the world has given a prominent place to the healing arts. Yet even now that science-based modern medicine has become the norm, countries vary greatly in how they deliver care and attempt to address health issues.

United States

The United States spends a great deal on health care—more in fact, than any other country in the world. It spends half again as much as Canada and more than twice as much as Sweden, both countries that have longer life expectancies, lower infant mortality rates, and overall better health.

Several factors go into making U.S. health care the world's most expensive. For example, U.S. physicians are among the best paid in the world, and hospital and insurance administration in the United States are costly. Technology is also expensive, and the United States is a world leader in advanced medical technology.

With such well-paid doctors and advanced medical equipment, why don't Americans fare better on overall outcomes? Over half of the U.S. expenditure on health goes into a person's last six months of life. Of course, it is hard to know in advance just when those last six months will be, but exceptional efforts to prolong the life of someone who is terminally ill can be very expensive.

Another factor is that the United States does not do as well as other countries in spending on preventive health care. It has by far the largest portion of its population uninsured or inadequately insured of any nation in the advanced industrial world. While some Americans receive outstanding care, those without private insurance often receive only emergency care, with little opportunity for regular checkups or prevention. This is especially true of uninsured pregnant women. They may have access to hospital emergency rooms and very sophisticated equipment in the event of an emergency for themselves or for their newborn child, but they may not be able to receive less expensive, ongoing prenatal care. Disparities in health care access often follow racial lines. While the infant mortality rate for white infants in the United States is on par with the lowest rates in the world, the mortality rate for black infants is comparable to the rate for Botswana in Southern Africa (Children's Defense Fund 2004).

While many have called for a national health care system in the United States, most reform plans are aimed at filling gaps in the present **private-pay** system. **Medicaid,** a joint federal and state program, provides care for the poorest people. Some states have added protection for the children of the working poor, who have jobs and may not qualify for Medicaid but often do not have work-related insurance and cannot afford other insurance. Attempts have been made to make insurance "portable" between jobs. Still, most Americans have their health insurance through an employer, and those who change jobs, are unemployed, or have jobs with no benefits are often left out of the system. Over 30 million Americans are in this situation.

Canada

Canada has used a **single-payer health care system** since the early 1970s. In this system, physicians are still in private practice, but except for a few specialists who work outside the system, they send their bills to the government in a program shared by the national and provincial governments. All Canadian citizens have a health card issued by the government that is their ensurance of access to care. This system allows patients to choose their doctors and to develop relationships with them over time.

This system is considerably less expensive than that in the United States, since emphasis is placed on preventive, rather than high-end, care. Also, duplication of services between hospitals is limited, and hospitals and doctors' offices only need to bill one source, greatly reducing overhead and administrative costs. The government sets fees for particular services and caps physicians' incomes, although Canadian doctors are still well paid.

The biggest downside of this system can be long waits for certain services, since facilities are run at full capacity and there is no incentive not to seek unnecessary care (except the deterrent of a long wait). Impatient Canadians sometimes seek care outside the government-payed system or in the United States. Yet most Canadians approve of this system, which provides broader coverage for less cost than the system to the south.

Sweden

One of the earliest efforts at **national health care** came in Sweden, which in 1891, instituted health care for all its citizens. The hospitals are government run, and most physicians are government employees. Their salaries are considerably lower than those of U.S. and Canadian doctors. While the care can be more impersonal, the technical level is quite high.

The Swedes have one of the longest life expectancies in the world, and their system costs considerably less than the Canadian system and less than half the

U.S. system. The Swedish system has been termed **socialized medicine** (a term sometimes wrongly applied to the Canadian system), since it is largely owned and operated by the national government.

Great Britain

Great Britain has used a hybrid system since shortly after World War II. The National Health Service provides health care to anyone who needs it, but an extensive private system remains in place for those who can afford to pay. The British system thus ensures care for all and preserves choice for some, but it does so at the risk of a two-tier system (not unlike the British school system), with better care for the better off.

Japan

Japan also retains private physicians, but most health care costs are paid by the government, as in the Canadian system. Private insurance makes up the difference. An extensive and well-regarded health care system, coupled with a traditionally healthy diet and exercise, have given the Japanese the longest life expectancy and the longest healthy life expectancy of people anywhere in the world.

The Japanese do suffer chronic illnesses related to high levels of smoking and occupational and educational stress. The influence of a higher-fat Western diet and greater dependence on cars, which reduces the amount of walking, are starting to add to the incidence of chronic illness.

Russia

The Soviet Union, not surprisingly, had a far-reaching system of socialized medicine. While the technology and expertise were not always at the highest level, the system did reach most everyone. Like many institutions in post-Soviet Russia, the health care system is in disarray. Physicians are paid very poorly, often earning no more than teachers or factory workers, and they are often paid irregularly. Over two-thirds of Russian doctors are women, reflecting an early opening of opportunities for Russian women as well as the fact that health care is not considered a very lucrative profession. Many physicians' training is comparable to that of a nurse–practitioner in the United States. Better care is offered in large cities and in military hospitals. The Russian system can be very impersonal, or at times, personal to the extreme.

The smoking rate is high in Russia, and the rate of alcoholism is one of the highest in the world. The Russian life expectancy has fallen to levels of fifty years ago, on par with some of the world's poorest countries (Farmer 2003). Russia seems to combine the chronic illnesses of the industrialized world with the infectious diseases and poor care of the undeveloped world. With a very low birth rate and relatively high infant and child mortality rates, Russia has one of the world's fastest-shrinking populations. Unlike most countries with shrinking populations, however, Russia will not have to worry about how to pay for all the retirees in an aging population. Unless health care and health practices change, many Russians will not live long enough to retire.

China

China is faced with limited resources and a huge budget. It first gained world attention by addressing this problem with a system of "barefoot doctors." Part paramedic, part nurse, and part public health official, these doctors traveled to rural villages to provide basic preventive health care and education.

Chinese health care is becoming more technologically proficient but also more unequal (Rosenthal 2001). The government owns and operates all the hospitals, as in Russia and Sweden, but as in Great Britain, people with cash can secure private care. Ironically, in China, the gap between the quality of government care and private care is often much greater than in Great Britain—sometimes, the difference between life and death. Chinese doctors, like British doctors, often "moonlight" in the private sector. In China, this can take new forms. Chinese surgeons, as in the United States, often stop by to reassure family members before the surgery of a loved one. One tradition has family members stuffing money into the pockets of the surgeon's white coat as he or she walks by with his or her sanitized hands and arms in the air. Some surgeons don't proceed into the operating room, where the already anesthetized patient is waiting, until their pockets are sufficiently filled!

While the Chinese health care delivery system is looking more and more Western, many traditional Chinese healing practices continue to prevail. A hospital may have a very Western-looking pharmacy, dispensing prescription drugs, and also a large kitchen, where healing herbs are carefully prepared according to ancient traditions. The Chinese contend that they have blended the best of the Eastern and Western healing arts. Indeed, many of these herbs have been found to have healing properties, and interest in ginger, gingko biloba, jasmine, and other traditional herbs and spices has grown in Western countries.

The ideals of balancing the forces of *yin* and *yang* and particularly of channeling the body's vital energy, or *chi,* have no direct parallel in modern Western medicine but continue to guide Chinese medical thought. *Chi* can be channeled through medicine and herbs but also through practices such as massage and exercise. A warm morning in any Chinese park will likely have many people, especially older adults, out practicing the slow and precise movements of *Tai chi chan.*

Tai chi is related to martial arts, but its main purpose is the improvement of health through the channeling of *chi*. It has gained wide following in the United States and Europe, as well. Similarly, *yoga*—an ancient Indian discipline that uses a combination of breathing, balancing, and stretching exercises to promote health, peace of mind, and well-being—has become extremely popular in North America and Europe.

Other Asian Countries

Both China and India have made great gains in lowering infant mortality and raising life expectancy, despite very low averages incomes. The southern Indian state of Kerala has combined socialized medicine with extensive village-level care, broad-based public health education, and particular attention to prenatal care and children's health. As a result, it has achieved a level of healthy life expectancy as high as the levels in the most industrialized countries. Sri Lanka, off the coast of India, has also achieved very impressive results with a very limited average income. Singapore has surpassed the United States in lowering infant mortality.

Continuing these successes will require continuing to ensure broad-based health care access while adopting new technologies. It will also be necessary to avoid the risk factors—lack of exercise, obesity, poor-quality environments—that can come with new technology and raise the risks of chronic illness.

Living Well, Staying Well

Many aspects of human physiology (how the body works) and pathology (what goes wrong) are still mysteries, but many others are not. We know the basic elements of individual health and well-being: A balanced, diverse diet that avoids excess fat, sugar, and alcohol; the avoidance of tobacco and dangerous drugs; an active lifestyle with regular exercise; meaningful work without extreme dangers or extreme stress; and healthy relationships are all key factors. We don't always follow all of these guidelines, however, either because we are unwilling or because we are unable.

We also know the basics of good public health—how to build healthy societies and communities. Health care must be available and affordable to all. And while new technologies and discoveries are important, the emphasis needs to be on prevention, particularly in the areas of sanitation and nutrition as well as early diagnosis. Prevention goes beyond health care access to education, both general education and specific public health education. People need to be able to learn about the basic elements of good health, in whatever context they nurture themselves and their families—rural or urban, Eastern or Western, traditional or modern. In this, women's education remains key, in part because it has been so long neglected in so many places and in part because in most places, women remain the primary caregivers for both the young and the old. An ironic relationship exists between health and population: The sickest populations with the most endangered lives and the least educated women and children also have the highest rates of population growth. As a result, seeing each person as unique, precious, and worthy of great investments of time and money goes hand in hand with slowing population growth.

We know what to do. Yet many societies remain unable or unwilling to make these investments in their people and their future. Developing countries must themselves make health and population control two of their top priorities. Wealthy countries must make access to healthcare for all—including poor, immigrant, and minority populations—one of their top priorities. Moreover, wealthy nations, foundations, and influential international organizations must recognize that the health of the planet respects national boundaries no more than does the latest epidemic. Whether these become global priorities will determine whether our future is as a dismal as the most nightmarish Malthusian projection or a continued transition to a healthy, stable population with hope for themselves and their children.

MAKING CONNECTIONS

Population Connection

■ Formerly called Zero Population Growth (ZPG), this group has changed its name to reflect a broader concern for population issues, including family planning, health care, and education, though limiting growth is still a major concern. The site at www.populationconnection.org contains a wide array of information, legislative action alerts, and other ways to get involved. Under the "Take Action" section, note information on e-mail contacts, local chapters, and their campus program, as well as their work for "kid-friendly" and healthy cities. What are their current projects at the community and campus level?

World Health Organization

■ This United Nations organization has been at the forefront of the campaign to eradicate disease, vaccinate children, and improve health care and health education around the world. Its site at www.who.int/en contains information on global health concerns and major campaigns. Special attention is given to HIV/AIDS and to global epidemics. Information can be found by country or by topic. In additon to AIDS, what are the current prime concerns of the WHO?

Health Clinics

■ What is available on your campus or in your community for health education and health care for the uninsured? Begin with your campus health office or campus–community office. Then visit local clinics and health offices. What are they doing to provide care and education? What are their main emphases and biggest challenges? How can individuals and groups become involved?

AIDS Services

■ Find out what is available in your community for AIDS services, HIV testing, and AIDS-prevention education. Are these programs offered on campus, in the schools, at community clinics, or through specialized agencies and programs? What types of services are offered, and how do they attempt to reach people in the community?

■ For further information on AIDS, HIV, tuberculosis, and efforts to combat related infectious diseases around the world, see the AIDS Education Global Information System at www.aegis.com.

CHAPTER 11

Technology and Energy
Prometheus's Fire or Pandora's Box?

Bhutan

Bhutan is not easy to find. This tiny country is tucked up against the Himalaya Mountains north of India and next to Nepal. Like Tibet to the north, Bhutan is a primarily Buddhist country, and devotion to this tradition permeates the culture. Bhutan is a very poor and remote state, and until 1999, it had another distinction: It was the last country on earth to have no television.

All that changed one day when the "cable guy" showed up. That's how he is known to the villagers, as he goes about connecting homes to the cable service that the government reluctantly agreed to accept. And since cable TV arrived, the country has never been the same.

Televisions are now everywhere, humming with foreign programming. One young boy now has a new topic to fight about with his older sister: He likes Cartoon Network, and she likes MTV. In the dirt schoolyard, the fights are more energetic, as young boys crash into each other in moves copied from the masked "heroes" of the World Wrestling Federation. An elderly woman, who grew up in a once peaceful land, shakes her head in dismay but also worries that she is neglecting her religious duties to watch soap operas.

Bhutan's mountains withstood millennia of invaders, but they were no match for the cable guy. Within a matter of years, the society has changed forever. Residents wonder, What has Bhutan gained? What has it lost? As the earnest young cable guy unrolls yet more spools, is he spreading civilization and culture or destroying it?

Seattle and Tahiti

Nicolas Lovejoy set off on a trek around the world with only his backpack and his girlfriend, Barbara. It was a wonderful experience, enjoying both the planet and the simple life. For one stretch, the two were on a sailboat, crossing the South Pacific en route from Tahiti to the Cook Islands. When they get off the boat, they were surprised that their millions of dollars in stock had tripled during the trip.

Nicolas and Barbara are not typical millionaires, if there is such a thing. He began as math teacher and feeling restless, took a pay cut from his $27,000 a year salary to go to work for a friend. His friend, Jeff Bezos, was trying to start a business on this thing called the World Wide Web. They decided to call the site "Amazon.com".

With their millions made, Nicolas and Barbara turned to philanthropy and began a multimillion-dollar foundation. Concerned about the community and the environment, along with low-income families, they sponsored some community gardens in Seattle (Verhovek 2000). While they were out gardening, their fortune was mostly lost: Amazon's stock plunged in the so-called dot-com crash.

What does it mean to live and work in an economy where millions can be made and lost before reaching the age of 30? Also, how can vast wealth be contained in a business that exists only in cyberspace and has never shown a profit? Have businesses such as Amazon transformed the world of opportunity or created a new boom-and-bust cycle akin to the bank failures and economic panics of the past? Will visionaries like Nicolas and Barbara be able to foster a sense of community and a better life, or have web business and web society already undermined face-to-face community?

Power Surge: The Advance of Technology

The ancient Greeks were fond of new ideas but also afraid of the changes they might bring. They told stories about these hopes and fears. The story of Prometheus tells of how he delivered fire to humanity in defiance of the gods, who feared that humans with control of fire would become god-like themselves. In another story, Pandora opened a box that was not meant to be opened and unleashed suffering and pestilence, along with an enduring bit of hope, on humankind. Similarly, the scientists who watched the world's first nuclear flash over the deserts of New Mexico in 1945 wondered whether they were seeing a new Prometheus's fire or opening a Pandora's box. As technology's power continues to grow at an exponential rate, questions about its value versus danger remain.

In one sense, technology has been around as long as humans have. None of us would last very long if we had to depend on our teeth and toenails to bring down game or dig up food. Humans need tools; they always have. For many millennia, the way to craft these tools was based on trial and error, and that experience was passed down through the generations. There were exceptions to this approach, but they were few.

The Greek mathematician Archimedes (c. 287–212 BCE)—known for his claim that with the right lever and a place to stand, he could move the world—came up with some clever inventions to build and defend Syracuse (on the island of Sicily). The story about him leaping naked from his bath and shouting "Eureka" at having found the principle of buoyancy may be true; the one about him burning invading Roman ships with giant mirrors is most likely not. The invading Romans admired Archimedes (although they killed him) and came up with some important engineering advances of their own: concrete, the self-supporting dome, arched aqueducts, paved roads, and so forth. But technical innovation continued to proceed slowly.

New attention to science came with the Italian Renaissance. Leonardo Da Vinci (1452–1519) designed everything from helicopters to submarines to tanks, although he never contrived a reasonable way to propel them. His inventions were impractical, but he was on the first wave of a new age, the age of science. Fellow Italian Galileo (1564–1642) studied the stars as people have done since the first human looked up, but he quickly adapted, refined, and employed a telescope. More important than any single invention, he refined and spread a hugely important idea: the experiment. Plenty of mathematics and a good measure of trial and error were still involved, but careful, systematic observation of a controlled event became one of the foundations of science.

The Fires of Industry

Science made Europe. Once the idea of technology took hold—wedding science, math, and craftsmanship to create new machines—Europe ruled the world. The Royal Academy of Sciences met in London with such greats as Isaac Newton (1643–1727), but tinkerers and craftspersons, if they understood science, also could join the elite club. In short order, they built everything from tea kettles to huge steam engines. Across the channel, French chemists conducted industrial espionage in China and then went to work fabricating new forms of porcelain, racing to keep ahead of the Dutch. In this atmosphere of rivalry, competition, greed, and inventive excitement, the industrial world was born.

Ancient Egypt and ancient Greece, as well as the early Chinese, Arab, and Mayan states, all had great mathematicians. Mostly they studied the stars and helped design monumental buildings. Later mathematicians built machines, and unlike Da Vinci, they devised ways to propel them, first with the power of falling water and then with the pressure of boiling water. The smelly, sooty, intensely productive age of steam was born.

The Europeans needed resources for their technology and markets for their mass-produced products. Just as with the creations of Archimedes and Da Vinci, as well as Galileo's telescopes, great inventions were employed in the service of war. Those who resisted the European expansion faced the brutality of science in bigger, deadlier guns, which were often mounted on bigger, faster ships and eventually driven by steam. Gunboat diplomacy forced the industrial idea on the rest of the world.

By the late 1800s, Germany, the United States, and finally Japan had joined the industrial world as major powers. The rest of the world succumbed to the power of what had been small states. The age of the machine had become the age of the machine gun.

But industrial technology was not all about brute force and raw power. Machines must be both powered and controlled. One of the first great inventions of the industrial age was the Jacquard loom, named for a French inventor. The design used punch cards, which looked like the IBM punch cards that guided the first computers, to guide the looms. And so a craft that normally took years to master and painstaking hours to execute could now be mechanically programmed and driven by water power. The English stole and perfected the idea, and soon England was producing more textiles than the rest of the world's countries combined. Competing textile mills quickly sprang up along waterways across Europe and North America. Clothing for the average person went from a single garment of homespun cloth to multiple possibilities, ending in the array that today fills our closets.

Booting Up the Electronic Age

Modernity is a slippery and elusive term, but in many ways, what became known as the modern world was the industrial world. The world of mass production, mass marketing, mass transportation, and mass consumption of industrial products dominated from the middle of the 1700s to the middle of the 1900s. But mathematicians, engineers, and tinkerers were already creating the beginnings of a new world. The might of Nazi Germany in World War II depended on a multitude of deadly machines—and a secret code to control them all, known as Enigma. Under this carefully controlled terror, much of European opposition collapsed. The British and Americans fought back with their own machines. Ultimately, the industrial capacity of the United States was unstoppable, but the key to an early turning of the tides of war was cracking that code. To do that, mathematicians and computing machines were needed. Crude but successful, the machines made their point: Computing power was global power.

Initially, computers filled entire buildings, requiring massive staffing and energy supplies, such as the enormous 1946 ENIAC computer in Philadelphia. In the 1950s and 1960s, computers were quickly put to military uses: guiding a global network of submarines and missiles. The transistor allowed the circuitry to become minute and cheap, and soon computers were found in all forms of industry.

The same electronic miniaturization and ultimate mass production—ultimately, millions of layers of "chips"—made other electronic items commonplace. The transistor radio brought music and ideas to the most remote locations. Television went from a curiosity to the central piece of furniture in U.S. homes in the 1950s. Today, from the heights of the Himalayas to the depths of the Amazon basin, the electronic eye of television is everywhere in the world. The same low-cost, miniature electronics could be launched into space and fit into someone's pocket, first as a calculator and then as a cell phone. Whether traveling by beam or by cable, the key to the electronic revolution, along with small size and low cost, is interconnectedness.

The idea of connecting computers in an **intercomputer network,** or **Internet,** was also born of defense considerations. But soon, universities found this a useful way to share information and resources. As late as the 1980s, pundits were arguing that only nerdy professors would ever care much about sending mail electronically and that certainly no one would pay for the privilege. But in the 1980s, first Apple and then IBM made computers small enough to fit on a desk: **personal computers,** or **PCs.** Miniaturization meant that these computers could do far more than the huge ENIAC of 1946. Yet their power was limited if they were used as isolated units. By connecting them in an Internet, it was like the synergy of connecting thousands of great minds.

Within a matter of years, commercial enterprises such as CompuServe and America Online (AOL) were offering everyone the miracle of instant, worldwide e-mail communication. The development of **HTML,** or **hypertext markup language,** meant that it would become easy to share much more than text messages. Any graphic image could be wisked electronically around the world, and so the **World Wide Web** was born.

Innovation has always thrived along complex networks. Originally, these were networks of trade, with caravans and caravels plying the deserts and the oceans to connect people, products, and ideas. In places where these networks were most dense, such as the crossroads of the Eastern Mediterranean and the Middle East, civilizations flourished, rich in both products and ideas. In the 1840s, the first network of cable, telegraph lines, began its march around the globe. In 1858 transatlantic cable connected the United States and Great Britain. "Glory to God!" wired Queen Victoria. Then the cable proved faulty and the system crashed. But even faulty technology can be powerful, and newer systems are created to replace the old. Telephone networks replaced the telegraph in the 1880s, along with the newly emerging radio.

Networks continue to flourish with newer cables and newer means of beaming messages, such as today's ever-present satellite dishes and cell phone towers. Sometimes, the systems crash. But they also intermingle to create new possibilities. Cell phones can receive e-mail messages and search the World Wide Web. Some can now take digital pictures, and others can take global positions from satellites. At the same time, personal computers have become laptops, downsized to notebooks that can be carried anywhere and plugged into the Internet, whether by cable or by microwave. **PDAs,** or **personal digital assistants,** combine the size of the cell phone and the data storage of the PC.

It is not hard to imagine a multiuse digital companion that merges all these uses into a single tool that will travel with everyone, like the six-shooter of the

Wild West or the communicators of *Star Trek*. Some version of a PDA or note-book computer will likely be the only thing many students will bring to class in the near future. Books, notes, even the whole library could be accessed from disks, from cables, or through the air. In time, Amazon will complete the transforma-tion: The old-fashioned idea of mailing a book that's been purchased will be ut-terly obsolete. Books will be ordered online and then beamed or cabled to their recipients, complete with full video and audio, if desired.

Industrial technology built the modern age, and now it seems that postindus-trial electronic technology is building a postmodern **information age.** Industrial modernism stressed uniformity, the interchangeable part that allowed U.S. inven-tor Eli Whitney to mass produce guns and cotton gins and that allowed Henry Ford to mass produce automobiles—inexpensive vehicles that all looked alike. There was also a certainty that there was a modern way, seen in the industrial West, that would uniformly transform production, urban environments, and ul-timately the people who worked and lived in these places. They would all be mod-ern and somewhat alike.

Postmodernism, based on the incredible diversity that is possible in the in-formation age, stresses a multiplicity of voices, centers, and different approaches. Power lies less in production and more in information. Every year, the United States and the postindustrial economies of Europe and Japan produce less and less that can actually be packaged and held. Instead, they produce designs, pro-grams, patents, and copyrights that allow them to direct and profit from the pro-duction of the industrializing world.

The Industrial Revolution of the nineteenth century displaced generations of farm laborers, and many rural dwellers were forced to seek industrial employ-ment, increasingly in urban areas. In the United States, farmers and agricultural laborers dropped from comprising over 35 percent of the population at the be-ginning of the 1900s to less than 3 percent by the end of the century. Similarly, postindustrial change has displaced millions of factory laborers, many of whom have had to scramble to try to find places in the service and technology sectors.

Technology has not only changed production and consumption, but even so-cial relations have been altered by e-mail, instant messaging, the chat room, and the cell phone. It is now easier to be in contact with others, but less of that con-tact is face to face. Proximity matters less, as people may participate in an inter-national chat room that spans the globe, but they have no idea of the names of their next-door neighbors. On "wired" campuses, roommates fixated on com-puter screens instant message each other across their dorm rooms, while at home, a teenager calls his or her parent across the house on a cell phones to ask to use the car. Technology can greatly reduce social isolation for those people in remote areas, for the very elderly, and for others unable to get out, and it can open a world of global contacts and new relationships. It can also be isolating in its own way, as coffeehouses give way to Internet cafes and ultimately to wireless laptops—all communication that is mediated by a keyboard. Virtual communities of virtual relationships are not always the most satisfying, any more than virtual travel to virtual locations to seek virtual romance!

For all its newness, the information age is repeating many of the patterns of the early industrial age. After commerce, one of its primary applications has been in war. In the industrial era, each new advance meant a deadlier weapon. The 1903 *New York Times* article that announced the flight of the Wright brothers noted that the army was interested in their success and that this new machine, just barely off the ground, might be useful for dropping torpedoes. Electronic technology has brought wars that are fought on video screens with weapons guided to their targets by laser beams and satellite signals.

The high tide of the industrial era was also a time of tremendous concentration of wealth and power in the hands of a few. Andrew Carnegie controlled steel, John D. Rockefeller controlled oil, and J. P. Morgan dominated banking. What had been local markets became national markets, and the potential for wealth was enormous. Whether these people were seen as philanthropists, contributing to a better society, or "robber barons," exploiting their monopoly of power, they dominated their era.

So, too, the information era is dominated by a few and now on a global scale, as national markets have given way to international markets. Of the ten richest multibillionaires on the *Forbes* list (2004), six have been closely related to technology, including the founders and leaders of Microsoft, Sun Systems, Oracle, and Intel. The remaining four are members of the Walton family, each with over $20 billion from the globalization of commerce that helped make Wal-Mart.

Mergers continue to put the largest media companies into fewer hands: AOL–Time Warner (combining what were once separate computer, print, television, and film operations), ABC–Disney (the Murdoch conglomerate that merged film, newspapers, and books), and then the Fox television network. The postmodern vision is comprised of multiple and diverse perspectives on the world, but increasingly, these are structurally merged in the hands of a few vast multinational corporations.

The musical styles of the times are drawn from the multicultural influences of a "world beat," but once packaged into global "pop," the music is popularized everywhere by MTV and marketed everywhere by a vast music industry. More music is recorded than ever before, but the global market is dominated by a handful of superstars. Similarly, more books are produced than ever, but the massive profits are confined to a few titles that are marketed globally, complete with movie and merchandise rights. Food products and styles are also drawn from all over the planet and then standardized by a few fast-food giants, which control the marketing to offer Taco Bell in Tokyo and Kentucky Fried Chicken in Guadalajara.

The industrial era created great opportunities for urban professionals and tradespersons at the same time that it displaced huge numbers of European peasants and rural people. So, too, the information age has created a **"digital divide"** between those who have access to the technological tools of the day and are comfortable using them and those for whom this is an alien and alienating world.

Electronic technology has also been a powerful force for cultural globalization. No place on the planet is protected from its influence. Some societies, such as Bhutan, are moving directly from the preindustrial to the postindustrial era. In parts of the world the leap, is even greater:

> Deep in the Amazon, the slow tropical twilight beckons villagers to join the fire circle. Here all gather to share the news, to learn of one another's lives, to hear elders tell the old stories, entertain and socialize the young into the right ways of living. Yet there are ever fewer young at this fire circle. The elders explain in hushed tones, "They have fallen to the ghost, the big ghost." For this jungle is haunted. As night falls, great clusters of bats swoop overhead blocking the moonlight, deep-throated frogs call, and the fleeting, flickering light of a ghost can be glimpsed in the village. The ghost prefers young people; one by one they disappear from the fire circle. Some are never seen in the circle again. Others return with a zombie-like glaze in their eyes. The elders know they have seen the Madonna—the one in strange underwear that is. The big ghost arrives by satellite dish, and brings Madonna and MTV to the Amazon along with cartoons and a world of other offerings. The Amazon's Kayapo Indians used money from gold and mahogany on the world market to install a small but effective satellite dish. Some wish they hadn't. The chief regrets his decision, "I have been saying that people must buy useful things like knives or fishing hooks. Television does not fill the stomach. It only shows our children and grandchildren white people's things." Bemoans an elder, "The night is the time the old people teach the young people. Television has stolen the night." (Sernau 2000, p. 140; see also Simons 1989)

It is incorrect to see these groups as powerless victims, however. In some cases, they have used technology to their own purposes. Kayapo fighters stalk their enemies silently through the forest. When they have them within range, they carefully site their favorite weapon and release the dreaded whir—not of a blowgun but of a video camera. They have effectively used video to capture the trespasses and violations of foreign oil companies and use this tape to support their complaints before the Organization of American States and other international bodies (Turner 1993).

In desperately poor rural Bangladesh, the Grameen Bank—a remarkable "microlender" known for its loans to small entrepreneurs, particularly women—is now lending money for cell phones. This sounds like the ultimate in waste and inappropriate technology. But cell phones can be extremely useful in places where regular phones are unavailable or unreliable. Women use the loans to buy phones and then rent them by the minute to villagers. The villagers can contact their relatives in neighboring villages, find out about prices for their commodities in nearby towns and cities, get medical advice, and otherwise access information in minutes that would previously have required a day's walk.

The Information (and Misinformation) Age

Technology typically has a double edge. High-speed computers can allow totalitarian dictatorships the means to monitor their populations and track dissidents. At the same time, e-mail and faxed messages can zip past censors to coordinate social movements and popular resistance around the world.

Postmodernists such as French social theorist Michel Foucault (1995 [1977]) note that we are experiencing both more sophisticated means of surveillance and social control and also more diverse and evasive means of resistance. Whether the first is positive or not depends on whether you see it in the hands of legitimate authority or the repressive hands of "Big Brother," which George Orwell portrayed in his novel *1984*. Likewise, the resistance may be "freedom fighters," dissidents and "free thinkers," or "terrorists," depending on the situation and one's point of view.

We must also face the fact the information age can be the misinformation age, where reality is packaged by corporate media, advertisers, and public relations campaigns. As stated by postmodern theorist Walter Truett Anderson in the title of his 1992 book, *Reality Isn't What It Used to Be*. The public is confronted with media-edited virtual wars that seem to have no casualties, carefully presented celebrity political candidates that have no unpopular policies, and idealized images of products and places that promise paradise in a package.

In such a context, the media is as likely to produce international misunderstanding as understanding. It also creates a climate of intense consumerism, in which people in richer nations are driven to spend beyond their own means and beyond the means of the planet to support their lifestyle. At the same time, new audiences in poorer nations are prompted to emulate the very behavior that is the cause of so many problems for richer, high-consumption countries.

Can the electronic media be harnessed to promote citizenship, rather than mere consumerism, and open dialogue, rather than cycles of repression and terror? The answer to that question will, in large measure, determine whether the information age will be a golden age or a very dark age disguised in golden tinsel.

Energy: Fire from Above and Below

The industrial age was built on the idea of using stored energy, the force of falling water, burning wood, or burning coal and oil to replace human and animal power. The electronic age is predicated on the availability of cheap and reliable electrical power.

When a massive power failure shut off the electricity to the northeastern United States and eastern Canada in 2003, economic activity came to a stop. People in tall buildings had no elevators. Urban commuters had no trains. Grocery stores had no refrigeration. Some cities had no water. And most significantly, unless one had batteries or generators, there was no access to the computers that ran everything else. Subsequent power failures in Sweden and in Italy likewise showed both how dependent we are on international networks of electrical transmission and also how fragile those networks may be.

Our industrial and electronic economies are all based on the use of large amounts of stored energy. Every year, humanity's appetite for energy increases (see Figure 11.1). Some economists use energy consumption as a proxy for level of economic development. Yet there is also a real danger here. Even as the world becomes ever more energy dependent, it has yet to settle on a safe and reliable energy source (see Figure 11.2).

Wood

Maybe it was fire that made us what we are. Many ancient peoples have stories about the coming of fire, such as the Greek tale of Prometheus bringing fire to

FIGURE 11.1   **World Primary Energy Consumption: 1970–2025**

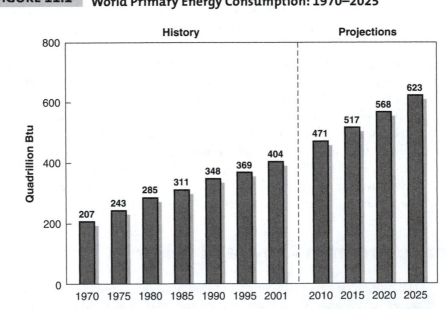

Source: U.S. Department of Energy, Energy Information Administration. Available online at www.eia.doe.gov/oiaf/ieo/world.html.

FIGURE 11.2 **World Primary Energy Consumption by Energy Source: 1970–2025**

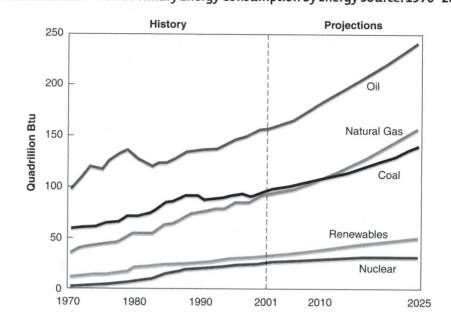

Source: U.S. Department of Energy, Energy Information Administration. Available online at www.eia.doe.gov/oiaf/ieo/world.html.

humanity from the gods. Fire allowed people to make food more digestible, to keep warm, and to ward off everything from predators to mosquitoes. Some people may even have used it to change tangled, brush-filled landscapes into the grasslands and open savannas that human hunters prefer.

In many places in the world, wood is still depended on as essential fuel. Herders in dry grasslands have long known that animal dung makes a very usable (if less than elegant) fire. But without enough animals on hand, there is little alternative to what wood can be found. All across the Sahel region of Africa, the dry country just south of the Sahara, on the fringes of the Kalahari Desert in Southern Africa, all across the dry plateau regions of India, and in the rugged highlands of Haiti, the land is being stripped of trees by people desperate for fuel (UNHCR 2003). When larger trees are not available or too difficult to harvest, people walk long distances to collect loads of gnarled sticks to haul back on their gnarled backs. The sticks feed small cooking fires and can be slowly burned in pits to create crude charcoal, which can be sold to urbanites to use as fuel. As the wood gets more scarce, the walks get longer. Many places are being deforested down to the last twig, not by great logging companies or raging forest fires but the slow, smoky burn of charcoal pits—the only energy and income source for poor and displaced people.

While back-to-nature North Americans and Northern Europeans investigate the idea of heating with high-efficiency wood stoves, many of the world's poor need to find alternatives. One option is **reforestation.** Fast-growing trees, such as the meleluca being tried in Haiti, can reforest slopes and provide a steady supply of firewood while also controlling erosion. For a long time, development workers doubted that poor people would take much interest in planting and protecting trees. Yet once the people have seen that a project will benefit them and their children in years to come and that they won't be denied access to the resource, successful reforestation projects have been undertaken in Haiti, in the Sahel, and in India.

A compatible option is to use the resource more efficiently. Open fires waste wood and can be replaced by high-efficiency stoves and ovens. The same technologies that allow people in cold, wood-rich climates to heat their homes efficiently can help feed people in hot, wood-scarce regions. Some stoves can use grasses for fuel, not unlike the method used by North American prairie pioneers, who found they could use twisted hay, and some can burn dung.

Finally, a hot, dry climate is the perfect place to use direct solar energy. Cookers that use curved mirrors to direct the sun's heat can replace wood all together.

Coal

Coal fired the industrial age. The age of coal saw huge surges in industrial production and the "dark Satanic mills" that blackened the skies of Britain, Germany, and the northeastern United States. Coal is vastly abundant. Great layers were created as ancient forests sank beneath new layers of sediment, trapping and compressing the carbon in the wood into coal.

The limitations of coal are apparent to anyone who has seen or seen pictures of a coal mine, a coal barge, and a coal furnace. Coal is difficult to extract, difficult to transport, and messy to burn. Large amounts of coal lie under some of the world's most energy-hungry countries, such as the United States and Russia, but it varies greatly in quality and ease of extraction.

The most accessible coal-like substance is peat, the black, dirt-like material that Irish peasants have long harvested from surface peat bogs and burned for fuel. Peat is coal in the making: still loose and crumbly, horribly smoky, but easily accessible and in some places still used. Coal grades improve as this substance moves from crumbly peat through bituminous to hard and cleaner anthracite. Abundant, easy-to-access coal tends to be of the dirtier sort.

Sulfur content is also a problem. Sulfur in the coal goes up as sulfur dioxide, mixes with water in the atmosphere, and comes down as sulfuric acid. It is a caustic component of **acid rain,** which kills trees and fish and eats away the facades of buildings and the finishes on cars.

Coal fires, especially lower-grade coal fires, also put out a lot of particulate matter: soot. The coal soot of early twentieth century London provided comic scenes in *Mary Poppins*. But coal soot so filled the air in parts of Eastern Europe that it blackened laundry that was hung out to dry and slowly blackened the lungs of adults and children alike.

Urban air in advanced industrial countries became cleaner as manufacturing went from coal- and steam-driven machinery to electrically driven production. Today, the majority of electricity in the United States and elsewhere around the world is produced by coal-fired electrical plants that sit just outside major urban areas. Higher-technology coal-fired plants use "scrubbers" to remove some of the particulate matter from the smoke.

Even the cleanest plant and the cleanest coal, however, mixes the carbon of the coal with the oxygen of the air to produce tons of carbon dioxide. Carbon dioxide has not been considered a pollutant, since it is harmless in small quantities, but it is the main "greenhouse gas." Carbon dioxide allows light to pass through but traps the escaping heat of the sun in the same way that the glass of a greenhouse or an automobile on a sunny day captures the heat of sunlight. Climatologists worry that over time, the carbon dioxide build-up in the atmosphere will lead to **global warming** and severe and unpredictable climate changes.

The other great problem with coal comes before it is burned: in the access and extraction. Cutting peat out of a bog gave way to extracting coal from deep mine shafts. Narrow, dark shafts into the black heart of the hills of such places as Scotland, Pennsylvania, and Japan became the daily abode of generations of miners in the 1800s. Young boys were preferred in the mines, since they could crawl into the narrower tunnels. Sometimes, they became the main income earners for their families after their fathers succumbed to "black lung" and other disabling diseases as well as frequent accidents.

Deep shaft coal mining in the United States shifted southward along the Appalachian Mountains and became the mainstay of rural West Virginia and eastern Kentucky and Tennessee by the 1880s. During the latter part of the twentieth century, coal mining in the United States began a massive shift westward, particularly after the Clean Air Act of 1970. Mines in the Rocky Mountain states contained lower-sulfur coal, and air quality in U.S. cities was becoming a major concern. But just as important, the great reserves in Montana, Arizona, and other western states could be accessed through **strip mines.** Huge excavating machines, some with tires taller than a typical bulldozer, could scour into the mountainsides and extract coal far faster than the old pick-and-shovel mines. This type of mining was also safer for the workers. New questions emerged, however, about what would be done with the great humanmade craters after the coal was gone and what would be done with the tons of rock, called **overburden,** that was hauled out to get at the coal.

Meanwhile, mining returned to parts of Appalachia in the 1980s and used western strip-mining methods. **Mountaintop removal mining** literally takes the tops off eastern mountains and ridges to get at the underlying coal, dumping the overburden down the sides to fill streams and valleys with mine tailings. At first, the unemployed Appalachian workers rejoiced at the return of their lost industry. Soon, however, residents realized the terrible environmental toll that had come with mining that literally tore down the mountains and fouled everything else downstream (Volles 1999).

Giant excavator mining has become the norm in many huge mines in developing countries, such as New Guinea. The production is vast, but the lifespan of most of these mines is short. Coal remains plentiful but hard to extract, hard to transport, and hard to work with. Its continued usefulness remains in question.

Oil

Coal fired the nineteenth century, but oil fueled the twentieth century. In many ways, the twentieth century was driven by petroleum and petroleum products: gasoline, kerosene, diesel fuel, jet fuel, and myriad plastics, even pharmaceuticals, that are petroleum based.

The century began with the internal combustion engine, a gasoline burner, becoming the dominant way to power automobiles, rather than steam or electricity. Lighter and more powerful gasoline engines made powered flight a possibility. Diesel fuel was used to power submarines and then gradually replaced coal-fired steam for ships and trains. By midcentury, oil dominated. World War II was fought with oil-burning machines and was often fought over oil fields: in North Africa, in the Soviet sphere, and in the Dutch East Indies, where Japan went to war in part over fears of a U.S.-led oil embargo (Yergin 1991).

The first oil fields were the easiest to tap. The "bubbling crude" came right to the surface. Easy-access fields in Pennsylvania (as the Drake well of 1852) and Texas (as the Lucas well at Spindletop, 1901) made the United States the leader in oil production. These fields were soon insufficient, and the search for new oil went global.

Substantial oil fields have been found in Alaska in North America; in Mexico and Venezuela in Latin America; in Nigeria, Chad, and other parts of West Africa; in the North Sea between Great Britain and Norway; in Indonesia (the former East Indies); in the Caucasus Mountains region of Russia and the new former Soviet Republics; and of course, in the Middle East. The area around the Persian Gulf may contain as much as two-thirds of the world's known accessible oil reserves. Accessibility is a key issue. No doubt, much more oil may exist in more remote offshore locations, but it would be very hard to reach and to extract safely and economically.

In advanced industrial economies, oil is power. In the 1970s, the Arab oil-exporting countries embargoed their oil exports to the United States and Europe in protest over these regions' support for Israel, which had fought a difficult war with Egypt and Syria in 1973 (Yergin 1991). The embargo was so successful in getting the attention of the Western industrial powers that oil-producing countries continued to work together to exploit this advantage. And so, **OPEC,** the **Organization of Petroleum Exporting Countries,** was born. The price of crude (unrefined) oil rose dramatically, and oil became the "black gold" of the world economy, promising an asphalt road to riches for oil producers. That road has proven bumpy for most, however.

Saudi Arabia has the world's largest oil reserves, and its very image is tied to oil and oil wealth. It is true that the Saudi royal family is wealthy with oil money and that Saudi Arabia uses its oil income to buy large quantities of industrial products, consumer goods, and top-shelf weapons. Yet the gross domestic product (GDP) per capita is around $8,000, placing Saudi Arabia as a middle-income country on par with parts of Latin America. Unemployment is very high, inequalities of both gender and class are extreme, and the quality of education and health care far below the standards of most of Asia (Energy Information Administration 2005). Oil has not brought broad-based development nor has it brought stability and democratic institutions.

A similar pattern can be seen in Kuwait and other oil-rich nations. Iraq's oil financed its weapons and disastrous wars, but it has not been able to finance the nation's recovery. Iran's oil wealth first financed the repression of the Shah and then the extremism of the Ayatollah Khomeini, but it still benefits only a few Iranians.

Latin America has fared little better. Mexico's dynamic President Lázaro Cárdenas nationalized the oil industry in the 1930s to secure the profits from primarily U.S.-based companies. But the national monopoly, Pemex, has been rife with corruption and mismanagement. While oil has financed some national programs and oil and petrochemicals are Mexico's leading exports, the entire economy now rises and falls on prevailing oil prices. Venezuela continues to face economic and political turmoil, in spite of large oil reserves.

Africa has had the most troubled times of all in the oil business. In Nigeria, oil revenues have topped $300 billion for the last twenty-five years, but the country remains desperately poor with a majority of its population surviving on less than two dollars a day (Onishi 2000). The oil revenues have been controlled by northern generals, who are not eager to strengthen their ethnic and political rivals on the coast. The only oil many Nigerians along the coast ever see is what leaks from the broken pipes. Some is collected in wheelbarrows and plastic jugs by desperate slum dwellers. In other places, the leaks foul water supplies and fuel deadly fires (Onishi 2000).

Chad, one of the world's poorest countries, is working with ExxonMobil, Chevron, and Petronas (the oil giant of Malaysia) on a huge pipeline to carry its oil though Cameroon to tankers on the Atlantic Ocean. The initial revenues have gone to buy weapons, and poor residents continue to wait for some benefit from the rest.

In the worst-case scenario, oil wealth has fueled bitter wars. For years in Angola, the government sold oil to arm its soldiers, while rebels sold black-market diamonds to arm themselves. The country was devastated. The potential of oil money to fill the coffers continues to bedazzle world leaders. The tiny islands of Sao Tome and Principe, off the equatorial African coast, have huge offshore oil reserves compared to their sizes. These long-overlooked entities are now being courted by the big oil companies. Will they become the next Qatar or Bahrain (both in the Persian Gulf), tiny and rich? Some have described the relaxed life on these small islands where the wealth was once in fresh fruit, as paradise. Will oil enrich them or bring paradise lost?

American oil companies have poured over $5 billion into neighboring Equatorial Guinea since oil was confirmed there in 1995. The man who has ruled the country since 1979, Teodoro Obiang Nguema, is now fabulously wealthy, as most of the oil revenue has gone to him and his family members. Most people in the country continue to live on less than one dollar per day.

The irony is that while oil producers struggle to find positive ways to use oil income to foster development, nonoil producers struggle under the burden of paying for oil imports in economies that are increasingly dependent on petroleum products for transportation, shipping, industry, and mechanized agriculture.

Oil poses many environmental as well as economic and political problems. Unlike coal, it is liquid, so it can be pumped rather than mined and piped rather than hauled. It can also be spilled. Oil drilling and pumping techniques have improved greatly since the days of flaming gushers, but spills and accidents are still common. As drilling moves to ever more difficult to reach and environmentally sensitive areas, such as the Arctic National Wildlife Refuge on the north slope of Alaska, these concerns will only increase. The greatest danger is in shipping the oil by tanker. In 1989, the Exxon *Valdez* caused enormous damage in its famous shipwreck off the Alaskan coast, but this was just the foulest of a continual problem. Earlier oil spills had fouled the California coast, and a huge spill contaminated large areas of the Spanish coastline. In each case, both the economy and the environment were devastated. Pipelines carry their own environmental problems and risks for accidents as well as sabotage and terrorism.

Oil poses major threats to the environment as it consumed, as well. Diesel fuel puts a lot of particulates into the air—that black, sooty, smelly smoke that belches from the exhaust of trucks and buses. Gasoline has fewer particulates but contributes a variety of harmful gases, including nitrous oxide. This comes back down as nitric acid and contributes to the acid rain problem. In certain weather conditions, it never escapes the urban atmosphere at all but hovers to create **ozone**, one of the major and most dangerous components of urban smog.

In this regard, the people in the cities in developing countries don't breathe any easier than those in richer nations and sometimes worse. While developing nations may have somewhat fewer vehicles, those vehicles are often older and in poorer repair. Many of the world's cities exist in a perpetual brown haze that smells like old tobacco (see Table 11.1). The burning of oil products is also a major contributor to the greenhouse gases suspected of causing global warming.

TABLE 11.1	Air Pollution in the World's Cities: 1995			
City	Population/ Million	Suspended Particles Levels (per mg m³)	Sulfur Dioxide Levels (per mg m³)	Nitrogen Dioxide Levels (per mg m³)
World Health Organization Recommended Max. Levels		90	50	50
Amsterdam	1.1	40	10	58
Athens	3.1	178	34	64
Beijing	11.3	377	90	122
Berlin	3.3	50	18	26
Brussels	1.1	78	20	48
Bombay	15.1	240	33	39
Cairo	9.9	—	69	—
Copenhagen	1.3	61	7	54
Dublin	0.9	—	20	—
Havana	2.2	—	1	5
Kuala Lumpar	1.2	85	24	—
London	7.6	—	25	77
Los Angeles	12.4	—	9	74
Moscow	9.3	100	109	—
Mexico City	16.6	279	74	130
Milan	4.3	77	31	248
Montreal	3.3	34	10	42
New York	16.3	—	26	79
Singapore	2.8	—	20	30
Sydney	3.6	54	28	—
Tokyo	27.0	49	18	68

Note: From this data it can be seen that the most polluted cities include Beijing and Mexico City which have high levels of all three pollutants. As well as this, Athens, Moscow and Bombay have high levels of suspended particles, Cairo and Moscow have high levels of sulfur dioxide and Amsterdam, Athens, Copenhagen, London, Los Angeles, Milan, New York and Tokyo have high levels of nitrogen dioxide.

Source: U.N. World Health Organization. Used by permission.

Oil often shares its underground cavities with a lighter fossil fuel relative: **natural gas.** Originally, natural gas was considered a waste product to be burned off in huge pillars of flame before beginning the serious pumping of oil. Oilmen remembered the dangers of gas buildup in coal mines. Over time, the handling of this fuel has improved, and it is now one of the fastest-growing energy sources (See Figure 11.3).

Natural gas is becoming an important international commodity, just as petroleum has been, and that will increase in this century. Canadian gas fields are already important to U.S. markets. Bolivia has been embroiled in intense controversy over the export of its natural gas resources, particularly to the United States, through a port in Chile (Rohter 2003). The gas could be a major source of revenue, but Bolivia's poor, largely indigenous population is not convinced. Bolivian silver traveled the world and made the Spanish Empire rich, but Bolivia remains South America's poorest nation. Can the people expect better from gas exports?

Natural gas can be delivered by pipe across the country and to individual homes. It is primarily just the gas methane and burns clean, giving off mostly just water vapor and carbon dioxide. This makes it safer and cleaner to use for home heating and allows for the open, unvented flame of a gas stove. Natural gas has

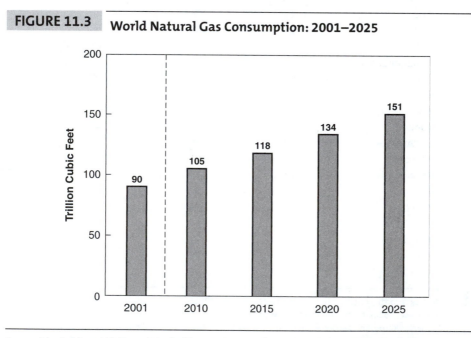

FIGURE 11.3 **World Natural Gas Consumption: 2001–2025**

Source: Adapted from U.S. Department of Energy, Energy Information Administration. Available online at www.eia.doe.gov/oiafa/archive/ieo04/world.html.

also become a popular fuel for electrical generation, again because it is high energy, easy to move, and clean. Some vehicles have been adapted to run on natural gas; they give off less hazardous exhaust, and while they typically have less power than gasoline vehicles, they are often ideal for urban stop-and-go vehicles, such as postal trucks.

Natural gas also has its limitations. It is in short supply, at least at our current rate of consumption, and harder-to-reach sources carry new dangers and environmental problems. Also to say that natural gas burns clean, giving off only water and harmless carbon dioxide, is no longer accurate on the global level when carbon dioxide is a major suspect in global warming.

Oil fueled the twentieth century, and the twenty-first is becoming increasingly dependent on oil and natural gas. These fuels not only fire our machinery, but petrochemicals made from these fuels are the basis for a vast array of synthetic fabrics, medicines, and plastics. The clothes on our backs and the plastic jugs that fill rich countries' landfills and poor countries' streets and hillsides are all based in oil. We wear it, eat and drink from it, put it on as cosmetics, and take it as medicine. Given the importance of these substances, it is the height of waste and recklessness to continue to burn them up or to spin them into products to be thrown away. Yet few places are developing effective plans for a postpetroleum age.

Nuclear Fission: The Power of Distant Suns

In one sense, all power is solar power, because our major energy sources are all means of stored solar power. Fossil fuels—oil, coal, and natural gas—release energy that was stored by ancient life that used solar energy to build molecules of carbon, hydrogen, and oxygen. Humanity's favorite fuel over most of its history, wood and charcoal, is this same storage process but occurs in living trees. Solar power also drives the wind, the waves, and the currents and evaporates the water that eventually returns as rivers—all sources of alternative energy.

The only exception to this is **nuclear power**, which releases the energy of atomic nuclei from heavy atoms such as uranium, fused in the supernova of primordial suns. And so perhaps it is the ultimate in stored energy. One other experimental energy source, nuclear fusion, imitates the processes of the sun itself in releasing energy as it fuses hydrogen into helium.

Manhattan Project scientists worked feverishly in the 1940s in Los Alamos, New Mexico, to develop a sustainable nuclear fission chain reaction to release the power of uranium and heavy atoms. Their goal was to beat the Nazis in the race to build an atomic bomb. Many of the scientists felt intensely conflicting emotions: the thrill of discovering a new and yet unknown source of vast energy coupled with the fear of what this tremendous energy source might do to the planet and the people who occupy it. Their fears were well grounded. Nuclear weapons hastened the end of World War II only to plunge the world into a cold war in which ever-deadlier "nukes" threatened to destroy whole cities and scorch the planet itself. Nuclear power, an attempt to tame this wild force, is similarly viewed with mixed hopes and fears.

A **nuclear fission** weapon uses an out-of-control chain reaction, in which each splitting atom produces high-energy neutrons to split other atoms. A nuclear power plant inserts carbon rods into the fuel to absorb the neutrons and slow the reaction. A slow reaction does not explode (one hopes) but produces intense heat. The heat produces steam that drives turbines, and the turbines drive dynamos, or electric generators. The process is as old as Michael Faraday's dynamo and James Watts's steam engine, only the fuel has changed.

Large amounts of water are used to cool the plant to a safe operating temperature. The only waste products are large amounts of steam (the great white plumes billowing from the hourglass-shaped stacks of many nuclear plants); a lot of warm water, which is typically pumped into whatever waterway the plant sits beside; and a small amount of spent fuel. This is the attraction of nuclear power: There is no dependence on great quantities of coal, oil, or natural gas, and there is no carbon- and particulate-laden smoke billowing into the air.

The United States built many nuclear power plants, particularly in the growth-oriented 1960s, and European countries, with less access to oil and coal resources than the United States, became even more nuclear dependent. France embarked on an ambitious nuclear program and now produces a majority of its electrical energy from nuclear power. Other countries have looked to nuclear power as an alternative to oil dependence, and many developing countries are eager to have nuclear plants to meet their growing energy demands.

As the hopes for nuclear power grow, so do the fears. Mining uranium is a difficult and dangerous operation, and it's only economical in certain parts of the world, such as South Africa. Only a certain rare type of uranium, the isotope U 235, is useful for fission, so the fuel must be enriched in a complex and energy-intensive process to increase the amount of fissionable uranium. This enriched form is highly radioactive, giving off dangerous radiation, and so must be transported and stored safely. A large area in the Caucasus Mountains of Russia shows evidence of severe radiation damage. Once thought to be evidence of a terrible nuclear accident hidden by the Soviet government, it may just be the result of careless practices in the handling, storage, and disposal of radioactive material—the nuclear equivalent of an abandoned open pit.

The process in the plant is highly regulated but not foolproof. The plant can't explode, but a runaway reaction could cause extreme heat and a "meltdown." Other errors could lead to the release of radiation. In the United States, the Three Mile Island plant had a series of mishaps followed by a radiation release that affected nearby areas and threatened to be far worse. The worst known nuclear disaster was the 1986 Chernobyl disaster near the city of Kiev in the Ukraine—at the time, part of the Soviet Union. Radiation was released and sickened and killed hundreds, perhaps thousands in the area. Radioactive particles also rode the winds into Eastern Europe and Scandinavia and ultimately circled the earth in the upper atmosphere.

Part of the fear of radiation is its invisibility, but more important is its durability. Many radioactive substances will emit radiation for thousands, even tens of thousands of years. (This is often reported as **half life,** the time it takes for half of the material to break down.) As you sit reading this, you have radioactive strontium and other materials in your bones, emitting minute quantities of radiation, as the result of nuclear accidents, atmospheric tests of nuclear weapons, and other radiation releases. For most people, the amount is too small to pose a health risk. Even so, questions as to how much material, of what kind and over what period, poses a health hazard are still hotly debated.

Time is another problem with nuclear waste. The quantities of material are small, but they are deadly. They must be stored under perfectly sealed conditions and essentially forever. One proposal is to bury nuclear waste in some very stable environment, such as a salt dome far from groundwater, earthquakes, and any other disturbance and preferably in a remote location. Plans to deposit nuclear waste at Yucca Mountain, Nevada, approved by President George W. Bush in 2002, have drawn a storm of controversy, not only from the residents of that state but also from others who live along the route that this material would travel by train or truck. Fears of terrorist attacks have only compounded the concern. The current alternative is to store the material onsite, allowing it to build up in the "cellar" of the plant itself. When the plant becomes obsolete after several decades of operation, the fuel will remain stored under its concrete protective dome, a huge monument to be guarded forever.

Nuclear power plant designs, such as the "breeder" reactor, solve part of the mining and enrichment problem by creating fuel as they operate. One process is to turn nonfissionable uranium into a fissionable humanmade element: plutonium. Like U 235, plutonium can be used in power plants and in bombs. In fact, the world's newest nuclear powers—that is, holders of nuclear weapons—developed their weapons by diverting technology and materials that were supplied for nuclear power plants. North Korea's nuclear program is about cheap energy but also about the production of nuclear weapons. In 1981, Israeli jets bombed the Iraqi nuclear power plant for fear it would be used to make nuclear weapons materials. Iran has nuclear power, largely of French design, and there is great suspicion about why an oil-rich nation is so eager to develop nuclear power; many suspect it is to become a nuclear power through weapons development.

Nuclear power offers a clean, smoke-free alternative to fossil fuels, one that contributes no greenhouse gases, and so it has stirred new interest. But it also poses the risks of accident, terrorist sabotage or theft of nuclear material, the world-wide proliferation of nuclear weapons, and the prospect of hazardous waste that will outlive us all.

Thermonuclear Power: Nuclear Fusion

The sun, like all stars, produces its energy by fusing hydrogen atoms into helium, a process that releases enormous amounts of heat. This is **nuclear fusion** or **thermonuclear reaction.** (The term is a bit misleading, since all nuclear reactions release intense heat.) In the 1950s, first the United States and then the Soviet Union built thermonuclear weapons. These weapons used a uranium-type fission bomb to create intense heat and set off a nuclear fission reaction—the hydrogen bomb.

Hydrogen bombs were soon being built that released enormous amounts of energy. The nightmare was that these weapons would be used against major cities in a thermonuclear war. The dream was that this energy could be harnessed for useful power. The small amounts of hydrogen needed (also a special isotope, known as deuterium) could be extracted from water, an endless source. The radioactive waste produced, mostly another isotope of hydrogen, was far less dangerous and only radioactive for a few years. This seemed to hold the promise of an unlimited, clean energy supply.

The problem has been igniting and containing this reaction. Fusion only takes place under conditions of intense heat. In a star, this heat is produced by huge gravitational pressures. In a hydrogen bomb, it comes from a fission bomb. Neither is practical in a power plant. Material this hot is also not easy to contain without vaporizing the container it's in. Attempts have been made to bombard material contained by a magnetic field with multiple high-energy laser beams. These and other designs remain experimental. Either they don't work reliably, or they take more energy to operate than they produce.

A brief stir was created over the idea that so-called cold fusion might be possible, but this has also proved unworkable. The tantalizing prospect of nuclear fusion energy remains, but whether it can be turned into safe and affordable energy is still unknown.

Alternative Energy: Sun, Wind, and Water

Why work so hard to create a "miniature sun" when we already have a big one shining down on our backyard every day? This is the idea behind **solar power,** the original energy source. The sun already grows our food and so indirectly powers us. It also warms our houses (some days, not enough perhaps, and some days, too much) and propels the weather. The amount of solar energy beaming down on the planet is huge, but the amount on any square meter of space is fairly small.

Therein lies the great difficulty: how to harness a power source that is diffuse when energy desires are often intense and concentrated.

Like coal and uranium, the sun can be used to generate electricity. Since the intensity in any one place isn't enough to boil water into steam, the usual means is a solar panel, what engineers call a photovoltaic cell. Light striking the substance begins an electric current, the same technique used in a battery-free solar calculator. One vision is to have a vast array of these solar panels in a sunny location to send the electricity to a major metropolitan area—say, from the Mojave Desert to Los Angeles. Cost is a problem with this arrangement, however, so most solar panels are used on the roofs of single buildings or pieces of equipment. They work well in cloudless spaces to power satellites but less well in cloudy and smoggy locations. A simpler technique for a building is to heat water as it winds through a rooftop solar collector and then use this to heat the building. This works best for places that are sunny yet cold enough to need heat. Still simpler is solar hot water, in which solar-heated water is used for bathing and other hot water needs.

Wind power—essentially an indirect form of solar power, since the sun drives the wind—has much the same promise and limitation. Windmills are ancient, having been used to pump water on the U.S. frontier and to drive mills in flat Holland, where there was no falling water to tap. Modern windmills are less picturesque than the Dutch mills and even the prairie farm mills, but they are far more efficient. Narrow airfoil blades spin on poles that turn to spin in even the slightest of winds. They can spin turbines, which in turn can generate electricity.

Again, this method works well for a single building or piece of equipment. Producing enough electricity to supply an entire metropolitan area would require a large "windmill farm." Experiments have tried placing these in windy mountain passes and open plains. (Downtown Chicago is windy enough but too crowded.) Some people complain that windmills are an eyesore, but the major limitation is cost.

Other efforts have been made to tap the resources of particular regions. Rising and falling tides can drive turbines, as can strong ocean currents. Both are powerful but also diffuse forces. Iceland draws most of its power from **geothermal energy.** Hot water just under the surface of this volcanic land, the stuff of geysers, can also heat homes in the cold Icelandic winter and provide the steam for electrical power plants. This system is clean, efficient, and safe for Iceland, but of course, it only works in areas that have geothermal activity. Each of the other forms also works best in special locations of high tides, strong currents or strong winds, intense sun, and so forth. While no one means will work everywhere in the world, each can contribute to global energy demands.

Not all uses of the sun, wind, and forces of the earth need to be high technology, however. **Passive solar systems** don't require pumps and photovoltaic cells but work on more efficiently capturing the energy that is already available. Many of these techniques are ancient. The Anasazi Pueblo peoples of the American Southwest have long built with walls of thick adobe mud. The walls insulate from the heat of the day, and then slowly release that absorbed heat during the chilly night. People living in hot, dry climates, such as around the Mediterranean, have often built with similarly thick walls and also made use of central courtyards that channel cooling winds. These techniques are often still used in Middle Eastern cities, in rural Spain, and in Mexico (and "Californian" styles), where Arab–Spanish styles are mixed with Native American styles. Even more efficient were the earth lodges of settled Plains Indian groups such as the Pawnee, a style later seen in sod houses on the frontier plains. Natural insulation, trapping or blocking the sun, and capturing or blocking the wind have long been features of traditional architecture. Only with the advent of central heating and air conditioning, typically powered by nuclear-produced electricity or fossil fuels, have some of these styles begun to disappear.

Passive solar techniques combine old forms with new ideas: south-facing glass to collect sunlight in greenhouse fashion, efficient insulators, heavy materials to absorb and radiate solar heat, and earth-sheltered walls to insulate from the wind and cold or the heat and sun. Carefully placed trees can shelter from the summer sun and in cold climates drop their leaves to allow in the desired winter sun.

The technology may be as modern as photovoltaic cells, as ancient as a tree-lined courtyard, or more likely, a combination of both. Regardless, a planet with a continually growing energy appetite will have to find better ways of using the energy that is showered on it, rather than burning the "stores" of millions of years in a matter of decades.

Chariots of Fire: Automobiles and Transport

Nowhere has our energy appetite grown more quickly than in transportation, particularly our ways of moving ourselves. Until the 1800s, all movement was driven by wind or current or powered by muscles—sometimes animal, most often human. Then the coal era brought the steam train and the steamboat. The internal combustion era, with gasoline and diesel engines, allowed people in the twentieth century to travel by plane and automobile. The first has revolutionized global interaction, and the second has completely reordered our lives.

Automobiles set in motion a cycle of sprawl that turned them from an oddity to a necessity all across North America. Europe shared the fascination with the car but needed a means of travel better suited to smaller spaces and more crowded conditions.

Diesel could also power trains. The first and finest diesel trains were American. The Pioneer Zephyr "Silver Streak" set a new speed record between Denver and Chicago in the 1930s, with a new modern, gleaming silhouette of stainless

Meeting transportation demands with ever more cars in Cairo, Egypt, and with the TGV bullet train in Avignon, France: automobile dominance continues to spread around the globe but cleaner, faster, and more efficient alternatives are being sought.

steel and a quiet, comparatively clean diesel–electric engine that drove the wheels and powered the air conditioning. The great trains were lost in the U.S. building boom of interstate highways and ever-bigger airports.

Train technology shifted to Europe. New designs, new seamless tracks, and new types of electric engines have made high-speed, high-comfort rail travel possible across much of Europe. The trains may no longer have the elegance of the Orient Express, but they provide an affordable and reliable system that has reduced the need for auto and air travel.

When U.S. Commodore Perry visited Japan in 1853, he brought a model steam train, and the Japanese have been fascinated with train travel ever since. Today's Japanese "bullet trains" are some of the fastest ever built, rivaling air travel between major cities. The Japanese, like the Americans and Europeans, have moved into the automobile business in a major way. Even so, fast intercity trains and efficient urban train transit have limited the need to own and use a car in Japan. South Korea also has entered the auto-manufacturing business but has more closely followed the Japanese pattern regarding domestic use of cars.

Train travel in the United States is most concentrated along the eastern seaboard between Boston and Washington and including New York, Philadelphia, and Baltimore. Yet aging systems and competition from air shuttles and interstate highways have made consistent rail service tenuous.

In Latin America, with a few luxurious exceptions, trains are often old and less than reliable. Partly as a result of this, automobile travel continues to increase dramatically, although buses remain the transport of choice for many. The contrast between Curitiba, Brazil, with its clean, efficient, and low-cost bus system that is used by most urbanites, and São Paulo, with its terrible traffic gridlock, is evidence that Latin America may do best not to imitate its neighbors to the north in automobile dependence.

Americans, who must travel long distances across regions with sometimes sparse populations (and who have a history of seeking independence), have been hard to coax out of their automobiles. They lead the world in oil consumption and will likely continue to do so (See Table 11.2). Even as gas prices climb, there is still

TABLE 11.2	World Total Gasoline Consumption for Transportation by Region, Reference Case: 1990–2020 (million barrels of oil per day)			
Region/Country	1990	2005	2020	Average Annual Percent Change, 1999–2020
Industrialized Countries				
North America	**7.6**	**10.2**	**13.0**	**1.7**
United States	6.6	8.9	10.7	1.4
Canada	0.5	0.7	0.7	1.0
Mexico	0.4	0.7	1.6	5.1
Western Europe	**2.6**	**3.0**	**3.0**	**0.3**
United Kingdom	0.5	0.5	0.6	0.5
France	0.4	0.4	0.4	0.2
Germany	0.7	0.7	0.7	0.3
Italy	0.3	0.4	0.4	0.2
Netherlands	0.1	0.1	0.1	0.6
Other Western Europe	0.7	0.9	0.9	0.3
Industrialized Asia	**1.0**	**1.3**	**1.3**	**0.4**
Japan	0.7	0.9	0.9	0.1
Australasia	0.3	0.4	0.4	1.1
Total Industrialized	**11.2**	**14.5**	**17.3**	**1.3**
EE/FSU				
Former Soviet Union	1.1	0.6	0.8	2.9
Eastern Europe	0.3	0.4	0.5	2.1
Total EE/FSU	**1.3**	**1.0**	**1.3**	**2.6**
Developing Countries				
Developing Asia	**1.0**	**2.6**	**5.5**	**5.2**
China	0.4	1.2	3.4	7.1
India	0.1	0.2	0.5	6.7
South Korea	0.1	0.2	0.3	2.0
Other Asia	0.4	1.0	1.3	2.4

Source: Energy Information Administration, *International Energy Outlook 2001,* March 2001, p. 248.

great allure in the car advertisements of sleek vehicles, humming along scenic highways that always seem devoid of any other traffic. The realities of smog, gridlock, and dependence on foreign oil have pushed some to seek alternatives, however. The question is whether the car must go or whether it can clean up its act.

Recent **gasoline–electric hybrids,** using a system not unlike those of midcentury trains, get twice the average auto mileage and cut emissions by as much as 90 percent. New hope has been offered for **fuel cell cars,** which use a fuel source to create electric current without combustion or batteries. The fuel may be a petroleum product or hydrogen. Much has been made of hydrogen cars, which have no exhaust but water vapor. The fuel cell combines hydrogen fuel and oxygen from the air to make water, generating electricity in the process. The limitation is how to get the hydrogen. This most abundant element in the universe, hydrogen, is not available in pure elemental form. It can be extracted from water, but that takes electrical energy which must be supplied by some other means. Hydrogen can also be extracted from hydrocarbons, such as petroleum products, but that would merely create just a new form of dependence on fossil fuels.

Fuel cell technology is promising. But we may need to face the fact that any car, running on any fuel, still takes too many resources to build and operate, too much space to park, and is too hard to recycle to ever be the daily transportation choice of most of the world's people. Some form of public transportation, combined with walking and biking, will likely be needed to have livable communities and sustainable economies.

Turning Down the Heat: Global Warming and Appropriate Technology

The local and regional effects of our desires for transportation and energy have been with us for a long time. England depleted the last of its great forests two hundred years ago in an effort to float the world's greatest navy; it needed wood for ships and wood for charcoal to smelt iron. Similarly, we are now seeing the global effects of our choices.

A huge hole in the high atmosphere ozone layer opened up over Antarctica several decades ago as a result of the release of various chemicals, such as the chloroflurocarbons (CFCs) in aerosol cans. This is not just a concern to geophysicists or a hazard to penguins. The high-altitude ozone layer protects us against damaging ultraviolet rays from the sun. Australia—a great, sunny island near this hole—already has the world's highest rate of skin cancer and ultraviolet exposure is a major concern.

At the other pole, things are also warming up. Adventurous travelers can now trek to the North Pole on Russian icebreakers, their tourist dollars supporting the ailing Russian navy. When they get there in midsummer, they may get to see something no human beings have seen before on or near the pole: open water. Glaciers are retreating in Greenland and Alaska, and now it seems that parts of the polar ice cap may be melting. Santa may need a snorkel.

Globally, the first years of the twenty-first century have been some of the warmest on record. Are people to blame? Tons of greenhouse gases, such as carbon dioxide and methane, pour into the atmosphere every day and trap the sun's heat from escaping. How much they contribute to the warming of the planet, no one knows for sure. The trouble is, no one will know for sure until the process is so far underway that it will take decades to reverse.

Global warming may not sound so bad if you are reading this in January in Minneapolis or Toronto, but its potential effects are worrisome. Already, residents of low-lying islands such as those of Palau are watching the waves sweep over their homelands. With another meter or so rise in sea level, their homes will be gone.

But this is only the beginning. Most of the world's population is crowded into cities along the seacoasts. If the polar ice were to melt enough to raise the ocean levels several meters, the waves would be in New York, Tokyo, Shanghai, Bombay, and hundreds of other major cities. A rise in ocean level of a few more meters would flood almost the entire country of Bangladesh, home to over 141 million people.

The irony of **global climate change** (a term that some prefer to *global warming*) is that some places might get colder. There is evidence that melting ice water is beginning to submerge the warm waters of the Gulf Stream, the current that flows from the Caribbean across the Atlantic and northward. It warms parts of the extreme eastern United States and Canada and much of Europe. It is the main reason that countries in Northern Europe, such as Great Britain, Norway, and Sweden, are as warm as they are, despite having latitudes as far north as Alaska and Siberia. Without the influence of the warm water, these countries could plunge into a decades-long deep freeze.

Also, while some parts of the world would experience flooding, others would likely experience severe drought as the global winds and weather patterns changed. Agriculture and ecosystems around the world would be disrupted.

We don't have to wait to know the effects of global warming to take action. The very steps that are needed to slow global climate change would also give us cleaner air to breathe, make us less dependent on limited fossil fuel supplies, and give us less need to damage fragile parts of the planet with drilling and mining. These steps include the following:

1. **Place greater reliance on efficient mass transit, most notably trains.** Reducing our dependence on automobiles and helping the developing world develop

The most efficient technology is not always the most complex. Bicycles work well for urban commuters in both Chengdu, China, and Haarlem, Netherlands.

alternative, more efficient means of transportation, rather than filling their roads with more cars, would do more than almost anything else to clear the air.

2. **Place an emphasis on energy-efficient homes.** Building homes that effectively use the forces of the sun, wind, and earth to heat and cool them and that rely on materials and designs that make the most of their environment (and thus have the least need for artificial heating and cooling) would greatly reduce the global demand for energy. Again, the wealthy nations may need to relearn the naturally economizing ways and designs of traditional societies, rather than encourage the developing countries to develop a desire for billions of units of central air conditioning.

3. **Alternative energy sources must be explored in earnest.** There is no magic sorcerer's stone that will provide all our energy needs. Using careful combinations of alternative sources, such as solar and wind, along with creative conservation will be needed.

4. **Reverse the trend toward disposable mass consumption.** We seem to be paving large portions of the planet in concrete and asphalt, and much of the remainder seems to be covered with plastic bottles. Plastic bottles and containers—recent additions to advanced industrial societies and now very recent additions to developing societies everywhere—have come to dominate landscapes around the world. They fill the beaches of Panama and float on the waves. They line the gorges of Mexico and bob under majestic waterfalls. They drift in remote reaches of the Amazon and choke the wildlife. In Africa, they have moved from a novelty to a necessity. Most plastic is a petroleum product, spun from oil and modeled to shape in processes that require large amounts of energy. Discarded, these products litter the land for centuries and must be replaced by still more fossil fuel inputs. Rich nations must lead the way in recycling and so reduce the energy and waste that goes into this process of turning limited resources into limitless litter.

Consumers in both rich and poor countries need alternatives to cheap breakable products in cheap disposable packaging.

Global technology has brought us a worldwide media that assures us that the way to a happy, healthy, rewarding life is through consumption: buying more, accumulating more, and then abandoning it in favor of a new and improved model. In the early 1900s, *consumption* referred to the ravages of diseases like tuberculosis that slowly drained a person, leaving him or her withered, gasping, and dying, or suffering from consumption. The planet is now suffering from consumption in its new twenty-first century meaning: withered, gasping, and in places, dying under the demand for energy and products. The truth is more likely that the way to a happy, healthy, rewarding life is by consuming less, making it last longer, and then recycling it into something new. The great challenge for twenty-first century technology will be to make this both a global vision and a global reality.

MAKING CONNECTIONS

World Watch

■ The World Watch Institute, founded by Lester Brown in 1974, now has global partners in over forty countries. Its site at www.worldwatch.org has an enormous amount of information on global issues related to population, energy, and the environment. From the site's resource center, select "Economy" for information on consumerism, information technology, consumption, and sustainability. Select "Energy" for information on climate change, energy sources, manufacturing materials, and transportation. Note also links to dozens of related organizations around the world. What are the topics featured? How does World Watch link its twin interests in environmental sustainability and social justice?

Energy Efficiency and Renewable Energy

■ The U.S. Department of Energy maintains a site with information on energy efficiency and renewable energy (www.eere.energy.gov). Note its discussion of these topics and the information it provides to groups and individual consumers to increase their energy efficiency and to learn more about alternative energy sources. What can individuals as well as communities do to use less nonrenewable energy?

ESTIF

■ For information on efforts in Europe, see the site of the ESTIF, the European Solar Thermal Industry Federation (www.estif.org). How are European efforts similar to those seen in the United States? In what areas are European nations taking new and innovative approaches?

APC

- The Association for Progressive Communications (APC) is a global network dedicated to open access to electronic communication around the world. Its site at www.apc.org explores issues of open, unfettered journalism and broad access to communications in an Internet age. Note efforts in various regions of the world: what changes are they seeking to bring about?

Transit and Energy

- What is being done in your community and on your campus to promote the use of public transportation? Are there ways that individuals and groups can advance these efforts? What are the barriers to greater use of the transit systems available?
- What efforts, both private and public, are being made to increase energy efficiency and reduce consumption on your campus and in your community? What resources are offered to help individuals and groups? Does your campus have an energy conservation plan?

CHAPTER **12**

Ecology
How Much Can One Planet Take?

DATELINE

Cameroon

The Baka have hunted and gathered in the rain forest of western Cameroon in Central Africa for more millennia than anyone knows. They are part of a broad cultural group that has been better known to outsiders simply as "pygmies." The Baka were one of the last of this resourceful group of people to hold on to their hunting-and-gathering lifestyle, which they managed well into the 1990s.

The Baka are now settled near a road that facilitates government aid and government control in a pattern familiar to native peoples in many places around the world. But they have not become completely sedentary. The Baka still walk great distances. They walk in ever-greater treks into the last remaining forest to hunt for game. No longer dependent on bows and blow guns, they have a rifle; one rifle with one bullet is all they can afford. Their chosen marksman, a young man of seventeen, is a lucky shot, and so for now, their one bullet has brought them a small forest buffalo. All members of the settlement trek into the forest to carve up and carry back the meat.

The Baka also walk into town, a small provincial outpost, to trade and to plead their case before local administrators. They win assurances that their forest will be protected. Yet within a few days, they note the marked trees and hear the deep-throated roar of the chain saw. The whole settlement turns out, but they can only stand and watch in silence, as loggers illegally remove the largest and most valuable trees and haul them down the dirt road.

Resistance is futile. The Baka are a courageous but peaceful people, and besides, they have already used their only bullet. They can again put on their size "small" suits and go in to plead for protection, but with little political clout and no money for bribes, they have little voice. ("Voices of the Forest" 2001).

Washington, D.C.

Moi went to Washington to talk to the president. He went to plead for help in stopping American-owned oil companies from carving up the last remaining forest home of his people, the Huarani of lowland Ecuador, known to outsiders as "Auca," or savages. Moi brought his eloquent language skills, speaking basic Spanish and English. He also brought his medicine pouch and his eight-foot-long spear. (The Huarani are not a peaceful people.) Simple horticulturalists, who both hunt and garden, the way of life that the Huarani have guarded from centuries of would-be conquerors is almost ended.

Without seeing the president and with receiving only empty assurances from the Ecuadoran ambassador, Moi returned to his South American home. He led a few raids, his young followers armed mostly with video cameras. A terrible oil well fire swept through their homeland, and his supporters thought Moi might have perished (see Kane 1996). But he is back—on the Internet.

Visitors to Moi's website can learn about the struggles of the Huarani and then go to a once-remote village to meet with the elders. The visitors will stay outside the village to preserve its character and participate in ecotourism activities to learn about the rainforest. It is hoped that they will return to North America, Europe, and Asia with a commitment to fight for Huarani rights.

Food: We Are What We Eat

What we eat, of course, matters enormously to our individual health. "We are what we eat," as the saying goes. But what we eat and how we produce it also matters enormously to our social health. In many ways, what we eat determines who we are as a society.

Hunter–gatherers searched for their sustenance from among a diverse supply of natural provisions. When both men and women were crucial to providing food, the genders tended to have more equal social power. Limited and shifting food supplies meant small, mobile populations. Mobility meant that possessions had to be few and had to be shared, and so members of the band tended to be fairly equal. Although life was dangerous, for many, it appears to have been quite satisfying. Food was uncertain but diverse and nutritious.

At some point, the growing population, declining resources, and changing climate caused many groups to begin growing food in communal gardens; they became **horticultural societies.** Their impact on their environment increased, as they now had to clear land for gardens, often by chopping or burning or both. But plots tended to be small and shifting, in part, to prevent soil depletion. Both men and women contributed; often, the men cleared and the women tended the land. Working together in common gardens, women were key to the economy and often held considerable power in the village.

Equal sharing was no longer possible with larger groups, and surplus produce had to be redistributed by some central authority, often a man of some influence and prestige. Still, nonperishable possessions were few and so inequality was not great. The most prized possession was often a respected family name, which would yield influence in community decisions.

In open grasslands and places too dry to garden, one way to survive was to herd grazing animals. As these animals grazed, they turned grass into protein for their herders. People first hunted these animals, including the wild ancestors of the horse and cattle. But as they came to control the movements of the animals, eliminate the competition of predators, and selectively manage the herd size, they shifted from being hunters to herders, forming **pastoral societies.** Smaller, more hardy animals probably were domesticated first: goats (known for eating anything), then sheep, then larger animals such as horses and cattle, and probably last of all, camels (ornery and harder to control) and their South American cousins, llamas.

Herders had to be tough. The animals had to be moved over large areas, especially in arid climates, so as not to exhaust the grass. They also had to be protected from predators and increasingly from other herders. Small animal herding probably involved the whole community, but eventually, large herds of large animals were controlled primarily by men, male warriors ready to protect their herds. Eventually, horses became more valuable as transportation than as food, and the mounted warrior rode onto the scene.

Large herds can be very hard on the environment, but traditionally, herders kept moving. If they mingled with local farmers, they also provided something valuable: organic fertilizer. Herders sometimes used their animals for meat, but that was generally considered too costly, as it reduced the herd. Others learned to extract protein from their animals in the form of blood or, more often, milk, and so keep them alive.

From food sources also come lifestyle and social patterns. Mobile herders had to make do with few possessions. Moving over large areas and among potentially hostile groups, they were often more militant than gardeners and gatherers. If men controlled the herds, they often controlled the society and its women, as well.

Each of these three groups has been discussed in the past tense because so few of them remain. When the Europeans set out to explore and conquer the world around 1500, many of these groups still existed. Hunter–gatherers lived in the harsh but bountiful forests of Canada and Alaska and throughout the North American Rocky Mountains. The highlands and grasslands of South America were also dotted with bands of hunter–gatherers. All of Australia was populated by aboriginal hunter–gatherers, whereas small but resourceful people of the pygmy cultural group lived in the rainforest of equatorial Africa. Further south, in the Kalahari Desert, were the San and Khoi peoples, whose simple but effective lifestyle was set in the popular imagination in the movie *The Gods Must Crazy* and its sequels. In the far north, Inuit (eskimo) peoples hunted caribou and seals and gathered roots and berries.

Some of these groups remained in remote locations well into the twentieth century, but their lifestyles continued to change due to contact, often forcible, with other societies. The few that remain, such as the Baka, have a lifestyle that is a blend of older traditions and new impositions. The means of survival that supported humanity for tens of thousands of years is now almost as extinct as the mastodon or, for that matter, the wild horse.

Many of the so-called primitive peoples that European colonizers and conquerors encountered were not true hunter–gatherers, though they often did hunt and fish. Rather, they depended on gardens; they were horticulturalists. Horticulturalists included the native peoples of the eastern woodlands of what is now the United States, as well as the peoples of the Amazon and the Pacific. When the Mayflower-bound Pilgrims came ashore in New England, they weren't saved by stores of meat or wild nuts but by finding stores of Indian corn in abandoned villages. The eastern woodland tribes survived on staples that had diffused northward from what is now Mexico: corn, squash, and beans. Together, they provide quite complete nutrition; also, corn and beans can be dried and stored for winter use.

Since horticulturalists typically leave large areas of the forest intact, the Europeans thought they were coming to wild lands inhabited only by a few wild people. But the eastern forests were laced with trails that connected villages whose residents hunted and gathered wild foods in the forest yet depended on small garden plots to ensure their survival. To the explorers, the Amazon seemed a great wilderness, but it was, in fact, home to plant cultivators who domesticated and eventually gave to the world black beans, peanuts, pineapples, and tapioca. In the Pacific, if Tahiti was a tropical paradise, ripe with beckoning fruits, it was only so because Polynesian seafarers had brought their plants with them and carefully cultivated new islands.

Like hunter–gatherers, horticulturalists are resourceful, and they utilize a wide range of both domestic and wild foods to survive harsh times. It was Squanto who saved the Pilgrims from starvation, not the other way around. Yet the number of horticulturalists was typically small in one area. They were ultimately no match for the large number of colonizers who coveted their open spaces. A few simple horticulturalists remain today, often in tropical rainforest environments in South America, Southeast Asia, and pockets of Africa, but these, too, are succumbing to the encroachment of other societies.

The reason that there were so few hunter–gatherers and horticulturalists in Europe and Asia, as well as North Africa, by 1500 is that most had already succumbed to more powerful neighbors. By 3,000 BCE, inventive farmers in the Middle East were learning a new way to put food in their stomachs. Instead of eating or milking the grazing animals, they put them to work pulling a plow. Cereal grains, such as wheat and oats, are grasses that produce seeds edible to humans.

It took a lot of land and the soil had to be turned up, but draft animals allowed large areas to come under cultivation. **Agriculture** was borne.

The impact on the environment was almost immediate. Large areas came under cultivation, and wild lands and wild animals were limited to remote reaches too hard to farm. Grain could be harvested in mass and stored, feeding larger populations and those not near the farm. Cities also became possible. But urban dwellers could only flourish by bringing more of the hinterland under cultivation and by ensuring, by trade or by force, that the bounty of land came to the central city. The agrarian kingdom and then the agrarian empire was born. **Agrarian societies,** with their larger populations and centralized governments, could field larger, more disciplined armies, and other societies were soon consumed.

The herders held out the longest, especially those who had learned to fight from horseback. Much of European and Asian history, the centuries from 3000 BCE to about 1500 CE, reflects the back-and-forth struggle for dominance between settled farmers on the fertile fringes (the Mediterranean and Europe, India and eastern China) and mounted herders on the great grasslands in between (such as the Mongols and early Turks). Firearms eventually settled the balance in favor of the agrarian states, and independent herding societies gradually dwindled away, coming under the control of more powerful states. A few, such as the Ottoman Turks, settled into their own firearm-equipped empires.

Sowing the Seeds of Civilization

Agrarian states and empires fed their growing populations through the intensive cultivation of a few strains of what had been wild grasses—grasses whose seed grains could be fed directly to humans. A Middle Eastern grass, wheat, was cultivated so successfully that it built the empires of Babylonia and Egypt, fed Rome, and ultimately fed much of Europe and the world. Its cousins—rye, barley, oats, and others—played a supporting role, but over time, wheat conquered the land.

In the wet lowlands of Southeast Asia, the preferred grass was rice. With a warm climate and increasingly sophisticated irrigation, rice could provide two or three crops a year and so came to support the world's most densely populated area. A dividing line still runs across Asia, separating the rice-based cuisine of wet Southern Asia from the wheat-based diet of the northern plains. Rice isn't very nutritious, but when combined with vegetables, and especially with protein-rich beans, it has served as the dietary basis of most of Asia's billions. Rice was brought to the tropical Americas by the Spanish and Portuguese, and rice and beans feed millions in Brazil and across the American tropics.

The Native American states that the Spanish found in place already had their staple grass: maize, or the American corn. Bred from tiny plants into tall stalks, this crop, combined with beans and squash, fed the great empires of ancient

Mexico and spread across the southern and eastern parts of North America. American corn now feeds much of the world, either through U.S. exports or through cultivation in China and Africa.

Africa originally built its great states on its own indigenous grains, millet and sorghum, but eventually adopted first wheat and then corn as staples. Ancient American horticultualists contributed to other key starchy staples: potatoes from the South American highlands and manioc from the tropical lowlands. Potatoes from Peru became the basis of diets from Ireland to Russia, wherever land was scarce and ill suited to grain production. Manioc, grown as cassava, feeds millions in tropical climates. The grains of these three grasses—wheat, rice, and corn—with some help from the starchy root crops, such as potatoes and cassava, and a few bushy legumes, such as peanuts, black beans, and increasingly, soy beans, now feed almost the entire world.

These three grains have a 5,000-year history of feeding growing populations, and the root crops and legumes have an even longer history. But how these are grown has changed dramatically. Agrarian states relied on vast fields under cultivation to feed the population, including urban dwellers who grew nothing, and to clothe the population in clothes made from fibers, such as the linen of Egypt and the Middle East. Cotton was apparently domesticated in slightly different varieties independently in Africa, India, and the Americas. Indian cotton produced beautiful gowns and saris, Egyptian cotton clothed Europe's armies and gained fame, but it was the cotton worn by Native Americans in Mesoamerica (now Mexico) and southern North America—which was used for everything from sun protection to royal robes to warriors' armor—that eventually traveled the world. The pastoralists contributed one other important fiber: wool. All of these fabrics were extremely labor intensive to produce. Cotton, in particular, was picked in clumps, cleaned of its seeds, and then spun and woven, all by many hands. Peasant laborers in India and Europe provided these hands; in the Americas, large plantations turned to African slave labor.

As demand grew, so did the desire to speed production. One of the world's first mass-produced machines was U.S. inventor Eli Whitney's 1794 cotton gin, which cleaned and processed the fiber. But turning it into clothing was still a slow process. In Europe, a French inventor named Joseph-Marie Jacquard came up with an ingenious way to operate looms using punched metal cards. The designs were encoded in the cards, rather than the memory of the master weaver, and the looms could run at high speeds and be operated by workers with simple skills. The great looms were run by water power and some time later by steam.

France, Germany, and Britain all began to build bigger textile plants. The British, eventually helped by power from English inventor James Watts's more efficient steam engine, took the lead and soon supplied much of the world with textiles. The natural resources were still agrarian products, but production was now fully industrial. The industrial age entered so quickly and completely that it has come to be known as the **Industrial Revolution.** Agrarian states became industrial societies—first in Western Europe, then in the United States and Canada in North America, later in Japan in Asia, and finally in scores of industrializing agrarian states around the world.

Industry did not replace agriculture but rather transformed it. Industrial machinery could dig irrigation canals and then pump water. With the internal combustion engine came the tractor and the harvester, increasingly larger machines that replaced the millions of hands once needed for farm production. In the early 1800s, most of U.S. society worked in agriculture. By the early 1900s, the number had dropped to one-third, and by the beginning of the 2000s, it had dropped to below 3 percent of the labor force (U.S. Bureau of the Census 2004). Industrialized agriculture, combined with global marketing of food, or **agribusiness,** feeds an ever-growing portion of the planet's billions (see Kimbrell 2002). It has also changed the face of the planet.

Growing Business: Industrial Agriculture

Flying over the central United States, one can see few natural land forms. Even the water that is visible is usually a dammed reservoir that turns a river into a source of irrigation and a transport route for grain (Brown 2005). What is visible is a great checkerboard of squares—green in the summer, brown the rest of the year, unless mixed with snow.

Most of the squares are filled with corn, which comprises over one-fifth of U.S. cropland. Corn grown in the United States feeds large portions of the world, including places such as Mexico, where corn was probably first cultivated. The hundreds of varieties of so-called Indian corn have been replaced by just a few varieties grown from hybrid seeds provided by large firms, such as Monsanto. Large tractors and harvesters are ideal for working these vast, unbroken fields. Herbicides and pesticides are used to maintain the fields, and most are irrigated, even in wet areas, so that periods of drought do not slow growth.

One allowance for an ancient tradition is made: Native Americans grew corn interspersed with beans to provide added nutrition and to replenish the soil with nitrogen, which was drawn out by the corn. These days, this is accomplished by rotating crops of corn with soy beans. Seeing these vast fields, one would suppose that Americans live on nothing but corn and soy beans. In fact, most of the production is either fed to animals or is turned by the food industry into syrups, sweeteners, and oils. Most of the remainder is exported.

American-grown wheat is also exported around the world, although it must compete with that from other industrialized agribusiness centers, such as Canada, Australia, and Argentina. The tremendous U.S. production is supported by large amounts of pesticides and huge amounts of water. In some parts of the western United States, the great squares give way to giant circles, visible only from the air. The circles are not alien creations but merely the result of giant rotating irrigation systems.

When mechanized agriculture covered the American plains with farm fields plowed "fence row to fence row," it helped create the great "dust bowl" of the 1930s. Amid unexpected drought, the turned-up soil simply blew away by the ton. The answer to the dust bowl was primarily **irrigation:** pouring on huge amounts of water from underground aquifers, essentially great underground lakes. These pools of groundwater, built up over thousands of years, are disappearing, however, forcing the need to find ever-deeper wells to tap. Wheat grown in Washington state uses surface water. Huge quantities are pumped from the Columbia River, water that is also sought by the salmon industry (note that even fishing is now an "industry") and rapidly growing communities.

More surprising to many than the United States' production of wheat or corn is that it is also a major exporter of rice. Half of this production comes from Arkansas, where large areas have been deforested or stripped of natural wetland vegetation to accommodate massive rice production. The wet clay soil retains the moisture that commercial rice needs, but it also breeds many pests, and so using a large quantity of pesticides is part of the process.

If developing countries in the global South are importing such large quantities of grains from the industrial agribusiness countries, what are they doing with their own land? Increasingly, it is also controlled by agribusiness and used for export crops. Coffee and cacao (the cocoa and chocolate plant) are major industries. Coffee, originally from East Africa but now dominating in the tropical Americas, is second in global trade only to petroleum. Chocolate, originally a Mesoamerican cultivation, now dominates the economy of Ghana and West Africa. In Brazil, black bean production has shifted to massive fields of soy to be turned into oil for export. In West Africa, the American peanut is grown to be pressed into vegetable oil for the European market.

Recent growth, however, is not just in crops that need tropical climates but also in crops that need cheap labor. Grains can be planted and harvested by enormous machines that outproduce armies of cheap laborers and so are increasingly concentrated in areas of heavily industrialized agriculture, such as the United States and Canada. This is not so easy with crops such as fruits and vegetables, which must be carefully harvested, often by hand, to avoid damage. The old means of achieving this was to import migrant farm labor. The Imperial Valley of California, acre for acre the most productive land in the United States, combines the sunshine of what should naturally be a desert with vast amounts of irrigation water from the Colorado River (largely draining it dry) and itinerant farm laborers to harvest the crops. This land, along with similar operations in south Texas and Florida, provide most of the U.S. fruit and vegetable production. But an ever-growing portion of that production comes from other countries: Mexico, Brazil, and Chile, in particular (Rohter 2004). And in the case of products that can be concentrated, frozen, or canned, they also come from Asia.

Agribusiness can transform almost any food product into a large-scale operation. Cotton is more likely to be grown in irrigated portions of California's central valley than in its traditional locations in the Southeast. California also just passed Wisconsin as the leading dairy state. But this is not your grandfather's dairy farm. The little red barns of family farms and children's books have been replaced by lactose mills. Dairy farms in Wisconsin average 80 cows; in California, the number is typically in the thousands, with new megaplants holding over 14,000 animals (NPR 2004). Most of these animals never see grass. They are housed in block-long open sheds, with apartment-sized blocks of hay. Drainage ditches carry the manure to vast holding lagoons. Old McDonald's farm has been replaced by electric machines and hoses operated by armies of migrant laborers.

These farms are typically located near communities of low-income people of color. The potential for air and water pollution, especially in these communities, is enormous, according to the Center for Race, Poverty and the Environment. In some places, the air—with its putrid mixture of manure, dust, and the exhaust of both machines and cows—is smoggier than that in Los Angeles (Grossi 2005). Yet regulations are rare, for this is farming, after all.

A similar shift in production has occurred with meat. Pork in the Midwest is now a product of huge hog farms, with over 5,000 animals. Hog waste is washed into great holding lagoons, where it fouls the air and threatens to leech into the groundwater. The hog's carcasses are shipped to huge factory-like slaughterhouses, where again, the workers tend to be low-income men and women of color. Consider this description by Le Duff (2000):

> It must have been 1 o'clock. That's when the white man usually comes out of his glass office and stands on the scaffolding above the factory floor. He stood with his palms on the rails, his elbows out. He looked like a tower guard up there or a border patrol agent. He stood with his head cocked. One o'clock means it is getting near the end of the workday. Quota has to be met and the workload doubles. The conveyor belt always overflows with meat around 1 o'clock. So the workers double their pace, hacking pork from shoulder bones with a driven single-mindedness. They stare blankly, like mules in wooden blinders, as the butchered slabs pass by. (p. 1)

As the world's best fishing grounds have been depleted, there is new interest in fish farming in both Asia and North America. The prospect of cultivating a new resource to replace an overtaxed natural resource is appealing. Yet the ecological and social costs can also be high. Farming American style means chemicals, mass production, and large agribusiness. All across the southeastern United States, hog production is now complemented by catfish farming.

Poultry has become a huge international operation. Chickens are stacked by the thousands in highrise wire compartments, their feet never touching the ground, from egg to market. The slaughterhouse emphasizes mass production, as described by Sernau (2000):

> Imagine an assembly line. The workers have all punched in, they are all in their places wearing their smocks, tools at the ready. The line starts up and down the conveyor come—chickens. Live chickens. They come squawking, pecking and attempting to get away. One can hardly blame them, I suppose. The workers are comprised almost exclusively of black women, many of them single mothers or otherwise the sole support of their families. The workers are poised in waders, calf-deep in blood, knives poised. Their task is to grab the chicken off the line and lop its head off without getting pecked or scratched or slipping in the blood. With deft strokes successive workers butcher the still-jerking chickens and send them down the line—quickly, without pausing. Knife strokes must be precise to deliver appealing looking filets, a difficult task since the chickens are odd-looking even before their heads come off. Many are covered in tumors. The chickens are fed a feed mixture that includes a variety of residual products, including the unused chicken parts. The company denies that any unapproved hormones or chemicals are used, but these chicken cannibals seem to develop in unusual— and unappetizing—ways. It doesn't matter, most will not go as whole fryers anyway but as filets to be frozen. They will be boxed and shipped to fast food outlets, to supermarkets, to schools, and overseas. (p. 87)

Tyson chicken has been battling union organizers, as well as facing Immigration and Naturalization Service (INS) investigations into hiring illegal immigrant workers in its U.S. plants. Tyson claims it is caught in an ever more competitive market. Even though it dominates the domestic market, it is being challenged in the lucrative Asian market by Thai chickens. Thailand is making a major push to develop its agricultural as well as its industrial exports. Chickens can be subcontracted: raised on small farms and then mass processed for export to Japan, Taiwan, and South Korea. Processed food now makes up 30 percent of Thailand's manufactured exports, meeting the demands of fast-growing Asian cities and helping Thailand establish itself not just as a NIC (newly industrial country) but also a NAC (new agricultural country)—Asia's new supermarket (McMichael 2000).

The origin of orange juice, once that symbol of all-American goodness and Florida sunshine, has also become mysterious. The container may say something like "Made from concentrate from one or more of the following: USA, Brazil, Belize." The label is even more mysterious for a common apple juice: "Concentrate from USA, Hungary, Argentina, and either Poland or Turkey." A package of chicken may soon require similar labeling: "Parts assembled from one or more of the following countries." In the ideal of global capitalism, product has become divorced from place. To be accurate, the label maybe should just say "Made on Earth, mostly."

"We are what we eat." The way a society gets its food supply is its **food regime.** We now have a global food regime based on industrial agriculture and controlled by corporate agribusiness and massive import and export. In one sense, this system is extraordinarily efficient. Production is massive, enough to feed all 6 billion of us and growing. Distribution is global, following prices to wherever there is demand for new items or lower costs. This is the principle of an **economy of scale,** or that more volume under mass production can lower costs.

Yet it is also extremely inefficient. Often, more energy is expended in fossil fuels to plant, irrigate, and harvest than is contained in the food. Rather than capture the sun's energy for human use, the entire process is merely an inefficient conversion of hydrocarbons into carbohydrates. The process also involves mining the earth of nutrients and topsoil, as well as groundwater, which are not replaced. The land, at best, is an unending monotony of monocropping; at worst, it is ultimately left barren and unusable.

People, especially rural dwellers in poor countries, are left vulnerable to the vagaries of the marketplace. If their export products thrive, they will earn enough cash to purchase the food they need for themselves. But, if their export commodity prices fall or if wages fall for agricultural workers, they will be left hungry or malnourished. Consumers in wealthy nations and cities gain choices, but these are often heavily packaged, heavily preserved, and heavily advertised choices that may offer little in nutrition or taste.

Food was one of the early battlegrounds for **development theory. Dependency theorists** saw export commodity dependence as one of the great legacies of colonialism and one of the great weaknesses of the economies of underdeveloped nations. **Modernization theorists** saw modern agriculture as finally banishing the age-old curse of hunger and famine. There is some truth in each perspective.

Humanity has been malnourished for the last 5,000 years. Hunter–gatherers had precarious food supplies but also assembled a diet rich in diversity: all those organically grown nuts, fruits, vegetables, and lean meats that dieticians encourage people to eat. Horticulturalists gained more control over their food supply at the price of variety (quite likely, a starch, such as manioc or sweet potato, made up many of their calories), but it was still supplemented by a rich diversity of both wild and garden-based foods. Devastation came with agriculture. Aggressive rulers drove their peasantry to produce more and more food, and crowded populations cleared more and more land. Wetlands were drained, forests cleared, wildlife exterminated, and soil depleted. Crops provided great food security in good times, but they were extremely vulnerable to drought, climate shifts, and the ravages of war. And so, the specter of mass famine was created.

The quality of the food supply also declined for most people. The wealthy and privileged ate better than ever before, but the peasants often subsisted largely on a single starchy crop: rice, wheat, corn, potatoes. The luckiest of them were able to maintain their own gardens to supplement the bounty of the fields. Colonial empires turned this system into a global food regime, with the finest delicacies, and the spices to keep them fresh, flowing into the colonial capitals, often at the expense of greater vulnerability to famine. The great Indian famines of 1630 and 1770 occurred while the ports were full of grain, tea, and spices (Sen 1999). The Irish potato famine that began in 1845 came from a blight that destroyed the peasants' food supply, yet pricier grains continued to leave Ireland, bound for London and the European capitals, at the height of the famine.

In many ways, our current food regime is merely an intensification of this system. Food flows in great abundance to centers of wealth, while the poor and peripheral areas are left extremely vulnerable. With land, seed, and fertilizer all at a premium, fewer of the world's people have access to their own gardens and so are entirely dependent on the cash economy of the global food regime. The question for the planet now is, Can we continue to feed our 6 billion plus, with 3 billion plus urban dwellers, yet also return to a more sustainable and equitable system? Can we find a place for "economies of detail," where small producers feed local markets, taking great care to ensure the long-term viability of the land and the food supply? Can we return to a more diverse landscape that is both healthful and beautiful?

Richer countries have sometimes been able to preserve a landscape of small farms. Japan's rice production is uneconomical in pure market terms, because rice

Contrast small-scale, mixed-use farming in the Canary Islands in the Atlantic (left) and corporate sugar cane production in Florida (right). How we produce our food has huge impacts not only on our health and well-being but also on the look and health of the land.

can be grown cheaper elsewhere. But the small rice farmer, along with the carefully tended orchard and other local production, is sustainable as well as traditional and provides a valued part of the Japanese landscape and food supply, one they are willing to subsidize. Similarly, the French countryside looks quite different than rural American regions with a similar climate, for France is dotted with small farms, vineyards, orchards, and pastures. The French maintain this only by limiting imports and subsidizing local production, but in doing so, they also retain beauty, an environmentally sustainable tradition, and some measure of food independence. Even with the dominance of U.S. corporate agriculture, farmer's markets, food cooperatives, alternative organic markets, roadside farm markets, and other arrangements have preserved some of the local landscape of small farms and varied production, as well as the taste of local produce.

Poor countries that will never be the highest bidders for global commodities need a basis of local production more than any other countries, yet they often find it the hardest to achieve. A major goal of rural development in the twenty-first century will be to feed growing populations with efficient and appropriate technologies, while helping rural communities and "green spaces" around cities maintain and revive diverse, small-scale, independent, local production. The health of the land and its people depend on it.

Pollution

Water: From Open Sewers to Toxic Canals

Our hunting-and-gathering ancestors must have enjoyed largely pristine waters, perhaps only facing the risk of a parasite like the *giardia*, which worries modern backpackers. This changed dramatically as people crowded into cities at the hubs of agrarian states. A few, such as the carefully planned cities of the ancient Indus civilization (modern Pakistan), had sewage systems, but most did not.

In medieval Europe, sewage and household waste was merely dumped into the street, sometimes from the second story, where chamber pots of human waste were emptied out the window. The overhangs of medieval buildings provided some protection, and a true gentleman always walked on the outside, allowing his lady the more protected path closer to the wall! But no one was safe from the stench or the disease. Rats, fleas, and bacteria flourished as bearers of the plague and other killers. Even worse was the water. Wherever a stream or ditch cut through the town, it was likely to be treated as an open sewer. Contaminated drinking water was and remains one of the world's greatest killers.

The greatest gains in life expectancy came not with elaborate medicines but with simple sewers and safe water supplies. Providing covered sewers and piped water systems is the simplest and most cost effective way to save lives, especially those of children. Yet the industrial age that brought the steel pipe and the concrete drain culvert also brought new killers. Industries poured chemical contaminants into the waterways. For example, the chemicals used in the preparation of fabrics and dyes often contained mercury. The Mad Hatter of *Alice in Wonderland* was quite familiar to those readers who knew of hat makers being driven mad by mercury exposure. As industry expanded, so did the wastes that spilled into the waterways.

Industrial sites were typically on rivers, both for transportation and for waterpower, but these rivers also served as toxic canals. Chemical odors replaced biological ones, as the Thames and the Hudson, the Seine and the Susquehanna, the Danube and the Ruhr all flowed with toxins. In the 1960s and 1970s, several rivers, including the Cleveland River, actually caught fire as combustible chemicals covered their surfaces.

Deadlier were the unseen killers. Chemicals dumped into Love Canal from 1920 to 1953 proved silent killers for residents of the area. Chemicals flowing from rivers and canals largely killed Lake Erie and threatened the other Great Lakes throughout the 1960s and 1970s. Warnings went out not to eat Great Lakes fish, which were laced with mercury and other heavy metals, as well as DDT and other humanmade toxins. In Japan, people who ate fish from Tokyo Bay developed strange and terrible diseases, also from heavy metals dumped into the water.

Then the water got cleaner, at least in some places. Cities in all of the advanced industrial countries strove to clean up their waterways. New sewage plants were more efficient and effective. New industries installed filters to capture wastes. But most important, the industry left. The once-filthy Baltimore harbor is now the bright and gleaming inner harbor shopping and entertainment district. The confluence of Pittsburgh's rivers was once a meeting ground of toxins, but now it hosts boats and picnickers along Park Point. The only heavy metal evident on Cleveland's gleaming waterfront is in the Rock and Roll Hall of Fame. London's formerly polluted dockyards are today prime real estate for development. Cities cleaned up old industrial sites and converted the waterways from industrial channels to attractions for recreation and commerce.

Of course, where the industry went, so did the pollution. Export processing zones around the world, often hastily built along waterways, often seethe with pollutants. The Rio Grande on the Texas–Mexico border receives pollutants from the industrial border cities, such as Juarez and Reynosa, where U.S. industry has congregated, and is now North America's filthiest river. The most dangerous part of a border crossing here may be getting into the contaminated water.

Of course, these rivers all carry their burdens to the sea, making the ocean a great global (dirty) sink. Hardest hit are the coastal regions, the continental shelf, which also contains most of the ocean's life. Persistent toxins, such as mercury and pesticides, build up in the food chain, contaminating fish and birds. The coast also receives the bulk of human activity and spills: from untreated sewage to devastating oil spills, which layer the water and cover the beaches. The great spill of the Exxon *Valdez* in Prince William Sound in 1989 captured the world's attention, but continued spills have threatened shorelines from California to Spain. The shallow waters off shorelines and islands are also the prime locations for coral reefs, perhaps the most abundant and diverse habitats on the planet, even surpassing the rain forests. Reefs have been damaged by boats and divers and polluted by spills and fish collectors stunning their quarry with cyanide.

Trouble on the land also quickly becomes trouble in the water. Erosion from deforested and mined lands spills down the rivers and washes over the coastal reefs in great toxic mudbaths. New concern has arisen that global warming may be part of the cause of a bleaching of reefs that is diminishing the once brilliant colors. Around the world, virtually every major reef has been damaged, and many are in serious danger of destruction (McGinn 2004). The coast, not the deep water, is the main habitat for most fish species. Great fisheries have supported entire human societies, both ancient and modern. Many of these fisheries are now collapsing under the weight of overfishing often with great factory ships, nets that capture and kill indiscriminately, and coastal pollution (Safina 2004).

The perils of the coasts are now reaching deep water locations, as spills and toxins travel the currents. Individual countries have tried to claim stretches of the coasts as their own: originally, the roughly three miles that could be defended with shore cannon and now, an agreed-upon twelve-mile limit, which some would like to see extended to two hundred miles. But no one owns the open ocean. Like the atmosphere that circles the planet, it is the ultimate shared commons. Only international agreement and enforcement can protect the waters that connect and nourish us all.

Solid Waste: A Planet in Plastic Wrap

Archeologists who study ancient societies must often rely on the few enduring remains they find—maybe a few bits of pottery or precious metal. Great communities built of wood and thatch and perishable materials can almost disappear. Future archeologists will have no trouble studying the artifacts of modern industrial society. The dumps, landfills, and ditches are filled with every detail of our daily lives, preserved in plastic, glass, and metal.

The coming of industrial society filled the world with products, and increasingly, the materials for those products were not agricultural, such as cotton, or wild, such as wood. Rather, they were mined as ores and coal and pumped as petroleum. As these products and their containers have proliferated, few places on the planet remain untouched. Remote waterfalls in South America kick up fertilizer-laden froth, on which bob the brilliant colors of hundreds of plastic bottles, the remnants of beverages and detergents marketed around the world. Remote beaches in Panama, where few tourists ever reach, are lined with great barrier walls of trash, particularly those same bottles, which float out to sea and drift back with the tide. Bottles and containers point the way to Mount Everest in the Himalayas. They fill the sides of gorges in Mexico and tumble across the savanna in East Africa. They freeze into the snowfields around arctic villages and even collect at the South Pole (where a U.S. field station has begun to implement a recycling program).

For millennia, the beverage container of choice was the gourd, grown and hollowed to carry water or sometimes the local beer. A few such containers can still be seen in Latin America and Africa. Once abandoned, it is eaten by animals and then decomposes. More sedentary people could depend on pottery. Once shattered, it returned to the soil. Glass and metal were more enduring, but as long as they were expensive, they had to be reused. Until a decade or so ago, the much loved *refrescos,* or soft drinks, of Mexico were often consumed right at the store, so that the bottle could be immediately returned. Then came the cheap and disposable plastic bottle, a petroleum product that lasts for centuries. With no incentive to return the bottles and often with erratic trash collection, the bottles have become one of the markers of our age.

Great trash dumps have long accompanied cities. When Jesus wanted a vivid metaphor of despair for his followers, he pointed to the trash dump that spilled down the hillside from Jerusalem: *Gehenna* was crawling with worms and punctuated by smoldering fires that never died out; it is often translated in the New Testament simply as "hell." Smoldering hells still fill the valleys, ravines, and hillsides of many cities: "Smoking mountain" outside Manila in the Philippines; the great Cairo dump, big enough to fill the pyramids ten times over; the massive mountainside dump of Rio de Janeiro, Brazil; the huge dumps of San Salvador in Central America and of Mexico City; and the growing Tijuana dump that has already filled its valley and now flows over settlements and cemeteries on the California border. (See Figure 12.1 for an idea of how much trash Americans throw away every year.)

Like the shopping centers that sell the products and packages that end up here, these dumps have an international sameness to them. Cardboard and rubber smolder and burn. Plastic bags rise up in great white clouds and drift on the wind until snagged by a tree or bedframe, to dangle like crackling ghostly sentries. Great clouds of gulls and vultures circle overhead, swooping down on choice morsels. And people—many who live in, on, or near the dumps—race over the heaps among the rats and the wild dogs, trying to get to resalable materials before someone else does. Children, bandanas pulled up over their grimy faces, are particularly effective at running and digging through the piles to claim prizes. These people are the original recyclers! Without them, the trash piles would be higher.

FIGURE 12.1   **Municipal Solid Waste in the United States: 2001 (229 million tons, before recycling)**

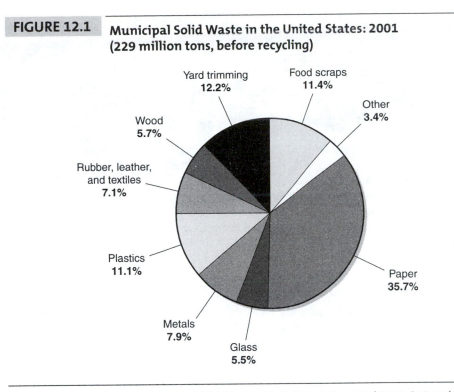

Source: Environmental Protection Agency (2001), *Municipal Solid Waste in the United States: Facts and Figures,* available online at www.epa.gov/epaoswer/non-hw/muncp/.

In some cases, they have moved beyond being mere independent trash pickers to form organized unions that contract with industrial recyclers. Yet one can't help but feel that these humanmade smoking mountains also represent an incredible waste of both natural resources and human potential.

The postindustrial electronic age has brought solid waste problems of its own. Computers and electronic equipment become obsolete quickly and are thrown away in abundance. Cheaply made appliances have short working lives and are often cheaper to replace than to repair. (New appliances are made with machines in remote, low-wage locations, while repair often takes human hands and must be done close to home.) Electronics and appliances are hard to recycle, since they contain many components, often an intermingling of metal and plastic. They also often contain dangerous materials, such as the heavy metal cadmium and chemicals such as PCBs. Discarded, these leech into the ground and water; incinerated, they go into the air.

Recycling is a viable option, if it is done with regard to human safety. Batteries filled with lead and acid, plastics that release toxins, and even radioactive

Trash dominates the view at Lake Windermere in the Lake District of England (left), once extolled by poets. Trash completely covers the water between homes in Brunei (right), a tiny country next to Indonesia. The popularity of cheap, disposable containers has littered even once idyllic and remote parts of the planet.

wastes have been flowing to the cities of low-income countries, such as India and Pakistan. The products are recycled to reclaim raw materials, but often the recyclers have no protection against the caustic acids and fumes and the dangerous chemicals. As early as 1993, Greenpeace reported that twenty-three shiploads of U.S.-made plastic soft drink bottles were shipped to India for this type of recycling. At the same time, this made lower-quality Indian bottles less desirable, and Indian cities were becoming choked with great mountains of plastic trash (Guruswamy 1995).

The good news is that the same technology that produces new products can be used to find new and more efficient ways to recycle old ones. Small European and Asian countries with nowhere to dump have led the way in recycling ever-larger portions of their waste streams. The ease of printing has meant that the electronic age uses more paper than ever. Yet the hope remains that electronic information can replace reams of unnecessary paper—information storage that could be recycled with the drag of a mouse. Ultimately, however, reducing the waste stream will require lifestyle and societal choices: producing and consuming fewer products and making those that are used to last.

Deforestation and Desertification

People have been making deserts for a long time. The vast Sahara was once a lush forest and grassland, with lakes and vast herds and flocks of wildlife. The desert has been growing ever since, perhaps due in part to natural climate shifts, but people have helped. Egypt once fed ancient Rome; now crops there only grow under intense irrigation. The Sahara continues its southward drift into the region of tenuous grasslands known as the Sahel. Sometimes, this drift is dramatic, as entire villages are engulfed in huge dunes of drifting sand. More often, the slow loss of scattered trees and grass allows the last of the soil to drift away, leaving a rocky crust.

Desertification often follows **deforestation.** Helped by the stripping of natural vegetation and the felling of trees, deserts continue to grow in Brazil, India, and Mexico (see Figure 12.2). The desert has only been tamed in the southwestern United States, where massive irrigation projects have drained the rivers dry.

Deforestation is also not new. Plato noted that the rocky treeless forms of many Greek islands had taken over from dense pine forests only with the introduction of people and goats. The brilliant sun of the Aegean islands is undimmed because all of the shade has been cleared. Likewise, Scotland and Ireland should be heavily forested. While we romanticize the heather-clad hills of Scotland and the green pastures of the emerald isle of Ireland, most of both should be covered with rich, moist forests. Most of England was also deforested—first for agriculture and pasture and then finally for wood for ships and charcoal for making steel. To keep the Royal Navy in towering ship masts, the British had to turn to North America.

FIGURE 12.2   **Distribution of Deserts Worldwide**

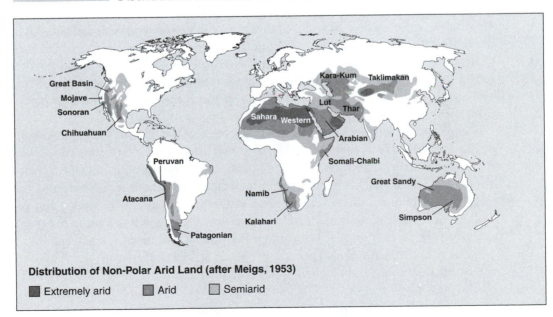

Source: Available online at http://pubs.usgs.gov/gip/deserts/what/world.html.

In turn, most of the eastern United States was also deforested. From precolonial times, when a hypothetical squirrel could travel from Massachusetts to the Mississippi without ever touching the ground, to the beginning of the twentieth century, vast forests of old-growth timber came down all across what is now the eastern United States. Land that is now endless farm fields and subdivisions, with an occasional shade tree or wood lot, was once endless forest, with only an occasional meadow or clearing.

Ironically, as more intense farming has moved westward with irrigation on the plains and in the dry basins of the United States and Canada, some of this land is becoming reforested. In some cases, animal species are being reintroduced, as well. This is **second-growth forest,** often of smaller and faster-growing trees, not the great stands of pine, maple, oak, and beech that once dominated. Likewise, most of the returning wildlife are smaller species that are more adapted to living with human neighbors: White-tail deer do well, but moose, elk, and woodland caribou are much harder to bring back. Coyotes expand into range once roamed by wolves, and feeder-friendly birds move into the habitat of extinct or disappearing native species.

In recent decades, the world's attention has been drawn to the tremendous loss of tropical **rain forests.** Much of the original rain forest has been cleared from Brazil and the Amazon basin, from Central America, from West and Central Africa, and from Indonesia and Southeast Asia (see Figure 12.3). The forest has sometimes been cut for timber. More often, it has been cut for farmland and pasture. Small farmers in Latin America, Africa, and Asia, often denied access to more fertile lands that are used for export crops, are driven ever further into the forest to clear trees and try to farm. Sometimes, the export agribusiness industries themselves lead the push. Millions of acres of tropical forest land in Brazil and Central America have been cleared for cattle, to be ground into hamburgers to feed a growing worldwide appetite for U.S.-style fast food. Coffee, tea, rubber, and even citrus can be grown amid tree cover but is often grown in huge plantations cleared of the original large trees.

The loss of the tropical rain forest is of particular concern, as this land is some of the most diverse in the world. The tiny remaining pockets of forest in Costa Rica have as many species of trees and birds as can be found in the entire eastern United States. When the eastern United States was deforested, plants and animals that were distributed over vast areas often survived in Canada and in rugged and less accessible mountain locations. For many endangered species in the tropics, however, there is no place to run. Deforestation will mean extinction.

The thin tropical soil also poses a problem. Stripped of tree cover, it bakes in the tropical sun into brick. Then, what was once the most diverse land habitat on the planet becomes desert. The most remarkable view of deforestation can be seen over Haiti, where land that was once dense forest has been stripped bare of trees and almost all vegetation. There, too, experiments in **reforestation** have been

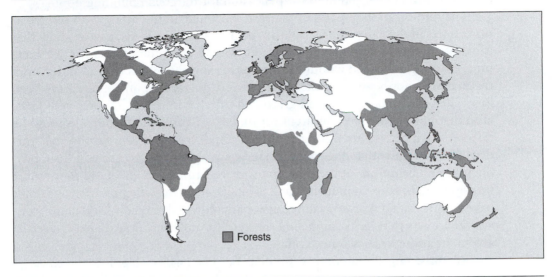

FIGURE 12.3   **Global Distribution of Original Forests**

■ Forests

Note: Source documentation for the Original Forest Cover map:

Map of *Ecoregions of Latin America and the Caribbean Scale:* 1 : 15,000,000. In: Dinerstein, E., D. M. Olson, D. J. Graham, A. L. Webster, S. A. Primm, M. P. Bookbinder and G. Ledec, (1995). A Conservation Assessment of the Terrestrial Ecoregions of Latin America and the Caribbean. Published in association with The World Wildlife Fund. The World Bank, Washington, DC.

White, F. (1983). *The Vegetation of Africa*. UNESCO, Paris. Scale: 1:5,000,000.

Source: Available online at www.unep-wcmc.org/forest/original.htm.

tried, but they have almost always involved introducing nonnative trees, such as the fast-growing Ipil-Ipil, to replace the unique species that have been lost.

Not all tropical forest is rain forest. Often, the most fragile lands are **dry forests,** where a delicate balance is maintained among trees, shrubs, and grass. In this environment, even subtle human pressures, such as the search for firewood, can tip the balance against the trees. With no trees to hold moisture and soil, dry forests quickly become deserts.

Neither is all rain forest tropical. From northern California along the Pacific Coast into Canada and Alaska is a vast region that once had huge stands of temperate rain forest. It often takes a biohistorian to know which California suburbs now sit on land that was once in the shade of the redwoods. This land has also been intensely logged. Flying over the Canadian and Alaskan Pacific Coast, the deep emerald of dense forest is often broken by vast, pale-brown clearings that often cover whole mountainsides and entire valleys. Douglas fir trees become stud walls for the new subdivisions built on these clearings, and the cedar and redwood trees end up as decks and deck furniture in the back. Much of the rest is pulverized into wood chips and pulp for paper and for the Asian building boom.

The reforestation of parts of the eastern United States, along with reforestation efforts in the Sahel, the Caribbean, the Himalayas, and elsewhere, show that it is possible to bring back the trees and to hold back the deserts. At the same time, planting rows and woodlots of fast-growing single species will not restore the majesty and diversity of the great old-growth forests, once these have been lost. The effort to keep the land green and thriving must be two pronged. First, land that has already been clearcut for timber, pasture, and farmland should be restored with careful attention to soil and conservation. Trees, shrubs, and gardens can be reintroduced to create a landscape that is tamed but still lush, productive, and beautiful. At the same time, the remaining stands of old forest must be preserved for their uniqueness and diversity and awesome presence. We don't have two thousand years to wait for new giant redwoods to grow. And in the tropics, the forests that have dominated the land for millions of years may never be able to be brought back, once gone.

Recently, rain forest conservation has become fashionable. It is the cause of international conservation organizations, local zoos, and even rock and film stars. Interest in the rain forest has also sparked new interest in **ecotourism**. More and more visitors to tropical locations are not content to sit on the sand or by the pool next to a planted palm tree but instead want to explore the forest interior. Visitors to the ultimate highrise hotel haven of Cancun, Mexico, increasingly escape hotel

Improper clearcutting in the Queen Charlotte Islands of British Columbia (right) erodes hillsides and fouls waterways. Meanwhile, in spite of government promises, logging consumes more land in the Mato Grosso state of the Brazilian Amazon (left), replacing the rich humidity with clouds of red dust. Old-growth rainforests face destruction from logging, wood chipping, and ground clearing both in tropical locations such as Brazil, and in temperate locations such as British Columbia.

row for trips to the interior to see the rain forest and the Mayan ruins. Costa Rica, with many beautiful beaches, has staked its claim on the ecotourism market. Visitors can choose between canopy tours on bridges or dangling from ropes and cables, and the numbers of nature parks, both private and public, continue to increase. In the Caribbean, places with few desirable beaches, such as the island of Dominica, promote exploration of the mountains, rivers, and rain forest of "nature island." In Hawaii, the more remote island of Kauai, "the garden isle," is now a fashionable destination, in part for its lush interior, which includes some of the wettest forest in the world. New resorts and parks in Malaysia and Indonesia likewise feature the natural attractions of the tropical forest and the ancient cultures of its people, largely village-based horticulturalists.

Ecotourism has also begun to discover the temperate rain forest. Ecolodges based on exploring the natural world have shown up on Canada's Vancouver Island, Alaska's Kenai peninsula, and points in between on the harsh but lush northern North American Pacific Coast. The savanna and dry forest of Africa have also received new attention, as safari tourism, based on "bagging" trophy game (much like that once common in western North America), is giving way to ecotourism, dedicated to understanding the land and its people.

At their best, these ventures are new ways for visitors to appreciate the remarkable beauty and diversity of the land and the history and diversity of the people who have shared it. Yet many of the parklands in poor countries are "paper parks," which show up on the map but remain largely unprotected, due to lack of funds and personnel. Poachers, loggers, miners, and others remain in these areas—some out of greed, many out of desperation. The quality of the ecotourist experience can also range from meaningful encounters to glitzy tours not much wilder than the jungle cruise at Disneyland. Litter from expeditions clutters the tropics and climbs the slopes of the Himalayas. It remains to be seen if new travelers will really tread lightly, leave with all their trash, and insist that governments and operators truly preserve these natural settings.

Transportation and lodging remain big problems. As more of the last wild places are cut by roads and airstrips, few locations are truly remote anymore. Just as urban sprawl consumes wild lands, so does tourist sprawl. The routes in and out of many U.S. national parks are cluttered with commercial sprawl, amusement parks, and so-called attractions that detract from the natural setting. Coastal locations around the world are often the most heavily targeted for development. In the tropics of the global South, natural vegetation, such as the mangrove forest, is stripped away to make room for open stretches of sandy beach, backed by highrise hotels. The posters promise tropical paradise, but the process is simply a continuation of deforestation followed by desertification—for what is an unbroken beach but a linear desert? Again, it remains to be seen whether a new breed of traveler will willingly give up the ocean view that's provided by a wall of windows in a beachside, highrise hotel for more environmentally friendly lodging that's set back to preserve the coast and that's attentive not just to the guests but also to the environment.

Who Invited You? Invasive Species

The travels of humans include a long history of hitchhikers, both intended and unintended. Early sailors took with them intended passengers, such as dogs and pigs, as well as unintended ones, such as rats. Unleashed on tropical island environments, which are particularly vulnerable, all three often devastated the local bird and plant life. Polynesian travelers across the Pacific established lovely horticultural and fishing settlements, which the Europeans in the 1700 and 1800s saw as paradise. Yet they exterminated many forms of native wildlife, such as the twelve-foot-tall flightless Moa bird, in their wake. With the bigger ships of European colonizers, the destruction increased. Islands, whose native wildlife develops free from outside competition, proved particularly vulnerable to outside invasion.

The brown tree snake, inadvertently brought from Southeast Asia sometime before 1952 thanks to its ability to hide in planes and ships, has destroyed most of the native bird life of Guam in a matter of years (Fritts and Leasman-Tanner 2001). Inspectors are trying to keep it out of Hawaii, where it would likely do the same to the already endangered Hawaiian native birds, many found nowhere else. Hawaiians are already having enough trouble coping with the cane toad, a large amphibian that is able to make itself at home in abundance in any subdivision or golf course. While amphibians worldwide are in deep trouble, this one seems to be thriving, taking over any habitat it can invade. Like many invaders, this toad was purposefully introduced to control pests and quickly became a pest itself.

The entire island continent of Australia is split by the world's longest fence, intended to keep feral (animals that have gone wild) dogs away from the sheep. The dogs were introduced to the island long ago, and the sheep more recently. European colonizers also introduced rabbits in the hope that they would multiply and provide food. The rabbits have multiplied, so much so that they now consume much of the limited vegetation needed by the native wildlife—the distinct marsupials, such as kangaroos, who are the original inhabitants—and the introduced livestock. For a time, societies of European colonists in New Zealand sought to introduce all the native plants and animals of Europe that they missed from home. However, these introductions quickly began to compete with and sometimes eliminated the unique island wildlife.

North America has also been hard hit by invasive species. Not an island but still largely isolated from the great landmass of Eurasia, North America has been particularly vulnerable to bioimports from across the Atlantic and Pacific. Sometimes the introductions were intentional. For instance, settlers released English sparrows and European starlings, just a few, to give the new world a bit of the feeling of the old. One society, calling itself Shakespearean, sought to introduce every plant and animal mentioned in the bard's plays. While some introductions failed, others succeeded too well. Introduced birds quickly became pests and took over the habitats of native species, which have seen drastic declines.

New plants also arrived with the new settlers. Dandelions, thistles, and tumbleweed quickly adapted to new homes. Sometimes, the introductions were intentional. Quick-growing kudzu was used to stabilize eroded banks and provide for a quick landscaping option. Multiplying beyond imagination, it has become "the vine that ate the South." Billions of dollars are spent each year fighting invasive plants; once established, they are hard to get rid of.

Insect invaders have been the most destructive. The boll weevil, an import from Central America, devastated U.S. cotton production in the early twentieth century. An Asian fungus transported tree to tree by a European beetle almost wiped out the American elm in the Northeast, starting in the 1930s. The gypsy moth, a native of Europe and Asia, introduced into the United States in the 1860s, defoliates vast areas of the northeastern United States each year and continues to spread, hitchhiking on trucks and cars. Seeming never to learn the lesson about intentionally introducing new species, the U.S. Department of Agriculture recently introduced a new type of lady bug, an Asian lady beetle, to control agricultural pests in the 1970s and 1980s. What seemed like an innovation in biological control has itself become a major nuisance, as the beetles have taken over from their native cousins. Each fall, they fill homes and commercial buildings with flying, foul smelling, biting bugs, trying to escape the onset of winter (Taubman 2002).

Stowaways also travel by boat. The sea lamprey moved into the Great Lakes with shipping along the St. Lawrence Seaway by attaching itself to native fish. It has plagued Great Lakes fishing since the 1950s. More recently, zebra mussels came in, probably released from the holds of cargo ships. They have filled the Great Lakes and continue to move into new waterways, often facilitated by human-built canal systems and the constant movement of pleasure boats. These foreign mussels take over from native species and grow in such abundance that they clog cities' water intake pipes. Their sharp shells make beaches hazardous, and their appetites take nutrients that would go to native aquatic life.

So far, all of the new species have actually been the old species of some distant location newly introduced. Biotechnology now has created the possibility of creating entirely new species, or at least old species with completely new characteristics. The possibilities are enticing: fruit that doesn't freeze, crops that grow faster than ever before, bacteria that are modified to attack other pests, and so forth. Our experience with introducing new species to new locations stands as a warning, however, of what can happen when an introduction is too successful and a plant or organism multiplies beyond the origin intent, taking over its own space. Could we create new superbugs or superplants that likewise spread far beyond their intended purpose?

Ecology and Economy: The Search for Sustainable Futures

Sustainability is the power to thrive and to endure. It is taking care of this generation and generations to come. Hunting-and-gathering societies survived for tens of thousands of years. Human hunters may have helped to drive some of the great massive mammals of the ice age over the brink of extinction, but for the most part, they endured by practicing a way of life that was indefinitely sustainable.

Horticultural, pastoral, and agrarian societies also survived for thousands of years. Some agrarian empires may have exhausted their soil with intensive farming and hastened their own collapse, but on the whole, this way of life proved sustainable century after century.

Industrial society is only two hundred and fifty years old and has dominated the globe for less than a century. Advanced industrial, or postindustrial, information-based society, the electronic age, is less than fifty years old.

As the people of the electronic age, are we already placing more strain on the planet than all other prior societies combined? Can our current way of life be sustained? Can it be globalized and shared by all the world's billions? Lester Brown (2003), of Earthwatch, estimates that it would take at least six Earths to provide all the world's people with the standard of consumption common in the United States. The demands of our ecology and the demands of our economy seem to be seriously at odds.

Ecology and **economy** both come from the same Greek word for "house." Keeping our global house in order will require careful attention to both. Environmental destruction is closely related to both poverty and violence.

This realization has come slowly. For decades, poor countries claimed that it was their turn to pollute—that they needed to exploit resources just as the rich countries had. Wilderness was dismissed as "the rich man's playground." The poor needed jobs, resources, and economic production. Yet the poor also need livable communities. Much of the world's dumping has been inflicted directly on poor communities (Bullard 1990, 1993).

The environmental justice movement has noted that it is the poor (and often, poor minority communities) that live among the untreated sewage, the piles of industrial and consumer waste, and the stagnant, toxic urban air. The wealthy can at least try to retreat to higher ground and a more secluded environ. They can move from one air-conditioned shell to another, dine on food gleaned from dozens of distant locations, and travel in search of an unspoiled locale. The poor must live, eat, and drink close to their earth and water, in whatever condition they may be.

It may be true that many rich nations became rich by exploiting the planet. But they exploited the resources of poor lands and then exported their worst environmental problems. Once again, the world's poorest nations find themselves last in line. There is no one else, nowhere else, left for them to exploit but their own land and people. Unlike rich and powerful colonizers, they have to sit in their own waste. For this reason, environmental concerns are of prime importance to poor nations and to poor people.

Environmental degradation is often directly related to inequality. The newly rich overconsume as they compete with one another in contests of conspicuous consumption. At the same time, the poorest citizens and refugees are often driven from the best lands to encroach on the last forests and the most fragile environments. Wealthy corporations carry off old-growth timber for greater profits, while poor woodsmen poach the last valuable trees and animals for a few dollars to survive. Wealthy mining companies move whole mountains to get to more profitable deposits, while poor independent miners destroy stream banks and fragile mountainsides in pursuit of a few ounces of salable material.

Environmental degradation is also closely related to violence. In his lectures, Arun Ghandi describes how his grandfather, Mahatma Gandhi, called environmental disregard "violence against the earth." Violence against one another also often claims the natural environment as so-called collateral damage. In ancient times, the Spartans burned and trampled crops to try to drive Athens to surrender, while Roman soldiers poured salt into the ground of Carthage to make it infertile. During the Indian Wars of the late 1800s, U.S. frontier forces slaughtered bison to starve the Plains tribes.

Modern arsenals are all weapons of mass destruction in regard to the environment. The United States sprayed the defoliant Agent Orange to destroy the rain forest of Southeast Asia during the Vietnam War, with lingering effects for both people and wildlife. Land mines turn former farmland useless. Refugees from war zones are often driven into remote border lands, where they strip the land of trees and wildlife in an effort to survive. The Gulf War released streams of oil into the Persian Gulf, and raging fires poured pollutants into the air from burning oil wells. Bombs and mortars destroy indiscriminately and chemicals linger. Nuclear fallout would be the most devastating of all.

We have thus come full circle. The only sustainable world is one in which people have regard for equity and for peace.

MAKING CONNECTIONS

Altria Group

■ Have you ever heard of the Altria Group? You probably have sampled several of their products this week. Altria is the parent company for Kraft Foods as well as Philip Morris and other subsidies. They control hundreds of food and tobacco labels, some with over a billion dollars of revenues annually. Go to www.altria.com and select "Our

Companies' Brands." Look at Kraft (North America and International) as well as Philip Morris. You might also note "Our Companies' Global Presence" with an interactive world map showing their global reach. Are you surprised at some of the familiar products listed? Why would one company have so many apparently competing brands? Are there parts of the globe they haven't yet reached?

Food Alternatives

■ What are the alternative ways to grow and buy food in your community? Is there a farmers' market or a buying cooperative? Some arrangements link consumers directly to local farmers in "you pick" arrangements or in cooperative arrangements, where everyone buys a share of the farm and then shares in the produce. Many communities are also developing community gardens, where neighbors work together to raise and share produce. Others offer help to those who want to turn some of their chemically maintained lawns into productive garden and wildlife space.

■ Find out what is available locally, and visit or participate in the operation. How is this group attempting to address concerns about nutrition, food safety, chemical pollution, and so forth?

Recycling

■ What is being done in your community and on your campus to promote recycling? How can individuals and groups advance these efforts?

Nature Conservancy

■ The Nature Conservancy operates worldwide, buying environmentally sensitive property and helping landowners preserve portions of their land. Increasingly, this group's efforts include ventures in biological "hot spots" and the "last great places" around the world. See the Conservancy's colorful site at www.nature.org and look for information on its activities, articles from its magazine, and contacts for upcoming conferences and local chapters. What types of habitats and environments are featured as central to the group's current focus?

Sierra Club

■ One of the world's oldest conservation organizations, the Sierra Club, has hundreds of local chapters and worldwide activities. These are highlighted at www.sierraclub.org, along with information on current environmental issues, letter-writing campaigns, upcoming legislation, and other activities including nature trips. What does the Sierra Club see as the urgent environmental issues of the day? What actions does it propose? Are there projects and activities near you?

CONCLUSION

Making a World of Difference

"How wonderful it is that nobody need wait a single moment before starting to improve the world."

—ANNE FRANK

"Never doubt that a small group of thoughtful committed citizens can change the world. Indeed it's the only thing that ever has."

—MARGARET MEAD

We have covered a lot of ground in twelve chapters. Perhaps you have the feeling that one sometimes has at the end of a long trip: It's good to be back home. Perhaps you're a bit overwhelmed. Maybe depressed. There is a lot of misery to go around, a lot of reasons to be discouraged about the present and even more pessimistic about the future. There are also many reasons for hope, however.

There is an old Chinese curse that simply says "May you live in interesting times." We certainly live in interesting times. But with that "curse," there is also endless wonder and growing opportunity. We can predict with certainty that we will continue to live in interesting times, but whether that is a blessing or a curse remains to be seen. The global stage has been set, but the play has not yet been written. And so, this is a good time to live, if you love high drama, rapid scene changes, and mounting suspense.

Economic globalization offers new opportunities for both entrepreneurship and innovation, yielding new solutions to old problems. It also offers the prospect of concentrating ever-more wealth in the hands of a few and of inflicting reckless schemes and ruthless monopolies.

Political globalization offers the hope that a world of war will be replaced by a world of law, of universal human rights, and of new respect for labor and the environment, built into new transnational agreements. It offers the prospect of petty dictators falling to the contagion of spreading democracy. Political globalization also offers the prospect of rule by a global elite, a powerful few who impose their will on the planet through repression, occupation, and the endless reach of bureaucracy.

Cultural globalization promises new opportunities to learn from one another and to respect, appreciate, and delight in our human differences. It also presents the prospect of the destruction of myriad cultural forms and local distinctive styles, to be replaced by bland uniformity or a crass commercial "pop" culture that is created, packaged, and imposed by a profit-driven media elite.

More likely than either the utopian vision or the opposite dystopian vision is that forces will continue to pull in both directions. We may have more say in setting the eventual course than we know. Perhaps we should add a fourth force to the global dynamic: **social globalization.** We have begun to see the globalization of social movements. Women's networks have moved from the extended family to the community, to the nation, and now to international partnerships. Environmental movements now span national borders, seeking protection for global ecosystems. The long struggle for civil rights at the national level has become embedded in a global struggle for human rights. Labor movements cannot remain national while capital goes international, and concern for work and wages now extends to sweatshops, child labor, and working conditions around the globe.

Don't be fooled! The real work is and has always been in our own backyards. It still comes back to how we cultivate our own spaces and lives—how we treat our own neighbors and tend our own neighborhoods. What has changed is that we now live if not in a global village then in some sort of postmodern, global cybercafe, where there is no limit to our reach and our contacts. Social networks span the entire earth. Insights and allies may come from different continents. Our challenge is to be open to many currents yet still be true to our core convictions.

Indian political leader and social reformer Mohandas Gandhi, known to his country as the *Mahatma*, or "great soul," said simply, "I do not want my house to be walled in on sides and my windows to be stuffed. I want the cultures of all the lands to be blown about my house as freely as possible. But I refuse to be blown off my feet by any." Assassinated for calling for the nonviolent accommodation of both Hindus and Muslims, with equal rights for both, he left a simple challenge: "You must be the change you wish to see in the world."

References

Abrahamson, Mark. 1996. *Urban Enclaves: Identity and Place in America.* New York: St. Martin's.

Air Force Technology. 2003. "F-16 Fighting Falcon Multi-Role Fighter Aircraft, USA."

Anderson, Elijah. 1990. *Streetwise: Race, Class, and Change in an Urban Community.* Chicago: University of Chicago Press.

Anderson, Walter Truett. 1992. *Reality Isn't What It Used to Be: Theatrical Politics, Ready-to-Wear Religion, Global Myths, Primitive Chic, and Other Wonders of the Postmodern World.* San Francisco: Harper.

Arendell, Terry. 1986. *Mothers and Divorce: Legal, Economic, and Social Dilemmas.* Berkeley: University of California Press.

Astin, Alexander W. 1992. "Educational 'Choice': Its Appeal May Be Illusionary." *Sociology of Education,* 65 (October): 255–260.

Baker, Pauline H. 1974. *Urbanization and Political Change: The Politics of Lagos, 1917–1967.* Berkeley: University of California Press.

Banfield, Edward C. 1970. *The Unheavenly City.* Boston: Little, Brown.

Barber, Benjamin. 1992. "Jihad vs. McWorld." *Atlantic,* March.

Barber, Benjamin. 1995. *Jihad vs. McWorld.* New York: Times Books.

Barnet, Richard J., and John Cavanaugh. 1994. *Global Dreams: Imperial Corporations and the New World Order.* New York: Simon & Schuster.

Barnett, Thomas P. M. 2004. *The Pentagon's New Map.* New York: Putnam.

Barone, Michael. 2001. "Dirty Diamonds." *U.S. News and World Report,* November 12.

Barth, Frederick. 1969. *Ethnic Groups and Boundaries.* Boston: Little, Brown.

BBC. 2000. "Anger Grows at US Jail Population." BBC News, February 15. www.news.bbc.co.uk.

BBC News. 2004. "Rwanda: How the Genocide Happened." www.news.bbc.co.uk/hi/world/africa/1288230. April 1. Retrieved July 10, 2005.

Becker, Gary. 1964. *Human Capital.* New York: National Bureau of Economic Research.

Bell, Daniel. 1973. *The Coming of Post-Industrial Society.* New York: Basic Books.

Bellah, Robert. 1957. *Tokugawa Religion: The Values of Pre-Industrial Japan.* Glencoe, IL: Free Press.

Berger, Peter. 1967. *The Sacred Canopy.* New York: Anchor Books.

Berger, Peter. 1974. *Pyramids of Sacrifice.* New York: Basic Books.

Berkey, Jonathan. 2002. *The Formation of Islam: Religion and Society in the Near East, 600–1800.* Cambridge: Cambridge University Press.

Bernal, Diaz del Castillo. 1963. *The Conquest of New Spain.* Translated by J. M. Cohen. Baltimore: Penguin.

Bernard, Jesse. 1981. "The Good Provider Role: Its Rise and Fall." *American Psychologist,* 36 (January): 1–12.

Bernstein, Nina. 2004. "More Teenagers Are Striving for Restraint." *New York Times,* March 7. www.nytimes.com/2004/03/07/nyregion/07TEEN.html.

Bhalla, A. S., and Frederic Lapeyre. 1999. *Poverty and Exclusion in a Global World.* London, England: Macmillan Press.

Blalock, Hubert M., Jr. 1967. *Toward a Theory of Minority-Group Relations.* New York: Wiley.

Blauner, Robert. 1972. *Racial Oppression in America.* New York: Harper.

Bluestone, Barry, and Bennett Harrison. 1982. *The Deindustrialization of America.* New York: Basic Books.

Bly, Robert. 1990. *Iron John.* New York: Addison-Wesley.

Bodley, John H. 1990. *Victims of Progress.* 2nd ed. Mountain View, CA: Mayfield.

Bourgois, Phillipe. 1995. "Workaday World—Crack Economy." *The Nation,* December 4.

Bradshaw, York, and Michael Wallace. 1996. *Global Inequalities.* Thousand Oaks, CA: Pine Forge.

Brady Campaign to Prevent Gun Violence. 2001. "Firearm Facts." www.bradycampaign.org/facts/factsheets.

Braudel, Fernand. 1979. *The Perspective of the World.* New York: Harper and Row.

Braudel, Fernand. 1984. *The Perspective of the World.* New York: Harper & Row.

Brodkin, Karen. 1998. *How Jews Became White Folks and What That Says about Race in America.* New Brunswick, NJ: Rutgers University Press.

Brown, Lester. 2003. *Plan B: Rescuing a Planet under Stress and a Civilization in Trouble.* New York: Norton.

Brown, Lester. 2005. *Outgrowing the Earth: The Food Security Challenge in an Age of Falling Water Tables and Rising Temperatures.* New York: Norton.

Bukharin, Nikolai. 1925. *Historical Materialism: A System of Sociology.* New York: International Publishers. Orig. pub. 1917.

Bukharin, Nikolai. 1973. *Imperialism and the World Economy.* New York: Monthly Review Press. Orig. pub. 1917.

Bullard, Robert D. 1990. *Dumping in Dixie: Race, Class and Environmental Quality.* Boulder, CO: Westview Press.

Bullard, Robert D. 1993. *Confronting Environmental Racism: Voices from the Grassroots.* Boston: South End Press.

Burch, Philip H., Jr. 1980. *Elites in American History: The New Deal to the Carter Administration.* New York: Holmes and Meier.

Bureau of Justice Statistics. 2005. *Substance Dependence, Abuse, and Treatment of Jail Inmates, 2002.* U.S. Dept. of Justice. July.

Burgess, Eugene W. 1967. "The Growth of the City." In Robert E. Park and Eugene W. Burgess (eds.), *The City.* Chicago: University of Chicago. Originally pub. in 1916.

Burowoy, Michael. 1979. *Manufacturing Consent: Changes in the Labor Process under Monopoly Capitalism.* Chicago: University of Chicago Press.

Businessweek. 2005. "Marine One, Sikorski Zero." *Businessweek,* February 14.

Cardoso, Fernando Henriuque. 1977. *Latin America: Styles of Development and Their Limits.* Occasional Papers Series, no. 25. New York: New York University.

Cardoso, Fernando Henrique. 1996. "Humanizing Growth—Through Equity." In United Nations, *Human Development Report 1996.* New York: Oxford.

Cardoso, Fernando Henrique, and Enzo Falletto. 1979. *Dependency and Development in Latin America.* Berkeley: University of California Press.

Cassidy, John. 1997. "The Return of Karl Marx." *New Yorker,* October 20 and 27.

Castaneda, Carlos. 1985. *The Teachings of Don Juan: A Yaqui Way of Knowledge.* Berkeley: University of California Press.

CBS News. 2003. "Pat Robertson Slams Bush on Liberia." July 11.

Chance, Norman A. 1997. "The Inupiat Eskimo and Arctic Alaska." *General Anthropology,* 2 (2): 103–124.

Chartrand, Luc. 1991. "A New Solidarity among Native Peoples." *World Press Review,* August.

Chase-Dunn, Christopher, Yukio Kawano, and Benjamin D. Brewer. 2000. "Trade Globalization Since 1795: Waves of Integration in the World-System." *American Sociological Review,* 65 (1): 77–95.

Children's Defense Fund. 2004. *The State of America's Children 2004.* Washington DC: Children's Defense Fund.

Chua, Amy. 2003. *World on Fire: How Exporting Free Market Democracy Breeds Ethnic Hatred and Global Instability.* New York: Doubleday.

Clinton, Hillary Rodham. 1995. *Remarks for United Nations' Fourth World Conference on Women.* New York: United Nations.

Clinton, Hillary Rodham. 1996. *It Takes a Village.* New York: Simon & Schuster.

Collins, Randall. 1977. "Some Comparative Principles of Educational Stratification." *Harvard Educational Review,* 47 (1): 1–27.

Constable, Nicole. 1997. *Maid to Order in Hong Kong: An Ethnography of Filipina Workers.* Ithaca, NY: Cornell University Press.

Coontz, Stephanie. 1992. *The Way We Never Were: American Families and the Nostalgia Trap.* New York: Basic Books.

Cose, Ellis. 1993. *The Rage of a Privileged Class.* New York: HarperCollins.

Cox, Harvey. 1965. *The Secular City.* New York: Macmillan.

Dahrendorf, Ralf. 1959. *Class and Class Conflict in Industrial Society.* Stanford, CA.: Stanford University Press.

Diamond, Jared. 1997. *Guns, Germs, and Steel.* New York: Norton.

Dillon, Sam. 2001. "Profits Raise Pressures on U.S.-Owned Factories in Mexican Border Zone." *New York Times,* February 15.

Dore, Ronald. 1976. *The Diploma Disease: Education, Qualification, and Development.* Berkeley: University of California Press.

Du Bois, W. E. B. 1903. *The Souls of Black Folk.* New York: Dover.

Duany, Andres, Elizabeth Plater-Zyberk, and Jeff Speck. 2001. *Suburban Nation: The Rise of Sprawl and the Decline of the American Dream.* New York: North Point Press.

Dugger, Celia W. 2004. "Deserted by Doctors, India's Poor Turn to Quacks." *New York Times,* March 25.

Duncan, Cynthia. 1992. *Rural Poverty in America.* Westport, CT: Auburn House.

Duncan, Cynthia. 1999. *World's Apart: Why Poverty Persists in Rural America.* New Haven, CT: Yale University Press.

Duneier, Mitch. 1992. *Slim's Table: Race, Respectability, and Masculinity.* Chicago: University of Chicago Press.

Durkheim, Émile. 1951. *Suicide.* New York: Free Press. Orig. pub. 1897.

Durkheim, Émile. 1964. *The Division of Labor in Society.* New York: Free Press. Orig. pub. 1895.

Eck, Diana. 2002. *A New Religious America.* San Francisco: HarperSanFrancisco.

Eck, Diana. 2003. *Encountering God.* Boston: Beacon.

Edwards, Mike. 1997. "Boom Times on the Gold Coast of China." *National Geographic,* March.

Ehrenreich, Barbara, and Annette Fuentes. 1981. "Life on the Global Assembly Line." *MS Magazine,* January.

Ehrenreich, Barbara, and Arlie Russell Hochschild. 2003. *Global Woman: Nannies, Maids, and Sex Workers in the New Economy.* New York: Metropolitan Books.

Ehrlich, Paul R. 1968. *The Population Bomb.* New York: Ballantine.

EIA. 2005. "Saudi Arabia." *Country Analysis Briefs.* Washington DC: Energy Information Administration.

Eisenhower, Dwight. 1961. "Farewell Address." *Public Papers of the Presidents.* Washington, DC: U.S. Government Printing Office.

Ellwood, David. 1988. *Poor Support: Poverty in the American Family.* New York: Basic Books.

Elsner, Alan. 2005. "U.S. Says Drugs War Hampered by Mexican Corruption." *Reuters,* June 14.

Evans, Peter. 1979. *Dependent Development: The Alliance of Multinational, State and Local Capital in Brazil.* Princeton, NJ: Princeton University Press.

Falk, William W., and Thomas A. Lyson. 1988. *High Tech, Low Tech, and No Tech.* Albany, NY: SUNY Press.

Faludi, Susan. 1991. *Backlash: The Undeclared War against American Women.* New York: Crown.

Fanon, Franz. 1963. *The Wretched of the Earth.* Paris: Presence Africaine.

Farmer, Paul. 2003. *Pathologies of Power: Health, Human Rights, and the New War on the Poor.* Berkeley: University of California Press.

FBI. 2004. *Crime in the United States, 2003.* Washington DC: Dept. of Justice.

Fernandez-Kelly, Patricia. 1983. *For We Are Sold, I and My People: Women and Industry in Mexico's Frontier.* Albany, NY: SUNY Press.

Firebaugh, Glenn. 2003. *The New Geography of Global Income Inequality.* Cambridge: Harvard University Press.

Fisher, Helen. 2004. *Why We Love: The Nature and Chemistry of Romantic Love.* New York: Holt.

Fishman, Charles. 2003. "The Wal-Mart You Don't Know." *Fast Company,* Issue 77. December.

Fitchen, Janet. 1981. *Poverty in Rural America: A Case Study.* Boulder, CO: Westview Press.

Fitchen, Janet. 1991. *Endangered Spaces, Enduring Places.* Boulder, CO: Westview Press.

Forbes Magazine. 2004. "The Forbes 400." October.

Foucault, Michel. 1995. *Discipline & Punish: The Birth of the Prison.* New York: Vintage. Orig. pub. 1977.

Frank, Andre Gundar. 1967. *Capitalism and Development in Latin America*. New York: Monthly Review Press.

Frank, Andre Gundar, and Barry K. Gills. 1993. *The World System: Five Hundred Years or Five Thousand?* London: Routledge.

Frank, Robert, and Philip Cook. 1995. *The Winner-Take-All Society*. New York: Free Press.

Freed, Josh. 2004. *Coat of Many Countries*. New York: Filmmakers Library.

Friedan, Betty. 1963. *The Feminine Mystique*. New York: Norton.

Friedman, Thomas L. 1999. *The Lexus and the Olive Tree*. New York: Farrar, Straus and Giroux.

Friere, Paulo. 1968. *Pedagogy of the Oppressed*. New York: Herder and Herder.

Fritts, Thomas H., and Dawn Leasman-Tanner. 2001. *The Brown Tree Snake on Guam*. Fort Collins: US Geological Survey. Available online at www.fort.usgs.gov/resources/education/bts/bts_home.asp.

Furstenberg, Frank F., Jr. 1988. "Good Dads—Bad Dads: Two Faces of Fatherhood." In Andrew Cherlin (ed.), *The Changing American Family*. Washington, DC: Urban Institute.

Galbraith, John Kenneth. 1958. *The Affluent Society*. Boston: Houghton Mifflin.

Gans, Herbert J. 1962. *The Urban Villagers: Group and Class in the Life of Italian-Americans*. New York: Free Press.

Garreau, Joel. 1991. *Edge City: Life on the New Frontier*. New York: Doubleday.

Garrels, Anne. 2002. "Child Labor in Pakistan." *All Things Considered*. National Public Radio. February 13.

Garson, Barbara. 1988. *The Electronic Sweatshop*. New York: Simon & Schuster.

Giddens, Anthony. 1999. *The Third Way: The Renewal of Social Democracy*. Oxford, England: Blackwell.

Giddens, Anthony. 2000. *Runaway World*. London: Routledge.

Gilbert, Dennis, and Joseph Kahl. 1982. *The American Class Structure: A New Synthesis*. Homewood, IL: Dorsey Press.

Gilbert, Dennis. 2003. *The American Class Structure in an Age of Growing Inequality*. Belmont, CA: Wadsworth.

Gilman, Charlotte Perkins. 1910. "Our Androcentric Culture." *Forerunner*, 1 (3): 12–22.

Gilmore, David. 1990. "Manhood." *Natural History* (June).

Gimbutas, Marija. 1982. *Goddesses and Gods of Old Europe, 6500–3500 BC: Myths, and Cult Images*. Berkeley: University of California Press.

Gimbutas, Marija, and Miriam Robbins Dexter. 2001. *The Living Goddesses*. Berkeley: University of California Press.

Goertzel, Ted. 1997. "President Fernando Cardoso Reflects on Brazil and Sociology." *Footnotes,* November.

Goode, William. 1963. *World Revolution and Family Patterns*. New York: Free Press.

Goode, William. 1992. "Why Men Resist." In Barrie Thorne and Marilyn Yalom (eds.), *Rethinking the Family*. Boston: Northeastern University Press.

Greeley, Andrew. 1972. *That Most Distressful Nation*. Chicago: Quadrangle.

Grossi, Mark. 2005. "Cows Emit More Organic Gas Than Cars, Studies Say." *Fresno Bee,* May 7.

Gupta, Avijit. 1988. *Ecology and Development in the Third World*. London, England: Routledge.

Guruswamy, Krishnan. 1995. "World's Waste Is Piling Up in India." *South Bend [IN] Tribune,* June 4.

Gutek, Gerald. 1997. *American Education in a Global Society*. Prospect Heights, IL: Waveland.

Gutmann, Mathew. 1996. *The Meanings of Macho*. Berkeley: University of California Press.

Hacker, Andrew. 1992. *Two Nations*. New York: Ballantine.

Hannigan, John. 1998. *Fantasy City: Pleasure and Profit in the Post-Modern Metropolis*. London: Routledge.

Hardin, Garrett. 1978. "The Tragedy of the Commons." *Science,* 162: 1241–1252.

Hareven, Tamara. 1982. *Family Time and Industrial Time*. Cambridge: Cambridge University Press.

Harrington, Michael. 1962. *The Other America: Poverty in the United States*. New York: Macmillan.

Harrington, Michael, and Mark Levinson. 1985. "The Perils of a Dual Economy." *Dissent,* 32 (4): 417–426.

Harrison, Bennett, and Barry Bluestone. 1988. *The Great U-Turn: Corporate Restructuring and the Polarizing of America.* New York: Basic Books.

Hayden, Jeffrey. 1996. *Children in America's Schools.* Columbia, SC: Saint/Hayden Company and South Carolina ETV Network.

Hechter, Michael. 1975. *Internal Colonialism.* Berkeley: University of California Press.

Hedges, Chris. 2003. *War Is a Force That Gives Us Meaning.* New York: Anchor Books.

Herrnstein, Richard J., and Charles Murray. 1994. *The Bell Curve: Intelligence and Class Structure in American Life.* New York: Free Press.

Ho, David. 2001. "We're #1: Population in Prisons Grows in US." *Common Dreams Newsletter.* October 29.

Hochschild, Arlie (with Anne Machung). 1989. *The Second Shift: Working Parents and the Revolution at Home.* New York: Penguin.

Hochschild, Arlie. 1997. *The Time Bind: When Work Becomes Home and Home Becomes Work.* New York: Metropolitan Books.

Horowitz, Donald. 2000. *Ethnic Groups in Conflict.* Berkeley: University of California Press.

Human Rights Watch. 2004. "Darfur Destroyed: Ethnic Cleansing by Government and Militia Forces in Western Sudan." *Human Rights Watch,* 16 (6).

Huntington, Samuel. 1996. *The Clash of Civilizations and the Remaking of World Order.* New York: Simon & Schuster.

ILO. 2002. *Every Child Counts: Global Estimates on Child Labour.* Geneva: International Labour Organziation.

Inglehart, Ronald, and Wayne E. Baker. 2000. "Modernization, Cultural Change, and the Persistence of Traditional Values." *American Sociological Review,* 65 (February): 19–51.

Inkeles, Alex, and David Smith. 1974. *Becoming Modern: Individual Change in Six Developing Countries.* Cambridge: Harvard University Press.

International Labour Organization (ILO). 2002. *Every Child Counts: New Global Estimates on Child Labour.* Geneva, Switzerland: ILO.

Isbister, John. 1998. *Promises Not Kept: The Betrayal of Social Change in the Third World.* West Hartford, CT: Kumarian Press.

Iyer, Pico. 1997. *Tropical Classical.* New York: Knopf.

Iyer, Pico. 2000. "Citizen Nowhere." *Civilization,* February/March.

Jacobs, Jane. 1970. *The Economy of Cities.* New York: Vintage.

Jacobs, Jane. 1984. *Cities and the Wealth of Nations.* New York: Random House.

Jaffee, David. 1998. *Levels of Socio-Economic Development Theory.* West Hartford, CT: Praeger.

Jenkins, Philip. 2003. *The Next Christendom: The Coming of Global Christianity.* New York: Oxford.

Jones, Christine W., and Miguel A. Kiguel. 1993. *Adjustment in Africa.* Washington, DC: World Bank.

Kane, Joe. 1996. *Savages.* New York: Vintage.

Kaplan, Robert D. 1998. "Travels into America's Future: Mexico and the Southwest." *Atlantic Monthly,* July.

Karakatsanis, Neovi M., and Jonathan Swarts. 2003. "Migrant Women, Domestic Work, and Sex Trade in Greece." *The Greek Review of Social Research,* 110: 239–270.

Keeney, Bradford. 1994. *Shaking Out the Spirits: A Psychoanalysts Entry into the Mysteries of Global Shamanism.* Barrytown, NY: Station Hill Press.

Keeney, Bradford 2004. *Bushman Shaman: Awakening the Spirit through Ecstatic Dance.* Rochester, VT: Destiny Books.

Kimbrell, Andrew. 2002. *Fatal Harvest: The Tragedy of Industrial Agriculture.* Washington, DC: Island Press.

King, Colbert I. 2001. "Pat Robertson and His Business Buddies." *Washington Post,* November 10.

King, Colbert I. 2001. "Pat Robertson's Gold." *Washington Post,* September 22.

King, Martin Luther, Jr. 1992. In James W. Washington (ed.), *I Have a Dream: Writings and Speeches That Changed the World.* New York: HarperCollins.

Kohler, Gernot. 1978. *Global Apartheid.* World Order Models Project, Paper no. 7. New York: Institute for World Order.

Konner, Melvin. 1991. *Childhood.* Boston: Little, Brown.

Korten, David C. 2001. *When Corporations Rule the World.* 2nd ed. Bloomfield, CT: Kumarian Press.

Kotlowitz, Alex. 1991. *There Are No Children Here.* New York: Doubleday.

Kozol, Jonathan. 1967. *Death at an Early Age: The Destruction of the Hearts and Minds of Negro Children in the Boston Public Schools.* New York: Houghton Mifflin.

Kozol, Jonathan. 1975. *The Night Is Dark and I Am Far from Home.* Boston: Houghton-Mifflin.

Kozol, Jonathan. 1991. *Savage Inequalities.* New York: Crown.

Kozol, Jonathan. 1995. *Amazing Grace.* New York: Crown.

Kozol, Jonathan. 2000. *Ordinary Resurrections.* New York: Crown.

Kristof, Nicholas D. 1996. "Who Needs Love? In Japan, Many Couples Don't." *New York Times,* February 11.

Kristof, Nicholas D. 1997. "In Congo, a New Era with Old Burdens." *New York Times,* May 20.

Kristof, Nicholas, and Edward Wyatt. 1999. "Who Sank, or Swam, in Choppy Currents of a World Cash Ocean." *New York Times,* February 15.

Kuznets, Simon. 1955. "Economic Growth and Income Inequality." *American Economic Review,* 45 (March): 1–28.

Lacey, Marc. 2003. "For Ugandan Girls, Delaying Sex Has Economic Cost." *New York Times,* August 18.

Lacey, Marc. 2004. "In Sudan, Militiamen on Horses Uproot a Million." *New York Times,* May 4.

Landsberg, Mitchell. 1998. "Changing America's Families." *South Bend [IN] Tribune,* April 7.

Le Breton, Binka. 2003. *Trapped: Modern-Day Slavery in the Brazilian Amazon.* Bloomfield, CT: Kumarian Press.

Le Duff, Charlie. 2000. "At a Slaughterhouse, Some Things Never Die." *New York Times,* June 16.

Le Duff, Charlie. 2004. "Mexican Americans Struggle for Jobs." *New York Times,* October 13.

Lenin, V. I. 1948. *Imperialism, the Highest Stage of Capitalism.* London, England: Lawrence and Wishart.

Lenski, Gerhard. 1966. *Power and Privilege: A Theory of Stratification.* New York: McGraw-Hill.

Lenski, Gerhard, and Patrick Nolan. 1984. "Trajectories of Development: A Test of Ecological-Evolutionary Theory." *Social Forces,* 63 (January): 1–23.

Lewis, Oscar. 1961. *Children of Sanchez.* New York: Random House.

Lewis, Oscar. 1968. "The Culture of Poverty." In *On Understanding Poverty,* ed. Daniel Patrick Moynihan. New York: Basic Books.

Lieberson, Stanley. 1980. *A Piece of the Pie: Blacks and White Immigrants Since 1880.* Berkeley: University of California Press.

Lipset, Seymour Martin. 1959. "Some Social Requisites of Democracy: Economic Development and Political Legitimacy." *American Political Science Review* 53 (March).

Lipset, Seymour Martin. 1996. *American Exceptionalism: A Double-Edged Sword.* New York: Norton.

Lipton, Michael. 1977. *Why Poor People Stay Poor: A Study of Urban Bias in World Development.* London, England: Temple Smith.

Loewen, James W. 1988. *The Mississippi Chinese: Between Black and White.* Prospect Heights, IL: Waveland Press.

Logan, John R., and Harvey L. Molotch. 1987. *Urban Fortunes: The Political Economy of Place.* Berkeley: University of California Press.

Lomnitz, Larissa Adler. 1977. *Networks and Marginality: Life in a Mexican Shantytown.* New York: Academic Press.

Lubiano, Wahneema, ed. 1997. *The House That Race Built.* New York: Pantheon.

Lucal, Betsy. 1996. "Oppression and Privilege: Toward a Relational Conceptualization of Race." *Teaching Sociology,* 24 (3): 245–255.

Lynd, Robert S., and Helen Merrell Lynd. 1929. *Middletown.* New York: Harcourt.

Lyson, Thomas. 1989. *Two Sides to the Sunbelt.* New York: Praeger.

MacLeod, Jay. 1995. *Ain't No Makin' It: Aspirations and Attainment in a Low-Income Neighborhood.* Boulder, CO: Westview Press.

Malthus, Thomas Robert. 1926. *First Essay on Population 1798*. London: Macmillan. Originally pub. in 1798.

Marshall, Alex. 2001. *How Cities Work: Suburbs, Sprawl and the Roads Not Taken*. Austin: University of Texas Press.

Massey, Douglas, and Nancy Denton. 1993. *American Apartheid*. Cambridge: Harvard University Press.

McGinn, Anne Platt. 2004. "Human Activities Threaten the World's Oceans and Coastal Regions." In Louise Gerdes (ed.), *Endangered Oceans*. San Diego: Greenhaven Press.

McIntosh, Peggy. 1995. "White Privilege and Male Privilege." In Margaret L. Anderson and Patricia Hill Collins (eds.), *Race, Class, and Gender* (2nd ed.). Belmont, CA: Wadsworth.

McLellan, David. 1977. *Karl Marx: Selected Writings*. Oxford, England: Oxford University Press.

McLellan, David. 1988. *Marxism: Essential Writings*. Oxford, England: Oxford University Press.

McLuhan, Marshall. 1964. *Understanding Media: The Extensions of Man*. New York: Mentor.

McMichael, Philip. 2000. *Development and Social Change*. Thousand Oaks, CA: Pine Forge.

McNeill, William H. 1963. *The Rise of the West: A History of the Human Community*. Chicago: University of Chicago Press.

Medoff, Peter, and Holly Sklar. 1994. *Streets of Hope: The Fall and Rise of an Urban Neighborhood*. Boston: South End Press.

Michels, Robert. 1967. *Political Parties*. New York: Free Press. (Orig. pub. 1911.)

Miller, D. T., and Michael Nowak. 1959. *The Sociological Imagination*. New York: Oxford University Press.

Miller, D. T., and Michael Nowak. 1977. *The Fifties: The Way We Really Were*. Garden City, NJ: Doubleday.

Mills, C. Wright. 1951. *White Collar*. New York: Oxford University Press.

Mills, C. Wright. 1956. *The Power Elite*. New York: Oxford.

Moore, Michael. 1989. *Roger and Me* [Film]. Filmography.

Moyers, Bill. 2000. *Surviving the Good Times* [Television program]. CBS.

Mueller, John. 1993. *Retreat from Doomsday*. Boston: Addison-Wesley.

Murray, Charles A. 1984. *Losing Ground: American Social Policy*. New York: Basic Books.

Myrdal, Gunnar. 1944. *An American Dilemma*. New York: Harper.

Myrdal, Gunnar. 1970. *The Challenge of World Poverty*. New York: Vintage.

National Geographic Television. 2001. *Africa: Voices of the Forest*. New York: Educational Broadcasting Service and WNET.

Nee, Victor. 1996. "The Emergence of a Market Society: Changing Mechanisms of Stratification in China. *American Journal of Sociology*, 101 (4): 908–949.

Nee, Victor, Jimy Sanders, and Scott Sernau. 1994. "Job Transitions in an Immigrant Metropolis: Ethnic Boundaries and Mixed Economy." *American Sociological Review*, 59 (December): 849–872.

Newman, Katherine S. 1988. *Falling from Grace*. New York: Free Press.

Nichols, Alan B. 2004. "Lockheed Martin, Sikorsky Aircraft Compete for Presidential Marine One Bid." *Washington Diplomat* (November).

North, Douglass. 1981. *Structure and Change in Economic History*. New York: Norton.

North, Douglass. 1990. *Institutions, Institutional Change and Economic Performance*. Cambridge, England: Cambridge University Press.

Nothdurft, William E. 1989. *SchoolWorks: Reinventing Public Schools to Create the Workforce of the Future*. Washington, DC: German Marshall Fund.

NPR. 2004. "California Becomes America's Biggest Dairyland." *All Things Considered*, November 12.

Nyabera, Emmanuel. 2002. "Sudan: Man-Eating Lions, Crocodiles, Famine . . . " *Refugees* 1 (126): 8–11.

O'Donnell, Guillermo. 1979. "Tensions in the Bureaucratic Authoritarian State and the Question of Democracy." In D. Collier (ed.), *The New Authoritarianism in Latin America*. Princeton: Princeton University Press.

Okano, Kaori, and Motonori Tsuchiya. 1999. *Education in Contemporary Japan: Inequality and Diversity*. Cambridge: Cambridge University Press.

Oliver, Melvin L., and Thomas M. Shapiro. 1995. *Black Wealth/White Wealth: A New Perspective on Racial Inequality*. New York: Routledge.

Onishi, Norimitsu. 2000. "In the Oil Rich Nigeria Delta, Deep Poverty and Grim Fires." *New York Times,* August 11.

Palen, J. John. 2005. *The Urban World*. 7th ed. Boston: McGraw-Hill.

Parenti, Michael. 1995. *Democracy for the Few*. 6th ed. New York: St. Martin's.

Park, Robert E. 1967. "The City: Suggestions for the Investigation of Human Behavior in the Urban Environment." In Robert E. Park and Eugene W. Burgess (eds.), *The City*. Chicago: University of Chicago. Originally pub. in 1916.

Park, Robert. 1914. "Racial Assimilation in Secondary Groups." *American Journal of Sociology* 19 (5): 606–623.

Park, Robert, and Ernest Burgess. 1921. *Introduction to the Science of Sociology*. Chicago: University of Chicago Press.

Parkin, Frank. 1979. *Marxism and Class Theory: A Bourgeois Critique*. New York: Columbia University Press.

Parsons, Talcott. 1964. *Social Structure and Personality*. New York: Free Press.

Pearson, Natalie Obiko. 2004. "Japanese Divorce Rates Rise as Stigma Fades." *South Bend [IN] Tribune,* January 18.

Peña, Devon. 1997. *The Terror of the Machine*. Austin: University of Texas.

Perlmann, Joel. 1988. *Ethnic Differences: Schooling and Social Structure among the Irish, Italians, Jews, and Blacks in an American City, 1880–1935*. Cambridge, England: Cambridge University Press.

Piore, Michael, and Charles Sabel. 1989. *The Second Industrial Divide*. New York: Basic Books.

Porrit, Jonathan. 1991. *Save the Earth*. London, England: Dorling Kindersley.

Portes, Alejandro, and Ruben Rumbaut. 1990. *Immigrant America: A Portrait*. Berkeley: University of California Press.

Portes, Alejandro, Manuel Castells, and Lauren A. Benton, eds. 1989. *The Informal Economy: Studies in Advanced and Less Developed Countries*. Baltimore, MD: Johns Hopkins University Press.

Prebisch, Raul. 1950. *The Economic Development of Latin America and Its Principle Problems*. New York: United Nations.

Przeworski, Adam, and Fernando Limongi. 1997. "Modernization: Theories and Facts." *World Politics*, 49 (2).

Reiman, Jeffrey. 1998. *The Rich Get Richer and the Poor Get Prison*. 5th ed. Boston: Allyn & Bacon.

Ricardo, David. 1996. *Principles of Political Economy and Taxation*. New York: Prometheus. Originally pub. 1817.

Riesman, David. 1953. *The Lonely Crowd: A Study of the Changing American Character*. New Haven, CT: Yale University Press.

Ritzer, George. 2000. *The McDonaldization of Society*. Rev. ed. Thousand Oaks, CA: Pine Forge.

Rohter, Larry. 2003. "Bolivia's Poor Proclaim Abiding Distrust of Globalization." *New York Times,* October 17.

Rohter, Larry. 2004. "South America Seeks to Fill the World's Table." *New York Times,* December 12.

Rosen, Bernard. 1982. *The Industrial Connection*. New York: Aldine.

Rosenthal, Elizabeth. 2001. "Without 'Barefoot Doctors,' China's Rural Families Suffer." *New York Times,* March 14.

Rostow, W. W. 1960. *The Stages of Economic Growth: A Non-Communist Manifesto*. Cambridge, England: Cambridge University Press.

Rowe, Claudia. 1999. "Saving Children from Sweatshops: One Teen's Crusade." *Biography Magazine*, November.

Royle, David. 1996. *Brazil*. New York: Quality Books.

Rubin, Lillian B. 1976. *Worlds of Pain*. New York: Basic Books.

Rubin, Lillian B. 1994. *Families on the Fault Line*. New York: HarperCollins.

Ruether, Rosemary Radford. 2005. *Goddesses and the Divine Feminine: A Western Religious History*. Berkeley: University of California Press.

Ryan, William. 1971. *Blaming the Victim*. New York: Vintage Books.

Safina, Carl. 2004. "The World's Ocean Fisheries Are Seriously Threatened." In Louise Gerdes (ed.), *Endangered Oceans*. San Diego: Greenhaven Press.

Sahlins, Marshall. 1972. *Stone Age Economics*. Chicago: Aldine.

Sanders, Jimy, and Victor Nee. 1987. "Limits of Ethnic Solidarity in the Enclave Economy." *American Sociological Review*, 52 (December): 745–773.

Sanders, Jimy, Victor Nee, and Scott Sernau. 2002. "Asian Immigrants' Reliance on Social Ties." *Social Forces*, 81 (1):281–314.

Sassen, Saskia. 2000. *Cities in a World Economy*. 2nd ed. Thousand Oaks, CA: Sage.

Scapinski, Helene. 1998. "Let's Talk Dirty." *American Demographics*, 20 (11): 50–56.

Scarr, Sandra, Deborah Phillips, and Kathleen McCartney. 1989. "Working Mothers and Their Families." *American Psychologist*, 44 (11): 1402–1409.

Schanberg, Sydney H. 1996. "Six Cents an Hour." *Life*, June.

Schell, Jonathan. 2003. *The Unconquerable World: Power, Nonviolence, and the Will of the People*. New York: Holt.

Schlosser, Eric. 2001. *Fast Food Nation*. New York: Houghton Mifflin.

Schumacher, E. F. 1973. *Small Is Beautiful: Economics As If People Mattered*. New York: Harper & Row.

Schumpeter, Joseph. 1949. *Change and the Entrepreneur*. Cambridge: Harvard University Press.

Schwartz, Felice N. 1989. "Management, Women, and the New Facts of Life." *Harvard Business Review*, 89 (January–February): 65–76.

Seiple, Robert. 1998. "Female He Created Them." *World Vision*, April–May.

Sen, Amartya. 1999. *Development as Freedom*. New York: Anchor.

Sernau, Scott. 1994. *Economies of Exclusion: Underclass Poverty and Labor Market Change in Mexico*. Westport, CT: Praeger.

Sernau, Scott. 1996. "Economies of Exclusion: Economic Change and the Global Underclass." *Journal of Developing Societies*, 12 (1): 38–51.

Sernau, Scott. 1997. *Critical Choices: Applying Sociological Insight*. Los Angeles: Roxbury.

Sernau, Scott. 2000. *Bound: Living in the Globalized World*. West Hartford, CT: Kumarian Press.

Sernau, Scott. 2001. *Worlds Apart: Social Inequalities in a New Century*. Thousand Oaks, CA: Pine Forge.

Shandy, Dianna. 2006. "New Americans: The Road to Refugee Resettlement." In James Spradley and David McCurdy (eds.). *Conformity and Conflict*, 12th edition. Boston: Allyn & Bacon.

Shostak, Marjorie. 2000. *Nisa: The Life and Words of a Kung Woman*. Cambridge, MA: Harvard University Press.

Sidel, Ruth. 1996. *Keeping Women and Children Last*. New York: Penguin.

Simmel, Georg. 1964. "The Metropolis and Mental Life." In *The Sociology of Georg Simmel*. K. Wolf (ed.). New York: Free Press. Orig. pub. 1905.

Simons, Marlise. 1990. "The Amazon's Savvy Indians." *New York Times Magazine*, February 26.

Sivard, Ruth Leger. 1997. *World Military and Social Expenditures*. Washington, DC: World Priorities.

Slater, Philip. 1970. *The Pursuit of Loneliness*. Boston: Beacon Press.

Smith, Adam. 1937. *An Inquiry into the Nature and Causes of the Wealth of Nations*. New York: Modern Library. Orig. pub. 1776.

South, Scott, and Glenna Spitze. 1994. "Housework in Marital and Non-Marital Households." *American Sociological Review*, 59 (June): 327–347.

South Bend Tribune. 2005. "Latinos Divided over Custom of 'Chaperonas' for Daughters." *South Bend Tribune*, June 14.

Southey, Robert. 2004. "Madoc." In *Robert Southey: Poetical Works, 1793–1810*. London: Pickering and Chatto. Originally pub. 1805.

Sowell, Thomas. 1993. "Middleman Minorities." *American Enterprise*, May–June.

Stack, Carol. 1974. *All Our Kin*. New York: Harper & Row.

Stapinski, Helene. 1998. "Let's Talk Dirty." *American Demographics* 20 (11):50–56.

Steinberg, Stephan. 1981. *The Ethnic Myth: Race, Ethnicity, and Class in America*. Boston: Beacon Press.

Stiglitz, Joseph. 2002. *Globalization and its Discontents*. New York: Norton.

Takaki, Ronald. 1993. *A Different Mirror*. Boston: Little, Brown.

Takaki, Ronald. 1994. *From Different Shores: Perspectives on Race and Ethnicity in America*. 2nd ed. New York: Oxford University Press.

Taubman, Stephanie. 2002. "Asian Ladybird Beetle." New York: Columbia University Introduced Species Summary Project. Available online at www.columbia.edu/itc/cerc/danoffburg/invasion_bio.

Tilly, Charles. 1975. "Reflections on the History of European State-Making." In Charles Tilly (ed.), *The Formation of National States in Western Europe*. Princeton, NJ: Princeton University Press.

Tilly, Charles. 1990. *Coercion, Capital, and Europeans States, AD 990–1990*. Oxford, England: Blackwell.

Timberlake, Michael, and Jeffrey Kentor. 1983. "Economic Dependence, Overurbanization, and Economic Growth: A Study of Less Developed Countries." *Sociological Quarterly*, 24: 489–507.

Toennies, Ferdinand. 1988. *Community and Society (Gemeinschaft und Gesellschaft)*. New Brunswick, NJ: Transaction Press. Orig. pub. 1887.

Toffler, Alex. 1980. *The Third Wave*. New York: Bantam.

Tolan, Sandy. 2003. "Sri Lanka: An Exodus of Women" [Radio program]. *Worlds of Difference*. Homelands Productions. Transcript available online at www.homelands.org/worlds/srmaids.html.

Trebay, Guy. 2000. "Shopping the Madison Avenue of Manhasset." *New York Times*, July 25.

Tumin, Melvin M. 1953. "Some Principles of Stratification: A Critical Analysis." *American Sociological Review*, 18 (August): 387–394.

Turner, Terrence. 1993. "The Role of Indigenous Peoples in the Environmental Crisis: The Example of the Kayapo of the Brazilian Amazon." In *Perspectives in Biology and Medicine*. Baltimore: Johns Hopkins University Press.

UNICEF. January 2005. "Monitoring the Status of Women and Children: Education." Available online at www.childinfo.org/areas/education.

United Nations. 1995. "The Cairo Conference." United Nations International Conference on Population and Development (ICPD). Available online at www.iisd.ca/cairo.html.

United Nations. 1996. *Human Development Report*. United Nations Development Program. New York: Oxford University Press. www.un.org.

United Nations. 2003. *Human Development Report*. United Nations Development Program. New York: Oxford University Press. www.un.org.

United Nations. 2004. *Human Development Report*. United Nations Development Program. New York: Oxford University Press. www.un.org.

UN AIDS. 2004. *Report on the Global AIDS Epidemic*. New York: United Nations.

United Nations, Food and Agriculture Organization (FAO). 2000. United Nations. www.fao.org. August.

UNHCR. 2002. "Wood: A Most Necessary Item for Survival." *Refugees*, 2 (127): 8.

UN Population Fund. 2000. *The State of the World Population 2000*. New York: United Nations.

Urrea, Luis Alberto. 1996. *By the Lake of Sleeping Children*. New York: Doubleday.

U.S. Bureau of the Census. 1995. *Current Population Reports*. Washington, DC: Government Printing Office.

U.S. Bureau of the Census. 1998. *Money Income in the United States*. Washington, DC: Government Printing Office.

U.S. Bureau of the Census. 1999. *Statistical Abstract of the United States*. Washington, DC: Government Printing Office.

U.S. Bureau of the Census. 2000. *American Fact Finder*. www.factfinder.census.gov.

U.S. Bureau of the Census. 2000. *International Data Base*. www.census.gov.

U.S. Bureau of the Census. 2004. *Statistical Abstract of the United States*. Washington, DC: U.S. Government Printing Office.

U.S. National Center for Educational Statistics. 1999. *Digest of Educational Statistics*. Washington, DC: Government Printing Office.

Verhovek, Sam Howe. 2000. "After Breaking the Mold in Business, the E-Wealthy Do It Again in Giving." *New York Times,* February 11.

Veterans for Peace. 2003. *Terrorism Is the War of the Poor.* www.veteransforpeace.org.

Vollers, Mary Anne. 1999. "Razing Appalachia." *Mother Jones,* July/August.

Waldinger, Roger. 1986. *Through the Eye of the Needle.* New York: New York University Press.

Wallerstein, Immanuel. 1974. *The Modern World System.* New York: Academic Press.

Walljasper, Jay. 1994. "Something Urban in Denmark." *Utne Reader,* September–October.

Washington Post, 11-2-01

Waters, Mary. 1990. *Ethnic Options.* Berkeley: University of California.

Weatherford, Jack. 1994. *Savages and Civilization.* New York: Ballantine.

Weatherford, Jack. 2006. "Cocaine and the Economic Deterioration of Bolivia." In James Spradley and David McCurdy (eds.). *Conformity and Conflict,* 12th edition. Boston: Allyn & Bacon.

Weaver, James H., Michael T. Rock, and Kenneth Kusterer. 1997. *Achieving Broad-Based Sustainable Development.* West Hartford, CT: Kumarian Press.

Weber, Max. 1964. *The Theory of Social and Economic Organization.* Trans. A. M. Henderson and Talcott Parsons. Glencoe, IL: Free Press.

Weber, Max. 1979. *Economy and Society.* 2 vols. Berkeley: University of California Press. Orig. pub. 1922.

Weber, Max. 1997. *The Protestant Ethic and the Spirit of Capitalism.* Los Angeles: Roxbury. Orig. pub. 1905.

West, Cornell. 1993. *Race Matters.* Boston: Beacon Press.

West, Cornell. 1997. "Afterword." In Wahneema Lubiano (ed.), *The House That Race Built.* New York: Pantheon.

Whyte, William H., Jr. 1956. *The Organization Man.* New York: Simon & Schuster.

Wiener, Myron. 1966. *Modernization: The Dynamics of Growth.* New York: Basic Books,

Wilson, James Q., and George L. Kelling. 1982. "Broken Windows." *Atlantic Monthly,* March.

Wilson, Kenneth L., and Alejandro Portes. 1980. "Immigrant Enclaves: An Analysis of the Labor Market Experiences of Cubans in Miami." *American Journal of Sociology,* 86 (September): 295–315.

Wilson, William Julius. 1978. *The Declining Significance of Race.* Chicago: University of Chicago Press.

Wilson, William Julius. 1987. *The Truly Disadvantaged: The Inner City, the Underclass, and Public Policy.* Chicago: University of Chicago Press.

Wilson, William Julius. 1996. *When Work Disappears.* New York: Knopf.

World Almanac and Book of Facts. 1991. New York: World Almanac.

World Bank. 1999. *World Development Report.* Oxford, England: Oxford University Press.

World Bank. 2000. *World Development Report.* New York: Oxford.

World Bank. 2004. *World Development Report.* Oxford, England: Oxford University Press.

Wright, Erik Olin. 1985. *Classes.* New York: Shocken.

Wright, Erik Olin. 1997. *Class Counts: Comparative Studies in Class Analysis.* New York: Cambridge University Press.

Wright, Erik Olin, and Luca Perrone. 1977. "Marxist Class Categories and Income Inequality." *American Sociological Review,* 42 (February): 32–55.

www.airforce-technology.com/project_printable.asp?ProjectID=1105. Retrieved 7/18/03.

Yergin, Daniel. 1991. *The Prize: The Epic Quest for Oil, Money and Power.* New York: Simon & Schuster.

Zakaria, Fareed. 2003. *The Future of Freedom: Illiberal Democracy at Home and Abroad.* New York: Norton.

Zinn, Maxine Baca. 1989. "Family, Race, and Poverty." *Signs: Journal of Women in Culture and Society,* 14 (4): 856–874.

Zwingle, Erla. 1998. "Women and Population." *National Geographic,* October.

Zwingle, Erla. 2002. "Megacities: The Coming Urban World." *National Geographic,* November.

Index

Note: Bold numbers indicate pages on which topics are defined as key terms.

Photo credits